MEN

AT

WAR

Other Books by
Robert Barr Smith

TO THE LAST CARTRIDGE
DALTONS! THE RAID ON COTTEYVILLE, KANSAS
THE LITERATE LAWYER

MEN AT WAR

TRUE STORIES OF HEROISM AND HONOR

ROBERT BARR SMITH

AVON BOOKS ◆ NEW YORK

AVON BOOKS
A division of
The Hearst Corporation
1350 Avenue of the Americas
New York, New York 10019

Copyright © 1997 by Robert Barr Smith
Interior design by Kellan Peck
Published by arrangement with the author
Visit our website at **http://AvonBooks.com**
ISBN: 0-380-78544-7

Library of Congress Cataloging in Publication Data:
Smith, Robert B. (Robert Barr), 1933–
    Men at war / by Robert Barr Smith.
        p.   cm.
    1. War. 2. Soldiers. I. Title.
U21.2.S62   1997   96-37375
355'.0092'2—dc21   CIP

First Avon Books Trade Printing: July 1997

AVON TRADEMARK REG. U.S. PAT. OFF. AND IN OTHER COUNTRIES, MARCA REGISTRADA, HECHO EN U.S.A.

Printed in the U.S.A.

OPM   10   9   8   7   6   5   4   3   2   1

In Memoriam

Long ago I came upon an inscription on a moss-covered headstone in an English churchyard. It is a lovely place, timeless and peaceful and wonderfully green, and it overlooks the ageless beauty of Dart Moor, in Devon. A weathered cross stands guard over the churchyard, and in the spring a whole regiment of daffodils nods above the graves. Except for the singing of birds and the hum of bees, it is silent there.

The headstone remembers two brothers. One disappeared in the night sky above Cologne with his bomber and never came back to England again. The other, a doctor with the British Airborne, was killed in action tending the wounds of a German soldier.

The inscription speaks not just for grieving families—God knows there are too many of those—but also for anybody who loves soldiers and understands the sacrifices they routinely make. It goes like this:

> *We who wear our names a little longer,*
> *do so by their courtesy;*
> *and should in courtesy remember,*
> *the reasons for which they*
> *and others from this village died.*

Dedicated to my best friend, Patty,
whom I had the great good fortune to
marry a long time ago

And to the officers and men of the 1st Battalion,
35th United States Infantry, the Cacti
Blue, who permitted me to join them for
some memorable days in Vietnam.

Contents

Introduction

This book is about soldiers, and only secondarily about wars and campaigns and generals' great decisions. It does not address cosmic theories of strategy. Such things are better left to great thinkers, who are as often wrong as they are right.

I am a storyteller, and make no pretense to great scholarship. The tales in *Men at War* are drawn almost entirely from secondary sources. A very few things in the book I know of my own knowledge; otherwise, I gratefully acknowledge the research done by other men, many of them long dead. A bibliography of the sources I used appears at the end of the book.

A couple of the chapters began life as magazine articles. Let me express my appreciation for the generosity of Cowles History Group and its fine publications *Vietnam* and *Military History*, and to the United States Naval Institute, for permitting publication of those articles in this book. My thanks also to the library staff of the University of Oklahoma Law Library, who magically obtained all manner of obscure books and microfilm for me. Thanks also to my very patient and expert editor, Tom Colgan, without whom this book would never have seen the light of day.

Whatever the literary merits of this book may be, it is written with profound respect and admiration for the men who are its subjects. They come from a multitude of times and places, nations and races. The one thing they have in common is an astonishing courage and determination. In courtesy, their devotion should be long remembered.

MEN AT WAR

CHAPTER ONE

THE ONCE AND FUTURE KING

Arthur the King at Badon Hill

Hic jacet Arturus
Rex quondam, rex futurus.

Here lies Arthur,
the once and future king.

IF YOU STARE hard enough through the shifting mists of time, you can catch just a glimpse of a formidable figure. He is a soldier, surely; a nobleman, probably; just maybe, he is even a king. He is a strong man, whatever his rank, a dominant figure on the island of Britain in the far-off sixth century. You can see the faint glint of his armor, perhaps the reflection of a silver collar, certainly the sheen of the naked sword he carries in his fist. But no man can see his face, for he stands always in shadow. He is called Arthur.

Britain in the early 500s is a battlefield. Great Rome is gone, her legions far-called, never to return. The native Britons carry on their long, heartbreaking battle against waves of North German invaders, Angles, Saxons, and Jutes. Their enemies are savage men, delighting in blood: looters, rapists, burners, destroyers.

The Britons are doomed. In time they will lose their long struggle, fighting bitterly to the very end. Some women will become slaves and bear Saxon children, and in time their descendants will become part of one British people. Many other Britons will die fighting, or lie murdered outside their burning homes. It is only the remnants of the British people who will in the end survive to people the West Country, Wales and Cornwall.

But before the final Saxon triumph there is an hour of shining victory for the British. That triumph will be a brilliant sunset in the fading day of old Britain; it will give the Britons a little time longer in the sun, another few decades to live. It begins a heroic legend that still lives today, a legend part myth, part history, part cry of the heart. It is the genesis of the legend of Arthur, the Once and Future King.

Arthur was real enough, although the principal man of the Britons in the early sixth century was not Arthur but one Ambrosius Aurelianus. Ambrosius might have been a king or a king's chief minister, but he was old, and he had delegated effective command of the Saxon war to Arthur, who might have been his nephew. The probabilities are, therefore, that Arthur was a war leader, noble or nearly so, but never a king. We do know he was a remarkable man, a charismatic commander, a winner, a thoughtful tactician who undoubtedly led from the front.

Before he died in battle he did what no Briton before him could do: in a series of hard-fought engagements—twelve, according to legend—his outnumbered men whipped the formidable Saxons repeatedly, hurting them so badly that the remains of western Britain were left in a sort of peace for half a century to come. Badon was the most important of all of Arthur's fights, a crushing repulse of the detested Saxons.

When Rome called its legions home about the year 410, military matters in Britain were left to the inhabitants. How the Angles, Jutes, and Saxons first came to Britain is not certain, but it is probable that they were invited guests and were offered East Anglia as their own for settlement. Some might even have cooperated in defending Britain before the last of the Roman legions left.

Although in time these fierce men brought their families to England, they came first as mercenary soldiers, perhaps called in by one British contestant for primacy to fight against his rival. All apparently went well and peacefully at first. However, as more and more of these Germans arrived in Britain, they began to reach out for what was not theirs. The Britons fought back, and the long twilight agony of Britain began.

We are not even certain exactly when Arthur lived, although we can place him with reasonable accuracy in the early years of the sixth century. Badon was probably fought in or around the year 518. That is the date given in the Easter Annals, the most reliable source of the history of those misty times. Easter being a movable feast, the Christian church kept records of when it fell each year. It became the custom to include on these calendars a little secular history as well, notations of important events that came to pass each year. The annals for 518 record:

> The Battle of Badon in which Arthur carried the cross of Our Lord Jesus Christ three days and three nights on his shoulders and the Britons were victors.

The reference to the cross surely does not refer to the literal carrying of a cross. It probably means a cloth cross sewed on Arthur's outer garment, a medallion hanging from his neck, or an emblem painted on his shield—for Arthur and his men were Christian. "Three days and three nights" may be a literal description of the length of the battle, but probably is no more than an attempt to describe the exhausting length of the actual fight.

A monk called Gildas, writing in the mid-sixth century, also mentioned the battle, although he said it was fought in the year of his birth, around 500, and he did not mention Arthur. Between Gildas and the Annals, we can at least place the battle with some accuracy in the first twenty years of the dark sixth century.

Just where Arthur fought the Saxons is also lost in those same chilly mists of time. Britain is covered with sites that might fit the descriptions of his battles. The locations of some of the more obscure engagements are wholly undiscoverable; there are not even similar names to be found in the British landscape. But for Badon it is different. There are at least five places called Badbury—and one, Badbury Rings, includes a likely hill fort of the proper antiquity. There is also the lovely city of Bath, a perennial nomination, and even a place in Scotland.

The most probable site, however, is a place called Liddington Castle, in Wiltshire, not far from the pleasant town of Swindon and hard by one of the Badburys, only a mile northwest. Liddington Castle is an Iron Age hill fort of approximately 200 by 150 yards that was used as a defensive work long before the days of Arthur.

Below it runs an ancient track, the Ridgeway, once a road for the Roman legions and for more peaceful travelers, a natural route the Saxons might well have used in their invasion west into Somerset. The England of the day was heavily and widely forested, and there was much swamp. A large army would surely have followed a major path, and the Ridgeway fills that requirement perfectly.

Moreover, this was a large Saxon war band, probably an army composed of detachments from three or even four Saxon areas of southern England. The ancient roads from the east would have brought most of them together just a few miles east of Swindon. The route for the East Anglian contingent joined the way west just below Liddington Castle itself.

The hill on which Liddington Castle stands rises some nine hundred feet, high above the surrounding countryside. It rises about four hundred feet higher than the ancient road called the Ridgeway, which ran across its shoulders time out of mind, making it a formidable piece of defensive high ground. Perhaps most significant, recent excavation has showed that the top rampart of the old hill fort was rebuilt and repaired *in the fifth century*. And the chroniclers refer to "Mons Badonicus"—*mons* is the Latin for "mountain" or "hill"—so it is reasonably certain the battle was fought on high ground. And Liddington Castle fits the physical description of the battle site very well indeed.

Arthur's outnumbered men seem to have been cavalry, or at least mounted infantry. That gave him a considerable advantage of mobility over his foot-slogging enemy. Nobody knows whether his men used stirrups, that simple innovation that gave the horse soldier the stability and leverage to fight effectively from the saddle with sword and spear. Since stirrups were in use by some of the Germanic tribes at least as early as the late fourth century, Arthur's men may well have used them, too. If they did, they probably fought from horseback; if not, the horse was chiefly a means of moving swiftly to the place of battle.

Arthur's men no doubt fought with much the same weapons as their Saxon enemy: the ax, the heavy spear, and the sword, probably double-edged. They may have used a smaller ax, too, designed to throw instead of chop, and perhaps light throwing spears. Some may even have used Roman weapons, reminders of the more peaceful days before the legions departed forever over the sea. Their defensive armament was probably sparse: wooden shields covered with hide, iron caps, probably jerkins of leather.

Whether they made great use of the bow is lost in history; it would be hard to believe they would not, however, even though it would not have been the great longbow of Plantagenet days. Some other footmen may have used slings at long range. Perhaps they even cast their own sling ammunition, slugs of lead of identical size; the Romans did so, and there had been tin mines in Cornwall time out of mind.

The fight at Badon probably began as a very large ambush, or as a meeting engagement. Arthur and his men approached from the north or northwest, perhaps sheltering in woods until the Saxons came close enough to strike. Then Arthur's horsemen charged this long column of Saxons marching west to harry, murder, rape, and rob. Since Arthur's enemies were probably using the old Roman path lying north of Badon Hill itself, the first clash of weapons echoed along the edge of the road.

Much of what we know about Badon comes from a twelfth-century manuscript by a cleric, one Geoffrey of Monmouth. Though Geoffrey was not above inventing what he could not gather from other works and tales, what he wrote about Badon has the ring of truth. The Saxons fought at Badon in wedged-shaped formations, he says, a sort of phalanx bristling with spears. That description sounds very much like the shield wall, the close-order hedge of spears that was a northern tradition. Or it may refer to the so-called swine formation, a sort of flying wedge often used by the Norsemen, a massed arrowhead of warriors tipped by berserkers or other notable axmen.

Arthur's men charged the Saxons again and again, closing to sword length when they could, perhaps hurling javelins and axes at close range when they could not penetrate the hedge of spears. What bowmen and slingers accompanied Arthur's cavalry would cover them with a flight of missiles as the horsemen thundered in to smash against the wall of shields.

The Saxon commander, an experienced fighting man named Aelle, formed his men in an easily defensible position about a thousand yards long, facing north. The Saxon line followed a line of higher ground just south of the road, its right flank anchored on a deep gully that ran southward behind them, on up the flank of Badon Hill. It was a reasonably strong position, for the gully would have protected their flank from any British cavalry charge. The Saxons' line probably followed the line of the ancient Roman road they had been tramping along when Arthur struck.

The fight raged all day, and the carnage must have been awful.

The Saxon enemy were doughty fighters, some swinging two-handed axes that could carve a man from scalp to breastbone in a single stroke. One chronicler says that Arthur's cavalry charged the Saxons repeatedly. They did terrible execution, but they could not break the wall of spears. Arthur's men also suffered heavy casualties, and they must have lost many horses to the wall of spears.

As night fell and it became too dark to see clearly, the two forces broke contact. Under cover of the darkness, the Saxons fell back uphill to the shelter of Badon Hill, which even then had ancient Iron Age earthworks cut into its grassy top. And it was very steep indeed, a fine defense against cavalry; over a stretch of some three hundred yards, the ground rose steeply, as sharply as one foot upward for every three feet forward. Mounted men could approach the hilltop only from the east, and then only with some difficulty.

For his part, Arthur pulled back far enough to find ample water, tend his wounded, and rest his weary men and animals. And always he kept watch on the Saxons, high above him. If we stare hard through the swirling vapors of time, we can see him standing silent in the gloom, a watch fire flickering behind him, his eyes on the dark mass of Badon Hill. Arthur watched and waited through the long hours of darkness, making his plans for the dawning. Somewhere deep in the West Country night, Arthur made his choice: he would attack.

Arthur might have left the Saxons to fester on Mons Badonicus. In spite of the hill's fine defensive attributes—it was the highest point for miles in every direction—the Saxons could not stay there indefinitely. When morning dawned next day, the Saxons would have had to choose to stay on their hilltop and eat themselves out of provisions or come down and face that terrible cavalry that waited grimly below.

Arthur could have waited, but he was not content to relax his grip on his enemy. One explanation for his decision is the fact that the fighting between Briton and Saxon was vicious and unforgiving, war to the knife, without quarter or pity on either side. To Arthur and his men, the only safe Saxon was a dead one, and Arthur was taking no chances that any of his enemies might escape. There might also have been another Saxon force somewhere in the vicinity. If that were the case, Arthur would have felt it necessary to exterminate the host on Badon Hill before it could summon help by beacon or messenger.

Arthur's men must have been veteran soldiers with immense confidence in their commander. They had fought hard through most of the day. Many of the men still in ranks were wounded; others had lost their horses. All had lost friends. They had to know that attacking the steep slopes of Mons Badonicus would be a bloody task with no assurance of victory at the end. Yet they were ready to follow their magnetic leader, whatever might lie at the end of the next long day.

And so, in the morning, probably at the break of dawn, Arthur's men started uphill, their weapons glimmering faintly in the first pale light of the coming morning. Many of his men must have advanced on foot, grimly slogging their way uphill toward the waiting hedge of spears. As they came, probably up the steep north slope of the hill, they were repeatedly charged by groups of Saxons, whose wild charges struck all the harder by reason of the speed of their downhill run.

The British left the ground behind them studded with the still forms of their dead and the writhing bodies of their wounded. The forays from the hilltop spilled much British blood; the Saxons would have hurled every missile remaining to them, and such stones as they could find. But still Arthur's men came grimly on, until they got within arm's reach of their blood enemies, and then the fighting went to hand-to-hand. Still the British fought at a disadvantage, trying to keep their footing on the steep slope and find leverage to hew and slash at burly enemies who towered above them.

Arthur now clutched his enemy tightly to him, and the infantry struggle went on and on through the day, swaying back and forth along the edge of the hilltop. Arthur was patient, waiting while his sweating, panting men struggled and died, pulling into the melee more and more Saxons from other parts of the hilltop.

And then, late in the day, when the Saxons were deeply committed to the ferocious infantry battle along the northern lip of the hill, Arthur struck. In the chronicler's words:

Arthur waxed wroth at the stubborness of their [the Saxons'] resistance, and the slowness of his own advance, and drawing forth his sword crieth aloud the name of Holy Mary, and thrust-

eth himself forward with a swift onset into the thickest press of
the enemy's ranks.

Arthur's charge, which he probably led himself, would have been
a cavalry rush, thundering in over the eastern edge of Badon's flat
top, the British horsemen shouting "Holy cross!" and their own
personal war cries, spearpoints down and forward, knocking aside
those Saxons who still manned the eastern edge of the perimeter.
The charge slammed into the mass of the Saxons from the flank and
rear, and the top of Mount Badon became soaked with blood.

The shock would have been tremendous, for the British horses
were bulky and strong, the result of generations of breeding between
the native ponies and the heavy horses of Rome. Many of the Saxons
were knocked down, some simply trampled to death by the burly
warhorses.

Arthur's shouting horsemen crashed into the Saxons, the riders
stabbing overhand at their enemies with their short, heavy spears,
clutching the reins with their shield hands, or perhaps gripping them
in their teeth. When spears were lost or broken, the British rose in
their stirrups for leverage to hack at the desperate Saxons with axes
or swords, slashing down through iron cap and leather jerkin, scattering blood and brains across themselves and their frantic horses.

Cornered, the Saxons fought back desperately, trying to pull their
enemies from the saddle, dropping to the earth to stab at the horses'
bellies and hamstrings. Those who did perished under the hooves
and heavy bodies of the horses, living and dead. The survivors were
exhausted, many wounded in the melee of the previous day. There
could have been little food to spread among that tired host the night
before, and perhaps no water at all. As the shield wall disintegrated,
their tired hearts began to fail as well.

Submerged by the relentless pressure of the cavalry, crushed
against the anvil of the infantry assault over the northern lip of the
hill, the Saxon resistance began to fragment, and fugitives started to
break away in ones and twos and threes, seeking refuge in flight,
looking anywhere for life and safety.

But there was no safety on that terrible hill—and none below it,
either. For most of the Saxons there was only a last spasm of whis-
tling steel and a bloody end to life. Arthur's men were paying back
fifty years of blood, fifty years of rape and kidnapping and ruthless

burning. They rode down every Saxon they could catch, killing and killing until their own exhaustion stopped them and there were no more living Saxons to cut down.

Thus the battle of Badon. Because nobody was present to write down what happened, because whatever contemporary chronicles there may have been are long lost, Badon is little known. It deserves better. For on that bloody hill Arthur the fabulous commander won a victory that bought a whole people another half century of life. And at Badon the legend of Arthur took deep root and began to grow. It is still very much alive today.

In spite of all manner of mean-spirited attempts to debunk the Arthurian legend, it does not die, nor will it ever. Arthur still sleeps, some believe, somewhere beneath the green, green earth in the West Country of England, or in Wales. He is surrounded by his men, like Barbarossa in the German legends. And like that fabled Teuton king, Arthur will ride out again, Excalibur in hand, when his country needs him the most. His memory does not die, any more than does the legend of Sir Francis Drake:

> *Take my drum to England*
> *Hang it by the shore*

And when the drum is touched, the legend says, in a day when England is at need, its beat will summon the long-dead sea dog, and Drake will appear again to help his country.

So it is with Arthur. For many centuries men of the West Country refused to believe the great soldier was dead. He was only sleeping, they said, and he would come again at need. The places associated with him are still visited by modern people who half believe, who perceive mailed shades even at noonday. There are still places in the West Country where it is easy to see such things.

The ancient hill fort at South Cadbury, in Somerset, is today identified with Camelot—and indeed it was the seat of some important commander during the years of Arthur's life. There were no soaring towers, of course, no knights clanking in and out in full plate armor. But a notable war leader did live there at about the proper time in history, and his fort was large enough to hold a formidable army . . . and its horses.

Not far away lies the sleepy town of Glastonbury, with the haunted

ruins of its beautiful abbey. Glastonbury may well be the Isle of
Avalon—in other days the sea inundated much of the surrounding
country and the area was called Ynis Witrin, the Isle of Glass. And
on the green and placid grounds of the ancient abbey there is a grave,
empty now, where legend says Arthur lay in peace for centuries.

It is easy to believe in Arthur at Glastonbury, too, for it is a mystic
place, closely linked to tales of Joseph of Arimethea and the precious
chalice called the Holy Grail. One pretty tale tells that Jesus came
to Britain as a boy, with Joseph, and stayed for a time in the West
Country. A thorn tree grows in Glastonbury—and only there—and
legend says its ancestor grew from Joseph's staff. This legend, too,
has been the subject of much scoffing . . . except that the tree grows
noplace else in England and is distinctly Mediterranean in ancestry.

And then there is Dozmary Pool, a desolate mere on Bodmin
Moor, where Excalibur may still sleep beneath the glassy surface. It
is an otherworldly place on the right kind of day. When the lonely
wind of the moor stirs the surface of that mere, one may wonder
whether that was a ripple of the wind . . . or could it have been the
slim white hand of the Lady of the Lake?

Thus the legend of Arthur, commander of the Britons. Although
we wish he were in fact a king, most historians conclude that he
probably was not. And yet, and yet . . . in 1190 the monks of
Glastonbury Abbey dug up Arthur's bones, or at least the monks
said they were Arthur's bones. The bones were reinterred with great
ceremony in a black marble tomb in front of the abbey's high altar.
They are gone now, God knows where, gone with the wind of the
dissolution of the abbeys all across England.

The monks showed visitors a lead cross that they said came from
the grave. On it was carved, in Latin: "Here lies buried the renowned
King Arthur in the Isle of Avalon." The cross is now lost—conveniently, some say. Still, many people saw it, wrote of it, and drew
pictures of it as late as two hundred years ago. Perhaps the whole
incident was faked by the monks to make Glastonbury more attractive
as a goal for pilgrims. Perhaps.

But modern archaeology has established that there was, in fact, a
grave where the monks said they found Arthur's bones, and the grave
might indeed have been as old as the fifth or sixth century. And the
Latin spelling on the cross was not the spelling of the twelfth century.

However much of Arthur's legend is invention or imagination, the fight at Badon was very real. Precisely what happened there nobody will ever know. It is even possible that it was fought on some ground other than Liddington Castle. No matter. The victory Arthur won there was one of the significant battles of any time. It deserves to be remembered.

CHAPTER TWO

THE HALLS OF MONTEZUMA
The United States Marines at the City of Mexico

WHEN TWO SMALL American armies wrested an empire from Mexico, the Marine Corps was still young, still eager to show its mettle. There was no naval war to fight, and so the marines, hungry for action, had to be content with a small part in the Army's hard-fought conquest of Mexico City. If they did not get all the action they wanted, they acquitted themselves well in heavy fighting action. And they had one incredible moment, a little time of glory that will live forever.

The goal of Winfield Scott's little army, so far from its base at Vera Cruz, was the enemy's capital. And when they faced the fortifications, Scott's tired, outnumbered men must have wondered whether the thing was possible at all. The heaviest of the fighting came in storming the formidable castle of Chapultepec, gateway to the city itself.

And for a while nobody was sure whether the stone walls of Chapultepec could be carried at all. Young Lieutenant James Longstreet was shot down as he swarmed up a scaling ladder carrying his country's colors; as he went down, Lieutenant George Pickett snatched the flagstaff and pressed on. Out in the open, a tall young gunner with piercing blue eyes was manhandling one of his pieces forward in a torrent of Mexican musketry. Miraculously untouched, the young lieutenant urged his men on. He was plain Tom Jackson in those days; one day men would call him Stonewall.

In bloody, protracted fighting, Chapultepec fell. George Pickett carried his flag all the way to the roof of the Mexican Military College, tore down the Mexican colors, and hoisted the Stars and Stripes in triumph. Now the battle for the city itself was on, a fighting advance across causeways swept with grapeshot and musketry. On the Americans pushed, on into the city, fighting their way from one house to the next through holes hacked in the connecting walls.

With the Americans coming ever closer, street by street, Santa Anna, the Mexican dictator, pulled out of the city, even though he still outnumbered his enemies. And as the shooting died away, a marine lieutenant named Augustus Nicholson climbed to the top of the National Palace, cut down the Mexican colors, and hoisted the flag of the United States.

Winfield Scott entered the City of Mexico that same evening. Bands played, everybody cheered and shouted, and the Americans celebrated an astonishing military achievement: their country had been vastly increased. Thanks to Scott and his handful, the United States had acquired new territory some five times the size of France.

And the marines had done their part, however small it had been. Ever after, the Corps would celebrate the day one of their own hoisted America's colors high above the Halls of Montezuma. In the 1840s, marine NCOs and officers began wearing a crimson stripe down the legs of their dress trousers; tradition says it commemorates the marine blood shed in storming Chapultepec Castle and the capital.

Historians have questioned whether that famous flag was raised by a marine or by somebody else. For most of us, whether it really happened is immaterial: the legend will stand as a symbol of the sort of gallant thing the marines have always done so well. Maybe Lieutenant Nicholson raised the colors over the Halls of Montezuma; maybe he didn't. You're free to decide that he didn't if you choose to.

Only don't tell that to a marine.

SEVEN FEET OF ENGLISH EARTH

Harold the King at Stamford Bridge

HAROLD GODWINSON WAS king of England. Though he sat on the throne of Alfred the Great, though he wore the crown of Edward the Confessor, his seat was precarious; the sceptre of England was slippery in his hands. He was ringed about by mortal enemies on every side, including the two most dangerous men in Europe. Harold's royal writ ran little farther than the length of his sword.

Across the English Channel in Normandy glowered William the Bastard, Duke of Normandy. With the indulgence of the late, inept Edward, Norman clerics and nobles had been infiltrating the English court for years—a Norman churchman had even been made Archbishop of Canterbury. The critical Cinque Ports—Dover, Sandwich, Romney, and the rest—were governed by Normans, even though these havens were the first line of defense against foreign invasion. Harold's father—Earl Godwin—had resisted the burgeoning Norman presence and been exiled for his pains.

Godwin's exile lasted only about a year. In 1052 he returned in triumph, supported by public opinion, driving out many of the Norman favorites, including the foreigner who held the see of holy Canterbury. Earl Godwin died in 1053, and his sons carried on: a more interesting band of brothers is hard to imagine. A certain amount of mythology surrounds the family to this day.

One of Godwin's sons is said to have ridden with the army that upset the usurper Macbeth in Scotland in 1054. Another respected history says that the stony heart of another brother, Leofwine, was responsible for the, ah, bareback ride of his saintly wife, immortalized as Lady Godiva (a pretty story, that, except that the lady's husband seems to have been, in fact, one Leofric, Earl of Mercia). Another brother, Sweyn, became enamored of a nun and carried her off quite against her will.

Tostig, the eldest, was also the blackest sheep of Godwin's unruly sons. He was, moreover, a worthless ruler, and he so mismanaged and oppressed his own northern earldom that his subjects deposed him and drove him into exile—with Harold's approval. However mythical some of the feats attributed to Godwin's hardy offspring, they were surely bold, tough, fearless men.

Foremost among them was Harold—intelligent, practical, ruthless, and courageous—a remarkable man born to rule and to lead. He seems to have been something of a patriot, too, although in those far-off days there was really no British nation, at least not in the modern sense. Harold was English and proud of it, and not a man to stand quietly and see his land ruled by men who came from across the sea in any direction.

Harold became a sort of executive to Edward, making many of the practical decisions for the otherworldly monarch. Harold was called "subregulus" (literally, "underking") and "Dux Anglorum," "chief of the British." His name appears with that of the king as co-signatory of royal charters; some vassals pledged their fealty to both the king and Harold.

We have no accurate picture of Harold, only a stylized image on a coin, but he was surely tough and burly, a man trained to arms and horses from childhood. He was tall and handsome as well, with the long hair and mustache of the professional fighting man. On his throat and right hand appeared the customary blue tattoos of the Saxon. We know he was an able soldier and an intelligent, tolerant ruler, ferocious in battle but capable of leniency and forgiveness in victory. He was popular, too, and well educated for his time: he spoke French, apparently quite well.

He had proved himself as a soldier. He had smashed the Welsh in a rapid, hard-hitting campaign in which he modified the arms and armor of his soldiers to give them speed and mobility among the Welsh mountains. And Harold had his tender moments, as well. His attachment to his mistress, Edith of the Swan-neck, persisted throughout his adult years and produced six children.

With Harold standing at the shoulder of King Edward, all might have gone well—had Edward behaved remotely as people expected a king to behave. Being bumbling, vague, and otherworldly was bad enough for a monarch, but taking an oath of perpetual chastity on his wedding day was a bit much for Englishmen to stomach.

It is not recorded what Edward's bride thought of this somewhat discouraging start to her marriage, but the leadership of England was not happy. Edward's oath meant that there would be no direct heir to the crown, a grievous failing that might well expose the island of Britain to all manner of bloody quarrels over the succession.

And so, when Edward died in the first week of the year 1066, Englishmen held their breath to see who would wear the crown. Harold had been named heir by the old king, although there were other claimants, including a small boy, a collateral heir of Edward's own family line. However, Harold was a man grown, a soldier and administrator of proven ability, and he was already running the country; the Anglo-Saxon noble council—the witan—elected him king.

William of Normandy protested immediately, claiming that Edward had long ago appointed him successor to the crown. Moreover, said William, Harold had once been shipwrecked on the Norman coast, becoming, so to speak, the property of the duchy with his ship and crew. At that time, said William, Harold had sworn to help William gain the throne of England; William had secreted all manner of holy relics in front of Harold, so his oath was binding before God, whether Harold had intended it so or not.

By Easter of 1066 England was full of the rumor of war. Toward the end of April a ghastly beacon appeared in the English sky night after night for a week, trailing a horrible tail of fire. It was Halley's Comet, but to superstitious men of the eleventh century it could be nothing but a dreadful omen of great and terrible events, "a portent such as men had never seen before." The "hairy star," as some men called it, produced awe, terror, and a torrent of vague predictions of doom, tragedy, and disaster. There would be, wailed the seers, much killing before this awful year was out. In that, at least, they were entirely right.

By that time King Harold knew that William was coming; the only question was when. The grim Norman duke had begun to gather troops and shipping, calling in his own vassals, offering English land to any restless younger son of European nobility who would pledge his sword to William. His army would not be large—there was not enough shipping for a really numerous force—but it would be a formidable mix of archers, mailed foot soldiers, and mounted men at arms in chain mail and steel caps.

King Harold's strength rested largely in Wessex and the other southern earldoms; the north was uncertain in its loyalty. In fact, the British of those days had no feeling of national identity; most men were apathetic, engrossed in local affairs or preoccupied by their own struggles to raise their families and wrest a living from the soil.

And Harold had other worries as well; his exiled brother Tostig, thus far sulking in Scotland or harrying the English coast (with William's connivance), had now done something even more flagrant. He had taken his simmering hatred to Norway, lair of England's ancient enemy. And now, at Trondheim, the Vikings were gathering men and long ships, their covetous eyes fixed on the island of Britain.

For the famous Norse warrior-king Harald Hardrada had offered Tostig assistance: his own experienced sword he would give, plus fighting men and long ships. Hardrada meant ''ruthless,'' and the Norse king was all of that. For centuries the Norse pirates had coveted English goods and English blood, and had regularly sailed south to kill and steal. If he could, the great Viking king would now make himself monarch of the whole island. Tostig's resentment of his brother had provided the Viking a perfect opportunity to invade and occupy the island of Britain.

Now Harold faced two lowering perils. If William was the nearer, the threat from the north was older. Ever since the sacking of holy Lindisfarne Island in 783, and the murder of its monks, the pagan Vikings had terrorized all Britain, gradually pushing their murdering way farther and farther south. ''From the fury of the Norsemen,'' ran the old English prayer, ''O Lord, deliver us.'' Now that fury was about to break over England again, a host of bright axes behind the black raven banner called ''Land-Waster'' by the fighting men of Scandinavia.

And so King Harold gathered his fighting men about him and watched, waiting for news and no doubt praying that both perils would not come upon him at once. He also had to worry about his own army, at least about those who were not his own personal retainers. His own men, his housecarls—or thingmen—ate his salt and would stick by him to the death. The other levies, however, had fields and possessions and families of their own to worry about, and a harvest coming. Harold could not hold his soldiers together forever.

His men are generally pictured as infantry soldiers, or mostly so. In England, however, horses had long been used to move a select fighting force quickly to the point of decision; the Briton commander Arthur apparently had done so five centuries or so before the reign of Harold. There is no reason to doubt that Harold's men not only marched but fought on horseback, although they also did much of their fighting on foot, at least when the terrain was at all rough.

The housecarls—the professionals—and some of the better-armed reservists wore chain mail tunics, called hauberks or birnies, reaching to the knees and sometimes below. Some of these chain mail shirts, and the best of them, were built up with as many as four layers of interlocking metal rings. The shirt was generally worn over a padded jacket.

The average weight of a mail shirt was about thirty pounds or a little less, and it was reasonably flexible. There was a hole for the wearer's head, a drawstring or buckle at the neck, and wide sleeves to give the soldier plenty of room to swing his weapon. Some men protected their legs with leather; a few had leggings of chain mail; most made do with the usual wrappings of cloth.

The warrior's head was protected by a steel helmet, sometimes including cheek pieces or a "nasal," a strip of iron projecting down the front of the wearer's face to give some protection to the nose and eyes. Most of these helmets were plain conical caps; the "Viking" helmet, with horns or a fanciful crest, was largely a ceremonial ornament and was not worn in action.

When he owned one, the warrior protected himself with a shield. According to the Bayeux tapestry, the illustrated history of the Norman Conquest, the Saxon fighting man, like the Norman, carried a shield shaped like a tall kite or elongated heart. It generally was made with an iron boss in its center to protect the left fist as it gripped the shield's inside handle. Shields were of wood—the wood of the lime tree was a favorite material—about a yard long and fifteen inches or so in width. They were reinforced with metal rims and covered with hide, often fancifully painted.

The ordinary soldier had to be content with lesser equipment, a quilted jacket or a leather jerkin. Sometimes his jacket was reinforced with plates of horn or iron, or had individual mail rings sewn to it. Many had only their workaday clothing, and no weapon more sophisticated than the keen billhooks they used to clear brush and prune trees.

Saxon fighting men used the bow, although it was a smaller and far less formidable weapon than the murderous longbow of the Plantagenet Edwards and Henry V. Harold's men were fond of closing with hand weapons: sword, mace, or ax. They made much use of a short, slender spear with a shaft of ash and a point of steel, iron, or even bronze, sometimes made to break away from the shaft so the weapon could not be thrown back. This spear could be thrown or used as a thrusting weapon, and some soldiers carried several of these spears and used them like javelins. Other warriors also carried a light, razor-sharp ax, designed to be thrown overhand at close range.

The sword was about thirty inches long and generally double-edged, although some had only one cutting surface; some fighting men wielded monstrous swords that could only be swung two-handed. Some warriors slung their shields to swing long-handled, two-handed axes, brutal weapons that could shear completely through both man and armor with a single stroke. Others wielded war clubs or maces with iron heads, or a deadly flail called the morning-star, a spiked iron head attached by a chain to a wooden staff.

The cream of Harold's army were his own household troops, the housecarls, professional soldiers with their own stout code of loyalty and responsibility to the king. Most of them were mercenaries, in fact, but mercenaries who felt a powerful sense of loyalty. Treason to their employer was punishable by death; once enlisted, a man could not even leave the corps of housecarls except on the first day of the year.

Harold could count on these men absolutely, to the death, but they were comparatively few. Far greater in number were the select reservists, men who were called up for sixty days in time of need. They were expected to appear for duty ready and equipped, armed in much the same way as the professional housecarls. Many reservists were experienced soldiers; all of them seem to have been a superior sort of man, both strong and willing. These reserve soldiers were apparently designated in advance, so that the same men answered the call each time; it may well have been a signal honor to be appointed as a member of this elite reserve.

The English kings had the power to call up one select reservist for every five hides of land. A hide was the area generally considered adequate to support one free family, and it varied in size from shire to shire, all the way from 40 to 160 acres. Each hide was also levied for four shillings for the man's wages and food for two months, the period of his obligated service. Towns were assessed a number of hides according to their size and population.

Thus, thriving Oxford, rated at a hundred hides, owed Harold twenty armed men; Leicester furnished twelve; Exeter, then a small town, was assessed at five hides and sent a single soldier to join the king's army. Even smaller towns could band together to raise a solitary soldier. These reservists were reliable fighting men, too, and well armed; they were not as experienced as the housecarls, perhaps, but they could be counted on to obey orders and stand their ground.

Finally, there was the "great fyrd," the general levy of all free men, the stout but inexperienced common citizenry. Some were able to bring along conventional weapons; others had to be satisfied with their own pitchforks and billhooks, scythes and cudgels and woodsman's axes. Virtually none of them possessed any defensive armor at all.

They were raised locally in any threatened area, and so generally some had incentive to fight for their own region and their own homes. Being unpaid, however, they had farms and trades and families to worry about; once the immediate danger had passed, or failed to materialize, they were moved to return home. Indeed, unless the king could afford to pay them, they were entitled to return home every evening, a fairly severe limitation on the range and mobility of the royal army.

As the summer of 1066 passed, and harvesttime approached, neither danger appeared. William's clumsy ships were pinned against the French coast by contrary winds while the duke raged impotently and tried to find provisions for his soldiers. Of vengeful, sulky Tostig and King Harald Hardrada there was no sign. Rations were running low for Harold's men, and for some of them the obligated term of service had expired. And so, on the feast of Mary's Nativity, September 8, Harold sent his reservists home and returned to Westminster himself. By the grace of God the wind would remain kind, he prayed, and England would not be troubled until the next year.

But the wind was not kind. Trouble was coming, coming fast on a brisk breeze from the north, swelling the bright sails of some three hundred war galleys heaving south from Norway. The very wind that kept the Norman duke in port blew fair for Viking invaders running down from the northern seas. In the lead was the huge dragon ship of Harald Hardrada, the Viking who would be king of England. Behind the king sailed as many as nine or ten thousand men, perhaps half the whole warrior strength of Norway. A number of rovers from Iceland and Ireland also had come along for the adventure and the loot.

If anybody had doubted that Hardrada was coming to stay, he doubted no longer. The huge Norwegian had brought much of his family, too, plus precious holy relics of St. Olaf. He also brought the royal treasury—which, according to legend, included a gold ingot so big it took twelve men to carry it.

Sailing ahead of Hardrada was Tostig, his heart seething with black hatred, leading a force of adventurers he had raised in Scotland. Both forces raided along the Yorkshire coast, burning and killing, virtually destroying the port of Scarborough and a dozen smaller places. The English survivors saved their lives by submission to King Harald of Norway.

Unopposed, the invaders at last turned into the great estuary of the Humber and sailed upriver toward York, metropolis of the north. Altogether, the invaders almost surely outnumbered the defenders; at nine or ten thousand, they were an enormous army for the time. The Vikings anchored at a place called Riccall, just below the junction of the Wharfe and the Ouse.

English opposition was gathering under the two northern earls, Edwin and Morcar, although the local levies could match the northmen neither in numbers nor in experience. They were up against the cream of the Viking marauders, men whose whole lives had been given to war and raiding. Still, outmanned as they were, the earls tried their best.

They met the northern horde on September 20, the eve of St. Mathias's Day, two miles south of York near a place called Fulford

Gate, drawn up between the river Ouse and a marsh. The English attacked, and for a while drove back one wing of Hardrada's host with considerable loss. Then numbers and experience began to tell, the Norsemen counterattacked, and the English force began to fall apart. The Viking bards sang that their enemy:

> lay in the fen, hewn down by the sword, so thickly heaped that they paved a way across the swamp for the brave Norsemen.

The *Anglo-Saxon Chronicle* sadly mentioned that "a great number of the English were either slain or drowned or driven in flight. . . ." Among the corpses lay a number of English priests, who died fighting the ancient enemy with weapons in their hands. Altogether, as many as a thousand Northumbrian fighting men may have fallen at Fulford Gate.

We know little of the details of the fight at Fulford Gate, but it may well be that the Vikings decided the day with a charge in their favorite swine formation, a sort of flying wedge tipped by a group of the boldest and most ferocious fighters. The point of the wedge, driven by the energy of many ranks behind it, drove deep into the English ranks, with everybody roaring war cries and blowing horns.

However the final disaster overtook the English force, the way to York was open. The Northumbrian army was scattered, what remained of it, and the earls were fugitives. Hardrada, intent on ruling all of England, would not open the city to pillage and killing in the old Viking style; instead, he took hostages and requisitioned supplies but left the city otherwise unmolested.

The Norse king ordered a further meeting with local representatives, a meeting to which they were to bring further hostages, this time from all over the shire. They were to meet at lonely Stamford Bridge, about eight miles east of York, a place where a number of ancient paths came together at the placid river Derwent, and thence led on to York. The Norwegian king was perhaps overconfident. He does not seem to have counted on the energy and decisiveness of the king of England—or the speed of his hard-marching army.

For Harold was on the way. Sometime toward the end of the second week in September he received intelligence that a massive invasion from the north was either imminent or actually under way. He may well have been alerted to the actual landing by a chain of fire beacons, a prearranged signal that his Norse enemy was ashore. In spite of the danger from William, awaiting only a fair wind, Harold chose to confront the immediate peril.

With his housecarls and as much of his local reserve as he could call up, he set out for York. Some, perhaps all, of his professionals rode horses; the common men no doubt walked. With a brief stop at his favorite church at Waltham, Harold hurried north along Ermine Street, the ancient road to York, his men swinging over the same stones that had echoed to the tramp of the long-vanished legions of Rome.

They had two hundred dusty miles to go, and Harold drove his army, as the chronicles say, "by day and by night" up the old trade road to the north. Pushing hard up the east coast, he passed through Lincoln, a long column of dusty men and tired horses and creaking carts loaded with provisions, exhausted stragglers trailing for miles behind him. He would have sent messengers galloping ahead of him, ordering local officials to call out at least the select fyrd to join him on the march.

On his men hurried, on through the rugged foothills of the Pennines into Tadcaster town, only a few miles from York itself. It was Sunday, September 24, and the corpses at Fulford were only four days cold. Harold had made a phenomenal march, almost two hundred miles in four to six days.

By then, he must have known of the Fulford Gate disaster. Messengers from the northern earls, and fugitives, would have reached him on the road well before his dusty soldiers swung into the town of Tadcaster and camped in the pretty meadows along the river Wharfe. Harold, the experienced soldier, no doubt soon knew where the Viking host was camped.

Harold would have known that his enemies were weary from the struggle at Fulford and somewhat weakened by the losses they had suffered there. Most important, Harold would have guessed that Hardrada and Tostig did not know an English army was only a few miles away. Harold, bold as always, would waste no time. The Norse king would get not his hostages, but steel.

Harold set his army in motion early on the next day, Monday, marching for York and then turning toward Stamford Bridge. As the day became hotter, the English army pushed quickly through Gate Helmsley, a village not far from the Derwent, and shook itself out into battle order. It advanced down a very slight slope across open ground, ahead of it the wooden bridge and the rush-grown, quiet Derwent. Beyond the river the ground rose again gradually toward the rolling Wolds . . . and behind them the sea.

Hardrada had left a guard with his ships at Riccall, some twelve miles from Stamford Bridge—in all probability, not a great number of men. There is some speculation that some of the Vikings might even have left their mail shirts behind in the ships, it being a hot day, but it is hard to imagine a Norse fighting man going anyplace without his full equipment. Moreover, though Hardrada had won a significant victory, he was an experienced soldier, and he had to know that Harold, also a veteran, might appear at any time.

In any case, the main body of the Norwegian army was apparently camped on both sides of the river. The first warning the Norsemen had of the death bearing down on them may have been an ominous cloud of dust rising into the clear morning air from the York road.

The Vikings ran for their weapons as the English battle line rolled down toward the bridge, attacking slightly downhill, and the Vikings on the west bank hurried to put the river between them and the advancing English. Some did not get across in time and died quickly on the west bank. Legend says that some of the Norsemen were attacked before they even had time to don their mail shirts.

For a brief moment the narrow bridge became a serious bottleneck as one enormous, ax-wielding Viking valiantly held the way all alone. Then he was gone, stabbed from beneath the bridge by one of Harold's warriors, who, legend says, floated under the structure in a wooden salting tub. (This legend lingered on into the present century in "spear pies," pastries shaped like little boats, eaten at an annual Stamford Bridge celebration about the anniversary of the battle.)

With the bridge cleared, the English were across the Derwent, forming quickly on the east side of the lazy river. They were faced by a rough shield wall, hastily assembled, snaking across a little rise about three hundred yards east of the river. By one Norse account, the Viking shield wall formed a complete circle, bristling with spears against the English cavalry. The place where the invaders made their stand is known to this day as Battle Flats.

Legend also says that Harold, as much as he valued surprise, still halted briefly to make one last attempt to save his traitor brother. If it happened at all, Harold's pause must have occurred as his men reformed and caught their breath in front of the shield wall on the east bank. Harold certainly struck the Vikings on the west bank without pausing; he was too good a soldier to sacrifice surprise to speechmaking, even to save an errant brother.

In any case, the legend goes like this: Either by messenger, or by personally hailing Tostig as he stood waiting in the Viking ranks, Harold offered his brother not only peace but the Northumbrian duke-dom. Sneering, Tostig retorted, "And what will you give my Norwegian friend?" This arrogant reply was too much for Harold.

"Seven feet of English earth," roared the king, "or as much as he is taller than other men!"

That, as the English say, tore it, and Harold's men went roaring in to attack, charging under a cloud of arrows and thrown spears. What followed was terrible hand-to-hand butchery, with sword and ax and mace and dagger. The English pushed on hard, never giving the Norsemen breathing room, the veterans among them well aware that a Viking attacked was far less formidable than a Viking attacking.

Some of the Saxon warriors probably charged on horseback, although as to this, historians cannot agree. The Norse historian Snorri Sturluson, writing his *Heimskringla* saga a century after, says the English advanced as cavalry, at least after the Viking shield wall failed. The level ground was surely fine cavalry country, solid and unobstructed. Although the details are lost in the mists of time, there is surely no reason to think the English did not charge mounted across terrain as favorable as this. They might even have used bows from the saddle, for the *Heimskringla* says the English "rode upon [the Vikings] from all sides and threw spears and shot at them."

The masses of struggling men heaved and surged against each other, the bloody blades catching a little of the autumn sun as they bit into wooden shields, or crunched into a mail shirt, or split and tore living flesh. The wounds were hideous, gaping cuts and slashes in heads and faces and shoulders, sometimes an arm shorn off like a tree branch by one of those terrible axes. Some men went down riddled with arrows or skewered on boar spears; others died with their skulls smashed by maces or morning-stars. Step-by-step, across sod sticky with blood, the English pressed forward.

Harold's housecarls were the spearhead, a solid, cohesive block of mail-clad professionals, their bloody axes rising and falling as they

slashed ever deeper into Hardrada's lines. Their terrible prowess
would long be celebrated in Norse legend, which knew them as the
men who were the equal of any two ordinary warriors. On and on
the struggle went, the air filled with the clang and crash of metal on
metal, the screams of hurt men, the terrible crunch of steel biting
flesh, the sound of a butcher chopping meat.

Deeper and deeper into the Norse ranks went Harold's banners,
the golden dragon of Wessex and the embroidered standard of the
fighting man. Dying men shrieked in agony and called out God's
name; gasping warriors howled their war cries and swung their weapons with leaden arms; blood and brains splashed across the faces of
the fighting men on both sides. In spite of their long, swift march,
the English were the fresher; the Norsemen had been badly mauled
in the Fulford victory, and now they fell back step-by-step, and their
wounded were trampled into the sod by the English.

And still the killing went on. The Vikings held out into the afternoon, but gradually those terrible English axes began to gain the
upper hand, and the shield wall crumbled. Hardrada, veteran of a
hundred fights and raids, fought on, his treasured vision of English
kingship only a mirage now. As his bard later sang:

> . . . the chief's heart never quaked, and the greatest courage was
> shown by the strong king amidst the war-cloud's thunder . . . by
> his bloody sword the men to death were wounded.

But courage was not enough anymore, not against the English axes.

Sometime after noon the Norwegian king went down, an English
arrow in his throat. With the mighty Hardrada died three centuries
of Viking terror; the "fury of the northmen" would trouble England
no more. Tostig fell somewhat later, still fighting, his head cloven
to the chin by a housecarl's ax. Whatever other unpleasant traits the
renegade displayed, he did not lack for courage. And as the shadows
began to lengthen, the Land-Waster fell and did not rise, and the
remains of the Norwegian army broke into panicked flight, leaving
a great heap of contorted corpses and writhing wounded on the
battlefield.

In the afternoon a Viking reinforcement under Eyestein Orre came
panting up from the ships and plunged shouting into the fray. They
charged fiercely into the melee—the Norse sagas called their attack

"Orre's storm"—but they could not turn the tide. They were exhausted from their forced march, and the English smelled victory. Orre's men died with the rest.

The *Heimskringla* says that late in the day Harold offered mercy to the surviving invaders—and that they proudly refused—but that is an unlikely possibility. For three centuries these Norsemen had raped and butchered and robbed in England. Thousands upon thousands of Saxons had died: men, women, and children; from toddlers to graybeards. Harold would have had no mercy in his heart for the ancestral enemy, and neither would his men. In any case, he gave the Vikings no rest, and he gave them no quarter.

And so the grim king drove his exhausted soldiers into pursuit, a ruthless, relentless hunting and killing that went on until the light was gone. It is likely that at least some of the English pursued on horseback, cutting down the fleeing Vikings without pity as the invaders ran wearily for their ships.

The *Anglo-Saxon Chronicle* somberly told of the end:

> While the English savagely harried their rear, the remaining Norwegians were put to flight . . . some were drowned, some were burnt to death . . . diversely they perished, until there were few survivors. . . .

Judging from the words of the *Chronicle,* some of the Vikings must have died floundering in the placid Derwent as they tried to reach their ships, for Riccall was on the opposite side of the Derwent, and the river is deep. More were killed when the English set fire to farmhouses or barns or churches in which the Norsemen had tried to make a desperate stand.

The rest were run down one at a time, or in small groups of two or three panting, desperate fugitives, slaughtered without pity and left for the ravens. As long as a Viking remained, the pursuing English killed and killed. The countryside around Battle Flats was littered with bones and rusty weapon shards for decades afterward.

Only a very few of the invaders survived, a small detachment left to guard the dragon ships heaved up on the riverbank. These men, including one of Hardrada's sons, got to their ships before the terrible axes reached them and pulled desperately downriver for the sea and safety.

Some versions of the fight suggest that Harold permitted these
survivors to flee, perhaps to carry the horror of Stamford Bridge
back to Norway. Maybe so. But considering the prevailing English
view—that the only good Viking was a dead Viking—this seems
unlikely. Harold would have reasoned that an invader killed now was
an invader who would nevermore return to England. Word of Hardrada's defeat and death would reach the northland sooner or later—
most effectively, perhaps, if no man of the great Norse host ever
returned to tell the tale in person.

In any case, some three hundred proud raiding ships had carried
Hardrada's host into Yorkshire. The surviving invaders needed only
twenty-four keels to take them home. Hardrada got his seven feet of
English earth; Tostig, as befitted a king's brother, even a treasonous
one, was honorably buried in York Cathedral.

The English had suffered heavy losses themselves. A good many
of their fighting men were dead; some could move only with great
pain and effort, or not at all; many others bore wounds that would
keep them from battle for many a long day. The trouble was, there
were not many days left in the autumn of Anglo-Saxon Britain.

For just three days after Stamford Bridge, William of Normandy
came ashore at Pevensey Bay in southeast England, two hundred
long miles to the south. As soon as word reached him, Harold put
his weary army on the road again, gathering reinforcements as he
went, sending messengers galloping ahead of him to rally still more
men. Only eight days after William's landing, after another astonishing march with tired and wounded men trailing behind him, Harold was back in London.

The longer Harold could wait in London, the more men he could
gather. It took time to notify local officials, who then had to call up
the reservists and the general levy and get them on the road to
Harold. He could ignore a series of challenges and taunts from
William; he was too cool a soldier to react to insults. But the
longer Harold waited, the worse became William's depredations
against the villagers and farmers in Sussex, Harold's own family
dukedom.

Torn between the agony of his subjects and his own anger—and
the obvious necessity to rest his tired troops and gather more—
Harold sought inspiration at his own Church of the Holy Rood, in

Waltham. There, the story goes, he offered God his lifelong service in return for victory over the Normans and laid himself prostrate in front of the cross. In that moment, a church official said afterward, the image of Jesus on the crucifix sadly hung its head (in another version, the church tower fell, symbolizing God's displeasure). No mortal can bargain with the Lord, not even a king.

Harold had worked a minor miracle thus far. Fulford Gate had been fought on September 20; York had surrendered to Hardrada on the twenty-fourth. Harold won his great victory at Stamford Bridge the next day. On the first of October, Harold learned that William had landed at Pevensey on September 28. On October 5, Harold was back in London, furiously raising more men. Had he waited there another ten days or two weeks, until his stragglers joined and the shires sent fresh men to join him, what then might have been the history of Britain?

In the event, however, just five short days after his return from the north country, Harold rallied what troops he had and marched southward for the sea, sixty miles to the grassy hillside called Senlac. There he would meet the mercenaries of William the Bastard in the battle we know as Hastings. Beside him rode his brothers Gyrth and Leofwine, and their household troops swelled the ranks of Harold's own housecarls.

In hindsight, Harold did not decide well. Much of his strength was still on the road and had yet to join him. No doubt many of the men who had fought with him in the north were still straggling south; on top of the almost two hundred long miles between York and London, there were another sixty from London to Senlac. Dismounted men could not have kept up with the mounted housecarls and the men of the select fyrd. In particular, most of Harold's bowmen must have been common men whose legs were their only transportation.

Harold's army probably amounted to no more than six or seven thousand men all told, and a great many of these were poorly armed peasants with little to offer but loyalty and courage. The shires around London had already been stripped of their best men before the march north to York; there could not have been many first-class fighting men left. What there were could not replace the troops sleeping under the sod in the north, the wounded, and those still trudging wearily south along Ermine Street. The army that marched toward

Hastings was only a shadow of the host that had won Stamford Bridge.

And so King Harold of England moved to meet a rested, professional army. With the banners of Wessex and the fighting man carried proudly behind him, Harold marched toward the sea, toward his own fate, toward the future of England.

He marched to his death.

CHAPTER FOUR

THE DEVILS IN THE FLESH

SINCE THE DAWN of time, every army has been haunted by the specter of venereal disease. Where soldiers are, there also appear ladies of leisure. And with the exception of a few devout, God-fearing forces—such as Cromwell's Ironsides—soldiers are not slow to seek the ladies, or the ladies to advertise their availability. The twain become one at every opportunity, and be damned to orders.

In World War I, officialdom's struggle against VD took a variety of forms. The Canadians went so far as to employ a well-known revivalist preacher to exhort Canadian troops to "remain continent." The British did nothing, reasoning, in Kipling's words, that "single men in barracks don't grow into plaster saints." The French also did nothing, and by the end of the war there were a million French VD cases. The Americans issued all manner of "thou shalt not" orders, put guards on every place in which a man could conceivably find some fun, and sent MPs lurking everywhere.

But the New Zealanders operated on the theory that if you can't beat 'em, it is better to join 'em. And so they organized something called the Venereal Prophylaxis Service, whose business it was to hand out condoms wholesale to soldiers on leave in England. Its attractive female supervisor made sure each New Zealander on leave in London got a box of six condoms.

"Six?" asked an American doctor.

"Yes," said the young woman. "Every New Zealander needs at least six his first night in London." And she added, perhaps unnecessarily, "We have some particularly sturdy specimens."

For sure.

In Vietnam, American forces tried various expedients, well aware that young soldiers did not put their hormones in storage during their year in southeast Asia. Fourth Infantry Division went so far as to sponsor its own little community of brothels, known locally as "Sin City." A soldier had to have a pass to go there, and he went only in daylight.

Sin City was covered by the guns of Camp Enari, where the divisional headquarters was, and the girls were regularly inspected by American doctors. If a prostitute became infected, the doctors closed down the entire house; such Draconian measures pretty well ensured that the madams made certain their girls did not stray from the fold and out among the microbes. Even the price was regulated: 300 piastres, soldier (if you were an officer, too bad; grit your teeth, you're not going to Sin City.)

Sin City worked fine for a while. The VD rate and the AWOL rate both stayed very low. The soldiers were happy. So were their commanders. All went merry as a wedding bell until an article in a national news magazine revealed the existence of Sin City. Some fathead reporter was engaging in bashing the Vietnamese army—a favorite pastime in those days—and alleged that one of its units spent its days guarding Sin City for the Fourth Infantry.

It wasn't true, of course. Either the writer had never been to Sin City or he made it all up or both. ARVN soldiers never went down there at all, in fact, except for the odd military policeman. But the cat was out of the bag, and all the do-gooders shed tears and called their congressmen, and that was that.

All that's left of Sin City is a cardboard sign hanging in a frame on this writer's wall. It's crude and hand-lettered, but it's a real piece of history. It says:

NOTICE

THE PRICE OF A WOMAN
IS **300** PIASTERS. IF
YOU ARE REQUIRED TO
PAY MORE NOTIFY THE
MILITARY POLICE.

DON JOHN OF AUSTRIA
GOES TO WAR

The Turkish Disaster at Lepanto

In that enormous silence, tiny and unafraid
comes up along a winding road the noise of a crusade.
Strong gongs groaning as the guns boom far,
Don John of Austria is going to the war.
Stiff flags straining in the night-blasts cold,
in the gloom black-purple, in the glint old-gold,
torchlight crimson on the copper kettle-drums,
then the tuckets, then the trumpets, then the cannon,
and he comes.
—*Gilbert Chesterton*, Lepanto

THE YEAR WAS 1571, and Christendom was in terrible danger. Just over a century before, great Constantinople had fallen to the Turkish enemy. The last Eastern emperor had died somewhere in the flaming night, sword in hand, and now the thousand years of Christian Byzantium were only a wistful memory.

The years afterward had been a time of war and hatred and much killing. The Turks had moved north, raiding and raping in Greece, in Albania, in Serbia, and in Hungary. Turkish cavalry pounded into northern Italy, and in 1499 a Turkish fleet beat the Venetians badly in the Gulf of Patras, off a place called Lepanto. After two epic sieges, the Turks captured Rhodes from the Knights of St. John, and Sultan Süleyman smashed a Christian army at Mohacs and occupied Budapest. In 1529 the Turks were beaten back from the very gates of Vienna.

Now the Turk was once more hammering at the gates of the West.

34

And as so often before, the Christian powers were not unified, but only childish gaggles of quarreling, jealous rivals, sharing little but a common faith. Not only would they not assist one another against the common enemy, they wasted their substance in vicious little wars among themselves. France, for example, so hated the Hapsburg dynasty of Austria that the French king sent a fleet to aid the Turks as they harried the Mediterranean. Spaniard fought Frenchman, Englishman, and Dutchman. A horrifying Moorish uprising in 1568 left Spain bathed in the blood of civil war.

Beginning in 1537, Turkey fought a protracted war against Venice, the queen of the Adriatic. In spite of Venetian prowess at sea, the sultan's men drove the proud republic from many of her possessions in and outside the Adriatic—except Crete, Cyprus, and Corfu.

In 1565, in a memorable siege, the Knights of St. John held tiny Malta against a huge Turkish army, leaving stinking heaps of Turkish dead stacked outside their battered walls. Otherwise, however, the Turkish armies moved on, pushing into southeastern Europe and occupying large parts of Austria, Transylvania, and Serbia. At last, in 1568, the Hapsburgs made peace with the sultan, by this time one Selim, called the Sot. Still, all the world knew it was only a truce, no more than a fragile intermission between wars.

And so it was. By the summer of 1570 the Turks were besieging the town of Famagusta, in Cyprus, losing thousands of men in futile attempts to storm the city's crumbling fortifications. At last, after a masterly defense, the Venetian commander, Bragadino, surrendered, assured by the Turkish general of honorable terms. What he and his garrison got instead was blackest treachery.

Most of the surrendered Christian garrison was either butchered or dragged away in chains to perpetual slavery, many of them to pull oars in the Turkish gallies that harried the Middle Sea. Bragadino himself was brutalized: his nose and ears were cut off and he was flayed alive, not dying until about half the skin had been stripped from his writhing body. Cyprus became yet another Turkish possession, with all the misery that status implied.

Long before Cyprus fell, it was obvious to the leaders of the West that the sultan's fleets would continue westward. The menace would grow and grow, and this year, or the next, or the year after that, the hated Turk would be at the very gates of central Europe. In spite of the deadly rivalry between Spain and the Italian cities, notably Ven-

ice, something had to be done to preserve Christendom from the
might of the antichrist. Pope Pius V saw the danger clearly and
pressed hard and fervently for a selfless alliance against the common
enemy. He was hard to resist.

The result was the Holy League, a confederacy of the Papal States,
Spain, and Venice, with contributions from several of the smaller
Italian states and a contingent of those formidable warrior monks,
the Knights of Malta. France would not join, her hatred of Spain
and lust for Turkish trade overshadowing any duty the French crown
might have felt toward the Church.

The league's members agreed to furnish two hundred war galleys
among them, a hundred or more other ships, fifty thousand infantry,
and forty-five hundred cavalry. The commander—the captain-gen-
eral—would be the Pope's own nominee, an able, charismatic twenty-
four-year-old, Don John of Austria, illegitimate half brother of the
Holy Roman Emperor.

Don John's own history was something straight from a romance
novel. His mother was Barbara Blomberg, a fascinating young
woman of Regensburg, in Germany. His father, the Holy Roman
Emperor Charles V, though he provided for young John, would not
recognize him. His mother, Charles's mistress, was married off comfortably to an imperial official; John was adopted by a retired court
musician, pensioned off to live quietly in bucolic Castile. Neither the
musician nor his wife knew the blood that flowed in the veins of
their new little boy.

John might have rusticated in Spain for the rest of his life. However, when his foster father died, a court official took the boy to his
own villa. John grew up there and acquired both the learning of
books and the art of soldiering; with his education, he also drank
deep of a passionate devotion to Mother Church. At long last, after
his real father's death, his half brother, King Philip, reluctantly recognized him and he took his place at court. His arrival must have been
something of a relief to the Spanish leadership, since Philip's only
son, Don Carlos, was more than a little demented.

Don John was a handsome, articulate man with an air about him;
he was of average size and was a considerable athlete. He was a
superb horseman and an avid tennis player, and he spoke three languages besides his own. And, as the Venetian ambassador somewhat
cryptically reported, he was "careful to seek his pleasure with those

women who are in the habit of intriguing with princes,'' apparently
a comment reflecting respect for the prince's judgment.

Now, pushed into the terrible burden of high command by the
Pope, Don John faced one of the most difficult leadership tasks of
all time. His enemy was unified, operating under a single will, vastly
outnumbering any force the West could bring against it. In addition
to some twelve thousand Janissaries, the elite shock troops of the
sultan, the Turkish forces numbered more than a hundred thousand
cavalry plus an uncountable horde of infantry.

At sea, sailing to join his fleet off Sicily, Don John learned for
the first time that his brother's directives required him to have all
orders countersigned by a senior Spanish officer, effectively ham-
stringing his ability to command. The Spanish king, jealous of this
bright young man, as well as fearful of the risks of battle, had also
managed to frame a petty edict slyly directing that John might be
addressed as ''Excellency'' . . . but never ''Highness,'' the preroga-
tive of royal blood.

Worse still, Don John's subordinate commanders were constantly
at odds, arguing heatedly over one thing or another; the requirement
that John's orders have a Spanish countersignature could only aggra-
vate those divisions. National rivalries among the crewmen ran nearly
as deep. To counter this divisive quarreling, Don John shuffled his
ships so that all three major divisions of his fleet contained ships
from every national contingent. He himself would command one
division; the papal and Venetian commanders became his assistants—
they would have no independent commands of their own. He assigned the two wings to a Genoese and a Venetian.

There was little time to prepare the Christian fleet. The festering
Turkish boil was about to rupture, for Selim's ships were ravaging
Venetian towns and islands up and down the Aegean and Ionian
seas, sailing far up the Adriatic to within sight of Venice herself.
Turkish flotillas struck at Crete, at Zante, and at Cephalonia, killing,
burning, and kidnapping. Don John issued orders for the elements of
the Christian fleet to rally at Messina, in Sicily. There was no time
to waste.

The fighting vessel of the day was the war galley—substantially
the same ship in which Ulysses clove the wine-dark sea on his way
to the siege of Troy. The fighting galley had been little modified in
two thousand years; Mark Antony would have felt perfectly at home

on the quarterdeck of one of the ships in Don John's fleet. The war galley was still a single-decked ship between 120 and 180 feet long, with a beam of perhaps 20 feet. The galley drew no more than 8 or 10 feet of water; this shallow draft made her a miserable sailor in any sort of sea but allowed her to maneuver quickly and operate in very little water.

She had two or three large lateen sails, but in action she was usually driven by oars alone. The power for those oars came from the wretched galley slaves, prisoners of war or criminals sentenced to toil, chained, in the stench of their own excrement. In a fog, you could smell a galley long before you could see it.

The rowers were condemned to heave at that heavy oar for a term of years, or forever, until they died of exposure or exhaustion or malnutrition and were fed to the fish. Conditions for the rowers were grim at the best of times and in the best of navies: in the galleys of the sultan, they were hideous.

In the Christian navies you could tell the status of an oarsman by his hair. If a man's head was completely shaved, he was simply a slave, probably a Moslem prisoner of war. The rower next to him, left with a small scrap of hair, was a criminal, serving out his years—if he lived—at an oar. A few men were allowed to wear mustaches; these men had voluntarily enlisted—it was better than starving to death ashore, though not by much.

The rowers generally sat five to an oar, naked or in rags, the port quintets separated from their starboard neighbors by a narrow catwalk. Along this gangway walked a vigilant petty officer with a whip to encourage laggards. The rowers stood up in unison on the backstroke, leaning toward the stern, then heaved back together until they were sitting back down at the end of the driving stroke. Their speed was regulated by the boatswain's shrill whistle, and God help the man who could not keep up the pace.

Like the galleys of ancient Greece, the sixteenth-century galley was armed with a large metal-clad beak, a ram, protruding forward from her bow for ten or twenty feet. If this beak could be driven deep into the flank of an enemy, the whole side of the foe might be stove in and the enemy galley would sink quickly, her planks smashed. The miserable galley slaves went down with her, screaming, still chained to their benches. By the time of Lepanto, the galleys also carried cannon, from two to five big guns pointing forward beneath the beak, and sometimes a few others sited to fire broadside.

The greatest maritime power of the Western world was the island republic of Venice, gilded, arrogant queen of the Adriatic, mistress of much of the Western trade in the Mediterranean and the Levant. In the 1570s, Venice kept thirty galleys always at sea, with another hundred ready to launch from the ways of her military heart, the great Arsenal.

The Arsenal was more than a storehouse. It was an astonishing production line of maritime fighting equipment from which skilled Venetian shipwrights could launch a new galley hull between dawn and sundown. Once the hull was complete, it was floated down canals from station to station, each of which added its specialty: masts, sails, rigging, artillery, and supplies. In the spring of 1570, the Arsenal produced twenty-five new galleys in a single month.

Everything a fighting vessel needed was produced within the Arsenal itself. Foundries and wood yards and a huge rope walk stood cheek-by-jowl with a hundred-man blacksmith shop and a loft in which four hundred women sewed sails for Venice's wooden walls. Eight hundred guns lay waiting to be hoisted aboard, and storehouses held enough weapons to equip fifty thousand men.

Venice could field sufficient galleys to meet the infidel, certainly. The question was whether enough crews could be found. Venetian crews were a mix of public-spirited volunteers, conscripted rowers, criminals, and hired foreigners. Most of the oarsmen were at least nominal Christians, however, and when the chips were down Don John would find a way to ensure their loyalty in a way the Moslem enemy could not match.

Aside from the technique of ramming, a sixteenth-century sea engagement was mostly a land battle fought on water, just as it had been in the days when Roman galleys grappled with their Carthaginian enemy. The opposing forces battered one another with fire from cannon and firelock, pots of fire and cast-iron grenades, clouds of arrows and crossbow bolts, then went roaring over the enemy's side with sword, pistol, ax, and boarding pike. Men fought in armor just as they did ashore, and the full-armed soldier who missed his footing on the enemy's gunwale went straight to the bottom, encased in his own steel coffin.

Don John of Austria had some experience of soldiering on land,

and now he showed his vision and leadership at sea as well. To begin with, he had the beaks removed from his galleys. Though this innovation must have horrified many of his more traditional sailors, it made sense. Whoever first suggested it, Don John saw clearly that, with this encumbrance removed, his galleys' five forward guns could be worked more easily and have a far better field of fire.

And the Spanish commander did something else. He unchained his Christian galley slaves and armed them with weapons and with rosaries. "Fight well," he told them. "Fight well for the faith against the infidel Turk and you shall have your freedom." In the event, these men, the dregs of the earth, would justify Don John's faith in them.

The Turkish enemy was near, in strength and well commanded. The Turkish commander was one Ali Pasa, ably seconded by an experienced North African pirate. This corsair, like so many of the sultan's officers, was a renegade, in this case an Italian. He was named Ochiali, and he was an intelligent, ugly, shrewd sailor, noted for his cruelty in a cruel age. He and Ali Pasa had gathered the fleet, three hundred galleys or more, in the Gulf of Patras, lurking on the edge of the Adriatic, the "Venetian Sea."

The Gulf of Patras, running east and west, separates the northern Greek mainland from the huge peninsula then called the Morea—like the rest of Greece, a Turkish satrapy. On the eastern side of the peninsula lay Negropont—modern Euboea—the great Turkish advanced base on the Aegean Sea. Negropont was connected by the ancient Corinth canal westward with the Gulf of Patras. Turkish ships and men could move quickly through the narrow canal to the Adriatic in both secrecy and safety.

Toward the western end of the gulf, near its junction with the Adriatic, lay a town called Lepanto, and there Ali Pasa collected the Turkish fleet. Within the arms of a little bay, covered by fortresses on both headlands, Ali could rest secure, menacing the whole Adriatic, even Venice herself.

Don John sailed from Barcelona to join his fleet off the toe of Sicily. His flagship, the galley *Real,* dropped anchor at Messina on August 23, 1571, and the rest of the fleet joined him rapidly. He was at sea with the entire Christian fleet by the middle of September, and off the island of Corfu by the twenty-seventh, pushing up the

Adriatic. There he received news: his foe was near, very near, in the bay of Lepanto.

Numbers of ships tell little about the magnitude of the clash that was now inevitable. For the galleys were crammed with men: there may have been as many as eighty thouand men engaged on each side. Of these, perhaps a quarter were soldiers. The sailors were armed too, and in Don John's ships the rowers were armed as well— at least the Christian ones.

Many, perhaps most, of the Christian soldiers wore armor, if only a steel cap and a breastplate; most of the Turks did not. The Turks' missile weapons were largely bows and crossbows; among Don John's soldiers were a substantial number of harquebusiers—matchlock men, who loaded their cumbersome weapons from a new-fangled device called the powder horn, an innovation that made the complex process of reloading faster and easier.

It was true that a Turkish archer could launch a dozen arrows in the time it took a harquebusier to reload. But arrows had little effect on Christian breastplates or steel caps, and nothing would stop a lead ball driven by gunpowder, least of all the robes of a Turkish soldier.

The best of the veteran Spanish infantry was away fighting the Dutch, so many of the Spanish harquebusiers were green troops, still learning the complex evolutions of loading and firing the heavy matchlock. Don John was not happy, writing from Messina that both the fleet and the army were poorly trained:

> fighting is not to be done with such men—a certain spasm takes
> me when I see with what materials I am expected by the world
> to do something of importance.

Still, if Don John's matchlock men were not as well trained as they might be, they would be firing at virtually point-blank range with pikemen and swordsmen to back them up. And they would have the protection of boarding nets to hold off Turkish assaults, a defensive wrinkle new to the war at sea.

To add to Don John's troubles, he was short of rowers. Both the Spanish and the Venetian galleys were shorthanded, and there was no source for more men. He would have to fight with what oar power he had. Most of his galleys would seat no more than three men to an oar, instead of the customary five.

There was an exception. Don John's fleet included a number of
ships called galleasses, big, hybrid, oar-and-sail battleships with cas-
tles at bow and stern. Don John had a special mission in mind for
these clumsy ships, and so he gave them seven men for every oar
to heave their bulk through the water. They therefore consumed many
rowers badly needed elsewhere, and they were so cumbersome that
they were generally towed into action by a pair of galleys. But they
had their advantages, too. Where the ordinary fighting galley carried
no more than five guns, the Venetian galleass boasted a murderous
broadside of forty guns or more. Some of these cannon fired fifty-
pound shot, which could break a galley in half. In the hours to come,
some of them would.

Also balanced against Don John's serious difficulties was a luminous, incandescent spirit of religious fervor, fanned to white heat by
the passionate oratory of the Pope and the preaching of the fleet's
chaplains. There were a good many of these, too: Don John had two
on his galley alone, a Dominican and a Jesuit.

And for once, thanks both to this urgent preaching and to Don
John's thoughtful leadership, enough of a feeling of unity prevailed
that the Venetians even accepted heavy reinforcements of Italian and
Spanish infantry to serve on board their galleys. And some three
thousand volunteers from all across the Christian world had come to
serve in Don John's fleet without pay, their only reward the chance
to give their lives for Christ. Marvel of marvels, some of these
dedicated foreigners were even Protestants.

The Turkish enemy was a mixed bag. The sultan's commanders
tended to be capable and experienced—many of them were Italian
or Greek renegades. The crews were often less experienced than their
Christian counterparts. The soldiers on board were solid for the most
part, and included a heavy percentage of the deadly, arrogant Janissaries. The Turkish galleys themselves were good enough; they were
slavish copies of Venetian warships—often built under the direction
of apostate Christians—though the workmanship was generally not
up to the standards of the great Venice Arsenal.

Just how good both ships and men might be was about to be tried
out in the crucible of battle. Out ahead of Don John's fleet sailed
four fast galleys carrying relays of rowers and commanded by an
experienced Knight of Malta named d'Andrade. His task was reconnaissance: he was to find and shadow the Turks. And on September

27, a small, fast vessel came rowing hard under the lee of Don John's *Real*—d'Andrade had done his job.

The Turks had raided Christian Corfu, said the messenger, killing and kidnapping, desecrating churches and strewing altars with filth. Now they had returned to the Gulf of Patras and lay under the guns of the sultan's fortresses at Lepanto. It was likely that they had returned there for the winter, too, for the time of the autumn gales was fast approaching.

The news of the Turks' depradations at Corfu ran quickly through the fleet, further hardening the determination of the soldiers and seamen. Perhaps more important, Don John was now reasonably sure where he could find his enemy. What he could not know, however, was that the Turks did not expect trouble from the west so late in the year. Ochiali had raided along the Italian coast, and a number of courageous landsmen had told him the same lie: the vessels of the league were still at Messina; they would sail no more this year. Ochiali, though John could not know it, had reported this falsehood to Ali.

Though Don John knew where his enemy anchored, he did not know how strong he was. The only intelligence he had was faulty and placed Ali's numbers well below the two-hundred-plus galleys now lying at anchor under the guns of Lepanto. Under the circumstances, however, none of that mattered. Don John, as befitted a soldier of Christ, was resolved to seek out the infidel enemy and fight him without regard to the lateness of the season, the shortage of rowers, or anything else.

Back at Messina, a council of war had urged caution, advising against Don John's proposal to strike directly at the Turks' Negropont base or at strategic Cyprus. In that event, Ali would have had to come out with his fleet to fight. But that opportunity had passed, and when the council met again the choice was simpler. Was the league to fight or slip away with its tail between its legs? Even then opinion was divided: some of the fainthearted voted to strike some Turkish island and then go home, and they were in the majority.

But the best of the Christian commanders supported Don John this time: Barbarigo, the Venetian admiral; Colonna, the Italian sea dog; Santa Cruz, the veteran Spaniard. The flaming words of the Pope still rang in their ears, and their hearts were wrung with anguish at

Turkish depradations against Christians up and down the Adriatic. They would fight.

And so Don John sailed for the gulf and the bay of Lepanto.

As for the Turks, it soon became plain that Don John was on his way, and Ali convened a council of his own. The choice was clear. The Turkish fleet could lie safely under the guns of the Lepanto forts, prepare for next spring's campaign, and let the Christians sail up and down and gnash their teeth. Or it could sail out and fight. Military wisdom dictated the first option. Let the bad weather pass; wait in safety for the spring. The Christians might well fall to quarreling, as they often had before.

However, the all-powerful sultan urged an attack on the Christians, and it was always wise for any Turkish commander to please the all-highest in Constantinople. Selim was vile and depraved, to be sure, and not very bright into the bargain. But his power was vast and unlimited, and a man of any rank who displeased him might lose everything in a heartbeat, including his head.

So it would be war.

Ali was confident. He believed he outnumbered his enemies in ships, and his twenty-five thousand or so soldiers included a substantial contingent of Janissaries, the iron soldiers of the faith. They were slaves, oddly enough, but privileged slaves. Most of them were Christian by birth—Greek, Albanian, or Serb—taken from their parents as a sort of tax by an official who used the local parish register as his studbook. On each visit he took away the cream of the crop of young boys, both assuring a supply of fine soldiers and diluting the breeding stock of the subject peoples.

The boys were then raised as Moslems, assured of a place in paradise. Their only allegiance was to the sultan. Their only calling was war. They lived a monastic life, forbidden to marry, but were fed well and paid regularly. Richly uniformed, with high hats of white felt, they carried the best of arms and armor. Even their ranks were unique, reflecting the excellence and abundance of their food: officer titles included "head cook" and "water carrier"; a senior officer grade translated as "soup kitchen." They were, in short, an elite, the reliable hard core of any Turkish army.

For a while, it appeared that there would be no fight: the autumn winds and fog hampered movement. And so, for most of the fifth of October, Don John's flotilla lay at anchor close to the waters off

Actium, where Antony and Cleopatra had been routed by the galleys of Rome. And while they were there news came, news that infuriated every man in the fleet, news of the fall of Famagusta and the agonizing death of Bragadino.

As the weather improved, Don John sailed for Lepanto, his ships moving in three divisions. The left-hand division, closest to the rocky shore, was largely Venetian, sixty-three galleys following the yellow pennant of that city's Admiral Barbarigo. Don John commanded the sixty-four galleys of the center, most of them Spanish. In one of these served a young, incurably romantic Spaniard who would fight well this day and do great things after: he was called Miguel Cervantes.

Three galleys went into action commanded by a pugnacious Englishman named Sir Thomas Stukeley. Sir Thomas, the epitome of the English sea dog, had fought all over the world. He was surely a ferocious fighter—and probably a former pirate. He might also have been a left-hand son of King Henry VIII by Jane Stukeley, Henry's mistress in the pre-Boleyn days.

Now, on the eve of action, Don John's thoughtful dispositions were bearing fruit. In his own division, the flagships of the papal and Venetian contingents were actually signaling compliments to one another. Veniero, the irritable Venetian commander, called Colonna, the papal commander, "the stoutest column which supported the church [a bit of pun on Colonna's ample figure]." Colonna, returning the compliment, quoted the Bible: "Yea, if I die I will not betray thee." Such friendly witticisms between such longtime rivals must have been more than Don John had dared even to hope for.

The galleys on Don John's right were a mixed bag, largely Genoese fighting ships under the green flag of Genoese Admiral Gianandrea Doria. Brigaded with the Genoese were ships from an assortment of other nations, among them devout Frenchmen who thought more of the cause of Christ than of the objections of their icy king.

A half mile in front of each division, galleys towed each of the galleasses into action; they would serve as heavily armed bastions, islands to disrupt the organization of the Turks' assault. In addition to their murderous complement of cannon, each of the six ships was stuffed with five hundred harquebusiers. The galleasses in front of the Venetian wing were Venetian, appropriately commanded by two angry seamen named Bragadino; they had much to avenge.

Don John's reserve was small: thirty galleys under the command of the experienced Spaniard Santa Cruz. Their function was to plug holes in the Christian line and intervene at the point and time of decision. Though Don John had ordered that his galleys attack no farther apart than necessary for neighboring ships to work their oars, loss of a ship or two might open a gaping rupture through which the Turks could stab into the Christian rear. Santa Cruz would deal with any breakthrough.

By the night of October 6, the fleets were close to collision. Doria, ever cautious, reminded Don John that he could still avoid a fight, and others murmured their concurrence. But Don John had decided, and he would not be moved. "Gentlemen, the time for counsel has passed," he said. "The time for fighting has come."

It had.

Early on Sunday, October 7, the Christian fleet moved south, closely skirting the north shore of the Albanian mainland into the Gulf of Patras, the wind in their faces. Mass had been celebrated before the fleet began to grope for its enemy. There had been absolution for the ranks of kneeling men, and the promise of pardon for those who fought with courage that day. Every man in the Christian host must have commended his soul to God with a particular deep and fervent urgency that morning. Nobody doubted that the decks of the galleys would run with blood before the sun went down that night.

All preparations for battle had been made. The Christian galley slaves' shackles had been opened, and each man had been armed. By contrast, the Moslem rowers had been fettered to their oars. If their Christian masters did not survive, neither would they, surely a certain motivation to pull hard at their oars. Ammunition was up and ready, checked and double-checked.

Those men with armor had put it on, and the burnished steel gleamed in the sun; their weapons were as sharp as stone could make them, and little wisps of smoke spiraled up from the slow matches of the harquebusiers. The boarding nets had been rigged and grease smeared anywhere a Turkish boarder might find a foothold to leap on board. More grease was rubbed on boarding pikes, just behind the points, so that no Moslem might grab and hold the shaft of a Christian weapon.

And then the enemy was in sight. Ahead, stretching from one shore to the other, was the Turkish fleet, spread across the gulf in its favorite formation, a long crescent. There were 274 vessels, including 208 fighting galleys, stretching all the way from the Albanian coast to the shoal water of Greek Morea to the south. Ali's line overlapped Don John's by at least a thousand yards to the south.

Fluttering over Ali's flagship was one of the most sacred of all Moslem emblems: a huge green flag, a copy of the banner carried into victory by Muhammad himself, embroidered in gold with Allah's name an astonishing 28,900 times. Where this banner went, said Moslem tradition, victory always followed. As usual, the Turks came with a great noise of drums, gongs, and cymbals; on the Turkish decks, men shouted and danced.

The Christian fleet was quiet. There was no firing, no dancing, no beating of drums, no brazen blare of trumpets. There were only the commands of the ships' officers and the urgent voices of the priests, urging the crews on to victory in the name of the Risen Christ.

Ali's vessels, the wind behind them, came down swiftly under sail. The admiral commanded his own center, ninety-six galleys. On his right, next to the Albanian shore and against the Venetians, moved fifty-six more galleys, mostly Egyptian. His left wing, sixty-three warships, attacked under the banner of the Italian renegade Ochiali; he had beaten Doria once before, off Tripoli. He saw no reason why he should not do so again.

As the two lines closed, the wind came clear around to the west and the Turks furled sail and went to their oars. Canvas broke out on the Christian masts, and the galleys of the league gathered speed—there could not have been many men in the Christian host who doubted that God had sent them a wind in their hour of need. And as they closed with the ancient enemy, each ship raised a crucifix, the immense banner of the league broke into the wind above *Real,* and a great cheer roared out from the Christian vessels.

Don John set his course straight at Ali's galley, with its monstrous gold-embroidered banner, and fired a shot at long range, as if in challenge. It did no harm, but the heavy cannon and murderous musket volley firing from the galleasses tore and hacked at the Turkish galleys as they rowed into action. The Turkish line warped and bulged as ships tried to pull away from those belching cannon and massed harquebusiers.

In the Christian galleys, the bow gunners, clutching their smoldering matches, grimly obeyed Don John's orders to hold fire until they could make out the faces of their Turkish targets. Then the prows of the Christian galleys spurted fire and smoke, and roundshot began to howl into the decks and bows of the Turkish galleys.

They were good, those Christian gunners, well drilled and unimpeded by the cumbersome rams Don John had ordered removed. They were getting off three shots to the Turks' one, their iron cannonballs smashing into the enemy's hulls near the waterline, tearing planks and ribs to let in the eager waters of the Gulf of Patras. More roundshot bounded like monstrous bowling balls through the soldiers massed on the Turkish decks, scattering bodies and limbs, weapons and turbans, like chaff in a high breeze. The Turkish return fire was generally high.

Real closed hard with Ali's *Sultana,* the Moslem's ram crashing into her forecastle, thrusting her own prow into the *Sultana*'s rigging, gripping her fast with grappling hooks under a hail of Turkish arrows. A rush of Turkish boarders was held up at the boarding nets, and *Real*'s harquebusiers fired in their enemy's faces, point-blank. Behind that terrible volley and a shower of sputtering hand grenades came the wave of Christian boarders, cheering, leaping onto the Turks' decks with swords and boarding pikes.

Eight hundred men fought hand-to-hand across the *Sultana*'s bloody, slippery decks, roaring in triumph, screaming in pain, calling out to God and to Allah amid the clash of steel and the hammer of pistol shots. The Christians, mostly Sardinian soldiers, hacked their way steadily into the press of Moslem defenders, twice driven back, twice pressing on again over the squirming bodies of the wounded, often stacked two and three deep, mingled with the gashed corpses of the dead.

Among the first Christians to board *Sultana* was a singularly graceful harquebusier, who killed the first Turk who approached with a single sword thrust. The soldier's name was Maria, *la Bailadora*—''the dancer''—serving side-by-side with her lover in the ranks of the Spanish. Don John himself, conspicuous in his gilded cuirass, fought sword-to-sword in *Real*'s bow, throwing back Turkish boarders clutching at the flagship's gunwales. Wounded in the leg, Don John laughed off his injury and fought grimly on.

As the Sardinian boarders pushed across *Sultana*'s blood-spattered decks for the third time, a harquebus ball smashed into Ali's forehead as the Turk stood on his poop, pouring arrows into the Christian boarders. As the Turkish admiral fell, a Christian galley slave slashed off Ali's head, impaled it on a boarding pike, and raised it high over *Real*'s deck.

It was the end for *Sultana*. Demoralized by the sight of their commander's eyes staring blankly at them from the top of a pike, the Turkish defenders lost heart. Down came the precious green flag covered with the name of Allah; up went the papal banner—to deafening cheers and a brazen blast of horns.

Close to *Real,* the crusty Venetian Admiral Veniero—white-haired and seventy-five years old—stood coolly on his quarterdeck driving crossbow bolts through Turk after Turk. It was beyond the old man's strength to wind his weapon; a soldier stood by him to cock it for him. But his eye had lost none of its skill. It would not be a bad thing, he said, to go to his God in such a fight; in the arrow shower, Veniero aimed quietly and feared no evil.

Over on the left, next to the Albanian mainland, the fight was touch-and-go for the Christians. The able Turkish commander, Mahomet Scirocco, pushed hard to cut between the Venetian galleys and the shore. Scirocco had the advantage of numbers, and he managed to swing through the shallows and turn the Christian flank.

For a little time the tide seemed to swing in the Turks' favor, and at one point eight Moslem galleys surrounded the Venetian flagship. Several Venetian galleys went down, but the seamen of the Doge did not think of quitting. They were face-to-face with the mortal enemy, the antichrist, and the memory of Bragadino's agonizing death was fresh in their minds.

And then, at the height of the battle on the left, a number of Christian galley slaves came boiling up from belowdecks in the Turkish galleys, hurling themselves on their Moslem masters from the rear. These men had somehow managed to conspire together, to file away their fetters in secret, and now all the fury of years of slavery was taken out in blood. They went after the Turks with fragments of their own slaves' chains, with captured weapons, and with their own strangling hands.

It was enough. Caught between the slaves and the Venetians, Scirocco's men were driven back, and the fight left the Christian decks to continue on the Turkish galleys. Scirocco himself was killed in the fighting. The Christians knew him for a deadly foe and able commander, and treated him as Ali had been treated, raising his severed head high on a pike. The fight just off the Albanian shore was won.

Out on the Christian right the issue was still in doubt. Ochiali, outnumbering Doria, lapped around his flank from the south, and Doria tried to extend his line far enough to prevent it. As his line grew thinner and thinner, a gap opened, and Ochiali led about a dozen galleys, rowing hard, through the hole and into the Christian rear.

Those that did not make it through the gap fought it out in a small vicious action, sixteen Moslem ships against eight Christian ships. Before Don John himself could get over to help, every fighting man on two Christian galleys was down, dead, or dying; on another, only fifty men remained unwounded out of five hundred. But the Turks were overwhelmed, cut down, drowned, chained as prisoners. Some managed to beach their vessels on the southern shore of the gulf and flee inland, but they had little future: the oppressed Greeks of the Morea had long memories.

Once behind Doria's line, Ochiali's galleys pivoted and raised their sails. They had the wind behind them then, and Ochiali led seven of them against a single ship, the flagship galley of the Knights of Malta, *Capitano*.

Capitano was commanded by the knight Pietro Giustiniani, all his life the mortal enemy of everything Moslem. He came of a famous name, this soldier of Christ: another Giustiniani had led the gallant defense of doomed Constantinople and had died with the ancient city a century before. Now Pietro led thirty of his knights and a contingent of men at arms in a ferocious hand-to-hand battle across the deck of *Capitano*.

The struggle could have only one ending. Fighting to the end against a swarm of attackers, every Christian fighting man fell on *Capitano*'s deck. Around the bloody bodies of thirty knights, all dead or dying but two, lay the heaped carcasses of some three hundred Turks. Giustiniani, stuck like a pin-cushion with five arrows, was carried onto Ochiali's galley along with his huge black-cross flag; his ship was taken in tow as well.

And Ochiali ran. He could see the day had gone against the Turks; more pirate than patriot, Ochiali had an important prize and an impressive prisoner. His reputation would soar, where his rivals' would suffer; it was enough.

But Ochiali had not reckoned with the Marquis of Santa Cruz and the galleys of the Christian rear guard, which quickly gave chase. A Spanish captain named Ojeda laid his galley alongside *Capitano,* and his men swarmed over the side to recapture Giustiniani's battered ship. Ochiali cut his towline and led thirteen Moslem ships out of the fray . . . almost the only survivors of the proud fleet that had followed Ali down the gulf that morning.

Don John's victory was total, an amazing feat of arms unequaled in all the centuries of bitter war against the infidel. Nobody knows how many men at arms and sailors actually fought at Lepanto. Estimates run anywhere from fifty thousand to eighty thousand on each side, though the lesser number is probably closer to the truth. The Turks had sustained a stunning loss of some twenty-five thousand, many of them the elite Janissaries and veteran seamen. By contrast, the Christian loss was on the order of seven thousand, of whom almost five thousand were Venetians from the embattled left of Don John's line.

Only twelve Christian galleys had been lost, but Ali's fleet was destroyed for all practical purposes: over one hundred vessels fell into Christian hands; the rest, with few exceptions, were sunk or burned. The Christian fleet remained in being—hammered about, to be sure, but seaworthy for the most part. Over twelve thousand Christian galley slaves had been liberated; thousands of Turkish prisoners would pull oars in Christian galleys for years to come.

There was no end of loot. There were gold coins by the thousands and over three hundred Turkish cannon, not to mention acres of rich clothing and weapons and the monstrous green banner of the faith, which Don John sent westward as a present to his king. He sent a large banner of the sultan to the Pope, who, after all, was the father of victory in more ways than one.

Don John, characteristically, also took great care of his men, especially the wounded, to whom he donated his one-tenth commander's share of the bounteous booty. He ordered that the Dancer, who survived the fight, be carried formally on the roster of her regiment, drawing pay like any other soldier; she had earned it. Among others he commended was the formidable Sir Thomas Stukeley, who had covered himself with glory in the desperate deck-to-deck fighting.

Christendom rejoiced. Venice first learned of Lepanto when a galley dashed into the city harbor trailing Turkish flags in the water behind her, her crew clowning on the decks in captured turbans. Well might the city celebrate: for the better part of a century afterward, Venice and her empire would have nothing to fear from Constantinople.

For the Pope, old and tired, it was the glorious end of years of preaching crusade. More than any other man but the fleet's commander, the victory was his doing. He had, after all, chosen Don John himself, and now, his old heart full, he quoted joyously from the Bible: "There was a man sent from God, whose name was John."

Perhaps the Pope was right.

CHAPTER SIX

THE SMITING OF THE INFIDEL

Saul and Allenby at Michmash Pass

PALESTINE, FEBRUARY 1918.

In this storied land, until very recently a satrapy of the Turkish sultan, a British army methodically hammered the Turks back, step by bloody step. The sacred city of Jerusalem had fallen to the British in December, and General Allenby had entered the city, on foot, to accept its surrender at the Tower of David. He would guarantee the safety of every religion's holy places, he said; not even a foreign flag would fly above the ancient town, and its gates would stand open. And he kept his word.

Then Allenby went back to the war, driving back with great slaughter a series of Turkish attacks aimed at recovering Jerusalem. Allenby's 60th British Division lay facing ancient Jericho and the way to the river Jordan. Joshua's ramshorns would not help this army; it faced a tough fight against Turkish infantry and machine guns dug in on the far side of a valley along a line of high ground. As a prelude to the assault, British 180 Brigade would strike a village on its front to straighten a kink in the British line. The place was called Michmash. It was to be frontal attack, and there would surely be casualties.

"Michmash," mused the Brigade Major of 180 Brigade. Where,

he pondered, had he heard the name? And in the heart of the night, as he lay reading his Bible by the light of a guttering candle, it came to him. The name appeared in the Old Testament, in the first book of Samuel's account of the Philistine wars, and he found it in chapters 13 and 14. This is what he read:

> Jonathan, the son of Saul, said unto the young man that bare his armour, "Come and let us go over to the Philistines' garrison" . . . and between the passages, by which Jonathan sought to go over to the Philistine garrison, there was a sharp rock on the one side, and a sharp rock on the other side: the name of one was Bozez, and the name of the other Seneh.

The major read on, engrossed in the account of Jonathan's daring raid on an overwhelming Philistine army. Jonathan climbed through Michmash Pass, the gut between the two huge rocks, and came to some open ground, about "a half acre of land, which a yoke of oxen might plow." There he and his armor bearer surprised a Philistine outpost and killed about twenty of the enemy. The Philistine army, terrified, began to waver, and when it was struck by the rest of Saul's small army it "melted away."

"I wonder," thought the major. "Geography changes little in this ancient land; nothing changes very much. I wonder if the rocks and the pass and the cleared space are as they were so long ago." And so he woke his commander, Brigadier Watson, and the two of them read Samuel again. Watson thought his scholarly major had something, and so he sent recon patrols to confirm the details of the Bible story.

So it was, said the patrols. Bozez and Seneh were still there, with a narrow gut of a pass between them, and there was a level patch of ground about large enough for a team to plow. It was also, said the patrol, only lightly garrisoned by the Turks.

Thus it was that in the dead of night a single British company slid between Bozez and Seneh, killing or capturing the Turkish sentries in silence. And when first light broke the skyline over against Syria, the British held the little patch of ground, and from it struck hard at Michmash itself.

The Turks broke, panicked at the sudden, silent appearance of their enemy virtually in their midst. Not a single Turk got away from

Michmash Village, and Allenby drove the struggling Turkish army back across the flooded Jordan. It had taken Joshua a week to overthrow Jericho; Allenby's men took it in a few hours, without ramshorns.

Allenby would push on to drive the Turks from Syria as well. By the end of October, Turkey was out of the war for good. Major Vivian Gilbert, a veteran machine gunner, thoughtfully recorded an ancient Arab fable, which warned:

> When the Nile flows into Palestine, then shall the prophet from
> the west drive the Turk from Jerusalem.

Considering that the Nile was some two hundred miles from Palestine, the Turks must have felt safe enough.

Except that much of the water the conquering British troops drank *was* Nile water, flowing up across the Sinai from Egypt. It was piped under the Suez Canal, filtered, and chlorinated. Then seventeen pumping stations pushed the precious liquid forward to the troops through pipes imported before the war by Standard Oil for more peaceful purposes.

Except for the fact that Allenby, soldier from the west, was commonly called "Al Nebi."

And *al nebi* means "the prophet."

CHAPTER SEVEN

THE WILD GEESE

1745: The Irish at Fontenoy

*We're not so old on the Army List, but
we're not so new at our trade, for we
had the honor at Fontenoy of meeting
the Guards Brigade.*

*Old days! The wild geese are flighting,
head to the wind as they've faced it before.
Wherever there's Irish there's loving and
fighting, and when we stop either,
'tis Ireland no more.*
—Rudyard Kipling, "The Irish Guards"

THEY WERE EXILES, mostly self-imposed. They had no country of their own now, not since the bloody defeat of a Jacobite army at the river Boyne in 1690. The Stuart cause died there, and there was no longer space in Ireland for Jacobites who were not willing to bow the knee to a foreign Protestant prince.

And so, like the beautiful, high-flying birds from which they drew their name, the Wild Geese left their native land behind, perpetually far from home, perpetually traveling on. They settled in France after a fashion, wore the French uniform, married French women, begat children whose native tongue was French. But still they ached a little inside for the green unattainable island that still was home, and for the gallant, illusory Stuart dream that had got its death blow at the Boyne.

The dream had begun dying then, and now it was almost gone, bright though it shone still in Jacobite hearts. Prince Charles Edward—the Young Pretender, as he was called—hovered in Paris even now, largely unrecognized by the French government, a penurious plotter with few resources and many dreams. Ignored even by his father, the jaded Stuart "king" in Rome, he still inspired a flaming loyalty in many Irish, Scots, and English hearts. The dream would crumble for all time only later in the very next year, when Bonny Prince Charlie's ragged Highlanders would die in windrows on the dreary moor of Culloden.

The Wild Geese were commanded by Irishmen, men named Dillon and Clare and Bulkeley. They would not have followed anybody else. And some of these officers grew great in the service of France. Such a one was a regimental commander this day, Arthur de Lally de Tollendal. Lally was every inch a French dandy—a count, in fact—from his noble toes to his larded, powdered hair. He was forty-three, born in France of a French mother, and he had seen the green shores of Ireland only once, but he remained at least as much an O'Mullally as a Frenchman.

Lally had fought at Dettingen, and fought well, and there he had seen the terrible British infantry with his own eyes. Others might wax enthusiastic about the drubbing they would give the Sassenach, but Lally knew his enemy. He knew both armies would wade in blood this day. Still, to his men he was all enthusiasm and panache, vaulting into the saddle with that athletic youthfulness for which he was famous.

James Dillon, a vigorous forty-six, was a regimental commander, and many of his men had been in the regiment very nearly all their lives. He was called the Chevalier de Dillon, and like Lally had been born French. His fractious, warlike clan had been scattered beyond repair by the winds of war. His brother had made his peace with Hanoverian George and returned to rule the family estates, but more than sixty clansmen had been attainted of treason at the end of the seventeenth century. Dillon was a consummate professional soldier, technically skilled, and idolized by his men.

The brigade commander, Clare—sixth Viscount Clare and ninth Earl of Thomond, as the Jacobites called him—was tall and aristocratic and dignified, and traced his ancestry back into the misty past and the legendary Brian Boru. He was an experienced and distinguished commander, much admired in the brigade. Clare was an O'Brien, a Catholic O'Brien, as distinguished from that branch of the clan that had become Protestant and sworn loyalty to the British

crown. Clare held the French rank of lieutenant general, and this day
he would command both the brigade and his own regiment.

These Irish wanderers were soldiers both by inclination and by
experience, and so they remained soldiers. It was not just that
Irishmen dearly love a fight of nearly any kind, although that surely
influenced their choice of work. Mostly, it was simply that soldiering
was what they knew, and following the drum gave them a chance
to strike once more at the hereditary Anglo-Saxon enemy. They
spoke Gaelic and English and French, and combinations of the same.
Some were new to the ranks; some had grown gray in the service
of France. There were six battalions of them at Fontenoy, about four
thousand men altogether.

Much blood and bitterness lay beween these men and the British
enemy, the legacy of a tortured land where even today you can find
people who speak of Oliver Cromwell as if he died last Thursday,
instead of three centuries ago. And many of the Wild Geese still
believed in the wonderful, threadbare Jacobite dream, the return of
the wandering Stuarts to their own, the double throne of England
and Scotland. And so there were a good many Jacobite Englishmen
in their ranks, men as hard as the Irish, plus a whole regiment of
Scots, the wild Highlanders of Lord John Drummond.

And the Wild Geese would have their fight. In the year 1745,
Britain and France were locked in yet another installment of their
perpetual struggle for world primacy, from Europe to India and back
to the great emptiness of North America.

Just now their great enemy—and France's—was Great Britain and
her hard-fighting field commander, the Duke of Cumberland. Cumberland was young, but he was a good, solid soldier, liked by his
men. He was famous for his courage even in an age when bewigged
officers rode casually into a blizzard of grapeshot with a jest and a
delicate dip of snuff (at Fontenoy, a seventy-eight-year-old veteran
commander named Campbell had his leg torn off by a French cannonball; carried dying to the rear, Campbell was heard to remark
matter-of-factly that his dancing days seemed to be over). It was
Cumberland's bad luck to be matched against a quite remarkable
opponent, the premier soldier of the time and one of the best who
ever commanded: Maurice de Saxe, Marshal of France.

Saxe was a German, the illegitimate child of Augustus the
Strong, the prodigiously potent Elector of Saxony and King of Po-

land. Being illegitimate was not much of a disability in those days, especially if you were of royal blood. And in any case, Saxe was not alone: his busy father provided him with no less than 354 siblings, only one of whom was born within the bounds of holy wedlock. Maurice was named for the castle of Moritzberg, in which, as Augustus somewhat indelicately put it, "I obtained the victory over his mother."

Perhaps in part because the Saxon exchequer was hard-pressed to provide for the abundance of offspring who threatened to inundate Dresden, Maurice got his heart's desire. He became a soldier at the tender age of twelve and saw action that very year at the siege of Tournai, serving in the army of John Churchill, Duke of Marlborough, the greatest soldier of the age. Surviving an encounter with a monstrous French cavalryman—whom young Saxe exterminated with a horse pistol—Saxe fought in the bloody action at Malplaquet before he was fourteen.

Saxe knew he had found his profession and never looked back. And he was no dilettante, this bright young man. Unlike many "social" officers of the day, he early on became a student of the profession of arms. By the time he was twenty-five, Saxe had fought the French, the Turks, and the Swedes of Charles XII. At seventeen, he had covered himself with glory by holding an inn against four hundred enemy with only twenty men of his own, and cutting his way clear after nightfall.

Saxe served France in the War of the Polish Succession in 1733, and again in the War of the Austrian Succession, during which he stormed Prague in 1741. He was made a lieutenant general in the French service, and in 1744 he received his marshal's baton and supreme command against the British under young Cumberland. Saxe had no great love for the Hanoverian rulers of Britain, either. His own uncle, Philip von Koenigsmarck, had disappeared in Hanover, presumably murdered by the Elector George, later George I of Britain (the murder was not without a certain provocation: Philip had been sharing the bed of Sophie, the elector's wife, a peccadillo that pleased George not at all).

But as the campaigning year opened, Saxe lay seriously ill in Paris, badly incapacitated with dropsy, his body ponderous and swollen with fluid. It was not even sure that he would survive at all, let alone be able to lead in the field. Voltaire, calling on Saxe, tried to reassure the sick man that he would survive. Saxe's reply was typical of the man: "It is not a question of how I am to live, but of how I am to set off on this campaign."

And set off he did, toward the end of April 1745. Typically, he chose to concentrate his eighty thousand men in Hainault, in Flanders, where he could menace all the "barrier fortresses," the line of fortified places that protected the low countries. And, as usual, he screened his movements and intentions so well that he had been besieging the city of Tournai for a week while his enemy thought he was threatening the fortress of Mons.

Saxe's enemy, Cumberland, was a prince of the blood, second son of George II. Cumberland is often portrayed as gross, crude, and a little dense, a portrait based in part on his later reputation as "the butcher" in the Highlands. But young Cumberland was no fool; though from childhood his consuming interest was military, he was something of a classical scholar. And he was a reasonable mathematician as well, a love instilled in him by none other than Sir Isaac Newton.

Nor was Cumberland insensitive. James Wolfe, later to win Quebec and an empire for Britain, privately described Cumberland as "ever doing noble and generous actions." Although the prince was a ferocious disciplinarian, his soldiers loved him because he was just and because he spared no effort to make sure they were taken care of.

Cumberland lay now near Brussels with an allied army only about fifty thousand strong, his cavalry probing to the east to locate the elusive Saxe. Cumberland's army was a mixed batch, with all the liabilities that go with a heterogeneous collection of nationalities who spoke no common tongue. One British officer neatly described Cumberland's dilemma:

> [A]n allied army like ours, with as many different commanders, each pulling their several ways and influenced by their separate interest, can never undertake what an army should do that has but one head, are under one interest, and understand all the same language.

The heart of Cumberland's force was his British infantry, about 12,000 of them organized in battalions of about 650 men each, plus some twenty 150-man squadrons of British cavalry. He could also count on his Hanoverians, about 8,000 in number, by and large tough and dependable soldiers. His artillery was excellent—at least the German and British batteries were. Though their pieces were of small caliber, they could do substantial damage with either roundshot or canister. Cumberland's numbers were rounded out by some 22,000 Dutch troops and 2,000 Austrians. Cumberland had no great opinion of the Dutch and Austrians. As it turned out, his misgivings were fully justified.

In retrospect, it seems quite clear that Saxe wanted to fight on the defensive, even though he substantially outnumbered Cumberland. Saxe knew his French troops were unlikely to do well head to head with the ferocious British infantry. If, however, he could induce Cumberland to attack him in a prepared position, he might hope to get the redcoats to take serious casualties attacking fortifications, then counterattack them with his superior numbers while they were bloodied and disorganized.

Besides the threat of the formidable British regiments, Saxe had serious irritations closer to home. His liege lord, Louis XV, appeared at Saxe's field headquarters, bringing with him an enormous retinue, in numbers a small army in itself. There were the great courtiers, the chamberlain, the first gentleman of the bedchamber and a handful of similar luminaries, plus aides, secretaries, valets, footmen, pages, doctors, apothecaries, and laborers by the dozen. There were also more than sixty servitors of "the King's Mouth," the apparatus charged with feeding His Royal Highness, plus cooks for every conceivable purpose, seven for coffee alone. There were horses by the hundred; all manner of carriages, wagons, and other equipage; baggage uncountable; and a large military escort. Saxe did not need this annoyance, sick and preoccupied as he was.

Worse still, Louis was surrounded by a cloud of courtiers, pomaded, perfumed dandies with red-heeled shoes and powdered faces. This numerous entourage contained a large contingent of "carpet soldiers," military amateurs both loud and opinionated, all of whom talked incessantly about attack.

Saxe would have none of them, which did nothing to decrease the jealousy they felt toward this foreign upstart risen so high in the royal firmament. "As long as I am the cook in charge of the stove," Saxe snorted, "I intend to deal with the British lobster in my own way."

He made no secret of his contempt for the arrogant dabblers who orbited around the king. Rouged, mascaraed, with beauty spots stuck to their powdered faces, these sissified fops were hardly Saxe's type of man. On one occasion, one of them had urged Saxe to undertake a small operation that would, he said, "only have meant the loss of twenty or thirty soldiers." "I'd have done it," Saxe replied, "if it had only meant the loss of twenty or thirty court generals."

Such talk was hardly calculated to win Saxe any friends among the sycophants of the French court. Fortunately, Louis stuck with his marshal. "I myself am under the orders of Marshal Saxe," he said, and that was that. The grumblers were not satisfied, but at least they were silent, which was better. Saxe went on with his plans.

Cumberland, fearless and pugnacious, was just the man to oblige Saxe, numbers or no numbers. Saxe soon learned that Cumberland's allied army was headed straight for him, and he made his preparations. He would meet the enemy around the village of Fontenoy, leaving about thirty thousand of his army to continue the siege of Tournai. He would still outnumber Cumberland by some six thousand men and have the advantage of prepared defensive positions. Saxe himself would be on the left, at the point of decision. Too sick with dropsy to ride, he was pulled around the battlefield in a sort of basket, a wicker cradle on wheels pulled by four horses. In it, Saxe could cover ground at amazing speed, albeit at enormous cost in pain.

As usual, Saxe had chosen his position well. It formed a sort of reverse *L* shape, his troops facing generally southeast, standing between Cumberland and besieged Tournai. His right flank was anchored on the broad waters of the river Scheldt and the substantial village of Anthoin. From there his line ran roughly east for two miles to the hamlet of Fontenoy, then continued north to the forest of Barri, which covered the French left flank.

Saxe strengthened that flank still further by building strong earth redoubts at the edge of the wood and filling the forest itself with skirmishers. His line ran along a gentle ridge that runs all the way from Anthoin and the Scheldt to Barri Wood. Saxe's men barricaded both Anthoin and Fontenoy and dug trenches in both villages. They also built three redoubts between the two towns.

Here occurs one of the mysteries of military history. Many later writers, including the thorough and reliable Sir John Fortescue, have asserted that the French infantry between the villages was dug in, awaiting the allied advance in entrenchments. Others deny there were field fortifications other than the redoubts and the defenses of the two villages. One writer asserts that the French occupied a sunken road, which would have been a common feature of the ancient and marshy Flanders farm country. In an age of many memoirs and much letter writing, it is surprising that there is no agreement on Saxe's defenses.

It seems illogical for Saxe to have permitted obstruction of the battlefield with trenches, for his plan was based on the mobile defense. It follows that he would have done nothing to impede the rapid advance of his reserves. Still, Fortescue, famous for his painstaking accuracy, states that the French dug not just one, but two lines of infantry entrenchments from Fontenoy to Barri Wood, and he is unlikely not to have carefully checked that critical fact.

The probability is, then, that Saxe, well aware of the terrible power of a British infantry advance, did dig in; at the least, he would have occupied a sunken road, if there was one. He must have been determined to give his defense every advantage; if he could not at least disorganize the British infantry, no counterattack could hope to succeed.

With or without infantry trenches, Cumberland's men faced a hornet's nest of massed artillery, fortified villages, and bristling redoubts, attacking uphill across clear ground. Protected down behind the ridgeline—"in defilade," as the soldiers say—Saxe held the bulk of his troops poised for his devastating counterattack on the bloodied and disorganized attackers. Farther back still, closer to the river, Saxe held further reserves.

Saxe paid special attention to his left. As he knew, the British and Hanoverian infantry would probably attack on the right of Cumberland's line—the place of honor. Wherever they struck the French line, there would the crisis of the battle come. There the line would be held by the cream of the French regiments and several battalions of Swiss Guards, backed by strong reserves. Saxe's first line was nine battalions strong, with a second line of eleven more battalions just behind them.

Waiting in reserve behind Barri Wood were more Swiss and the best troops Saxe possessed, the six battalions of the Wild Geese. Each of the Irish units was made up of twelve companies of fusiliers and one of elite grenadiers, and each company numbered about fifty men. Like their Swiss allies and their British opponents, the Irish regiments wore red coats; only the distinctive colors of their cuffs and lapels told one unit from another.

Cumberland, coming up from the south, had to decide how best to get at his enemy. The allies' purpose was to relieve Tournai, and the most direct route to the besieged town was between the Scheldt and Barri Wood. Cumberland's immediate subordinates did nothing to inspire his confidence. The senior Dutch officer was Prince Waldeck, himself only twenty-five. At the other end of the spectrum was the Austrian, Marshal Koenigseck, sick and worn out at seventy-six, who had already asked his queen to relieve him so he could "resume the course of hot baths and asses' milk" on which his health depended. Still, Cumberland consulted both him and young Waldeck. Waldeck seems to have voted for a frontal assault, but old Marshal Koenigseck was not so sure. He wanted to try to turn the enemy's left, going through or around the wood of Barri to threaten Saxe's communications.

Cumberland was an experienced soldier, and he must have known he had a tough nut to crack. He had a good eye for ground, and no doubt could read the difficult terrain he would have to surmount to get at the French. And he knew Saxe by reputation. Still, Cumberland chose the bulldog's path, a head-on frontal attack on the French position.

Cumberland issued his orders. His battle plan had at least the great military virtue of simplicity, even if it did not show much imagination. As Saxe had predicted, the British and Hanoverian infantry would strike the French left. Fontenoy itself and everything south of it were left to the Dutch and the Austrians.

On the far right flank of the British, at the corner of Barri Wood, Brigadier General Ingoldsby would lead four battalions, including the formidable Black Watch, against the very strong earthworks of the Redoubt d'Eu. Ingoldsby's mission was critical, for d'Eu's cannon and muskets were sited to fire straight south into the flank of Cumberland's main attack.

And so, at two in the morning on May 11, 1745, the Duke of Cumberland's army began to move. The early start was essential, for there were many narrow roads to cover; it took a long time to get everyone in position. Once there, Cumberland's mailed fist, his British infantry, would simply march straight at the dug-in French across a thousand yards of open ground.

Once out of the tight defiles from which they deployed, the British shook themselves out into line. French roundshot skipped and bounded through their orderly ranks, smashing into bloody hash five and six men at a time. The British guns hammered at the French artillery, but even after they had found the range, they could not entirely suppress that galling, destructive fire. French Huguenot general Ligonier commanded the British infantry attack, and in time sent a courier galloping to Cumberland: the infantry was ready (the officer who carried the message was an ardent young captain named Jeffrey Amherst, one day to be the hammer of the French in America).

All things being ready, the Dutch and Austrians advanced against Fontenoy itself, but the attack went nowhere. The Dutch fell quickly back and took cover from the French artillery, and nothing could persuade them to come again. To compound their failure, some of the Dutch cavalry went madly galloping clear off the battlefield, screaming as they went that the day was lost.

Nor did anything go as planned on Cumberland's right. Ingoldsby, apparently confused about what the Duke wanted him to do, did exactly nothing, permitting the Redoubt d'Eu to spout roundshot and grape unmolested, a hive of deadly hornets enfilading the flank of any British attack. And here Cumberland blundered, unaccountably, for he was a better soldier than that. Instead of again ordering Ingoldsby forward, and waiting for his attack, the duke put in his main attack, straight into a hell of artillery flaming from front and flank.

The front rank of the British advance consisted of ten battalions, including a battalion each of foot guards, the proud regiments known today as the Grenadier, the Coldstream, and the Scots Guards. Marching beside them were battalions of seven line regiments, including the Royal Scots—the oldest of the line regiments—the King's, and two Yorkshire regiments.

The morning sun flashed and flickered on the long bayonets and on the blades of the officers' espontoons and the NCOs' halberds. The senior company of each battalion carried the colors, two standards to a battalion. Behind the leading units were ranged seven more battalions. This line included the Buffs, the Royal East Kent Regiment, which traced its lineage from 1572 and to this day is one of the few units privileged to march through the city of London with bayonets fixed, drums beating, and colors uncased. Behind them, as a third rank, marched the Hanoverian battalions, veteran units with a proud heritage of their own. All the battalions brought their artillery with them, two guns to a battalion, the men heaving the light field-pieces forward by hand.

As the infantry came abreast of Fontenoy and the Redoubt d'Eu, the murderous cannonade from both positions began to tear into their flanks. Where before a cannonball might hurl down two or three files, now it might tear a dozen men to pieces as it bounded from flank to flank. Cumberland, to his credit, sat his gray hunter in the midst of his men, paying no attention to the hail of fire that fell all around him. From point to point he rode, calling out to his men, urging and encouraging them.

Behind the British battalions the ground was littered with crumpled red dots. But still the scarlet ranks came impassively on, never changing that deliberate pace, quickly closing the gaping holes left by the French artillery. There was something inhuman, incomprehensible, about that slow, deadly advance. Sir Charles Petrie, historian of the Jacobite dream, put it vividly:

> Whole ranks were swept away, but still the dense mass contin-
> ued to press forward over the heaps of dead and dying, while
> the sergeants dressed the ranks with their long halberds as if
> they were on parade . . . in spite of the terrible flanking fire
> from the redoubts, and of the efforts of one French regiment
> after another, the British moved steadily on. . . .

Now the British reached the crest of the gentle ridge of Fontenoy, and finally their quarry was in view, lines of French and Swiss infantry standing in their trenches, muskets at the ready, blue coats, white coats and red, depending on the regiment. And still the Britsh came on, their muskets at shoulder arms, without noise other than the steady hammering of their drums. The range closed to fifty yards, and still the scarlet soldiers came on at that inexorable pace.

And then they halted. Their drums stopped.

About here the wonderful mythology of war has created an engaging scene, a baroque picture of exaggerated gallantry and de Bergerac panache. The legend, related by Voltaire, is that an officer of the English guards stepped forward, doffed his hat, and invited the "gentlemen of the French guards" to fire first. *"Non,"* replied a French officer, *"nous ne tirons jamais les premiers."* It's a wonderful moment in the history of warfare, but of course it didn't happen that way. Nobody can say whether the whole pretty story is Voltaire's invention (he was not above inventing), or whether some French officer misunderstood what he heard. The truth is hidden far down the dim corridors of time.

What actually took place was a lot less romantic than the myth—and a lot more English. Out in front of his men, jaunty and smiling, stepped young Lord Charles Hay of the Grenadier Guards, and in his hand he held his silver flask. He raised it to his enemies, drank to them, and called out mockingly in French:

> I hope, gentlemen, that you are going to wait for us today, and
> not swim the Scheldt as you swam the Main at Dettingen?

It was a mortal insult, delivered with a mocking smile, and Hay's tough guardsmen would have laughed. Hay turned to his men and spoke again:

> Men of the King's Company, these are the French Guards, and
> I hope you are going to beat them today.

The British answered Hay with a thunderous cheer and stepped off again toward the French lines. The range was down to a brutal thirty yards, and one English guardsman is said to have murmured:

> For what we are about to receive, may the Lord make us truly
> thankful.

About this time the Guards did receive, for the French fired a point-blank volley, and many of the British fell. But now the scarlet ranks halted again, and finally the musket barrels swung down to the horizontal. And at last the British fired, a stunning torrent of lead balls that slashed and tore at the French ranks. That first terrible blast is said to have killed or wounded more than seven hundred Frenchmen, and the hell was just beginning. Volley followed rolling volley, one battalion firing while two more loaded, and the French went down in windrows. The British light battalion guns joined in, pouring in grapeshot literally in the faces of the French.

The British were firing slightly downhill, where the tendency is to fire high—their regimental officers walked down the ranks, using their canes and sword blades to tap down the barrels of men who aimed too high. The French infantry crumbled before those terrible volleys; Saxe fed in more and more battalions, but none of them could stand against that murderous musketry.

Now Saxe threw his cavalry in, charge after charge against the front and flanks of the advancing British, but none of them could close with that terrible infantry. Dillon's Irish regiment tried but was driven back with its commander wounded. Even the famous Maison du Roi, the troops of the French royal household, were driven back in a rabble of fugitives.

The ranks of the French cavalry positively dripped with gold braid, pomp, and circumstance: five princes of the blood and their entourages, to say nothing of a whole gaggle of surplus officers and divers noblemen and hungry courtiers. All their rank and privilege could not stop those terrible muskets. One French courtier described that:

> dreadful hour in which we expected nothing less than a renewal
> of the affair at Dettingen; our Frenchmen being awed by the
> steadiness of the English, and by their rolling fire, which is
> really infernal . . . enough to stupefy . . .

Even Saxe was discouraged by the brutal British fire: "Is it possible," he said, "that such troops should not be victorious?" But the French marshal kept his head. In front of Fontenoy the Dutch were inert; Cumberland's British and Hanoverians were fighting the whole battle alone, and taking terrible casualties from the French artillery, tearing at their ranks from ahead, both flanks, and even at an angle to the rear as they advanced. They were now in the heart of the French camp, both flanks bent back to protect against assault from the side, so that they now resembled a gigantic hollow square. "It was like charging two flaming fortresses," wrote a French officer, "rather than two columns of infantry."

But Saxe was buying time, time to reinforce and reorganize. His enemy was now isolated, ringed with French fire, and without help. The Dutch had tried again at Fontenoy, and again had failed completely. Saxe was able to move still more artillery from his right, and the British fell back to the ridgeline. Once more they advanced into the teeth of the French fire, assailed now by more French reinforcements. More and more troops crowded in against their flanks, and now, at last, Saxe launched his best weapon.

The Wild Geese came in yelling, at the charge, the remains of
Dillon's men among them; they shouted "Remember Limerick!" a
reference to the shameful failure of the British government to honor
the provisions of a treaty made when the Jacobite defenders of that
town surrendered more than fifty years before. Running into the teeth
of the British fire, the Irish were cut down in heaps by another of
those terrible volleys, but they trampled over their own dead and
dying to close with bayonet, sword, and musket butt.

The British met them with the same weapons, and for a little while
the old enemies fought ferociously in the smoke and dust, hand to
hand, a wild melee of shouting, screaming men, of spattering blood
and cries to God and the roar of point-blank musketry.

As the ranks closed, a young Guards officer ran out in front of
his men, closing hand-to-hand with a soldier from County Clare
named MacDonough. In a flurry of shimmering steel MacDonough
slashed the young officer's sword arm and made him prisoner. In
the melee that followed, many more redcoats were overrun by the
shock of the Irish charge; many fell and did not rise again.

But the Irish casualties were terrible, too. More than 270 of the
Wild Geese died in that charge, including 13 officers; almost 400
more were wounded. Their losses were higher in proportion to their
strength than those of any French unit engaged that day; one man
in six was a casualty. And among the Irish dead was one who simply
could not be replaced: the Chevalier Dillon himself.

The wild attack of the Wild Geese had been enough, just enough.
Saxe had bled the British advance white, and now even Cumberland
realized that he had no options left. If he left his British and Germans
where they were, encircled on three sides, he would lose them all.
There was nothing left but retreat. It was a bitter pill, especially
because the red regiments had to leave behind their battalion guns,
fifteen of which fell into the hands of jubilant Irish.

The great red column faced about and fell back, back across that
terrible field it had given so many lives to cross. As they fell back,
they were charged by the French household cavalry again. The
Guards and a Hanoverian battalion let loose another of those murderous volleys, virtually exterminating one regiment and killing or
wounding all the officers of a second.

Saxe did little to pursue, a decision he was criticized for afterward.
But the veteran Saxe was right: "As we had enough of it," he said,

"I thought only of restoring order among the troops." Saxe's army was bloody and exhausted, and the country ahead was cut up with woods and ravines. The redcoated rear guard—dour Yorkshiremen and borderers—were still full of fight, and the hedgerows lining the Flanders roads were infested with those kilted hellions of the Black Watch. Behind his rear guard and a cavalry screen, Cumberland retired, and saved his army. At the next day's roll call, no man of the Guards Brigade was missing but the dead and badly wounded.

But Saxe had his victory, and he owed it to Lally and his Irish, mostly, as well as to his own clear vision and the supine behavior of the Dutch. And if the British had inflicted terrible casualties on Saxe's army, they had taken an awful hammering themselves, especially among the officers, who led from the front no matter what their rank. One major general had been wounded in four places; another, Ponsonby, lay dead (another Ponsonby would die for his country at Waterloo). Young Charles Hay had been badly wounded, but would survive to help take Louisburg from the French.

The twenty English battalions left some 4,000 dead and wounded on the field. Alone, the three Guards battalions in the first line had lost some 250 men apiece. Altogether, in the allied army 7,000 to 8,000 men were down, mostly British; French casualties were about the same. "We gained the victory," said Saxe, "but may I never see such another." And Lally, sitting on a drum after the fighting was over, would shrug off the congratulations of a French nobleman: "Monseigneur, they are like the words of the evangelist; they fall on the one-eyed and the lame."

The battlefield was the usual scene of terrible carnage, made all the worse by the lack of any medical service worthy of the name. And the French, contrary to their usual custom, treated Cumberland's wounded with indifference if not downright cruelty. In the end, Cumberland sent angry messages directly to Saxe, and the greathearted marshal gave orders that the surviving British wounded be decently cared for.

Cumberland himself had contributed to Saxe's victory. Saxe knew his enemy, his bulldog tendency to batter straight ahead, in this case to thrust his finest troops into a three-sided box of fire. A Marlborough or a Wellington would have cleared his flanks first or not advanced at all. And it is hard to understand why Cumberland did not turn part of his force on the Redoubt d'Eu or the flank of Fontenoy Village once he had taken the French camp.

Moreover, Cumberland's advance to contact with the French had been nothing short of glacial. He had taken eleven days to cover forty-eight miles; even by the leisurely standards of the eighteenth century, he could have done much better. In 1809, for example, one of Wellington's divisions, marching over bad Spanish roads, covered sixty-two miles in just twenty-six hours, with very few stragglers, and was ready to fight on arrival.

In fairness, it is significant that Cumberland had to fight without much of his heavy artillery. At the time of Fontenoy, although artillerymen were soldiers, the men who transported the guns were not. Early in the action at Fontenoy, Cumberland's civilian contract drovers had fled with their horses, leaving the cannon immobile.

Most of those British guns became French property, adding to the delirious joy of the French court and nation. Te deums were sung in French cathedrals, jubilant crowds thronged the streets, and the royal family basked beneath a brilliant sun of public popularity. Voltaire, ever alert for a profitable opportunity, quickly cranked out an epic poem about the battle that sold over twenty thousand copies in a matter of days, and in time went through eight editions.

Cumberland had no choice but to retreat, collecting his Flanders garrisons as he went. Saxe, now in possession of Tournai, had almost twice the force remaining to Cumberland. After Fontenoy, under confusing orders to defend everything, Cumberland ended up by defending almost nothing. Saxe cut his communications repeatedly, and took both Ghent and Ostend. In August, in the midst of this crisis, came urgent orders to send troops back to England—first ten battalions, then nearly the whole army—in spite of the disastrous effect this withdrawal would surely have on the allied effort in Flanders.

For Bonnie Prince Charlie had made his grand gesture. Toward the end of July he had landed in western Scotland with a handful of supporters, and had raised the Jacobite standard at Glenfinnan on August 19. And Charles Edward had chosen his time well. As supporters rallied to him, the royalist response was feeble. The only royal troops remaining in Scotland were green and poorly trained; there was not a single able-bodied artilleryman in the whole country.

After Fontenoy, there were many promotions and honors for the Irish. MacDonough, whose bright sword had cut down the young British guardsman, was also promoted, and sent off to County Clare to recruit for the brigade. MacDonough found recruits all right, but he also found love; he would not return to the brigade. It is pleasant to relate that he died at eighty and left MacDonoughs to carry on that hardy line.

One of those promoted was the gifted, gallant Lally, but his promotion proved to be a curse. Sent to India to rescue French fortunes there, Lally failed to take the British fortifications at Madras and was badly defeated at Wandiwash (by an Anglo-Irishman, Sir Eyre Coote). The French were entirely ejected from India in the very next year. Lally, sent to England a prisoner, was paroled and returned to France in 1761. There, a grateful government threw him into the Bastille, and six years later judicially murdered him for his failure in India.

Lally's fate infuriated the Irish, who had already begun to realize that the futile, effete Stuarts would never rule in England. Fontenoy proved to be almost the last hurrah for the Wild Geese, for Irish recruiting for the French army steadily decreased. And in time, more and more Irishmen enlisted to fight in the British army, which knew their quality and was glad to have them.

Saxe retired in 1748, rich in honors. He would live in spectacular Chambord Castle, opened to him by the king of France. There he entertained in almost royal style and indulged his fondness for the ladies. Before his death in 1750, a lovely star of the Paris opera graced Saxe with a daughter, whose own daughter would be the famous novelist known as George Sand.

Perhaps the finest compliment paid the Irish came from their enemy. "Cursed," said King George II, "be the laws which deprive me of such subjects." Which echoed a member of Parliament, arguing for Catholic emancipation:

> We met our own laws at Fontenoy. The victorious troops of
> England were stopped . . . by the Irish Brigade which the Penal
> Laws had shut out from the ranks of the British Army.

But that would change. In the end, many more Irishmen would follow English colors than ever served France, and Irishmen in numbers serve Her Britannic Majesty to this very day.

About all that remains of the Wild Geese in France is a legacy of gallantry. The French army has not forgotten its old allies, and three French regiments have "companies of honor" that carry on the lineage of regiments Dillon, Clare, and Walsh.

CHAPTER EIGHT

THE WILD GEESE, STILL FLIGHTING

And the Irish Move to the Sound of the Guns,
Like the Salmon to the Sea

BRIGADIER MIKE CALVERT, a soldier's soldier, led British 77 Brigade to the epic 1944 capture of Mogaung, in Burma. He told me this story in London several years ago.

One of 77 Brigade's units was a company from the King's Regiment. The King's, of venerable lineage and glorious history, is a Liverpool outfit, but Mike's company was almost all Irish—southern Irish. One of his enlisted aides had been a sergeant in the infantry of the Irish Free State. And when England's fortunes seemed low, about the time of Dunkirk, the sergeant led his whole platoon on board the ferry to Anglesey. Debarking on the English side, the unit enlisted en masse in the British army, which was delighted to have them.

"They all fought extraordinarily well," said Mike, whose chief intelligence officer was also Irish. "They were completely uncomplaining." And the old enmity between the south of Ireland and Great Britain? It was never mentioned. The Irish fought for a good cause, and that was enough for them.

Any echoes of old anger were drowned out by the sound of the guns.

CHAPTER NINE

AN END TO THE DREAMING: CULLODEN MOOR

THE DAY HAD been bright and shiny, like a new gold sovereign, when the old red-and-white silk standard snapped in the clean air at Glenfinnan. There had been nothing but hope then, that glowing August day, when Prince Charles Edward Stuart had come in down the road from the Isles. Then there had been much cheering and tossing of Highland bonnets into the air. It seemed so long ago now, and the shining time was gone, and there was hunger, and wet, and cold, and many a good comrade's face missing from the ranks.

For a little while after the bright morning of Glenfinnan, the Stuart cause had seemed to thrive. Prince Charles Edward, Bonnie Prince Charlie, had been gallant and gracious, and there had been piping and brave speeches and bright claymores raised in the sun. Lochiel the Younger had brought the strength of Clan Cameron to add to smaller groups of MacDonalds, Grants, MacLachlans, McGregors, and Stewarts, and the men of Atholl.

If fewer Highlanders rallied to the prince than he had hoped, his enemies were also few, and they were untried. There were no more than three thousand government troops in all of Scotland, and these included some garrison soldiers who were for all practical purposes invalids. Some cannon there were, but not a single Royal Artilleryman in the whole country. The prince had timed his return perfectly.

But there was also a little cloud in that brilliant sky: save for Lochiel, none of the major Highland leaders joined. Sympathize they might, and did. But the memories of the disasters of the rebellion of '15 were still green, and the canny clan patriarchs wanted no part of another gallant lost cause. However much cheering there may have been, they saw that the prince had landed with only nine companions and with no arms or money to speak of.

Yet there was success, at first. Most of the British army—and the best of it—was in Flanders, fighting the perpetual wars against the French, and a hastily collected Hanoverian force had been routed by the Highlanders at Prestonpans in September of 1745. The whole affair took about ten minutes of fighting and was settled by a rolling, roaring, howling Highland charge, all waving claymores and ferocious war cries, a "hideous shout" that froze the hearts of King George's men. It had all been too much for the Hanoverians, who got off a single, ragged volley and took to their heels, leaving about a thousand prisoners behind. At least they ran fast enough that the Highland reserve never caught up with the battle.

The Hanoverian commander, General Sir John Cope, was swept willy-nilly from the field by the river of fugitives. And thereafter—while the sunlight of the rising lasted—the pipes would play a catchy little air about the disaster. "Hey, Johnny Cope" would remain a favorite with the Highland army. The government troops had been humiliated, badly whipped in about the time it takes to read about it.

Maybe they had been too badly whipped. For panic spread through the lowlands and the north country, and the rank smell of it reached all the way to London. The government immediately began the transfer from Flanders of some twenty regiments of infantry under the command of the king's chubby younger son, the Duke of Cumberland. Cumberland was no military genius, and he would show a deep streak of brutality. But he was a disciplinarian, he feared nothing, he was careful, and he would fight. His soldiers admired him and would follow him anywhere. Trouble was on the way.

But for now the prince's troops basked in the sun of victory. New recruits came in, the army lived well for a change, and the leadership debated the next move. The Young Pretender, encouraged by victory, was certain that England would rise in his behalf. And so the decision was taken to move south, and the army packed its kit and moved out from Edinburgh in the first week of November 1745.

They were headed for Carlisle, and the town fell to them on the fifteenth. A British relief column under General George Wade tried to reach the city but was frustrated by heavy snow and a lack of reliable transport. Virtually unopposed, the Highland army pushed on south through the cold, reaching undefended Manchester on the twenty-ninth.

The prince enjoyed an enthusiastic welcome from some of the populace—but no real help. Though there were many cheers, there were few reliable recruits, mostly some two hundred ragged men without jobs who admitted they had been prepared to join whichever army reached the city first. These unimpressive replacements did not begin to make up for the hundreds of men who had deserted on the way south.

Nonetheless, the prince pushed on. He moved more slowly now, much of the spark gone out of his movement, reaching Derby on December 4. And here even Charles had to face the great danger ahead. Cumberland's veterans waited for him just to the south; Wade was moving to join Cumberland; and a third army was prepared to defend London. There was nothing for it but retreat, retreat to Scotland where at least there was real support—and replacements.

The prince left a four-hundred-man garrison behind him in Carlisle. He did so against nearly everybody's advice, for "he would have a town in England." He did not have it long, just a bit over a week, before Cumberland's guns forced the Jacobites' surrender. To the north of lost Carlisle, the Highland army marched into Glasgow. It was Christmas Day.

Cumberland followed, deliberate, stolid, sure of himself. On December 18 he made contact, and the Highlanders fought a series of vicious little skirmishes with British dragoons up and down the narrow roads around Clifton Village. And if the dragoons fell back at the end of the day, they did not run. These were not the men of Prestonpans, and they would be back.

But for the time, things were easier for the prince and his loyal Jacobites. They had crossed safely into Scotland, and here there was food for empty bellies and good news to cheer the heart. For at Perth reinforcements were waiting, Highlanders under Lord Strathallan, and 750 wild Irish troops under Lord John Drummond. One Highland contingent had been raised by Lady Mackintosh, a stout Jacobite, whose husband, the clan chief, was an officer in the royalist Black Watch.

In addition to reinforcements, there was food in plenty for a change, and sympathetic people, and a chance to rest. While most of his troops rested, the prince laid siege to Sterling Castle, bashing away at that fabled old pile with heavy guns brought all the way from France. Meanwhile, he watched still another Hanoverian army coming north; fortunately for the prince, this new set of enemies was commanded by yet another military nonentity.

Lieutenant General Henry Hawley, a noted martinet without noticeable military talent, had brought some eight thousand men across the border. He groped his way toward the prince's forces, arriving on the sixteenth of January at a place near the town of Falkirk, about midway between Edinburgh and Glasgow. Charles Edward left a screen of men to maintain the blockade of Sterling and moved to meet this new threat.

Hawley, thus far all energy and bustle, was now strangely hesitant. Nobody knows just why, although his reluctance to move farther north may have had something to do with the Countess of Kilmarnock. This lady, wife to a prominent Jacobite, entertained the general in high style at Callendar House. The countess was apparently a woman of considerable attraction, and there is some reason to think she might have seduced the general—all for the cause, of course.

In any case, he was still with the countess in the warmth of Callendar House when bad news arrived. He was startled to find that the Jacobites were near at hand and looking for a fight. In fact, they were already within cannon-shot, on favorable ground neither the general nor his officers had reconnoitered, or even seen. There were about eight thousand of them, too, roughly the size of the general's own force.

Southwest of Falkirk, about a mile from Hawley's camp, a ridge rose out of the moorland. Lord George Murray, commanding the Jacobite army, had instantly recognized the position for what it was, the perfect launching pad for the Highlanders' favorite wild downhill charge. One end of the Highland line was protected by a bog, the other by a ravine. In the center a hill rose above the surrounding moor. It was an ideal place to fight.

The two forces met in a driving rain, the Highlanders occupying the ridgeline; Hawley, too late, sent three regiments of dragoons forward to do the same. Behind them plodded his infantry, English and Scots loyalists, the rain driving into their faces as they came.

Before the rest of the British force could align its ranks, Hawley sent his left-flank dragoons charging through the downpour toward the Scots' right. They galloped head-on into a murderous volley fired into their ranks from about thirty feet away. Some eighty men went down together, and the rest rammed home their spurs and sought safety at the gallop. Those who were not quick enough were pulled down by shouting Highlanders wielding dirks and claymores, and the dragoons were routed. Oblivious of everything but their terror, they rode down the infantry of their own left wing, scattering them in all directions.

In the center the Highlanders reached for their broadswords. They had fired a single volley and could not load again in the rain. Fair enough, it would be cold steel, and they rolled down the slope in a roaring wave, bounding down the rough moorland toward the Hanoverian infantry, already shaken by the disaster on its left. It was too much for Hawley's disordered foot soldiers. Those whose wet muskets would fire managed a single puny volley, and then the whole force took to its heels. It was Prestonpans all over again.

Except on the right. There three regiments, protected by a ravine in their front, held their ground, then moved forward, changed front, and fired volley after volley into the flank of the advancing Highlanders. Their cool, destructive volleys convinced many of the Jacobites that they had been defeated, and some of them began to leave the field of battle. At this moment the Irish came up from reserve and the three Hanoverian regiments fell back to join the retreat. But they had fought well, and they continued to show their teeth whenever pursuit came too close. They would be heard from again, these stubborn regiments: Ligonier's, Price's, and Barrel's.

Both sides had had enough. The king's troops were in full retreat; the Scots stopped to loot the riches of their enemy's camp. They had lost only some fifty dead and perhaps eighty wounded. The king's soldiers left about three hundred and fifty still corpses on the field, and at least three hundred prisoners. The fight had lasted only twice as long as Prestonpans, and that only because of the three hard-nosed regiments of the right wing.

General Hawley reported that he had administered "a severe check to the Highlanders," but he did not come again, nor stand upon the order of his going, nor tarry more with the lovely countess. Now was Charles Edward's golden opportunity to pursue and destroy. But he did not see it, and instead returned to the siege of Sterling, fumbling his chance away. It would not come again.

By February the Highland army had fallen back north to Moray Firth, near the town of Inverness. There would be no campaigning during this time, the worst of the winter, save for the occasional raid. A force of Irish under Brigadier Walter Stapleton moved against Hanoverian posts along the Great Glen. Stapleton took Fort Augustus on the first of March and then turned against Fort William. It turned out to be a considerably tougher nut, and the siege was abandoned in the first week of April. Still, it had been a successful winter. Now that the spring was almost upon them, the prince's men would be on the road south again to harry the king's troops and perhaps to bring Charles Edward to his own again.

But a hundred miles or so southeast of Inverness, in Aberdeen, William, Duke of Cumberland, was already preparing for the new year. He was careful and determined, and he was coming north— and he would bring with him a tough, experienced army. If he was no Marlborough, he was not Johnny Cope, either. There would be no more Prestonpans.

William moved early in the year, long before he was expected. He crossed the fine natural barrier of the river Spey without a fight, and by April 14 he was in Nairn, just eight miles away from the Jacobite army. Only then did the prince realize how near the enemy was; only then did he realize the very great danger so very close to him.

The Highland army was scattered and shrinking. Food was very short thanks to an unforgivable failure in the Jacobite commissary; many of the troops foraged desperately far and wide just to survive. Others had gone home, just walking off. Some had had enough of war and hunger; many others had business of their own to care for before the next campaign. The prince hastily called in whatever forces he could find, but he had left it far too late.

For there was no time to reorganize, no time to wait for laggards.

The enemy was too close. The prince called a council of war and gathered what remained of his army on Drummossie Moor—now called Culloden Moor. He counted some five thousand men, ragged and cold, many of them still hungry. About a third of the army had still not joined, although some contingents were coming in steadily and others were on the way.

Drummossie Moor was not a place to give battle, not for this army, at least. Lord George Murray, the best of the prince's officers, knew it: "There could never be more improper ground for Highlanders," he said, and he was right. But the prince, never a competent tactician, listened to others, and Murray's advice went unheeded. Drummossie Moor it would be, although Murray had found and recommended a patch of rough, broken ground near Dalcross Castle, fine terrain for infantry to resist an enemy strong in cavalry and guns.

And now ignorance was compounded by fantasy. Somebody suggested a night attack on the duke's encampment, and the prince endorsed the idea. And so this disorganized, tired, hungry army set off into the night, and things immediately began to come unstuck. Almost instantly the troops began to straggle, and before long soldiers were wandering everywhere in the gloom. All organization was lost, and in time there came the beat of drums from the English camp. There would be no surprise; the enemy was alert and ready.

So Murray wisely called off what should never have been attempted in the first place, incurring the wrath and distrust of the prince in doing so. The tired Highlanders straggled back to Drummossie Moor, where many threw themselves on the wet ground and fell instantly into a deep sleep. Other men wandered off to forage, until the prince could muster no more than five thousand men on the field. He himself made for Culloden House and fell into an exhausted sleep without even taking off his boots.

The prince would have no more than an hour's rest, for Cumberland was coming on. Confident in the training and discipline of his own veterans, he would not let the Highland army recover from its exhausting night march. His only fear was that the Highland army would not stand and fight.

He need not have worried. The prince certainly should have ordered a retreat. Retreat would have bought time to regroup and bring in food. More stragglers could be collected, given a little time, and there were reinforcements marching hard from the north. At worst, a retirement would at least have moved his army onto more defensible ground. But the prince made up his mind to fight, apparently refusing to recognize his weakness, intoxicated with the sad illusion that his Highlanders were invincible.

And so Charles mounted his fine gray horse and galloped off to grim Drummossie Moor. In personal command for the first time, he would not listen to the excellent advice of several of his veteran officers, including the able Murray. The moor was too open, they warned the prince; it was too flat, too smooth, too open. It was made for English artillery and cavalry.

Prince Charles' professional officers urged him to withdraw across the river Nairn and fight from the rugged high ground on the other side. But the prince chose to listen to other advisers, including one superannuated favorite whose last fighting experience was over half a century old. Above all, he listened to his Irish confidante, one Colonel O'Sullivan, a nitwit of the first magnitude. Cumberland could not have wished for better Scots dispositions had he arranged them himself.

As the Highland army fell in on the moor, the prince's officers knew there was hell to pay and no pitch hot, but there was little they could do. Murray spoke for them all: "We are putting an end to a bad affair," he said, though he could not know then just how very bad it would be. Though the pipers played stoutly in the rain—"Hey, Johnnie Cope" was one of the airs—there was only gloom in Murray's heart.

The front ranks were mostly Highlanders—Camerons, Stuarts, Frasers, and Mackintoshes among them. Clan MacDonald claimed the honor of holding the right of the line but was relegated to the left, an apparent slight that did not sit well with those proud men. Nevertheless, the army was shaken out into two lines, together with their artillery, a miscellany of twelve guns of different calibers and indifferent crews. And so they waited while the orderly lines of red coats in front of them came steadily on.

It was raining again, a slashing squall driven by a northeasterly wind. This time it bit into the faces of the Highlanders, as it had done to their enemies at Falkirk. It was more than miserable, for it made it very hard to keep powder dry, more for the Scots with their old-fashioned powder horns than for the English with their cartridges.

And so the two armies stood in silent ranks until, at about one o' clock, the Scots artillery began a halting fire.

The prince's tired men faced fifteen battalions of regular infantry, also fallen in in two lines with a small reserve. They were supported by the Scots Argyle Militia and several hundred dragoons. In the British first line were the familiar uniform facings of Price's and Barrel's regiments, in the second line the silent ranks of Ligonier's. Each second-rank regiment covered a gap between two front-rank units.

There would be no exposed flanks for the Scots to find and roll up. Cumberland's right flank was covered by marshy ground. Along the far left of the Hanoverian line ran a little stream that rose from a spring later named—with reason—the Well of the Dead. There stood a regiment called Wolfe's, a well-disciplined unit positioned to wheel to its right to enfilade the wild Scots charge everyone knew was coming. The men of Wolfe's were grim and determined; they had not behaved well at Falkirk, and they knew it. This time, they told themselves, things would be different.

Many of these scarlet regiments were veterans of the hard wars against the French in Flanders. Some had fought in the desperate action at Fontenoy. They remembered the shame of Falkirk and Prestonpans, and they had heard a rumor that the Highland command had ordered its men to give no quarter. Well, then, said the experienced English, war to the knife it would be. And as the cannonade began, they gave a great cheer and then stood silent, protecting the pans of their muskets with their coattails, waiting for the Highland rush. Their enemy stood silent in the rain, perhaps five or six hundred yards away across the moor.

Spaced in five pairs between the duke's first-line regiments were the Hanoverian guns—easily handled three-pounders manned by expert royal artillery crews. They were supported by two three-tube batteries of big coehorn mortars. And now this artillery began to return the Scots fire, their gunners experienced, their accuracy and rate of fire much greater than the Highland guns could achieve.

Hanoverian cannonballs tore great bloody lanes in the Highland ranks, and here and there men began to edge away. A ball ripped the head from the prince's groom, and anxious officers persuaded Charles Edward to retire to a little safer place. The prince was a courageous man, but he heeded this advice. It was a mistake, for it took him too far from the front ranks and the heaviest of the action. He was supposed to be in personal command, but he could not see the battle. He might as well have been back in France.

And so the prince gave no order to attack, though in attack lay the only chance for the Highland army and the Stuart cause. For twenty minutes the suffering Highlanders stood this galling fire; the prince was too far back to appreciate what his men were enduring until finally Lord George Murray appealed to Charles Edward to let his men advance.

And then, finally, the order to charge was given. As the Highland lines started to move, the British gunners switched to grapeshot, and the foremost Scots ranks began to dissolve into bloody ruin. That wild, terrifying attack, so often irresistible in the past, began to roll across the flat moorland, first the center, the right wing a minute or two behind it. On the left, however, the MacDonalds held back. Perhaps they were still deeply insulted by their assignment to this end of the line; perhaps, and more probably, they were only a little late in reaching the battlefield.

The charge swept down on the motionless scarlet lines of infantry, who stood in silence until the range closed. Into the teeth of the sleet the Highlanders came roaring on as British grapeshot tore great bloody holes in their ranks. And then the infantry volleys crashed into the Highlanders running through the rain toward the British infantry, strewing the sodden ground with kilted figures.

Still the prince's men came on, the mass of them drifting to their right and into the murderous flanking fire of Wolfe's regiment. Caught up in the fury of battle, the Highlanders kept coming, stumbling over their own dead, until their momentum carried them into the ranks of Barrel's Regiment—the Royals—and Munro's Regiment next to them. Doughty Colonel Munro—a Scot and clan chief himself—had been killed at Falkirk, and his men had something to repay.

Now the prince's men could go to cold steel, and the red broadswords began to rise and fall. Some of the charging Highlanders passed all the way through the English regiments. The front-line regiments were staggered, but this time they would not break. This time the king's infantry stood their ground, fighting it out man-to-man with bayonet and musket butt and the officers' espontoon, a sort of wicked boar spear.

And for a little while it was very hot and very bloody. One British officer spitted a Scot on his espontoon, then went down with his head split in two pieces. The commander of Barrel's Regiment fell with one hand cut off and six head wounds. But the red infantry would not back up, the second line closed in to help, and the bayonets took a dreadful toll of the Highlanders.

Cumberland had issued orders that each soldier should ignore the Scot directly in front of him. Rather, he was to attack the Scot just to his right, where his long bayonet could go in under the sword arm and behind the small shield most of the Highlanders carried on their left arms. The troops had practiced this tactic and learned to trust their left-hand neighbors; this day they would discover that Cumberland's battle drill worked.

Of the five hundred or so Highlanders who had broken through the leading regiments, very few came safely back again. Most of them were down and dying, and hundreds more behind them on the sodden turf. One huge Highlander, a MacGillivray, is said to have cut down a dozen soldiers with his broadsword. He died in the British second line in spite of the efforts of an admiring English officer to save his life. Another Highlander used a cart shaft to knock over his attackers until an English bullet put him down forever.

Two second-line British regiments came up to deal with the men who had gotten past the first-line units, and suddenly the heart went out of the Highland charge and men began to throw away their arms and run. Some fell back stubbornly, fighting for every yard. Lord George Murray, his horse killed under him, was one of the last to leave the field, fighting on foot at the head of his Athollmen.

The MacDonalds had farther to go than the rest of the Jacobite line, over worse ground, and so they came late to the fight. Even so, they closed to within a hundred yards of the British line; but with the rout of the Highland center their right flank was exposed, and British cavalry was coming in on their left.

And so that proud clan ran with the rest, or most of them did, the whole army streaming back, away from those terrible bayonets, and the Highland corpses stacked in heaps on the dreary moor, and the old Stuart dream dying there in the rain. A few of the MacDonald leaders ran forward into the British lines and fell there among the bayonets, but their men would not stand, and Cumberland's infantry came steadily on.

And now, as the Scots recoiled, Cumberland's redcoats began a deliberate advance. Ferocious hand-to-hand fighting swirled around the clan standards, as clansmen struggled and died to keep the precious talismans from the hands of the English. One Scot, rejoicing in the name of "Hairy Donald," got away with the Appin banner, cut from its staff and wrapped around his body.

In the retreat that followed, many of the MacDonalds owed their lives to the grit of Stapleton's Irish infantry, who held up the pursuing dragoons long enough for the MacDonalds to get clear of the rout on the moor. The price was high. Stapleton received his death wound there, and more than half his men would remain on the moor forever.

Over on the Highland right a series of stone walls were occupied by British dragoons and the loyalist Argyle Militia. They were behind the Jacobite flank, and their musketry hammered the retreating Highlanders as they passed. The Campbells caught sight of their ancient enemy, Lochiel's Camerons, falling back, smashed three volleys into the exhausted men, then charged with cold steel. And then there was more killing there in the cold rain.

On the other end of the line British dragoons were also lapping around the Jacobite flank, and there was no stopping the retreat. Most of the Highlanders ran for their lives, but some of the prince's soldiers kept a little cohesion. Some fought on in small groups until they won to safety, or the cavalry rode them down, or the crimson bayonets caught them.

Most of them simply plodded on across the sodden moor, seeking safety anywhere. But there was no safety, no sanctuary, from Cumberland's pursuit. For the duke was determined to finish the rising there and then, and he urged his men on to destroy the Highland army utterly. He very nearly succeeded.

The prince won clear, mounted and covered by his devoted men. But more than twelve hundred of his men died out there on the moor, many of them cut down by Hanoverian cavalry during the merciless pursuit. Many more were prisoners, and the rest were scattered beyond rallying. The whole affair had lasted about an hour, and the grand old cause was lost forever.

Cumberland had won his victory, quite competently and certainly thoroughly. But in the doing of it he had permitted and indeed encouraged the grossest brutality. His triumph was greeted with enthusiasm in England, where he was called "Sweet William," and there was even a flower named for his obese self. In the Highlands he was seen somewhat differently—and more accurately—as "Butcher" Cumberland—or, more simply, "Stinking Willie."

There was much indiscriminate killing during the retreat. Some was by Hanoverian soldiers with scores to settle for Falkirk and Prestonpans. Some was by loyalist Scots allies with old debts of their own. Prisoners died, and wounded men, and even a few civilian noncombatants; and Cumberland's name was forever blackened as a result.

Cumberland himself had shown great courage during the fighting, as he had in the carnage of Fontenoy, sitting his horse calmly as cannonballs flew past. And he gave prompt orders for the careful care of his own wounded; later he would reach deep into his own pocket for gold sovereigns to reward his hurt soldiers and the men who had captured Scottish standards.

But on the battlefield the duke proved himself a butcher indeed. At one point he saw a captive Scot watching him, and asked to whom the Scot belonged. "To the prince," replied the courageous Highlander, and Cumberland was outraged. Turning to a slim young captain on his staff, he ordered the officer to shoot the Scot. The officer shook his head.

"My commission is at Your Highness's disposal," said the captain, "but I can never consent to act as an executioner." It was typical of the man, young James Wolfe, who thirteen years later would find immortality—and death—before Quebec and would win a whole new world for his country. Cumberland found a soldier to do his killing and rode on into Inverness.

In that newly liberated town, British troops freed a number of loyalist captives, mostly Argyle Militiamen. And Cumberland took up residence in the finest house of the town, the residence of the dowager Lady Mackintosh. The prince had stayed in the same house, and the owner was not enchanted with either of her royal guests. Later she would put it plainly:

> I've had two king's bairns living under my roof in my time, and to tell you the truth, I wish I may never have another.

"Bonnie Prince Charlie" got safely away, covered by a handful of his faithful officers, hounded by Hanoverian pursuit. He would travel west across the Highlands, calling for a futile rally at Fort

Augustus, a rally to which no one came. It was then, it seems, that he finally realized how low his cause had fallen. And it was then that his messengers carried the word to what remained of his supporters: "Let every man seek his safety the best way he can."

Most of the prince's officers escaped, many hiding for weeks or months in the Highlands. Most left the country in time, and many of these ended up in France, where several were granted commissions in the French army. The inept O'Sullivan fell out of favor at last, but made a rich marriage and lived out his days in comfort. Murray, the able officer whose advice the prince ignored, also escaped to Europe and settled in Germany. He was safe, but he would never see Scotland again.

So it was every man for himself, and the prince for himself too. For Charles, the only safety lay west over water, to the outer Hebrides. There he met Flora MacDonald, who hid the prince, dressed in women's clothing, as Irish Betty Burke. Flora took him farther still, to the Isle of Skye, where lay safety, at least for a while. If his escape to Skye produced one of the loveliest of songs, it produced no improvement in his fortunes.

The prince would return to the mainland by early July, kissing Flora's hand and bidding her a smiling good-bye. "I hope," he said, "I hope we shall meet in St. James yet." But they would not meet in St. James, or Holyrood, or anywhere ever at all, for the old cause was nothing anymore but a fading, bittersweet memory. The pipes might play "Will ye no come back again?" but the Stuart prince would not, and his claim on the throne was dead forever.

The prince stayed but a little time on the mainland, hunted and hounded, until he was glad to take to the sea again, this time to leave the British Isles forever. He would die in Rome in 1788, a sodden sot, a shadow of the young, proud man who stood beneath the scarlet-and-white standard at Glenfinnan, so many years gone.

It was a great pity that he did not go down beside his men on dank, dreary Drummossie Moor, for it was mostly his bad judgment that led them to their deaths. Had he stood and fought and fallen beside them, the warm bright legend would have bloomed untarnished for all time, instead of dying by inches, old and tired, in pain and drunkenness in a far-off, alien land.

CHAPTER TEN

THE HORSE MARINES

I'm Captain Jenks of the Horse Marines
And I feed my horse on pork and beans
And I often live beyond my means . . .

BACK IN THE HALCYON days before the world wars, service with the marine legation guard at Beijing (then called Peking) was considered something of a plum. In the first place, all the heavy work was done by hired coolies. The ordinary marine passed his time in training and sports and the pursuit of pleasure. There was plenty of all three.

Back in 1907 the legation guard had raised a mounted detachment, known to one and all as "the Horse Marines." They became an elite unit, very impressive on ceremonial occasions, and very useful as well. Mounted on tough Mongolian ponies, they were an effective crowd-control force, and they could move quickly to warn isolated pockets of Americans of the riots and other tumults endemic in early twentieth-century China.

The Horse Marines never lacked for recruits, even though their ponies were sometimes hard to handle and there was currying and grooming to do. The reason was quite practical. It seems the Horse Marines were generally used as the "enemy" during field exercises outside the city. More mobile than their foot-slogging comrades, they made it back to town much more quickly at the close of the field problem, thus ensuring themselves first crack at the coldest beer and the prettiest whores.

The marines have always been a practical lot.

A TORCH TO THE ENEMY
Rogers' Rangers at St. Francis

IT WAS A place of blood, of horror. Men and women by the hundred had been dragged there as prisoners, and many had died there, their last ugly memories the laughter and jeers of their murderers. The lucky ones died quickly, in hot blood; for others, death came slowly, in agony, over slow fires. Hundreds of dried human scalps swung in the wind from poles imbedded in the earth of this ugly place, and some of them had come from the heads of little children.

The place of death and fear was an Abenaki Indian town, named, with supreme irony, for the gentle St. Francis. It lay in a pretty site, with the forest at its back, on the bank of the St. Francis River, a few miles above its confluence with the mighty St. Lawrence. To add to the irony of its bloody reputation, St. Francis called itself a Christian town, and indeed it had its own Roman Catholic church and its own French priest. In this year, 1759, St. Francis remained a nightmare horror to colonial New York and New England, even though a skinny, redheaded British brigadier named Wolfe was even then shaking the foundations of great Quebec.

For decades, war parties had trekked south from St. Francis, to strike at the tiny English settlements and the scattered farmsteads, murdering, kidnapping, slaughtering stock, leaving the towering smoke from burning homes and crops and barns to dirty the sky behind them. At last, the British command had decided something was to be done about this running sore in the flesh of the northern colonies. Lord Jeffrey Amherst, the British commander-in-chief, decided to exterminate this nest of vipers for all time, and he had just the keen-edged instrument to do it.

The man was Robert Rogers, a big, deadly bear of a New Hampshire frontiersman. Born in 1731, he was the fourth son of a tough pioneering family of immigrant Ulster Scots. The Rogers settled along the Merrimack River in Massachusetts Bay Colony and moved northwest into New Hampshire when Robert was still a small boy. Like most frontier youngsters of his time, Robert's life was one of dawn-to-dark farmwork and precious little education.

For a time, the Rogers family's only foe was nature: wresting a new farm and a living from virgin nature was work and worry enough. But then, in 1744, France declared war on England and the ominous threat of Indian raids began to loom over New Hampshire like a thundercloud. By late 1745 threat became reality, as parties of French and Indians out of St. Francis, Crown Point, and Montreal struck along the frontier in a series of brutal surprise assaults. New cabins and hard-won crops burned while farm families banded together so that some could work while others kept watch.

In this time of fear and danger, Robert Rogers grew toward manhood. At fourteen he served in the local militia, which vainly chased the murderous, elusive enemy into the back country north of the Merrimack Valley settlements. In 1748, the Rogers homestead was burned out, their precious stock slaughtered, even their fruit trees destroyed. Robert and other frontiersmen were learning more than woodcraft and bush combat; they were learning to hate. The raiders from the north had sowed the wind; in time they would reap the whirlwind.

Rogers was a huge man for his time, strong and level-eyed, plain-spoken and direct, that singular sort of man designed to lead good soldiers in bad places. He had little schooling but was educated quite well for a man of his day. His spelling was not always correct, but then, virtually all men of the eighteenth century spelled phonetically. But Rogers was intelligent, and he had the soldier's virtue: he expressed himself well and clearly and in few words.

Born of the frontier, Rogers was entirely at home in the woods, and he knew and understood the Indians well. He admired them in a way, admired their lack of avarice and ambition, their sense of oneness with nature. But he learned to fight them, too, learned to move and shoot in the woods and wild places, learned how to kill and how to survive. He led and fought against the French and Indians, and he soon attracted the attention of Sir William Johnson, the great father of the Iroquois confederation. Johnson knew talent when he saw it, and he sponsored Rogers, even to suppressing allegations that royal funds entrusted to Rogers as a commander had somehow stuck to the ranger's fingers.

By the spring of 1756 Rogers was captain of a ranger company, already voted a gift of money by the New York Assembly for "his extraordinary courage, conduct and diligence against the French and their Indians." Most regulars considered provincial militia to be weak reeds in a fight. Level-headed James Wolfe spoke for most professional soldiers: "[T]he Americans are in general the dirtiest, the most contemptible cowardly dogs you can conceive." If there was considerable truth to this comment as it applied to the generality of colonial levies, Rogers and his men were distinctly a different breed of cat; they had the respect of the British regular army. Wolfe himself asked that a company of rangers, commanded by Rogers himself, be attached to Wolfe's army for the assault on Quebec. And Rogers' commanders realized what an irreplaceable asset Rogers was. As General James Abercrombie put it:

> With regard to Rogers himself, I do think him so necessary and useful a Man, that I should be extremely Sorry to part with him . . . Without him these four Companies [of rangers] would be good for nothing.

Rogers and his men were acquiring a reputation, not just for hard, ferocious fighting—his rangers could scrap with the best of them— but for something infinitely more important.

For Rogers provided what the British army needed most: information, hard intellgence on which a commander could act. It was invariably reliable, as information from friendly Indians tended not to be. Johnson and British commander Sir Jeffrey Amherst depended utterly on Rogers' reconnaissance; the big ranger did not disappoint them. Penetrating deep into territory dominated by the French and Indians, Rogers and his men became the eyes and ears of the British and colonial forces, scouting winter and summer against the lowering threat from the north. And the exploits of Rogers' green-clad men did much for the colonies' morale: for the first time, British woodsmen were carrying the war to the enemy, ambushing war parties bound south to kill and burn in the settlements.

He went on his first scout in 1755, when only four men followed him. In time his little band became eight complete companies of rangers. At first, a ranger's uniform was whatever he could provide; rangers dressed in green-dyed buckskin, mostly, and many of them favored a Scots glengarry bonnet. In a 1776 painting, Rogers himself is pictured wearing a British Light Infantry cap, a little like a baseball cap with the brim turned straight up in front.

Later on, the rangers adopted a uniform especially designed for the wilderness: a short sleeveless jacket, its armholes extended and reinforced by "wings" of the sort worn by regular army drummers. Over a shirt they also wore a long-sleeved waistcoat. Both waistcoat and jacket were lined with green, so that their collars and cuffs contrasted with the rough wool of the garments. The uniform was closed with white metal buttons, and officers were distinguished by silver cord piping on clothing edges and buttonholes. Over drawers of canvas or linen they wore a curious sort of short skirt, rather like a kilt, which covered the tops of their thigh-length leggings or gaiters.

They traveled light, their food no more than a bag of cornmeal and a little jerked meat. A powder horn hung under their right arms, suspended from a shoulder belt; at the other hip they carried a canteen. At the front of their waist belt hung their bullet pouch, made of leather or sealskin, or a regular army cartridge box. They must also have carried several made-up cartridges, prepared paper-wrapped loads that had only to be bitten open and rammed home. The officers carried compasses, often affixed to the bottoms of their powder horns.

The rangers' arms were musket and bayonet, hatchet and scalping knife. The knife was generally carried at the belt; the tomahawk and bayonet hung in a sling suspended from the right shoulder and hanging at the left side. The officers and sergeants were generally armed as their men were, though some probably carried a pistol or two as well as the musket. For close-range work, the muskets were often loaded with several buckshot, as well as the lead ball, conveniently combining the virtues of both musket and shotgun.

No doubt there were also some rangers who carried rifles, but they were probably few. A rifle was far more accurate than a smooth-bore musket: above eighty or a hundred yards, most soldiers considered a hit with a musket to be purely accidental. On the other hand, a rifle took a great deal longer to load than a musket: you had to force the ball down the barrel, sometimes hammer it down, in order for it to fit tightly enough to engage the rifling in the bore of the weapon. In a close-range fight, the extra time it took to reload a rifle could get a man killed.

They went into terrible danger, these hard men in green buckskin. A quick death was the best they could hope for if they were cornered, for they took their share of scalps and the Indians feared them. Some, captured, died under terrible torture. Those who went back, and back again, would follow nobody but the best. That was Rogers, Rogers and the men he trained as his own officers. Most of these were frontiersmen, men like Israel Putnam and William Stark; but some were British regulars, men who came to study under this master of bush warfare so they could learn and teach other soldiers.

Good men were eager to serve under Rogers, for his exploits were legion. Over the evening fires and around tavern tables, men talked of his capture of a French schooner on Lake Champlain, of his single-handed capture of French prisoners for interrogation, of his daring, of his care for his men.

They talked, too, of the epic winter battle in 1758, when Rogers and his men fought a vastly superior force of French and Indians on Lake George. Understrength, Rogers had advanced with great care, carefully screening his main force with scouts, some of whom "went before him on scates," in Rogers' words. He and his Rangers ambushed and defeated a force of Indians, only to discover they were the advance party of a much larger force.

Battling odds of seven to one, Rogers' men beat a fighting retreat, during which some 150 of Rogers' 180 rangers were killed or captured. Wounded, Rogers himself won clear, an escape so miraculous that the Indians attributed it to intervention by the Great Spirit. Before he set out, Rogers had warned his superiors that his mission required twice as many men as he had; that any rangers escaped at all was a tribute to Rogers' leadership.

If there was any question about the efficiency of his men and their training, it was answered the next summer, when Rogers' rangers badly beat a strong force of Canadian woodsmen near the ruins of Fort Anne.

Rogers and his men had a certain panache about them, too. On Christmas Eve, 1757, under the noses of the French at Crown Point's Fort Carillon, Rogers set fire to the garrison's wood supply and butchered a number of cattle. And then, to the intense irritation of the French commander, Rogers left a receipt for the dead bullocks stuck in a cleft stick where the French would find it, a note that sent his compliments to Montcalm, the French supreme commander. If the French commander was not amused, the British Army laughed.

Now the ultimate test for the rangers had come. St. Francis had been a scourge to the British for some seventy years, long, long years of murder and torture and kidnapping. Many of Rogers' men had personal scores to settle with the Abenaki. Rogers himself did, for St. Francis Indians had burned the Rogers family farm, and he personally knew of some four hundred colonists killed or kidnapped to misery or death in the north.

Amherst's orders were quite secret; nobody but Rogers knew his objective. But nobody could keep secret the fact that some sort of expedition was being organized; among other things, it was simply not possible to draw thirty days' rations for more than two hundred men without the army grapevine humming with word that some sort of show was on. Rumor—perhaps intentionally started by Rogers—said the objective was someplace called "Suagothel," although nobody could say where that might be.

If General Amherst's orders were secret, they were also specific: Rogers was to destroy St. Francis and every male of fighting age, root and branch. The town was to be obliterated, not a stick of it left standing; it would burn to ashes, along with all its goods, chattels, and food supplies. At the same time, however, Amherst was careful not to descend to the level of his enemy. His orders were clear:

> Remember the barbarities that have been committed by the enemy's Indian scoundrels. Take your revenge, but don't forget that, though these dastardly villains have promiscuously murdered women and children of all ages, it is my order that no women or children be killed or hurt.

Which was all very well for Sir Jeffrey to say, and no doubt quite laudable. It was quite another thing for the man who was to carry out the orders. Still, the orders left to Rogers' discretion who might be "children" and who not, and that would have to do. Rogers was not an indiscriminate killer, despite his years on the bloody frontier, and he was quite conscious of his reponsibilities as a King's officer.

His orders in hand and his men ready and eager, Rogers planned his raid. He faced a formidable task. Ahead of him waited some 150 miles of wild country, unmapped, hostile, and largely empty. What information there was about the terrain and the enemy came from prisoners and a few scouting parties, moving fast and furtively. What was known about the way north was not encouraging.

On Lake Champlain lay a French fleet, quite considerable for the place and time: a brigantine, two schooners, and a flotilla of smaller craft. These were fighting ships; they carried cannon that could reduce Rogers' whaleboats to kindling without a chance to fight back. Once past the French vessels there was Fort Isle aux Noix to pass, and still seventy miles to go, and other French posts beyond that. And then there was the French stronghold at Montreal, not far off the line of the rangers' advance.

Assuming that his force managed to avoid all contact on the way north, and assuming that all went well at St. Francis, Rogers knew his route home would be swarming with strong parties of French and Indians panting for revenge. Rogers had a plan for that, too, but nobody could say whether it would work or whether the whole command might perish under the weight of converging French and Indian forces.

Rogers started north from Crown Point after nightfall on the thirteenth of September. Though he could not know it, it was the very day on which, far to the north, Wolfe's red-coated regulars fired two murderous volleys and won an empire before Quebec. Leading about two hundred rangers and friendly Stockbridge Indians, Rogers moved up the long arm of Lake Champlain in his whaleboats, rowing softly through the autumn night, pulling through the gloom until just before first light. Before sunup, the whole force was ashore and hidden in the timber, boats and all. Recon parties moved cautiously north while the main force rested.

Not far to the north, the French were cruising off the mouth of Otter River, and Rogers reasoned that the shoreline was also under surveillance by foot patrols. The sensible course of action was to wait, and wait Rogers did. But while he did, illness and injuries from a musket discharge and a small gunpowder explosion cut his force by about 20 percent. Without hesitation Rogers sent his casualties back south; where he was going, there was no room for a hurt man or a sick one. Only the strong would survive, if anybody survived at all.

And then, after all the ill fortune, Rogers had some good luck. The weather turned foul, rainy and cold, and Rogers used the bad visibility to slip past the French vessels into the northern reaches of the lake. He may have rowed up East Bay, a skinny arm of water between the east shore of the lake and Grand Isle, protected by shallows and a bar.

The rangers' water journey ended on the marshy shores of Missisquoi Bay, at the north end of Lake Champlain. There Rogers cached his whaleboats and a stock of rations, and there he left two friendly Indians to watch and give warning if the boats were discovered. And then, in the early morning of September 23, the column struck off on foot into the wilderness, northeast toward St. Francis.

And wilderness it was, a boggy, flooded country of spruce swamps, empty of people, where the rangers were perpetually wet and chilly. There was seldom a dry place to rest except a tree limb, if a man could find one, or a crude lattice of spruce branches wedged in the crotch of a tree. There was no game, and great clouds of gnats and mosquitoes made the days and nights a misery. And on the night of the second day of slogging through this miserable country, Rogers' two Indian sentries overtook the column after hours of running. The fat was in the fire, they said; a column of French, more than twice the size of Rogers' column, had found the precious boats and supplies. Both were gone, burned to ashes. Worse, half of the French force was even now baying on Rogers' trail.

Rogers called his officers together, and together they grimly examined their few options. There was no going back. With their supplies and transport gone, the lake route meant only death or captivity. Rogers' clear tactical sense told him to push on. His pursuers could make no better time than his rangers could; they could not catch him before he reached St. Francis, nor could a messenger alert the town before he reached it, even if the enemy behind him correctly guessed where he was going.

Press on, Rogers ordered; press on ahead of their pursuers; press on and destroy St. Francis before that vile place could be warned. And then, he said, then the force would return another way, a great circle to the southeast through the vast empty spaces, down past remote Lake Memphremagog, south down the Passumpsic River, all the way to the great Connecticut.

Rogers sent an officer, Lieutenant McMullen, already limping, south to Crown Point with a small escort. Make your best speed, he told McMullen, and ask Lord Amherst to send supplies up the Connecticut River as far as its confluence with the Wells River . . . "that being the way," Rogers said, "I should return, if at all . . ."

McMullen, lame or not, made remarkable time through hostile country, reaching the British fort at Crown Point just nine days after parting from Rogers. Amherst reacted immediately, ordering a ranger officer, Lieutenant Stevens, to collect men and provisions and move north at once. Amherst's orders were dated October 4; Stevens was on the move the same day.

Far to the north of Crown Point, for Rogers and his men the die was cast. They would drive hard for St. Francis, scouts far out on all sides of the green-clad column, everybody's senses reaching out for any fleeting sight or sound of hostile men. For Rogers and his 140 men walked now in the shadow of death, in the enemy's very backyard.

Rogers had his men on the move before daylight and kept them at it till after dark. It was a murderous march, a test of stamina that lasted seven more exhausting days, days of short rations and little sleep, scanty meals of jerky and cornmeal . . . and sometimes of nothing at all. It was cold, and no ranger carried more than a single light blanket; all fires were forbidden. The countryside was flooded; for most of the way the water was a foot deep.

But Rogers was not seen and he was not overtaken, and in time the ground began to firm up until the column struck the southwest bank of the swift, icy St. Francis River, some fifteen miles upstream of the Indian town. The river runs from southeast to northwest, and the town lay on the northeast shore. And so Rogers' men forded the St. Francis, the tallest, strongest rangers locking hands and arms to form a human chain across the swift water. They got over without losing a man, and then they had "good dry ground to march upon."

Still undetected, they moved closer to the town as the light faded on the fifth of October, twenty-two weary days since they had left

Crown Point. Rogers climbed a tree and observed the town, and then
the swift night came down and the rangers, 142 of them, began their
preparations for the dawn.

St. Francis was a considerable town, fifty houses at least. Some
were apparently of bark; others were substantial structures made of
squared timbers; still others seem to have been of frame construction.
A few were apparently built of stone, and there was a church, occupied by a French priest.

As his men made their dry camp and looked to their weapons,
Rogers and two of his officers crept closer to the town, thoroughly
reconnoitering their target for the morning. And again they had some
luck, for the St. Francis Indians were celebrating something or other,
engrossed in a "high frolic or dance," as Rogers put it. What the
occasion was has never been clear; various accounts say the village
was celebrating the conclusion of a hunt, the gathering of the harvest,
a wedding, or the return of a war party. Whatever the reason for the
festivities was, the Abenakis were quite oblivious to the death lying
in the woods so near to their celebration.

One account says that Rogers himself, wearing Indian dress, entered the town alone after dark to find the inhabitants still singing
and dancing. Maybe so; probably not. Rogers was certainly capable
of that sort of nervy act. But he was also a thorough professional,
and it is unlikely that he would have imperiled the whole mission
by taking the chance of discovery. Rogers did not look like an Indian,
and his size would surely have attracted some attention in the village.

Whether Rogers did his final reconnaissance from inside or outside
the village, he was satisfied. Rogers must have smiled in the darkness, watching the long hours of dancing in the village. Nobody
would be rising early next morning at St. Francis . . . nobody but
Rogers' own men.

Rogers gave his final orders and had his men on the move by
three. Packs were stacked, muskets freshly loaded. The officers would
have carefully supervised, making sure each man was ready. And
then, in absolute silence, they approached the town in the lonely
hours well before dawn, that cold, dreary time when even fighting
men are least alert, the hours in which people die. They moved like
shadows through the gloom, a patchwork of darkness and tendrils of
mist reaching up like tentacles from the banks of the chilly river.
Following their officers in the murk, the rangers would have checked

their priming and their flints again, for that was the careful ranger way.

And then, as the darkness began to pale ever so slightly, these silent men slid the long, triangular bayonets onto the muzzles of their muskets, loosened the hatchets in their belts, and rose to their feet. The time had come.

They padded silently into the village, where no man watched. There was nobody awake to see cold-eyed death stalking St. Francis town. After all, the shoe had been on the other foot for so very long: St. Francis men had done all the killing, all the torturing, had staged all the horrible predawn raids on sleeping farms and villages. Now the cycle of slaughter had come full circle; now the terror was coming home to roost.

Methodically the rangers broke in the doors of house after house, killing every man and older boy who emerged. They used the bayonet and the hatchet at first, killing silently, until shots were fired somewhere, and then the muskets began to flame in the gloom, and little eyes of flame sprang up here and there as men kindled torches and began to repay seventy years of terror to the south.

As women and children ran from the burning buildings, Rogers' men spared them—or most of them, at least, for those were the major's orders. Some of those who died were no doubt killed in error—it was unhealthy to hold your fire too long in the predawn darkness. In other cases, the killing must have been deliberate: there was no man of the rangers who did not know of the things the Abenaki had done to women and children in the ruined villages to the south.

The resident priest was also spared. Rogers did not make war on men of God, however tolerant they might have been of the cruelty and horror for which St. Francis stood. Father Pierre Joseph Antoine Roubaud's wooden church, however, was consigned to the flames with everything else. Churches had been burned in the colonies, and there seemed no good reason to spare this one. Before the church burned, one ranger thoughtfully removed a silver icon of the Virgin from the altar; it weighed ten pounds, and the soldier saw no point in throwing away perfectly good loot.

For two hundred or so men and older boys of St. Francis, there was no mercy. Most died as musket balls tore into their bodies or under the hatchets and bayonets and musket butts of these yelling,

hard-eyed men. Some never got out of their flaming cabins, burning
to death in cellars and lofts. For those who escaped the flames,
rangers waited outside amid the stench of burning flesh, waiting to
finish what the fire did not.

Other Indians ran for the St. Francis River, dove in, and swam for
safety. A few managed to launch canoes and paddle desperately away
from their flaming town. By that time, however, the rangers had
shooting light, and most of the fugitives died in the river, their only
memorial a swirling cloud of blood in the clear waters. There had
been revenge in plenty, and only ashes remained of St. Francis town.
The Abenakis, those who remained, would long remember this terrible dawning in a plaintive lament:

> I am lonesome, I am lonesome.
> Our village grows up to trees.
> Marina is very lonesome.
> There is no friend anywhere.

In the unlikely event that any of the rangers were moved to mercy,
reminders of what St. Francis stood for were all around them. A
forest of poles swayed in the breeze above the town, and from them
hung between six and seven hundred scalps, ripped from men,
women, and children, nearly all of them taken in raids on the colonies. The rangers also recovered a handful of terrified English prisoners, survivors of Abenaki brutality and the slave labor they had been
forced to do.

Even as the rangers took vengeance, however, their officers stayed
in tight control. So much of the stored food of the Abenakis as was
useful to the rangers was carefully saved; the rest was burned with
the village. Twenty Indian prisoners were herded together in the
center of the village: Rogers kept five—two boys and three girls—
to take south; the others were turned loose.

Rogers had had only a single man killed in the attack, a Mohican
ally. The seven ranger wounded were seen to, the food was distrib-
uted, and the column formed again quickly, bayonets wiped and put
away, muskets reloaded and ready. As the flames still roared through
the remains of St. Francis, the rangers were on the move. They had
taken their vengeance; they had finished their mission. Now it was
time to get clear and survive if they could.

They could not return to the lake. That way lay pursuers in unknown numbers, and the boats and supplies had been taken or destroyed in any case. And so Rogers turned the other way, marching up the St. Francis River *away* from the St. Lawrence and away from safety, headed through trackless wilderness for lovely Lake Memphremagog, which lies along the present-day border between Vermont and Canada.

It was a dreadful march. The long column, moving fast, could not hope to kill big game unless it could halt and send hunting parties out into the silent forest, away from the disturbance of the line of march. And it could not halt, for death was close behind. As the captured corn ran out, Rogers split his force into smaller parties, faster moving and harder to find, appointing a rally point at the junction of the Connecticut and Wells rivers. There the survivors might find safety and supplies from Lord Amherst . . . if Lieutenant McMullen had made it safely to Crown Point, if a relief party could find the rendezvous, if the French and Indians did not, if . . .

Some small parties struck out on the direct route home, the perilous march directly for Crown Point; most took the long eastern circle toward the Connecticut River rendezvous. All of them grew weaker for lack of food as the brutal terrain took its toll of them. Steep, brushy high ground, thick timber, more of the vile, mucky swamps. A howling north wind tore at them, and a slashing rain soaked their uniforms, which froze on their bodies. They ate mushrooms and beech leaves, some of them, and others ate nothing at all, and they grew steadily weaker. Many went days on end without anything whatever to fill their bellies.

Most men ate roots, the leather of their cartridge boxes, leather thongs from their coats, anything to keep hunger at bay another few hours. One detachment admitted later that it not only ate portions of some corpses it discovered but took some of the flesh along for rations on the march.

The enemy was always close behind. Just days after Roberts split his men into small parties, a large band of Indians surprised one exhausted group trying to snatch a little rest, capturing seven of them. Two of these managed to escape and rejoin Rogers; two others were later exchanged; the others died miserably in captivity. Another group, eighteen men together, was attacked by a band of pursuers;

both ranger officers—one a British regular—were killed, along with ten of their men. The rest escaped.

On the twentieth of October Rogers himself led his own small party to the rendezvous point. The men heard shots in the distance and hurried on to meet the help they supposed was waiting. Cruelly, it was not. There was a fire still burning where help should have been, but there were neither men nor provisions.

In fact, the shots had been fired by a pair of hunters. Lieutenant Stevens was not there. He had come north, as Amherst had ordered him, but he had simply given up too soon. He had gone south only hours before Rogers' exhausted men stumbled into the rendezvous. And he had taken the precious provisions with him.

Rogers remained a tower of strength to his men. Ordering them to dig groundnuts and lily roots and boil them into a sort of porridge, Rogers left an officer in charge and rafted down the Connecticut with two rangers and an Indian boy. Losing one raft in a rapids, Rogers and his men laboriously built another. Without an ax, they burned down trees, and then painstakingly burned them into manageable lengths.

Back on the river, they reached the British post called Number Four. In less than an hour, Rogers had a relief party headed upriver for his men; after a very short rest, Rogers went up himself, collecting every survivor he could find and sending search parties deep into the woods to bring in every exhausted straggler still on the march south.

When the final tally was made, Rogers' small force had lost three officers and forty-six NCOs and rangers, some dead, some captured. Of the missing, only two survived. Even so, the wrecking of St. Francis, and the devastating casualties inflicted on the Abenaki, moved all the northern colonies to transports of joy. Perhaps because retribution had been such a long time coming, it was doubly sweet. And Lord Jeffrey Amherst, who as a soldier was keenly aware of the terrible obstacles Rogers had overcome, was doubly appreciative. He wrote Rogers:

> I . . . assure you of the satisfaction I had on reading [your report] as every step you inform Me You have taken, has been very well Judged, and Deserves my full approbation.

For the miserable Lieutenant Stevens, there was no happy ending. He had not carried out his orders, and Rogers was unforgiving. He believed Stevens had heard shots fired by Rogers' starving men, "but would not return, supposing we were an enemy." A court-martial sentenced Stevens to be cashiered from the service. He would no more be a ranger, and it is not recorded that any of his one-time comrades regretted his departure.

Robert Rogers stood at the zenith of his career. He was one of the legitimate heroes of the struggle against the French; nobody could forget his extermination of the dreadful scourge of St. Francis. The British army even granted him an indefinite leave on full pay. And after the end of the French war, Amherst sent his trusted ranger west to take the surrender of the French posts along the Great Lakes. Along the way, Rogers met and spoke with Pontiac, who would soon lead the greatest of all Indian uprisings against the encroaching white man.

Although Rogers played a notable part in the desperate fighting against Pontiac's besiegers of hard-pressed Detroit, the years that followed were largely unhappy. Rogers was repeatedly denied money owed him and his men by the colonies; he was endlessly pursued by debtors. Rogers himself was much to blame for his misfortunes; to repair his financial woes, he had turned to trading with the Indians and to land speculation, neither of which prospered.

Shortsightedly scorned and distrusted by the patriot government during the Revolution, Rogers took a king's commission again, leading a new unit of "rangers." The new men were mostly inexperienced recruits, however, and never became more than a pale imitation of his old frontiersmen. And Rogers himself had slipped badly, still deep in debt and increasingly given to the solace of the bottle. In the end, he fled to England to escape a storm of debts.

The last days of Rogers' career are mostly lost in shadows. His Majesty's government remembered his services, if his creditors did not, and Rogers was put on the half-pay list. He could live at least, scraping out a dreary existence in Southwark, south of the Thames, on five and a half shillings a day. At least once he served time in debtors' prison. Alcohol was his only solace, and he sank deeper and deeper into the comfortable oblivion of cheap booze. In his drunkenness he would sometimes imagine himself back with his rangers again; his landlord heard him pitifully shouting out names from the old days.

And in May 1795, in cheap, depressing Southwark lodgings, Robert Rogers passed at last far beyond humiliation and disgrace. He was buried in a dreary rain in the churchyard next to the ancient and famous Elephant and Castle. He lies there still, finally at peace.

He deserved much better. It is pleasant to think that in his last twilight hours his mind might have formed again a picture from the happy, heroic old days, the vivid martial picture he painted in the only poem he is known to have written:

> And see! and see! on yonder plain
>   The long and glittering line;
> The red coats glow in the evening rays
>   the bustling bayonets shine;
> How, 'twixt those shadowy western hills,
>   Upon the bright array
> The sinking sun pours duskily
>   His last departing ray!

CHAPTER TWELVE

IN FEW WORDS

CONFEDERATE GENERAL JUBAL Early was a cantankerous sort, albeit a ferocious fighter. Early wasted no words on useless explanation or discussion; for that matter, he spent precious few on ordinary courtesy, even to his military superiors.

The feisty Early had the misfortune to be assigned to the corps of Stonewall Jackson, whose Old Testament fighting spirit was matched by his punctilious insistence on discipline. There were bound to be fireworks.

Jackson was famous for his spectacular marches. His "foot cavalry" covered tremendous distances with few stragglers, and Jackson expected other officers' commands to do the same. On one occasion, perceiving that Early's division had shed more stragglers than it should, Jackson told his adjutant, Sandy Pendleton, to find out why. Pendleton composed a simple note to Early that went like this:

To Major General Early:
General: General Jackson desires to know why he saw so many of your stragglers in the rear of your division today?

Signed: A. S. Pendleton, A.A.G.

Early, irascible as always, or maybe more than usual, answered thus:

Dear General Jackson:

In answer to your note I would state that I think it is probable that the reason you saw so many of my stragglers on the march today is due to the fact that you rode in the rear of my division.

CHAPTER THIRTEEN

FIRE IN THE FOREST

The Royal Americans at Bushy Run

FOR GREAT BRITAIN, 1759 was the year that rained victories. King George's men whipped the French enemy everywhere across the world, in the New World, in India, in Germany, at sea, in the very ports of France herself. Bonfires flared in jubilation the length and breadth of Britain, and Englishmen lustily sang "God Save the King" in the streets of English towns and villages. Two terrible volleys from James Wolfe's red regulars won an empire at Quebec, and the lilies of France fluttered down all across the vast, rich emptiness of New France. Montreal was English, too, and so were the lonely little forts that had once flown the colors of France.

But now, only four short summers later, bloody trouble stalked the dark, endless land that Wolfe and Amherst had won from France. It was trouble of the worst and least expected kind, a huge conspiracy involving many of the most warlike of the Indian nations; worse still, it had a leader of real genius. He was a charismatic Ottawa, a brilliant speaker and wilderness politician. He was called Pontiac.

Terribly reduced by a penny-pinching Parliament, the postwar British army was stretched far too thin. The entire force amounted to fewer than fifty thousand men all together, at home and abroad. Of these, a paltry fifteen thousand men were supposed to hold Gibraltar and Minorca in the Mediterranean and all of the West Indian islands, as well as maintain garrisons in New York, Quebec, Mobile, Pensacola, and Halifax in Nova Scotia. At the same time, they were to keep open the tenuous line of isolated forts that led three thousand miles from Quebec all the way to the lower Mississippi valley. It was an impossible task for so few soldiers, and still the political opposition whined ceaselessly about the expense of imperial defense.

Most of the tiny garrisons west of the Pennsylvania colony were garrisoned by men of the Sixtieth Regiment of Foot, the Royal Americans. Many of them were colonial recruits, and of these many were foreigners, especially German immigrants. They lived at the end of a very long, very uncertain supply line, bored, friendless, quite alone. Even their rations were poor and monotonous, as one German soldier wrote from Fort Presque Isle on Lake Erie:

> We have no kint of flesh nor venison nor fish, and that we could suffer with patience; but the porck is so bad that neither officers nor men can eat it . . . and self lief [I have lived] more than seventeen weeks upon flour and peace-soup, and have eat no kint of meat but a little bear at Christmas.

Many of the Royal Americans were green soldiers; some were in poor health. Above all, there were never enough of them. In 1762 a weary British officer described the pitiful garrison of dreary little Fort Ligonier, on the southern shore of Lake Erie:

> Rogers, unfit for any kind of fatigue, Davis, improper to be entrusted on any duty, Shillem, quite a little boy, my servant, an inactive simple creature . . . and one more. Two stout fellows would beat the whole five of them.

Although Ligonier might have been worse staffed than some of the other little posts, none of them were strong enough to withstand any sort of determined assault. And the storm was surely coming.

Trouble had been brewing in the New World almost since the surrender of Quebec. After Montreal fell in 1760, a tiny British force had been sent west into the emptiness to carry the King's Peace along the Great Lakes. Robert Rogers had led the expedition, Rogers, the fabulous ranger officer, the scourge of the French and their Indian allies, the terrible destroyer of St. Francis. In his travels Rogers met Pontiac—in Rogers' words "the king and lord of all this country."

Pontiac asked Rogers why he had come into the west country, and the ranger replied that the French had given over the entire region to Britain. It was not news calculated to please the Indian nations. Save for the Iroquois, most of the tribes had supported France, and they still had memories of bloody wilderness struggles against the redcoats and of the killing of Braddock.

The old French allegiance died hard, and some of the Frenchmen who lived among the Indians lost no chance to fulminate against the British. And there was the matter of pride. This was Indian country, after all, time out of mind. One white nation had simply given it away to another, an old enemy who had killed many of the tribes' young men.

And so, when Pontiac preached war along the Great Lakes, his words fell on fertile ground. He was a talented orator, this dynamic man. By birth a Catawba, he had been captured as a child and raised by the Ottawa, a tribe despised by many whites as "infamous and cowardly." Now, in full manhood, he was Ottawa to the core, and he sent a wampum belt for war and a tomahawk painted red all along the lakes, up and down the Ohio country, even down the great Mississippi.

A great Indian confederation began to take shape, a mighty force of warriors that would destroy the British forts. The red soldiers were very weak; everyone could see that. They would all die, and the rest would fear to come to the lake country again. In addition to his own Ottawas, Pontiac was joined by Chippewas and Mingos, Delawares and Pottawatomies, Hurons and Shawnees, even some Senecas under an able leader called Guyasuta.

Wherever Pontiac spoke, men responded, for his words had great power. There had been signs and portents, too. In the autumn of 1762, men said, a black rain had fallen about crucial Fort Detroit. It came down from frowning, ugly clouds of an inky blackness, and it stank of sulfur.

And so, in the spring of 1763, Pontiac's plan began to unfold. The little British posts were not only feeble but spread too far apart for any sort of mutual support. They stretched from Fort Niagara, at the eastern end of Lake Erie, down the southern shore of the lake: Forts Presque Isle, Le Boeuf, and Sandusky. The next and strongest of the chain, Detroit, held the passage from Erie up to Lake Huron. Isolated Michilimackinac guarded the narrows between Huron and Michigan. Below on Lake Michigan lay Fort St. Joseph. Outanon lay far down on the Wabash, and Miamis between Outanon and Lake Erie.

This long, lonely line of little forts could depend on only one real link to help: a line of posts connecting western Pennsylvania and the Ohio: Cumberland, Bedford, Ligonier, and Pitt. Fort Venango lay north of Pitt, in theory holding open the way to Presque Isle and Niagara. The whole system was as fragile as a spider's web.

The storm broke in May 1763, and it came with little warning. Pontiac had laid his plans well. Earlier in the year he had held a meeting of the tribes and won general agreement to a simultaneous attack on the English forts. Each tribal representative left the council with a bundle of sticks, one for each day between the close of the conference and the day of the uprising. One stick was broken and discarded with each passing day, and when the last stick was gone the British would be destroyed.

They would be overcome by treachery wherever possible. Warriors could enter their forts during the day at will. They would conceal their weapons under their blankets, or have their women bring them into the fort. Some even cut down the muzzles of their muskets, the better to conceal them. Surprise and overwhelming numbers should make the whole enterprise simple.

And so it would be at most of the little forts.

Detroit, the pivotal post, was another matter. Detroit was well built and was garrisoned by two understrength companies of the Royal Americans and one of the Queen's Rangers. They did not amount to more than 120 men all told, but even that was a substantial strengh along the undermanned British frontier.

And so Pontiac himself would deal with Detroit, entering the post for a council in company with sixty chiefs; each would carry a cut-down weapon beneath his blanket. At the right moment, he would proffer to the British a peace belt of wampum, green on one side, white on the other. He would present it white side up; when he turned it over to green, the chiefs would shoot down the British officers and other Indians would push in to destroy the soldiers of the garrison.

Pontiac's plan seemed foolproof. On the morning of the "council," however, he and his chiefs entered Fort Detroit to find the whole garrison alert and under arms. Hedges of gleaming bayonets lined his way, the British officers bristled with swords and pistols, and behind Pontiac the fort's gates slammed shut. Fort Detroit's commander, a tough, experienced captain named Gladwyn, had been warned.

It has never been clear just how Gladwyn learned of the plot to murder him and his garrison. The most common tale—and the most engaging—is that Gladwyn was warned by his Ojibway mistress, Catharine. However the English commander had learned, it was clear to Pontiac that his plan had miscarried. One account tells that Pontiac hesitated with the wampum belt in his hand, as if he were ready to give the signal for massacre. Gladwyn, watching closely, made a gesture of his own, and the fort immediately echoed with the long roll of drums and the "clash of arms." Pontiac and his chiefs left Detroit frustrated and angry.

And so Detroit settled down to a siege. Pontiac's warriors managed some casual murdering of local settlers and expended thousands of rounds of musketry on the fort, but they did Gladwyn's men little harm. In the weeks to come, the garrison would more than hold its own, running in supplies and mounting repeated sorties to burn all nearby cover behind which their besiegers might hide.

For all their energy, Gladwyn's garrison had their hands full. For weeks they remained on permanent stand-to, sleeping on the fort's fire step, under arms. As one officer wrote in early July:

> We have been besieged here two Months, by Six Hundred Indians. We have been upon the Watch Night and Day . . . from the 8th of May, and have not had our Cloaths off, nor slept all Night since it began . . . The Day before Yesterday, we killed a Chief and three others, and wounded some more . . .

In time Gladwyn would receive reinforcements, including a small band of rangers commanded by the redoubtable Major Rogers. In spite of losses incurred in an ill-conceived sortie against Pontiac's camp, Detroit would not lack for men or munitions. Gladwyn would hold vital Detroit.

But if Pontiac's conspiracy was thwarted at Detroit, it was a bloody success elsewhere. Pontiac's waves of warriors submerged the little posts at Miamis, Venango, Ouatanon, Michilimackinac, St.

Joseph, and Sandusky. Most of the men in the tiny garrisons were killed; a few became prisoners, and some of these were tortured to death. By the middle of June no king's troops remained on the Great Lakes west of Niagara except at hard-pressed Detroit.

Farther east, the news was somewhat better. At the great junction of the three rivers, Fort Pitt still held out. So did Fort Bedford and the twelve-man garrison of tiny Ligonier, strengthened just in time by a meager reinforcement from Bedford. In between these tiny islands of resistance, however, there was only fire and death, and long straggling columns of frantic civilians streaming east in panic. Behind the terrified refugees, lazy clouds of smoke marked the graves of friends and neighbors, butchered stock, and treasured homes and barns and fields of standing crops, wrested from the wilderness with years of work and sweat.

The Pennsylvania frontier flamed with war, and there seemed to be little to prevent Pontiac, flushed with victory, from pushing east as far as he chose. Pennsylvania, eager to be defended, even so was unwilling to provide men to stand up to Pontiac. Few of the able-bodied men fleeing east would stop to help the little garrisons. Ligonier's tiny twelve-man garrison could not find a single colonist to stay and help. As so often happened in the past, the work would be left to the red-coated soldiers of the regular army, and they were precious few.

Sir Jeffrey Amherst, the British commander-in-chief, had few resources with which to stop this terrible flood from the west. His army, already understrength, had been bled white by expeditions to Martinique and Havana. Thousands of men had died of sickness, and many more were unfit for duty without a substantial rest. He would send what he could, sick and well, and trust in his soldiers' hearts and his commander to work a miracle.

And Sir Jeffrey did have an extraordinary leader to command on the frontier, a professional who understood fighting in the wilderness and led always from the front. The man who would have to deal with this chaos was a foreign-born career soldier in British service, a Swiss named Henry Bouquet. Bouquet was a native of the Vaud, the area north of Lake Lausanne, and had been soldiering since 1736, when he turned seventeen. He had fought for Holland and for Piedmont, joining the British service about 1754. He was one of a number of German-speaking officers given king's commissions and intended to command in the 60th Regiment of Foot, otherwise known as the Royal Americans.

The Royal Americans were raised specifically for service in the colonies, regular line soldiers who were lightly equipped and trained to fight in the woods. Many of the men recruited for the 60th were German and Swiss immigrants with very little English; hence the need for leaders like Bouquet and other European Protestants with names like Ecuyer and Haldiman.

Bouquet commanded the first of four battalions of the Royal Americans, each of ten hundred-man companies. Though each battalion's official complement was one thousand men, none of them ever approached full strength, and sickness and battle casualties reduced their numbers still further. The Royal Americans were new at their trade, but they were well commanded, and they had a brilliant future, a life that lasted long beyond British rule in the New World. For they would become the King's Royal Rifle Corps, the premier light troops of the British army; as the Royal Green Jackets, the regiment lives on today.

The Royal Americans were also different in another way: they were specially trained for what they were about to do. From the time the regiment was first raised, they trained in the light infantry tradition, wearing cut-down coats and streamlined equipment. They were taught patrolling, and flank and rear security, and how to move quickly and quietly in the forest.

For, contrary to legend, the British command in the New World was not inflexible. Early on in the French and Indian wars, British regulars were trained to use the terrain, to reload while kneeling, and to fire from the prone position. "I must confess," wrote a British commander,

> wee must comply and learn the Art of Warr from Ennemy Indians or anything else who have seen the Country and Warr carried on in itt.

And they did. More than fifty British volunteers served with Rogers' rangers, learning from the master the art of war in the bush and carrying those lessons home to their own units. "Tree all!" was a new command—meaning, quite literally, "Find some cover and fight from behind it." At the same time, British officers realized that

European obedience and steadiness were their chief assets; there would be no relaxation of discipline. Colonel Bouquet was about to take full advantage of both the new tradition and the old.

Nobody had forgotten General Braddock's terrible defeat by the French and Indians near the forks of the Ohio in 1755. More important, its lessons were not lost on the British commanders who came after Braddock. Dying, a soldier to the bitter end, Braddock had murmured, "We shall know better how to deal with them next time." The next time was coming, was here, and Colonel Henry Bouquet was about to show how much royal commanders had learned. He had been over this very country on the way to take the forks from the French, the vital ground on which Fort Pitt now stood. He knew the terrain; he knew the enemy; he knew precisely what he had to do.

First, however, Bouquet had to find the troops to do it, a nearly insurmountable task in itself. Parliament's perennial penny-pinching had almost denuded North America of anything like enough force to turn back Pontiac's confederacy. But by the end of June, Bouquet had scraped together some five hundred men. They were good soldiers; at their core were men of the famous Black Watch—the 42d Highlanders.

There were also several companies of the Royal Americans and Scots of the 77th Foot, better known as Montgomery's Highlanders. The 77th was a new regiment—something of an experiment, in fact—for it was raised largely from clans that had been "out" in the Highland rising of 1745, strongly Jacobite in sympathy. Worries about its loyalties had proved groundless; once Montgomery's ate King George's salt, it fought for him loyally and well. It was about to prove its loyalty again.

With these men, few enough for the enormous task ahead, Bouquet moved west. At least sixty of Montgomery's Highlanders had to be transported in wagons, so debilitated were they from recent service in the fever-ridden West Indies. Bouquet left these men to reinforce the tiny garrisons along the road west. He next pushed on to little Fort Bedford, picked up a small but welcome reinforcement of frontiersmen, and moved on. Arriving at Ligonier on August 2, he left his cattle and wagons and pushed on two days later, carrying his supplies on 350 packhorses. Much of the provisions he carried for Detroit was in the form of bags of flour; Bouquet would soon value that flour out of all proportion to its worth as bread.

Bouquet was in dangerous country. He could expect attack at almost any time, and his way west was made for ambush. It was very bad terrain indeed, a confusing country of hills and steep defiles, everywhere thick with brush and timber. He kept his flanks, front, and rear constantly covered against surprise, sometimes moving with the advance guard himself, musket in hand.

The first night out of Ligonier, Bouquet pitched camp early. He got an early start next day, the fifth of August, intending to halt and rest near a stream called Bushy Run, some seventeen miles away. After dark he would move again, passing in darkness through an ugly, ominous defile at Turtle Creek, a little way beyond. Bouquet could smell trouble; the woods stank with danger, a lurking menace that could strike his column any time.

It came just short of Bushy Run, a spattering of musketry up ahead, quickly rising to a roar of firing. The advance guard stood its ground, and a two-company rush with the bayonet cleared a little space in front. But very soon the firing had spread all around the long column; there were Indians everywhere, on both flanks and in the rear, and Bouquet's men began to take casualties.

His men held their ground wherever they chose to take a stand, and their disciplined rushes temporarily cleared the ground in front of them. But it was like fighting water. As one section of the Indian line gave way before those terrible bayonets, the pressure increased elsewhere. Through the trees and the dense brush, it was difficult to get a clean shot at the screaming, taunting Indian enemy. Men saw little but flashes of movement and the wraithlike puffs of white smoke from Indian muskets.

Bouquet pulled his long column together on a heavily wooded little rise, forming a rough perimeter around the packhorses and their vital supplies. Some of his men off-loaded enough flour bags to build a low wall to protect the increasing number of seriously wounded men. But there was no shelter for the screaming, terrified horses. Many were killed or wounded, thrashing in agony among living men and dead; many more broke loose and fled in panic through the brush. The Indians made the day hideous with their war cries, and some, notably one Kukyuskung, shouted taunts and insults in broken English.

On through the afternoon the battle raged; it was a hideous, broiling-hot day of desperate conflict and death. All of Bouquet's men were thick-tongued and cotton-mouthed, for there was no water on their small hill and their own bottles were empty. What little of the precious stuff remained was saved for the wounded. After dark, as the firing died away to a few spiteful shots, some of the frontiersmen crawled to a spring and brought back a little more water for the wounded. But for most of the exhausted troops there was nothing to drink through the whole, long night. Thousands of voracious mosquitoes tormented them all through the dark hours, and jeering Indian voices promised them agony and death with the coming of the day.

With the morning, the Indians came on again, and Bouquet's men fought on, still waterless, and more men went down within the defensive circle on the hill. More horses were hit, more bolted, and the drovers whose duty it was to take care of the frantic animals hid in the brush, useless and "stupified by fear," in Bouquet's scornful words.

The British troops maintained their discipline in spite of terrible thirst and mounting casualties, saving their ammunition, firing only when they had a target. It might have been the low volume of fire by the Highlanders and the Royal Americans that moved the Indians to press closer and closer on the perimeter. Perhaps they took it as a sign that British resistance was slackening or that ammunition was running low.

Bouquet knew he had to do something to break the terrible deadlock. He could not leave his wounded or his precious supplies. Nor could he stay where he was. His men were close to their limits from the terrible thirst—in Bouquet's words, "much more intolerable than the Enemy's Fire." He had to close with this elusive enemy, and so he decided to capitalize on the increased enemy pressure.

And so Bouquet determined on that most dangerous of military maneuvers, a feigned retreat—"to Entice them to Come Close upon Us," as he later wrote. Pulling two companies out of his defensive circle, he quite deliberately opened a gap in his perimeter. It was an extraordinary maneuver under fire for tired soldiers, dripping with sweat, half mad with thirst, and in close contact with a confident enemy. But their discipline held; they fell back in order, fighting; and Bouquet's bluff began to work.

Sensing victory, the Indians pushed into the inviting hole, and Bouquet turned on them. Instead of a demoralized, fleeing enemy, the Indians met a murderous, close-range, two-company volley and a line of red-faced, angry men, some of them roaring in Gaelic, coming in at the double behind a hedge of gleaming bayonets and waving claymores.

The Indians turned and fled, only to run into a carefully laid ambush—one company each of the Black Watch and the Royal Americans—that raked them with another terrible volley and charged with bayonet, sword, pistol, and dirk. The Indians ran for dear life, and the British gave them no chance to reload, "nor even to look behind them." Kukyuskung, he of the loud voice and arrogant insults, died on a British bayonet along with many of his men, and the entire Indian force dissolved in flight. Bouquet's men took only one prisoner . . . temporarily; he was quickly shot by a soldier who could not stand the sight of a living Indian enemy.

Bouquet quickly collected his wounded, buried his dead, and prepared to move on. He destroyed the flour he could not carry, rigged litters for his wounded, and advanced to Bushy Run, where there was cool water and lots of it. As his men and animals drank deeply for the first time in two days, the column was fired on again. It turned out to be no more than a halfhearted effort by only a few Indians, and some of Bouquet's men easily drove the snipers off.

It was over.

Bouquet's men had paid heavily for their victory. Bouquet's own report listed fifty dead, sixty wounded, and five missing. Among the dead were three of his officers, and four others were wounded. Indian casualties, never easy to establish, were at least as great, and the moral effect of the British victory was enormous. Bouquet relieved Fort Pitt four days later, just in the nick of time. Several days before, its commander had written, "I have but four legs of beef and no flour." Detroit was next, where stout Captain Gladwyn still held on. Most of the hostile Indians fell back beyond the Ohio, and for a while there was a little peace. The Lake Country was British again.

In the next year, however, war parties again pushed east, stabbing at the settlements along the lakes. Because none of the major posts were in danger, the British took their time in responding. This time, however, they would make an end. And so, in late summer, Bouquet left Fort Pitt with a force of some fifteen hundred men. It was the Black Watch and the Royal Americans again, plus contingents from Virginia and Pennsylvania. They marched southwest for the Delaware country along the Muskingum River, moving a hundred miles in a sort of monstrous hollow square, with squads of axmen to clear their way and vigilant security pushed well out on all sides.

It was obvious to the Indian leaders that there was no stopping this juggernaut. The great Bouquet was coming, and with him were many of the same men who had killed so many of their warriors at Bushy Run. Bouquet was going to go wherever he pleased, and where he pleased was the heart of the Indians' own country. Quite aware that Pontiac's rebellion was a failure, the chiefs sought to cut their losses, and asked Bouquet for a council. He agreed, but he was not moved to forgiveness. The Ohio country and the lakes were soaked with too much British blood.

"Deliver all your prisoners," Bouquet told the chiefs; "all of them, without exception, and then perhaps we will talk of peace." Or, he said, they could choose more fire and slaughter instead; this time, however, the blood and the burning would be in the Indian towns. They could expect no help from the French, said Bouquet; there was peace between Britain and France. And the terrible warriors of the Iroquois had joined the British as well. No one at the council doubted that this grim redcoat meant precisely what he said; this was the great warrior, the victor of Bushy Run. There was no argument.

And so Colonel Henry Bouquet enforced the king's peace. The killing was over, and the prisoners began to come in, women and children mostly, some held so long that they were more Indian than white. The process of sorting them out was joyful and bitter by turns. Some families, come in hope to find a relative, found only news that their loved one had died in captivity; some could learn nothing at all. Others went home rejoicing, bringing one or more relatives back from the dead. Even for some of the lucky ones, the reunion was a trial of souls.

One German woman appeared at Bouquet's camp to search for her little daughter, kidnapped as an infant. Hers was an especially poignant search, for the rest of her family had been massacred, even to the family watchdog, who had died with his jaws locked on a warrior's throat. But the woman could identify nobody, and the little girl had been too young to remember. As hope faded, Bouquet himself took a hand. "Did you not sing to your daughter?" he asked. "Is there no hymn she loved?"

There was, said the woman; I sang her to sleep with an old German hymn. "Sing, then," said Bouquet, and the woman softly sang the opening words—"*Allein, und doch nicht ganz allein* [Alone and yet not all alone]." And a tiny child among the ex-prisoners cried out "Mother!" The two embraced and together sang the rest of the verse. It's a pretty story, probably even true; even if it isn't, it symbolized the return of peace and a chance to live and build again. The inexorable march west would continue, and there was no stopping it. The Indian lands would never be the same.

Neither would Pontiac. That magnetic leader had lost most of his influence. Bushy Run had destroyed his dream of turning back the white man, and now the tribes would reap the whirlwind. As Bouquet advanced along the southern edge of the lakes, another British force brought the peace to the north. The tribes would no longer listen to Pontiac's counsel, and he fled into the Illinois country, where French traders still inveighed against the English and promised French help that would never come.

Pontiac was able to rally a little help there, but the steam had gone out of the rebellion. Deep in the west country, the realization came that the lilies of France were gone forever. There would be no help, and the new masters of this land were there to stay. There would be much trading again, and it appeared the English were making a real effort to confine civilian traders to the forts, where fair dealing with the Indians could be enforced.

And so Pontiac's followers lost faith and fell away, and in the spring of 1766 he made the long journey up the lakes to Fort Oswego, where he too made his peace in council with the great Sir William Johnson. In later days he again began to preach resistance against the English, but without any widespread support. He was murdered in a village on the Illinois in the spring of 1769.

Bouquet was back at Fort Pitt by the end of November 1765. A peace had been concluded; the Indians had even given hostages to ensure its keeping. Bouquet dismissed his provincial soldiers with praise for their good conduct. Still, peace and praise did not prevent an ungrateful Virginia from trying to saddle Bouquet with the burden of personally paying its own levies. Surprisingly, Pennsylvania, belatedly thankful, assumed the Virginia obligation so that Bouquet would not have to.

And King George paid his Swiss officer the ultimate compliment. Though a foreigner, Bouquet was promoted to brigader general in the British army, an honor that delighted Bouquet and nearly everybody else. As a Royal American officer wrote Bouquet:

> [T]he townsmen . . . stop us in the streets to ask if it is true
> that the King has made Colonel Bouquet a general; and when
> they are told it is true, they march off with great joy . . .

Montgomery's Highlanders were disbanded in the year of their victory. Jacobite or not, they had been true to their salt, and a great many of them left their bones in the New World. The Black Watch departed for Ireland in the summer of 1767; in seven years of service to these struggling new colonies, almost a thousand of them had been killed or wounded. Like the Royal Americans, the Black Watch lives on today, rich with the battle honors of three and a half centuries.

Henry Bouquet did not long enjoy his welcome promotion and his enormous popularity in both America and England. With his new rank came a new assignment, command of the southern department. And at pestilential Pensacola, within three years of his return from the Illinois country, he died of fever. He was only forty-six.

As much as any man in history, he had won a continent.

CHAPTER FOURTEEN

THE EAGLE OF ST. MIHIEL
Frank Luke, the Arizona Cowboy

FRANK LUKE WAS a bit of a maverick, something of a loner. He wasn't very popular with his squadron mates in the 27th Aero Squadron, and when he first arrived most of the pilots just plain disliked him.

Luke didn't smile much, and he didn't laugh at all. He didn't talk much, either, and when he did he was liable to be brash and loud. He kept mostly to himself, something of an oddity in a closely knit fighter squadron. He was also undisciplined and insubordinate in a business in which men's lives depended on everybody's flying as a team. At one point his squadron leader grounded him for a month to teach him that formations were to be flown in and orders were to be obeyed. Some of his squadron mates thought Luke was too often someplace else when the fighting was hottest, and even believed he lied about his first claimed combat victory, never confirmed.

Luke wasn't much of a pilot, either, at least not at the beginning. But he was an excellent shot. And as his squadron mates would soon learn, Luke was absolutely fearless, aggressive to the point of recklessness, bold to the point of death.

Maybe Luke's truculent, lonely nature was due to his frontier blood, or maybe it was his German heritage, a matter for suspicion and distrust in the Kaiser's War. Or maybe it was because he didn't

121

like the service; he had only left Phoenix for the army because of the taunting of his sister. He didn't cut much of a figure during his first months at the front, but all that would suddenly change.

For Frank Luke was about to embark on his spectacular career as a balloon buster. Observation balloons were conceded to be the toughest targets a pilot could attack, gigantic sausages tethered high above the German lines, with a bird's-eye view of anything that moved behind the American front. Unless the weather was foggy, nothing could move in daylight that the balloon could not see.

In a wicker box slung below each one rode an observer with binoculars and a telephone. Only brave men rode balloon gondolas. When incendiary bullets turned his balloon into a flaming pyre collapsing upon him, the observer either fried or dove over the side, trusting in the rudimentary parachute strapped to the side of the gondola and the suspension lines that connected his harness to it. It might save him . . . if it opened—and if the inferno above him did not catch up with him on the way to the ground, or on it.

On the twelfth day of September 1918, American, British, and French aircraft took off into a clear dawn to begin the biggest air offensive of all time. A single officer, American Colonel Billy Mitchell, commanded almost fifteen hundred aircraft, a little over half flown by British or American pilots. Their bombing and strafing played a major role in the brilliant American advance that cleared the Germans from the salient.

And so, when the offensive moved to the Meuse-Argonne region, the air over the front was again packed with allied aircraft. There were about eight hundred of them this time, but almost three quarters were American. The target this time was the deep and formidable Hindenburg Line, five deadly miles of wire, pillboxes, trenches, and deep dugouts.

Mitchell made the balloons a priority target. And if they were immobile and unarmed, the balloons were a very dangerous target indeed, for they had many friends. Antiaircraft units guarded them on the ground, and the still-powerful German air force watched over them from above. *Drachens,* the Germans called their balloons—"dragons"—and they were fearsome targets indeed.

Only three pilots in the squadron showed Luke any respect at first. One of them was Joe Wehner, also of German blood, and the two formed a team to strike at the eyes of the German army, the critical observation balloons. Luke would go for the balloons, they decided, and Wehner would fly cover for him. And so was born one of the most successful—and short-lived—aerial teams that ever flew for America.

When Luke announced his intention to attack balloons, most of his squadron mates took his statement as pure boast. "You couldn't get a YMCA hut if it was nailed down," one of them sneered, but those words were made for eating. Luke followed his first balloon almost to the ground as its crew frantically winched it toward the earth. The observer died in the flames; it was his first day on the job.

Luke got his second *Drachen* with Wehner keeping eight German aircraft off his back, and got a third in spite of a hail of antiaircraft that cut his sturdy Spad almost to pieces. On September 12, Luke and Wehner went out again but split up over the German lines. Before the day was out Wehner had killed a ballon and two aircraft; Luke's score was three more balloons and another wrecked Spad.

Next day the two were at it again, but they could find no quarry. That evening, however, Luke made his most audacious boast. They would go after three balloons, he said, and told his commander the *Drachens* would go down in flames exactly ten minutes apart. As the commander and Colonel Mitchell watched in the dusk, three blossoms of red flame burst out in the evening sky. The first was on time; the last was only six minutes late.

On the eighteenth, Luke and Wehner were back, flying through a cloud of Fokker D-VII fighters. Luke got two more balloons, a pair of fighters, and an observation aircraft . . . but Joe Wehner did not come home. He never would, and he had been covering his friend Luke when the end came. Luke went into depression, which even a spell of leave in Paris could not cure. He was back early, thinking of nothing but more balloons.

Within days he lost another wingman, a youngster named Roberts. Luke again went into black depression, left the field without permission, stayed away overnight, then returned without explanation after flaming still another *Drachen*. And then, against orders, he took off again, intending to refuel at a forward strip.

His commander had had enough. Sending word forward to arrest Luke when he landed for gas, the squadron leader made a solemn promise: "First, I'm recommending him for the Distinguished Service Cross, and then, by God, I'm going to court-martial him!"

Luckily for Luke, or perhaps unluckily, his old commander arrived at the forward strip before Luke could be arrested. Luke pleaded with him for permission to attack three balloons near Verdun. All right, said his officer, but only after sunset. Even then, he took time to fly over an American balloon unit and drop a message: "Watch those three Hun balloons along the Meuse. Luke."

The soldiers watched, and they were not disappointed. One *Drachen* flamed in the sky, then Luke dove through a formation of German fighters to turn a second one to cinders almost on the ground. And then he headed for the third balloon, antiaircraft reaching out for his Spad from all sides. And some of it must have hit, for Luke's fighter was fluttering and shaking as he pressed home his attack.

The third balloon fell in a pyre of foul black smoke, and Luke turned away. He made no attempt at evasive action; he did not try to find cover in the smoke and gain altitude. He probably had already been wounded, perhaps mortally, but he took time out to strafe a column of German infantry on the march.

And then he was down, slipping the reeling Spad into a meadow on the edge of the village of Murvaux. There Frank Luke staggered from his airplane to the shelter of a churchyard wall. He might have been looking for shelter or trying to get water from a nearby stream. In any case, when a German platoon closed in on him, Luke turned on them, and there among the tombstones he drew his side arm and fought his last fight. The Germans called to him to surrender, but he answered with pistol fire until a German soldier's bullet pulled him down.

Frank Luke still sleeps near the village of Murvaux. He had been a meteor, a brilliant flash across the heavens that vanished in a heartbeat. He had shot down fifteen balloons and four aircraft, and it had taken him just seventeen days.

He never got to wear his Congressional Medal of Honor.

CHAPTER FIFTEEN

THE SHORES OF TRIPOLI
Lieutenant O'Bannon Finds His Glory

LIEUTENANT PRESLEY N. O'Bannon was a glory hound. Everybody in the fledging Marine Corps knew it; O'Bannon himself proclaimed it. But most people liked O'Bannon anyway, for he was genuine, and he was very good company. He was a womanizer par excellence—in an engaging way. And he was a first-class fiddle player, to boot, and so, one way or another, the big Virginia lieutenant was a welcome visitor nearly everywhere.

He was something of a curiosity, too, being a United States Marine officer, for that was something very new indeed. The United States Marine Corps was only seven years old in 1805, the year of this story, and nearly all of the Corps' lustrous history was still to be written. O'Bannon was itching to write his own chapter. Trouble was, he was a born soldier with nobody to fight.

Just then, the Marine Corps was a force in search of a tradition. It had done well with those few chances it had been given. In February 1804, for example, marines had been part of a daring night raid into the North African harbor of Tripoli, a strike that succeeded in burning the American frigate *Philadelphia*, captured by the resident pirates after she had run aground. Britain's Lord Nelson, who knew a thing or two about daring, called the raid "the most bold and daring act of the age."

Still, the *Philadelphia* raid had been mostly a navy show, led by a navy officer. The Marine Corps still searched avidly for chances to show what it could do. To find them, it badly needed a war.

Its only hope just then was the sporadic but continuing trouble along the south shore of the Mediterranean. The difficulty was with a particularly unpleasant group of sailing men from the North African littoral whose joy, profession, and hobby were piracy. They had long been an irksome thorn in the side of honest seafaring men everywhere in and outside the Mediterranean, capturing ships and robbing their cargoes, and often enslaving their crews as well. Their bases were Tripoli and Derna and a dozen smaller ports, called, in the words of the old sea chantey, "High Barbaree."

The pests who inhabited this benighted land were generically known as the Barbary pirates. By 1801 the United States had had quite enough of them, and so the fledgling U.S. Navy was directed to abate this seagoing nuisance. One instrument was a quite extraordinary adventurer named William Eaton, sometime United States consul in Tunis.

Eaton, by trade a teacher, came from Connecticut by way of Dartmouth College. He had served his country first as an NCO in the Revolution and later as an officer out west in the Ohio country under Mad Anthony Wayne. He had a gift for languages, did Eaton, and was a crack shot and a superb horseman, to boot. Long odds were only a challenge to him, and he feared nothing under the sun. He and O'Bannon might have been hatched from the same clutch of eggs.

Eaton detested the Barbary pirates, all their works and all their friends. He especially abhorred his government's payment of a large tribute to these bloody-handed outlaws, at one point demanding he be recalled from Tunis and replaced by "a slave accustomed to abasement." Perceiving that the French consul at Tunis was in league with the pirates, Eaton horsewhipped that worthy on a Tunisian street. A determined man, this Eaton.

Eaton sold his government—Thomas Jefferson was president—on a scheme to topple the chief pirate, one Yusuf Karamanli, who rejoiced in the title of Bashaw of Tripoli. Yusuf, a thoroughly loathsome sort, had gained the throne by way of murdering his eldest brother. The American plan was to replace the bashaw with his exiled next older brother, Hamet Karamanli, whom Eaton had known in Tunis. Eaton wanted several hundred marines to get the job done, but he got only eight for a bodyguard: seven enlisted marines and . . . Presley N. O'Bannon.

O'Bannon and his corporal's guard were supposed to protect Eaton and a substantial bag of American gold, intended to finance an army led by Hamet. Nobody seemed interested in finding out whether Hamet had any real support among his own people (he did). Neither Eaton nor O'Bannon seemed to greatly care. The play was the thing. Neither man was going to miss a six-hundred-mile expedition into exotic lands, especially with a chance of martial glory at the end of the road, just because the man they supported might be a paper tiger.

To begin with, nobody knew for sure that Hamet was even willing to undertake the perilous reconquest of his own throne. He was somewhere up the Nile in a lawless no-man's-land inhabited by feuding Mameluke warlords and units of motley Turkish troops who frequently doubled as bandits. The Turkish viceroy's writ did not run far beyond the metropolitan areas of Cairo and Alexandria. The viceroy was genial but without much real power; the only friends Eaton had were the British, who extended themselves to help him.

Dramatic enterprises tend to attract peculiar people, and Eaton's quixotic quest was no exception. In addition to the eager, flamboyant O'Bannon and Eaton himself, Eaton recruited one of the most astonishing characters in all the history of the exotic Levant. He had a lot of names, but the one by which the Americans knew him was Eugene Leitensdorfer. He was Tyrolese, in fact, although he had begun life in the faraway Alps under still another name.

Leitensdorfer spoke German, of course, and in the course of his travels in the Mediterranean he had also learned Arabic and Coptic. His French was excellent, too, since he had twice served in the French army, deserting in between hitches. He was a veteran of the Austrian and Turkish armies as well, and at other times had been a novice in a Capuchin monastery, a wandering conjurer, a dervish traveling to Mecca, and a coffee shop owner in Egypt.

At one point Leitensdorfer renounced Christianity and became a Moslem dervish, circumcising himself in public with his own razor as a demonstration of faith (flimflam man he might be, this Leitensdorfer, but he certainly did not lack for courage). During his wanderings he had acquired—and shed—several wives, and had broken most of the laws of God and man. And this was the man Eaton chose as his emissary, organizer, and chief of staff. Remarkably, Eaton chose very well indeed.

Leitensdorfer's first mission was to find Hamet. He forthwith departed south into the desert by camel, snatching moments of sleep as the beast traveled. And he found Hamet deep in the interior, a guest in a Mameluke camp in upper Egypt. Leitensdorfer delivered a letter from Eaton saluting Hamet as bashaw and inviting him to reclaim his kingdom with the help of the United States.

Whatever was in the letter, whatever blandishments the wily Leitensdorfer might have added, Hamet packed his possessions and rode for Alexandria, followed by a motley retinue of some 150. In spite of opposition from a number of local sheikhs and from the French, who suspected everybody of being in league with their implacable British enemy, Hamet made his way north. He and Eaton finally met at a place called Damanhur, near Alexandria, helped by the good offices of the Turkish viceroy and British diplomats. There the two men renewed acquaintances and plotted the overthrow of the incumbent Bashaw Yusuf.

One of the problems was an army, an essential tool the conspirators lacked altogether. Lieutenant Isaac Hull, commanding the American man-o'-war *Argus* at Alexandria, put the difficulty clearly to Eaton:

> The plan you have formed for taking Derne, I think rather a hazardous one, unless the Bashaw can bring into the field from Eight hundred to one Thousand Men, particularly as we are destitute of every article necessary for an expedition of the kind.

It was indeed a hazardous undertaking, and Hamet had no immediate hope of raising anything like five hundred fighting men, let alone a thousand. Still, Eaton and O'Bannon were not much interested in wise counsel, and they forged ahead with their meager preparations.

One major problem was foot dragging and outright opposition by the local Turkish authorities, and for an unusual reason: it seemed that their best men, weary of the dull, degrading life of a Turkish soldier, were ready to go AWOL to take service with these demented Americans. A number of Arab sheikhs, it was said, had to be put in irons to prevent their desertion. There was, moreover, the ceaseless opposition of the French. Reinforcing their appeals was a considerable distribution of good French gold, a persuasion that spoke a good deal louder in Egypt than the tiny voice of Moslem unity or the rights of man.

In spite of these tribulations, Eaton continued to gather a sort of army. One of his more exotic volunteers was a young Englishman named Percival Farquhar, younger brother—or perhaps the son—of a British merchant on the island of Malta. Young Farquhar seems to have been a man of unusual courage and ability—at the end of the expedition, Eaton paid the Englishman the ultimate compliment of recommending him for a commission in the Marine Corps, and Hamet referred to the youngster as "like my son."

By this time Eaton was being called "General" by Hamet and his people, and Eaton seems to have succumbed sufficiently to find himself a plumed hat and epaulettes to wear. In spite of Turkish opposition, his "army" was growing, and young Farquhar was successfully scrounging provisions all over Alexandria. O'Bannon left the brig *Argus* to join Eaton with six men and a sergeant named Campbell, and *Argus* also contributed a midshipman with the wonderfully euphonious name of Pascal Paoli Peck.

Argus herself would weigh anchor and sail west to wait for Eaton's army in the Gulf of Bomba, on the shore of which lay Derna, the first objective. Her cannon would be a welcome assistance if Eaton ran into trouble at Derna. And there was every chance that he would find lots of trouble; even as his little expedition got ready to march, a Tripolitanian force commanded by the bashaw's chief Mameluke, Hassen Bey, set out to meet this threat from the east, accompanied by the usual blessings and exhortations from the resident holy men.

And so, on the nineteenth of February, Eaton's army set forth, not a forlorn hope exactly, but a pitifully small hammer to break the teeth of the bashaw of Tripoli. Including his strange staff, and O'Bannon and his handful of marines, Eaton presided over a peculiar collection of eleven nationalities, about four hundred men altogether.

There were some three hundred Arab cavalry—Hamet's own supporters and the followers of two perpetually irritating sheikhs called Tahib and Mahomet. In addition, Eaton commanded about seventy Christian volunteers recruited in Alexandria—Englishmen, Italians, Germans, Spaniards and divers Levantines. The equipment and stores were carried by a baggage train of one hundred camels or so.

Of the local hires, about twenty-five were supposed to be gunners,

mostly mercenaries under the command of Lieutenants Rocco and
Connant, both men probably Europeans. There were thirty-eight
Greeks led by Captain Ulovix and Lieutenant Constantine; there was
also a doctor, and a handful of footmen and camel drivers. And that
was all.

Up to see them off was the British consul, who must have wondered whether anybody would ever see Eaton or his weird following
again. It was a thousand miles to Tripoli, over some of the worst
desert country on earth; even Derna was five hundred miles away.
To get there, Eaton would have to cross the blasting waste of the
Desert of Barca, a northern projection of the murderous Sahara.

Eaton's force wasn't much to take on all of Tripoli, and it was
easy to suspect that the "army's" heart was not entirely in its mission. Almost immediately the Arabs panicked at the rumor of a
Turkish force, which somebody said was advancing to attack them.
O'Bannon and his hard-bitten marines cocked their muskets and
scowled at the timid Arabs, and the army did not run after all.

This incident was minor, but it did not bode well for the future.
The whole army had been ready to run away before it found out that
the Turkish "threat" was simply the result of Eaton's having forgot
to bribe the correct local official. With the help of the British the
matter was quickly smoothed over. Still, Eaton and O'Bannon must
have wondered what might happen in a similar situation deep in the
desert, with no urbane Englishman around to help out.

Things did not go well from the start. For one thing, food was a
constant problem. The men got by on a little rice and dry biscuit,
the expedition's only meat consisting mostly of indigenous wildcat
plus the occasional tough, stringy camel. The weather was ugly, too,
the season of "the winds of fifty days," which whirled a skyful of
tiny, abrasive sand particles out of the southwest into the faces of
Eaton's column. This was the devil's wind, the *Khamsin*, which
clogged and lacerated men's lungs with sand and sometimes gave
birth to enormous moving clouds that seemed alive, ominous specters
that turned high noon into twilight.

Then there was water—or, rather, the lack of it. Everybody was
perennially thirsty, and much of what water there was, was foul and
evil-smelling. One cistern they found occupied by two corpses; they
drank their fill anyway. At their very first halt Eaton's men found a

dry well, and they suffered through a long night before they were able to dig down to a remnant of vile liquid.

The Arabs were avaricious and unpredictable, too, as anybody could have told Eaton Arabs were likely to be. They would steal anything that was not red-hot or nailed down. And early on, they staged the first of many strikes: before they would go another step, they said, they wanted more money in camel rental. Eaton, forever short of cash, ran a successful bluff: if the Arabs persisted in their demands, he said, he would simply march back to Egypt, and there would be neither rent nor loot, nothing for anybody. Flavored with a little coin the Marines chipped in, Eaton's threat averted mutiny. For the time being.

The Arabs started out nervous and got more so, constantly ready to bolt at any sign of trouble. The news of a relief army on its way to Derna produced a positive snit in all the Arab leaders. For his part, Hamet went into a blue funk at any rumor of Tripolitanian resistance, and he even seized Eaton's officers' horses to mount his followers for flight.

At one point, a courier from Derna reached the head of the column bringing the joyful news (which wasn't true) that the whole province was in revolt in Hamet's favor. In the best Arab tradition, these good tidings were greeted with a *feu de joie* from the sheikh's men, who galloped madly about firing into the air. The tail of the column, convinced that they were under attack, came close to murdering the nearest Christians and stealing all the baggage they could carry.

Still, once he got rolling, Eaton marched west at a very respectable twenty miles a day, following the steps of a couple of millennia of fighting men, from the formidable legions of Rome to the lean Tommies of Montgomery's Eighth Army. They were fortunate to find water enough in ancient wells along the way, although food remained in short supply.

By the fourteenth of March, Eaton's tatterdemalion column had left Egypt and marched into Tripolitanian territory, slogging through a desolate region studded with ruins, forts and towns dead and buried time out of mind. Another money strike by the Arabs was ended with blandishments and promises of largesse to come, and by the eighteenth the column had reached the settlement of Massouah, a dirt-poor community where they were able to buy a few provisions.

And at Massouah the Arab camel men struck again. This time

nothing would induce them to continue. They would promise only to march on for two days more, and only in return for almost seven hundred dollars, all the money Eaton had and could borrow from the marines and the Greek Christians. In the event, the Arabs immediately broke their promise, pulling out eastward in the dead of night. To make matters worse, it was becoming plain that the Arab lack of cooperation was being fomented, aided, and abetted by Sheikh Tahib.

And now Eaton showed what he was made of. He called a conference and spoke bluntly to his Arab allies. The velvet glove was gone. They could cooperate, he said flatly, or they could starve. There were no other options. He was prepared to fort up in Massouah Castle with his Greeks and his marines and the food, send a messenger to the American ships, and wait for help. What the Arabs ate in the interim—if anything—was their affair entirely. The Arabs were not pleased, and said so long and loudly, but Eaton had both the muskets and the provender. The gruff American had made his point. Fifty camels reappeared as if by magic, the Arabs agreed to continue west for two days more, and for a while the alliance was repaired and functioning.

Meanwhile, although he could not know it, help for Eaton was on the way. *Argus* and the new sloop *Hornet* were indeed sailing toward the Gulf of Bomba, bringing provisions and a very welcome war chest of some seven thousand dollars. The warship *Congress* was under way, too, sailing to Messina in an attempt to procure some artillery for Eaton. There would not, however, be any reinforcement of marines, the help Eaton's little column needed the most.

The letter announcing this welcome news—written by Commodore Barron—would not be delivered to Eaton for another three weeks, however, and perhaps it was just as well. For it also included a warning that the United States would not hesitate to abandon Hamet and support his repulsive brother if satisfactory treaty terms could be reached with the usurper. The United States was chiefly concerned with ransoming the crew of *Philadadelphia*, imprisoned in Tripoli with other luckless mariners.

And President Jefferson had made some other decisions, too. First, America would not continue to pay tribute to these pirates as she had in the past. Instead, the United States would keep a frigate, at least, on permanent station off Tripoli to cover American trade in the Mediterranean. Moreover, if the naval forces now operating against Tripoli could not put an end to the Barbary trouble this very summer, they would be withdrawn. Eaton's expedition, though he could not know it, was America's last real chance of quickly ending the Tripolitanian threat by military force.

On March 22, Eaton's army reached a large Bedouin camp whose tribesmen were loyal to Hamet. Although Eaton was out of money, the expedition was able to barter for a little fresh food, and it acquired another two hundred or so desert horsemen by way of reinforcement. Eaton and O'Bannon had some reason for satisfaction, but their sense of well-being did not last long.

For the odious Tahib now inspired another mutiny, and actually started back toward Alexandria with part of Eaton's measly force. When Eaton kept on marching west, Tahib called down a variety of curses on the Christian dogs . . . but he still reversed his course and rejoined the column, boasting about his influence over Hamet's followers.

Then it was Hamet's turn to get cold feet, and after considerable dithering he also started back toward Egypt. Eaton, nothing abashed, told Hamet what he thought of backsliders and pushed off west again with his marines, his Greeks, his mercenaries, and his strange group of officers.

That brought Hamet to heel again. He rejoined the column, flattering Eaton and praising his loyalty. That night, however, Tahib ran away once more, this time taking with him part of the Arab contingent that had just joined this ragtag army. Eaton sent an Arab officer to bring them back, or try to, and pushed on to an oasis, where his remaining men gratefully spent the day resting. Eaton devoted his time to composing a ringing proclamation to the people of Tripoli, a rambling two-thousand-word epistle damning Yusuf the usurper and his admiral, Murad Reis, a nasty piece of work who was, in fact, a Scots-Irish renegade.

Before the proclamation had time to have any effect (it never did have much), there was more trouble. It was Sheikh Mahomet this time. In a fit of pique because Tahib had defrauded him, he left the camp, headed back toward the fleshpots of Cairo. This time, however, Hamet himself gave chase. While both men were away, Tahib made yet another attempt to dominate what remained of the camp. When he threatened Eaton, that unflappable hardcase simply told the sheikh that if anything like mutiny happened in camp, he would shoot Tahib

quite dead. With the gleaming bayonets of O'Bannon's marines close
at hand, Tahib believed him.

And that was that.

Miraculously, Hamet soon reappeared with a mollified Mahomet
in tow, and the whole circus got under way again. By now Eaton
commanded—or tried to command—a total of about seven hundred
men, not to mention several hundred more camp followers, all of
them short of food, out of money, and without the faintest notion of
what awaited them up ahead.

The column slogged on, however, supplementing their meager rice
and dates with the occasional shoe-leather camel, plus wild fennel
roots and sorrel leaves. About ninety miles from Bomba, Hamet
again became recalcitrant, calling a halt until he could discover
whether American ships really *did* await the column with supplies.

Eaton was having none of this. The rations were nearly exhausted,
he explained; they must push on. Hamet, annoyed, declared his intention not only of leaving, but of taking the food supply with him. At
this, Eaton formed up his marines, his Greeks, and his other Christian
mercenaries, literally drew a line in the sand between the food and
the Arabs, and announced that the food was not going anyplace.

For a few moments things were very tense indeed. At one point
about two hundred Arab cavalry thundered down at the leveled muskets of Eaton's men, then wheeled abruptly away. The Arabs then
halted and pointed their own weapons at the Christians—somebody
in the Arab ranks even shouted "Fire!" but cooler heads prevailed.

Eaton, O'Bannon, Ensign Peck, and the Englishman Farquhar
stood coolly together at the center of the line. Eaton later said the
young Briton behaved "with manly firmness," and the others must
have, too. With the grim-faced marines and Greeks just behind them,
these four faced down the Arabs with every evidence of confidence.
As they calmly watched hundreds of Arab horsemen galloping
straight at them, God only knows what they were thinking.

At last, this emergency also passed. Eaton agreed to issue a rice
ration, and Hamet agreed the whole force would resume its march
the following morning. And so it was through a half dozen other
crises, until finally, beyond hope, the Gulf of Bomba was reached.
Here everybody's hearts sank again, for the brilliant blue of the gulf
was empty. But next day the vastness of the ocean was broken by

tiny white sails, sails that turned out to be USS *Argus*, standing in to help as she had promised.

With decent food, and lots of it, the army's morale soared. O'Bannon, fearing recall to his service on *Argus*, took the initiative by requesting permission to continue with the expedition, and got it. Peck was not so lucky; he was retained on *Argus*, his place taken by Midshipman George Mann, who successfully got his captain's leave to join up.

Resupplied, the army pushed west for Derna, now only some sixty miles away. The country became verdant as they marched, heavily cultivated, even planted in places with ancient red cedars. With plenty all around them, Hamet cautioned his men not to disturb the harvest, encouraging their good behavior by promising to cut the hand off any vandal he caught. As they neared Derna, however, Hamet and his Arab leaders caught another severe case of cold feet, a combination of alarm that a relief army was approaching Derna from the other direction and fear for Hamet's family, imprisoned in Tripoli.

Much palaver did nothing to still the Arabs' fears, and once again Mahomet and Tahib collected some of their followers and took the road back toward distant Alexandria, more than five hundred miles away. This time, however, Eaton tried something even better than O'Bannon's bayonets: money. Two thousand dollars from his newly filled war chest miraculously soothed the Arabs' fears, and sweet unity again prevailed.

And then, at last, there was Derna, the jewel of Yusuf's crown, set on a bay a mile from the sea, surrounded by trees and crops, watered by a never-failing river. It was built of stone, mostly, squared blocks salvaged from the ruins of Greek and Roman buildings that had gone before it, for this was a very ancient place indeed.

And it was defended. A water battery faced the sea, mounting eight nine-pound guns. The rest of the city was covered by the walls of its houses and by temporary barricades thrown up by its governor, one Mustifa, who kept a ten-inch howitzer parked on his terrace. Loopholes had been punched through the houses' walls, and some eight hundred men were available to defend the town.

Mustifa was not in a mood to negotiate, either. When summoned to give Hamet passage through the town, he replied succintly: "My head or yours. Mustifa."

The relief army from Tripoli had not arrived yet but was reported to be drawing near. Fortunately, the U.S. Navy was also drawing near. *Argus, Hornet,* and *Nautilus* anchored in the bay, and *Argus* began to unload what Eaton needed most: two brass fieldpieces with all their equipage and ammunition. At last the little army could deal with stone walls. Though only a single gun could be gotten ashore, the Christian gunners who had tramped five hundred miles from Egypt would at last have something to do.

The first step was the water battery, and that job took about an hour. *Argus, Nautilus,* and *Hornet* all opened on the hapless Tripolitanian gunners and simply blew the Moslem artillery crews away from their pieces. The ground assault could then go in, and Eaton sent his army to the attack from two directions.

Hamet's Arab horsemen, now totaling about a thousand, would assault the town from the south and southwest—that is, the side away from the sea. Attacking from the southeast was the hard core of Eaton's force: O'Bannon led it, sword in hand and joy in his heart. Behind advanced Sergeant Campbell and his six marine privates, the thirty-eight Greeks, the motley collection of artillerists, and a handful of Arab infantry. With them, they rolled up the single fieldpiece the navy had been able to get ashore.

It was tough going. Hamet's multitude of cavalrymen did a good deal of yelling and prancing, and achieved absolutely nothing. The load would have to be carried by O'Bannon's handful, and they were under very heavy fire and making no real progress. At that point, the polyglot gunners with O'Bannon somehow managed to fire the cannon with the rammer still in the bore. Cannonball and rammer flew away together into Derna, and that was the end of artillery support. Worse, the navy's cannonade had cleared the waterfront of defenders, most of whom ran back to join the Arabs holding the walls against O'Bannon. The attackers had started out outnumbered; now the odds were worse still.

The crisis of the fight had arrived. There was no place to maneuver; the artillery was rammerless; there were no reinforcements; there was no time to regroup and fight another day. Eaton and O'Bannon knew it was now or never, and they chose the only option open to them: they charged. The marines went in shouting, dark blue coats, brass buttons, and red facings vivid against the glaring sand.

O'Bannon was in his element, out in front, cheering his men on, saber gleaming in the sun. Behind the grim marines panted the

Greeks and the Arab footmen. "We rushed forward," wrote Eaton later, "against a host of savages more than ten to our one." He did not exaggerate.

And the defenders broke. Nobody wanted to wait to meet those terrible bayonets and that bunch of crazy foreigners who did not realize that they were beaten. The marines, the Greeks, and the Arab infantry drove through the abandoned defensive positions and kept right on going—an astonished navy watched in delight as O'Bannon and Midshipman Mann raised the American flag over the city. Mopping up continued in the narrow, twisting streets as O'Bannon's gunners turned the deserted water battery against what resistance remained, and the navy hammered anybody who still showed any sign of fight. Hamet's cavalry cut off any enemy fleeing the town and at last escorted Hamet to the governor's palace itself.

Derna had fallen.

The cost had been astonishingly low. Not surprisingly, the marines had suffered the worst—in proportion to their strength, at least. One was dead, another dying; a third lay wounded. Fourteen of the Christians had been killed or wounded, mostly Greeks, who had fought exceedingly well. Eaton himself had been shot through the wrist, an injury from which he would never entirely recover.

The victory created a sensation at home, particularly once the astonishing details were known. It even inspired John Greenleaf Whittier to produce a sort of heroic ode called "Derne," which lavished Homeric praise on the victors in this vein:

> *Vain, Moslem, vain thy lifeblood poured*
> *So freely on thy foeman's sword!*
> *Not to the swift nor to the strong*
> *The battles of the right belong;*
> *For he who strikes for Freedom wears*
> *The armour of the captive's prayers,*

And much, much more of a similar stirring nature.

Eaton was fulsome in reporting on the men who had done most to win the day. He again complimented Farquhar's conduct, and suggested he be commissioned a marine officer. For O'Bannon, that "intrepid, judicious and enterprising Officer," there was unstinted praise.

Praise and celebration were all very well, but within four days
Eaton and O'Bannon had another threat to deal with. At long last
the relief army, a considerable force of five thousand or so, had
arrived from Tripoli. Their Mameluke officer, Hassen Bey, was aggressive and likely to be a tougher customer than Mustifa had been.
A spirited action followed, fought mostly by Hamet's outnumbered
Arabs against the Tripolitanian cavalry. Eaton retained his dependable marines and Christian troops in the city fort, relying on the guns
of the captured water battery and the cannon of *Argus* to keep control
of the battle.

It was enough. Even as Hamet's men began to waver, a round
from one of Eaton's guns plowed into a group of Tripolitanians and
scattered bodies and pieces of bodies in all directions. The attackers
broke and fled, leaving eighty dead or severely wounded behind
them. Hamet's men, who had suffered only twelve casualties, left
their entrenchments, pursued for a while, and then returned rejoicing
to celebrate their victory.

There followed a lull while Hassen sulked in his tent outside the
town and awaited reinforcements. Once these arrived, he tried again,
and the result was a full-scale DeMille-epic cavalry battle outside
the walls with several thousand well-mounted Arabs hacking away at
one another. The Christians were largely spectators, a most gratifying
position considering what they had been through. And, most pleasing
of all, Hamet won his fight. The only unhappy man in the city fort
was O'Bannon, who had sought permission to take his marines and
the Greeks out to join the battle and had been refused.

Next day, big *Constellation* put into the harbor of Derna, and the
sight of her broadside so discouraged the Tripolitanian besiegers that
they packed up and departed. However, any jubilation that Eaton and
his men felt on *Constellation*'s arrival soon turned to gloom. For
Eaton and O'Bannon quickly discovered that the United States had
sold Hamet out, rather cynically concluding a treaty with the degener-
ate Yusuf. Eaton was ordered to pack up and leave, abandoning
Hamet to his own devices, without support.

So now, at the moment of victory, Eaton and his men prepared to
slink away as if they had lost, not won, the bitter fighting for Derna.
Hamet realized immediately that he was abandoned; he was as good
as dead if he remained in Derna to fall into his brother's tender
hands. He, too, he said, would leave with the navy to return to exile.

As one of his last acts, he gave O'Bannon his own jeweled sword, a lovely weapon with the gracefully curved Mameluke hilt.

And so the expedition left Derna like thieves in the night. Ship's boats took them out to *Constellation*, the Greeks, the other Christian mercenaries, Hamet, and his personal suite. By the time the townspeople and Hamet's Arabs realized they had been betrayed, it was too late. They rushed down to the waterfront only in time to scream and curse and shake their fists at the departing rear guard: O'Bannon and his faithful marines. Eaton was the last man off the dock.

Eaton had the last word, and it was a bitter one:

> . . . this devoted city . . . has experienced as strange a reverse in so short a time as ever was recorded in the disasters of war. . . . Six hours ago the enemy were seeking safety . . . from them by flight—this moment we drop them from ours into the hands of this enemy for no other crime than too much confidence in us!

Eaton returned home, understandably disillusioned, settling in Brimfield, Massachusetts, after a little time spent in Washington, D.C., damning the perfidy of his government. In Brimfield, he ran a small mill and lived quietly for the most part, although he became a justice of the peace and a state representative. He was not well-to-do, for he had spent all he had ever owned in the service of his country. He died in 1811, a very tired forty-seven.

And in Brimfield, one day in 1809, appeared the remarkable Leitensdorfer, having in the meantime experienced Turkish slavery, still another temporary wife, and a stint before the mast in an American merchantman. Eaton, ever loyal, opened doors for his old chief of staff in Washington, where Leitensdorfer served for years as a sort of janitor and night guard. In time Congress granted him 320 acres in Missouri, some money, and a mileage allowance for his colossal desert march.

The spectacular O'Bannon left the Marine Corps in 1807, perhaps in resentment over the shabby, faithless treatment his country had accorded Hamet. Virginia, his native state, recognized its famous son with a jeweled sword, a beautiful weapon bearing much engraving and the gracefully curved hilt borne by Hamet's own saber.

In 1809 O'Bannon and his wife moved to Kentucky, where his

brother, a distiller, already lived. O'Bannon became something of an ornament to his adopted state, sitting in both houses of the Kentucky legislature. In later years his fame was perpetuated in the names of two United States Navy destroyers, the second of which served with great distinction against Japan. O'Bannon would have liked that. And he would probably have been even more pleased to know that today's unique Marine officer's sword is the direct descendant of Hamet's gift, his own graceful Mameluke blade.

In Frankfort, Kentucky, a plaque records the memory of Lieutenant Presley O'Bannon's greatest deed:

> As Captain of the United States Marines he was the first to plant the American Flag on Foreign Soil.

And so he was. He would not be the last.

CHAPTER SIXTEEN

THE INCREDIBLE RUN OF HOLDFAST GAINES

EVERYBODY KNOWS THE story of Phidippedes, the Athenian soldier who carried to his city the joyful news of the Greek triumph over the Persian horde at Marathon. Phidippedes' run is the stuff of legend, for at the end of his epic trek, the gallant Athenian gasped out his message—"Rejoice! We conquer!" and promptly dropped dead.

Phidippedes' run was twenty miles long, or maybe a little more (much later the "marathon" distance was tinkered with by the British, the story goes, so that during an Olympic competition in England, the race would end near Windsor Castle). The gallant Athenian will never be forgotten . . . but his run was mighty small potatoes alongside the journey of a remarkable man few people have ever heard of. He was named Holdfast Gaines.

Gaines was a full-blooded Mohegan Indian whose tribal name was Sleeping Bear. He was a noted runner, and it was to Gaines that General Andrew Jackson turned in the turbulent year of 1814. Jackson was marshaling men at New Orleans, and he badly needed reinforcements. The only source of men in any numbers was the gathering of Tennessee and Kentucky volunteers under General Wil-

141

liam Carroll at Nashville. Get there, Jackson told Gaines; tell Carroll to hurry south; you have just ten days to make Nashville.

Nashville was six hundred miles away.

And so Holdfast Gaines ran and ran, pushing himself north by day and by night, up the Tombigbee River and then along the old Nachez Trace toward Nashville. He began his first leg on November 7.

On the evening of November 12, General Carroll had his dinner interrupted; there was a message for him. He read the note the haggard messenger handed him, then began to bark his orders for the downriver journey to New Orleans. He would get his three thousand men under way at once, and they would reach Jackson's lines in time.

Holdfast Gaines heard none of the tumult and shouting; he neither knew nor cared. He was asleep by the fireplace.

CHAPTER SEVENTEEN

THAT ASTONISHING INFANTRY

The Miracle at Albuera

"THEY WERE COMPLETELY beaten," said a bewildered Marechal Soult:

> They were completely beaten, the day was mine, and they did not know it and would not run . . . they could not be persuaded they were beaten . . .

The veteran Soult had every reason to be depressed. He had fought a brilliant battle. He had seized the dominant high ground. He had thoroughly outgeneraled his opponent. He had destroyed regiments and captured guns . . . but now, in a dreary spring rain, the remnants of his army were in full retreat through a hostile Spanish countryside. For all his brilliance, for all the courage his veterans had showed, Soult had been soundly whipped, whipped by a handful of English regiments who didn't know they were beaten.

It was May 1811. Napoleon's marshals strove to hold rebellious Spain for the emperor. Portugal was lost already, torn from the empire by a polyglot army under a tough and brilliant enemy: Sir Arthur Wellesley, first Duke of Wellington. The Iron Duke had cleared Portugal of French troops and was heading into Spain's province of

Estremadura. The action was centered along the Portuguese frontier, where Wellington menaced a French garrison at the town of Almeida.

On May 5, French Marshal Massena moved west with thirty thousand men from his Spanish base at Ciudad Rodrigo, intent on relieving Almeida. Instead, at a place called Fuentes d'Onoro, he ran head-on into the duke leading a British-Portuguese force of about the same size. Fighting from a strong defensive position, as he liked to do, Wellington beat off Massena and took Almeida.

But the duke, victorious again, still worried. He could not do everything and be everywhere. He could not personally oppose all of Napoleon's marshals at once. On May 15, he spoke plainly in a letter to his brother, "I am obliged to be everywhere and, if absent from any operation, something goes wrong." Even as Wellington wrote, something was going very wrong indeed to the south. It was going wrong just below the critical border town of Badajoz, near a village called Albuera.

As Wellington won his fight at Fuentes d'Onoro, an allied army lay besieging critical Badajoz. This force was a curious mixture of British, Portuguese, and Spanish troops, an unwieldy mixture of starkly different traditions, speaking three languages. The commander of this odd lot was General William Carr Beresford, later Lord Beresford. He was a competent combat leader, the spit-in-their-eye, hold-your-ground sort of commander who led from the front and, accordingly, did well commanding in close combat.

Beresford was a towering, bluff, honest man, and there surely was nothing wrong with his courage. Indeed, this very day he and his staff would fight hand-to-hand with the French cavalry, and the general would personally yank a Polish lancer from the saddle and hurl him under the horses' hooves.

In short, Beresford was a fine subordinate, a simple slugger in an army famous for blunt, fearless commanders. Everybody in Wellington's army would have accepted as quite ordinary the story of Sir Andrew Agnew at Dettingen. Turning to his Royal Scots Fusiliers, Sir Andrew had issued a famous operations order: "My lads, you see they loons upon yon brae-face? If you dinna kill them, they'll kill you!" And his Scotsmen forthwith threw "they loons" off the brae-face. Beresford was that kind of commander.

High courage, however, was no substitute for tactical sense in high command, as Beresford's boss knew well. There was nothing on earth, Wellington wrote, so stupid as a gallant officer. Poor Beresford, as gallant as they came, would shortly demonstrate his unfitness for independent command.

Immediately after his victory at Fuentes d'Onoro, Wellington turned south, marching hard to reach Beresford outside the walls of vital Badajoz. Wellington knew that another French army was nearby, experienced and fit and well-commanded by Marshal Nicolas Soult. Wellington, for all his haste, would be too late. For Beresford, lifting his ineffective siege of Badajoz, turned to meet Soult, who was marching hard up from the south with a veteran army of a little over twenty-four thousand men. He was heavy in cavalry and artillery, a special strength in the open cornland around the village of Albuera.

Beresford hastily pulled together a force of about thirty-five thousand. It was not an altogether happy combination, however. As many as fifteen thousand of these men were Spaniards, brave enough as individuals but slow and unwieldy in the mass. For the rest, Beresford commanded some twelve thousand Portuguese, British-led and getting stronger with every battle. The hard core of his men were British, but there were only ten thousand of them.

Beresford chose to fight along a low north-south ridge lying just west of the little Albuera River and about a mile south of the town. It overlooked not only Albuera but also the river and the bridge that crossed it a little south of the town. It would not have been a bad position—had the French obliged by giving battle there. The veteran Soult, however, wanted no part of fighting British infantry holding high ground—he knew about that murderous musketry from hard experience. Instead, he would maneuver.

And maneuver he did, superbly.

Soult immediately saw the flaw in Beresford's position. The allied force was oriented to defend against an attack across the river from east to west, and its right flank—its southern end—had been left hanging invitingly in the air. Moreover, Beresford's southernmost piece of high ground was overlooked by an even higher hill slightly to its right rear, a hill that overlooked the British line from no more than five hundred yards.

In fact, Beresford intended to occupy that dominant ground with his fifteen-thousand-man Spanish contingent, still moving ponderously to join him. They were a weak reed, these Spanish, mostly willing young soldiers, very raw and very poorly led. In the event, the Spanish units would never be an effective force in the battle, suffering comparatively few casualties and achieving nothing much that mattered. Throughout the coming fight they would be as much a burden as an asset.

And so Soult massed his men, collecting almost five sixths of his force opposite Beresford's right flank under cover of darkness. Soult was able to concentrate this mass of men—and forty guns—behind a hill within about ten minutes' march of Beresford's vulnerable right, and Beresford was blissfully unaware of his peril. For Beresford was blind. The allied cavalry was heavily outnumbered by the effective and experienced French horse, and the British commander could not see the danger that lurked behind the high ground just to his south. He would soon be terribly surprised.

Soult opened the battle where Beresford expected it, at the major crossing of the Albuera River. A French division—General Godinot's—bore straight in at the bridge, concentrating on it although the stream was fordable on both sides of the structure. The British artillery tore at their struggling ranks, and the attack stalled.

Beresford, noticing that Godinot's assault at the bridge was not closely supported, finally began to smell a rat. Wondering whether the real French attack would not come from his right after all, he sent word to the Spaniards to change front and face south. He met rank insubordination, a plain refusal to obey by their commander, a Spaniard with the unlikely name of Joachim Blake.

Twice Beresford sent messengers galloping to Blake; twice his aides met arrogant refusal. The real attack was at the bridge, Blake insisted, and he adamantly refused to shift his men. Even when Blake finally, grudgingly, began to obey, the realignment proceeded with glacial speed. Finally Beresford himself rode hard to the southern pillar of his line and began to realign Blake's bewildered troops himself.

It was too late. For swinging in behind the misaligned allied line came a cloud of French cavalry, and behind them loomed solid columns of gleaming bayonets. Beresford was appalled. Almost without warning, the French were crowding in on his open right flank. The way to his rear was open, and massed French artillery ripped at Beresford's men as they tried to shift their ground.

The Spaniards were immediately thrown into confusion. Some of their units began to fall back. Others milled about fecklessly as they strove to manage maneuvers almost brand-new to them. The army's only possible salvation lay in the British Second Division, marching hard to meet the threat.

As the Second Division arrived at the rear of the ridge, behind the floundering Spanish, the pandemonium on the crest was plain to see. Unfortunately, General William Stewart, leading the division, appears to have been another of Wellington's gallant numbskulls. Stewart certainly compounded the confusion. Instead of deploying his regiments into line, where they could make maximum use of their destructive musketry, Stewart sent a brigade of the Second Division straight into action as it had marched, in column of companies.

Attacking in a driving rain that reduced visibility to a few hundred yards, the British companies charged into a yawning trap. Out of the downpour galloped four regiments of French cavalry, including Polish lancers. For a moment there was indecision in the British ranks— somebody shouted that the oncoming horsemen were Spanish.

Then the cavalry struck like an avalanche out of the curtain of rain, driving into the rear of the slogging red infantry before they could shift from column into line. There was no time to react, much less to form the hollow square that was the only sure defense against a cavalry charge.

The result was disaster, the loss of six guns and the virtual destruction of three battalions of the brigade. The East Kents—the famous "Buffs"—the Northamptonshire Regiment, and the Berkshires were simply swamped by cavalry, reduced to scattered fragments fighting on in a sea of horsemen.

As the British columns broke apart under the onslaught of cavalry, some soldiers were taken prisoner. Other little knots of men fought back-to-back with musket butts and bayonets, then disappeared under the wave of French horse. Beresford and his aides were in the thick of the melee, hacking at the triumphant French cavalry with their sabers.

The only unit not immediately ravaged by the cloud of French cavalry was the 31st Foot—later the Huntingdonshire Regiment. This regiment stood to its work against enormous odds, driving steady volleys into the French, providing a little nucleus around which survivors of the other units rallied. The 31st Foot would lose 155 men out of 398 this day, but they provided the hard rock to which clung what remained of their sister regiments.

In those days, British regiments went into action carrying two colors—the regimental and the king's. As the Buffs fought and fell in their tracks, the French carried off the regimental color in triumph, killing the sixteen-year-old ensign who died trying to save it. The king's colors fell to the keeping of a lieutenant named Latham who, like the rest of that red infantry, did not know when he was beaten. Latham fought a multitude of French horsemen all alone. He was horribly mutilated in the process, but he would not let loose of the precious color. The left side of his face and his nose were virtually cut away, and he lost his left arm entirely.

Still Latham fought on, slashed with sabers and pierced by lances, until he was knocked from his saddle. Even then he managed to rip the colors from their staff and conceal them under his coat. The lancers stabbed him again and again as he lay on the ground, but they never laid hands on that precious, tattered flag.

Meanwhile, a second British brigade had gone in to plug the gaping hole in the allied line. It could make no progress under the hail of French fire, and its commander died at the front of his men. Almost 80 percent of this brigade fell that day, but the survivors stood their ground doggedly, pouring musketballs into the French at point-blank range. The remnants of the second brigade were joined by the third brigade of the division, marching in through the torrents of rain and the hovering smoke to close with the French.

All of the regiments in this desperate melee were English, and among them were many of the most famous names on the Army List. The Devons were there, part of the last brigade to engage, the regiment that almost single-handedly whipped an enormous Indian army at Plassey in 1757. They had won a continent for Clive and Britain, and proudly bore on their badge the legend "Primus in Indis [First in India]."

Fighting near them was the 28th Foot, the Gloucestershire Regiment, which in the 1801 Egyptian campaign had fought back-to-back against a mass of French infantry outside Alexandria. For their gallant and victorious stand, they won the honor of wearing their regimental badge on both the front and back of their caps. In an eerie echo of their great day at Alexandria, later Gloucesters would fight back-to-back again against heavy columns of Germans in Belgium—

they got a little larger badge for that one—and once more against hordes of Chinese in Korea.

The remains of the Second Division were in line together, trading murderous volleys with the French in clouds of acrid smoke and torrents of cold rain, torn by French canister and repeatedly charged by French cavalry. Five days later, when Wellington arrived on the battlefield, he found the British dead still lying as they fell, in ranks, with all their wounds in front.

Hoghton, commander of the second British brigade, was hit repeatedly but stayed on horseback, cheering on his men. He was a difficult man on normal days, a man who "worked himself into misery and daily visited Beresford with lamentations." But this bloody day he was spectacular, calling to his men even after his horse collapsed beneath him . . . until at last a French bullet pulled him down, dying but still defiant.

British battalions shrank to companies, but still their men fought on. Great gaps appeared between regiments as the soldiers closed ranks on their colors in the center of the line. Still they poured that terrible musketry into the French at ranges as short as twenty yards.

The fight of the 57th Foot was typical. This veteran outfit—now the Middlesex Regiment—went into the fight at Albuera with 570 men. When the smoke cleared they had lost their commander—Colonel William Inglis—twenty-two other officers, and over 400 soldiers. The story goes that, on the next day, the rations for Number Two Company were drawn by a single drummer . . . who carried them back to the unit in his hat.

But the 57th would not give an inch. Colonel Inglis had been dressing his regiment's ranks when his horse fell dead beneath him. The doughty colonel bounced out of the saddle without, it is said, ever taking his eyes off his men. When Inglis was finally mortally wounded by a grapeshot, he insisted on remaining at the front of his suffering troops. And he roared a last order to them before he died: "Die hard, my men, die hard!" They did, those nameless red soldiers; they died very hard indeed—and the Middlesex have been called "the Diehards" ever since. On the anniversary of Albuera, the Middlesex still publish an account of the fight in Battalion Orders. Colonel Inglis' dying words are included.

Even with all the gallantry, even with all the selfless dying, the day still seemed lost to Beresford and his beleaguered men. Casual-

ties had been hideous in all the units. The colonel of the 48th—the
Northamptonshire Regiment—was killed, the overimpetuous General
Stewart was twice wounded, the colonel of the Worcesters was
shot down.

Although they outnumbered their red-coated enemy by at least two
to one, the French were also suffering terribly. Three generals had
fallen to the British muskets, and dozens of other officers were down:
"The dead were piled in heaps, and the men, bitterly discouraged, cried
out not unjustly that they were being slaughtered to no purpose . . ."
But the French were veterans, too, and they stood their ground while
the French grapeshot tore gaping holes in the British ranks.

Beresford, for all his personal courage, was seriously considering
retreat. He had tried vainly to get the Spanish to advance to the
assistance of his hard-pressed English. The burly Beresford had personally dragged a Spanish colonel toward the raging fight, but the
Spaniard's men would not follow, and the officer himself went back
to his unit as soon as Beresford turned him loose.

Beresford had also called on a Portuguese unit to back up the
tortured British lines, but that unit was already heavily engaged
against Godinot, down by the bridge. There seemed to be no help
for his English regiments, and the general began to give preliminary
orders to pull his army back.

Whether Beresford could have withdrawn successfully is not at all
certain; his British units were closely engaged. Quite probably, any
general retreat would have meant the destruction of his whole army,
falling back over bad ground at the mercy of the excellent French
cavalry.

In the event, however, Beresford was saved the terrible choice of
retreating or hanging on. The vital decision that salvaged Albuera
for the king's men was made by a pugnacious thirty-nine-year-old
Irishman named Lowry Cole. Cole was a major general who had once
competed with the duke himself for the hand of Kitty Pakenham,
now Wellington's happily wedded wife. On this dreadful day Cole
commanded the 4th Division, and retreat was the farthest thing from
his mind.

One of Beresford's staff officers, a quartermaster colonel named
Hardinge, had galloped to Cole on his own motion, urging the Irishman to attack the victorious French. Cole needed little urging; in
fact, he had already been pondering exactly such an advance. And

so without orders, entirely on his own good tactical sense, Cole sent in his men.

Cole's command was a mixture of English and Portuguese troops, and in it was a brigade of real hard cases, famous in an army full of very tough soldiers. It was called the Fusilier Brigade, and it contained two renowned regiments, the Royal Welch Fusiliers (the 23d) and two battalions of the 7th, the Royal Fusiliers or City of London Regiment. The brigade, only about two thousand men strong, was commanded by Sir William Myers, colonel of the Royal Fusiliers.

Both fusilier regiments were storied outfits. The Royal Welch was among the six regiments, called the Minden Boys, who picked roses to wear in their caps on their way into battle in 1759. These were the extraordinary infantry regiments who at Minden advanced alone against a mass of French cavalry, smashed it utterly, and drove the French army from the field with heavy losses. To this day they wear roses in their caps on August 1, in remembrance.

They had also been among the devoted regiments that attacked the village of Blenheim, pinning the mass of French infantry inside the town, making possible Marlborough's smashing attack through the weakened French center. They would continue to fight all over the world for centuries more, imperturbable and very conscious of their own heritage.

In 1914, for instance, one battalion halted during the bloody retreat from Mons to stage a full military funeral for its mascot, a shaggy goat. It did not matter that huge masses of Germans were close behind, or that the Belgian civilians were scandalized. Things would be done properly if the world ended meantime; that was the way of the Royal Welch.

The Royal Welch would do it properly at Albuera, as usual. So would their equally famous comrades, the Royal Fusiliers, the first formed of the fabulous fusilier regiments. This veteran unit was, and is, among the very few regiments permitted to march through the city of London with bayonets fixed, drums beating, and colors uncased. They were originally named for the type of musket they carried, the fusil, or fuzee.

The mass of French up on the high ground were a very tall order, even for the fusiliers. A sergeant of the Royal Fusiliers, waiting to attack, calmly surveyed the enemy and accurately assessed the situation:

> The day was apparently lost, for large masses of the enemy had
> gained the highest points . . . and were compactly arranged in
> three heavy columns . . . ready to roll up our whole line . . .
> Sir William Myers had urged the . . . Commander to allow us
> to counter-attack; and, permission given turned to those near,
> and said: "It will be a proud day for the Fusiliers."

And so it was. Fusiliers fell by the hundreds, but nothing seemed to phase those stolid red regiments. They simply kept coming, closing toward the center as men steadily fell, coming on grimly through the rain behind those wicked bayonets. They fired steadily, their disciplined volleys tearing the French lines apart. Great clouds of white powder smoke belched out at every volley, and those well-guided lines of implacable infantry emerged from the swirling clouds of smoke looking, as one historian wrote, "like the holy men from the Assyrian's furnace."

The French showered the fusiliers with everything they had, masses of musketballs and a point-blank rain of grapeshot, but nothing seemed to make any difference. Albuera was down to a simple slugging match now, and the fusiliers and fragments and bits of the Second Division regiments bowed their backs and pushed on doggedly into that hail of French missiles.

There was no stopping them. The French were pushed back step-by-step across that vital, commanding hill, until at last they plunged down the reverse slope in a confused mixture of beaten units. Cole's men recaptured five of the six guns lost in the first French attack, the French attack at the bridge collapsed, and by three o'clock the fighting died away to a bickering of skirmishers. The British historian Napier waxed positively eloquent over this miraculous triumph:

> Then was seen with what a strength and majesty the British
> soldier fights . . . nothing could stop that astonishing infantry . . .
> their measured tread shook the ground, their dreadful volleys
> swept away the head of every formation . . . and fifteen hundred
> unwounded men, the remnant of six thousand unconquerable
> British soldiers, stood triumphant on the field.

Maybe Napier had a right to exult, after all. The outnumbered British infantry had indeed been astonishing, nothing less. Soult, still wondering how his perfectly fought battle had gone awry, fell back in full retreat. He had lost almost a third of his twenty-four thousand, and the damage to French morale was incalculable.

Beresford's army was intact, although it had been badly hurt. His losses had been fewer than Soult's, about six thousand, but most of them were taken by his best troops. Over forty-four hundred casualties had been suffered by the British infantry, who numbered no more than sixty-five hundred to start the battle. The Portuguese troops had lost about four hundred men out of ten thousand; the Spanish losses were roughly fourteen hundred out of fourteen thousand. It was plain to see who had borne the brunt of the fighting.

Now began the melancholy business of bringing in the wounded out of the steady rain and saving whoever could be saved by the crude medicine of the day. One surprising survivor was the redoubtable Lieutenant Latham, who by rights should long since have passed to his reward. He was very much alive, however, soaked with blood but still clinging to his regiment's precious color when a sergeant of the Royal Fusiliers found him in the mud.

Latham was horribly disfigured, but he would recover to live long years after. In those days before regular decorations for gallantry, Latham was specially honored by his brother officers, who clubbed together to present him with a gold medal commemorating his courage and devotion.

Both sides lay exhausted through the seventeenth. On that day a fresh British brigade joined Beresford by forced marches, and the British retook some lost ground west of the village of Albuera. On the eighteenth Soult wisely called it quits, falling back toward Seville. He left behind several hundred wounded men too badly hurt to move.

Wellington learned of Albuera from a despairing dispatch written by the depressed Beresford. The duke was appalled. "This won't do," he said. "It will drive the people in England mad. Write me down a victory." And so Beresford's report was altered before it was sent on, and the British public never knew what a close-run thing Albuera had been.

In truth, Albuera had, after all, been a victory. Soult had taken some prisoners and a gun, but he had been driven off south, foiled from his objective, the relief of Badajoz. That siege, lifted by the British for only a few days, was immediately resumed.

Wellington's Third and Seventh Divisions, marching fifteen miles a day down from the north, reinforced Beresford's battered forces May 24. About ten thousand of them pushed on under the able Rowland Hill, driving Soult's tattered forces far down the Andalusian Highway, to the south. At a place called Usagre, some forty-four miles south of Albuera, British cavalry ambushed a large force of French horsemen and won a fine little victory, inflicting three hundred casualties for a loss of less than twenty of their own troopers.

Wellington rode the battlefield when he arrived and drew his usual accurate conclusions about how it had been fought. Some of his redcoats still lay on that muddy hillside, still in ordered ranks as they had fallen. The Iron Duke grieved for the terrible losses his devoted infantry had suffered. "Another such battle," he wrote later, "would ruin us." Also, he quite clearly saw the magnitude of Beresford's terrible errors. "The battle of Albuera was a strange concern," said the duke:

> They were never determined to fight it; they did not occupy the ground as they ought; and they were ready to run away at every moment from the time it commenced till the French retired; and if it had not been for me . . . they would have written a whining report upon it which would have driven the people of England mad.

"They," of course, was Beresford. And yet Wellington, with his talent for handling men, wrote kindly to Beresford, all too aware of the horrible losses his English regiments had suffered.

"You could not be successful in such an action," the duke wrote, "without a large loss, and we must make up our minds to affairs of this kind sometimes, or give up the game." Perhaps because his commander did not condemn him, Beresford would serve well thereafter, although never again would he be entrusted with a major independent command.

In his heart, surely, the clear-sighted duke knew exactly who had been responsible for the miraculous victory at Albuera. Years later, on the eve of his greatest success at Waterloo, he sat in a Brussels park with a friend, watching a sight-seeing British private looking at the ranks of statues in the park.

Wellington nodded toward the soldier. "There," said the duke:

> There, it all depends on that article whether we do the business or not; give me enough of it, and I am sure.

There had been just enough of "that article" at Albuera. Even without the duke's presence, that astonishing infantry had won again against daunting odds. It had suffered hideous losses, but it had won more than a battle. After Albuera, as eminent historian Sir Arthur Bryant wrote:

> The French, gallant and experienced soldiers though they were, never wholly recovered from the effects of that terrible day. Thereafter the memory of it haunted them in the presence of the British infantry like a blow across the eyes.

Perhaps some of those same haunted French soldiers never forgot those terrible red soldiers who did not know when they were beaten. It may be that the memory of that astonishing infantry still lingered in French minds on another miserable wet day in 1815, when the empire collapsed forever at a place men called Waterloo.

DIRTY WORK

DURING WORLD WAR I, British and German troops fought an unspectacular, unheralded war for control of east Africa. It was a campaign the British eventually won, in spite of the genius of the German commander, General Paul von Lettow-Vorbeck. The British success was due in no small part to the ingenuity of a young British captain named Meinertzhagen, an intelligence specialist who was years ahead of his time in waging the dirty war . . . literally.

Meinertzhagen developed an effective network of native agents, some three thousand of them by the end of the campaign. And he relied heavily on information from a source, ah, very close to his enemy: he called it the DPM—the Dirty Paper Method.

Toilet paper being an unknown luxury in the wilds of east Africa, German officers used whatever paper came to hand. That paper included maps, operation orders, and other notes. And so Meinertzhagen's agents raided officer latrines, and their gleanings provided a substantial amount of useful information for their boss and his superiors.

Meinertzhagen was not above dirty tricks of another kind. When he learned that a sophisticated Arab agent was furnishing the Germans extensive intelligence about British railway movement, Meinertzha-

gen sat down and wrote a personal letter to the Arab. He thanked
the German agent for the useful intelligence he had provided the
British, enclosed a fistful of German marks, and gave the message
to his own most incompetent agent. And when that agent was captured by the Germans, the Arab ceased to trouble the British.

War is a dirty business in lots of ways.

CHAPTER NINETEEN

REGULARS, BY GOD!

The United States Infantry on the Niagara

THE WAR OF 1812 was a stupid undertaking, a tragic farce that should never have been fought. While there was much talk of British impressment of Americans into Royal Navy men-o'-war, trade with Britain was booming, and New England was largely content. In fact, young America drifted into war largely at the urging of bellicose western senators who coveted the endless timber and lush wheat land of British Canada. Bombast and chest beating in and out of Congress took the place of common sense and negotiation.

All that hot air might replace clear thinking, but it could not replace an army. The long and short of it was that America had no army worthy of the name; a pinchpenny Congress had seen to that. The fledgling United States was not ready for a war with Luxemburg, let alone imperial Britain.

True enough, Britain was stretched to the limit in a death struggle with Napoleonic France; that was, after all, the basis for the quarrel. Simply put, the survival of Great Britain was the reason the Royal Navy resorted to impressing foreign seamen to fill out its crews. But even if the British had their hands full elsewhere in the world, fighting a war took soldiers—regular soldiers, as time would show. America's minuscule force was wholly insufficient. Never mind, blustered the congressmen, standing armies were for European despots. Why, said Henry Clay, the militia of Kentucky alone would be enough to wrest Canada from Britain.

But it wouldn't, and neither would all the rest of the militia anybody could scrape up. Fortunately for the young United States, Great Britain could spare very few regulars for this sideshow war. When hostilities began, in June 1812, the British had no more than five thousand troops in all of Canada, plus some militia about as unreliable as their American counterparts. Even more fortunately, Americans made good soldiers, as they still do, and a tiny cadre of talented officers was available to whip them into shape.

The regular army had an authorized strength of some thirty-five thousand, mostly in seventeen regiments of infantry, each of which had anywhere from ten to eighteen companies of about ninety men at full strength. When war broke out in June 1812, only seven of the infantry regiments, one of dragoons, and two of artillery had anything like a full complement. Congress also voted to raise thirty thousand federal volunteers, all of whom had to be trained, and asked the states to stand by with eighty thousand militia.

Everything was in short supply, even winter clothing for the regulars. Especially lacking was high-level leadership, since the general officers' average age was about sixty, and most of them were veterans of the Revolution. In command in the Northeast was bumbling Henry Dearborn, whose most noteworthy characteristics seem to have been ineptness and sloth.

Transport was in short supply, too, and so was food, which tended to be spoiled even when it arrived. The militia was about as efficient as it had been in the Revolution, which is to say, not very. An early American attempt to invade Canada failed in part because some of these citizen soldiers refused even to cross the border. So much for Henry Clay.

Still, by the end of 1812 America had managed to put almost seventy thousand men in the field, about half regulars and half militia, largely because of a boost to recruitment caused by British forays into the United States. Since the British were not strong enough to mount a serious offensive south of the border, the American forces had time to grow and learn, and some of the ancient generals were replaced by younger, more vigorous men.

Still, very little went right when American forces faced even small bodies of British regulars. British training had proved itself again and again, as it had against the revolutionary armies of France. The redcoats fought in a double line rather than the French column, a formation in which every British musket was brought to bear. The British infantry were famous for their steadiness in spite of bloody losses, and for their ferocious volley firing.

Fat Henry Hull surrendered Detroit to the British in August 1812, and superannuated Henry Dearborn dithered while the British marched rings around him and beat him badly at Queenston, where a fierce young American officer was forced to surrender with most of the rest of the Yankee force. That officer's name was Winfield Scott. Dithering Dearborn was replaced, but only with another ancient, Major General James Wilkinson, a change in which, as historian William Ganoe neatly put it, "age and infirmity gave place to age and fatuity."

Some bright spots there were. William Henry Harrison won a solid victory over a mixed force of British and Indians in which the formidable Tecumseh was killed. Andrew Jackson destroyed the power of the great Creek Nation at Horseshoe Bend. And on Lake Erie, Oliver Hazard Perry's scratch American naval forces won a victory that assured American control of the lake. Most of the modern upper Midwest was now assured of remaining American. Still, no American attempt to invade Canada came anywhere close to real success.

And in spite of the successes of Perry and Harrison and Jackson, nobody had yet won anything like a victory over a substantial body of redcoat infantry. The methodical ferocity of the British infantry had beaten American contingents again and again, often against odds. In a long list of humiliations, the 1814 Bladensburg rout was doubtless the worst. That was the day the British routed a large body of militia—and the president and his cabinet—and went on to occupy and partially burn Washington.

Even the American regulars lacked real training in tactics and battlefield evolutions. They badly needed real tactical training, and the time was coming when they would get it. For America was learning; the list of new general officers for 1814 included Andrew Jackson and two men who figure largely in our story: Jacob Brown and, especially, Winfield Scott.

Scott was a huge man, a regular. He had been captured by the British during the early charade of a campaign that ended at Queenston. Exchanged, he was back in action in 1813. Although subsequent campaigning did little to cover the United States with glory, everything Scott himself did was marked by signal gallantry and energy. This was an officer who could lead men; perhaps even more important, he knew how to train them.

In the spring of 1814, Scott took command of a small regular force at Buffalo, a force intended to be part of still another attempt to clear the vital Niagara peninsula, between Lakes Erie and Ontario. Scott's superior was Major General Jacob Brown. Brown was an amateur, a farmer in civilian life, and without any particular military training. He was, however, a formidable scrapper—and wise enough to let his better-trained subordinates use their own initiative. Scott's men were soldiers of the 9th, 11th, 21st, 22d, 23d, and 24th Regular Infantry. Most of them were still relatively green, but Scott would fix that. He immediately set to training.

Scott proceeded as von Steuben had at Valley Forge during the Revolution. Train the officers first and have them train the sergeants; then everybody trains the troops. This simple system worked for Scott as it had for the Prussian drillmaster, and his men learned quickly the tactics of the British line. Each man learned his evolutions individually. Then they worked together by squads, then by platoon and by company, and, finally, by regiment.

There was no blue cloth for Regular Army uniforms, but Scott found some common cloth and had it cut; at least his men would be uniformed and uniform. And, as it turned out, his troops looked rather natty in their sober gray uniforms set off by tall black shakos and white cross belts. You can see their uniform, virtually unchanged, any day at West Point.

Scott's training was hard. Repeat, repeat, repeat, ten long hours every day. One more time, men; then do it again. And again. Those who preferred desertion to duty soon lost their appetite for French leave after Scott drew up his men in hollow square and executed four deserters. His troopers might gripe and grumble, but they stayed. And they learned.

And so, when General Brown ordered his men across the Niagara in July, he led two highly competent regular brigades, one commanded by Scott and the other by New Englander Eleazar Ripley.

A Pennsylvania militia brigade filled out the force, following ex-warhawk congressman Peter Porter. Altogether, the little American army numbered somewhere between thirty-five hundred and forty-five hundred men. Opposing them were three thousand or so British troops, regulars and militia, widely spread over a long, difficult frontier.

The British commander, able Sir Gordon Drummond, immediately began to pull his scattered troops together. Before Drummond could oppose them, the Americans captured Fort Erie, just across from Buffalo, New York. Brown's men quickly pressed on north along the west bank of the Niagara, looking for trouble.

And on the fourth of July they found it.

The Niagara River runs north from Lake Erie into Lake Ontario. It is about twenty-seven miles from one lake to the other, although the winding course of the river itself is three or four miles longer. The east bank is American; the west shore belongs to Canada.

At the river's southern mouth lies Buffalo, New York; across the river from it stood Fort Erie, on the Canadian shore. About halfway up the river lie the famous falls. The Chippewa River falls into the Niagara from the west a little way south of the falls. The mouth of the Niagara, at Lake Ontario, was British on both banks. Fort George secured the west side, Fort Niagara the east.

Drummond's subordinate, General Phineas Riall, had moved swiftly himself, pulling in his scattered detachments up and down the Niagara. He was waiting for Brown with about two thousand men just eighteen miles north of Fort Erie. The terrain was open there, a smiling land of fields and orchards and pastures, level and civilized. Riall had chosen a solid position behind Chippewa River, at a point near its confluence with the broad Niagara. There was a bridge there, and on the south bank a tiny settlement of perhaps fifty homes, also called Chippewa.

Scott was leading the American advance, and the burly brigadier knew a tough position when he saw one. The Chippewa was unfordable for miles upstream, and the British held the only bridge. Riall had a bridgehead battery established there, and his redcoats waited on the other side. Scott did the only sensible thing and pulled back, more than a mile to the south, behind a run called Street's Creek. There he camped while the rest of the army came up. Tomorrow would do for fighting.

So it would.

Between Street's Creek and the Chippewa lies almost a mile of open ground bounded on the east by the Niagara; to the west lies a forest. And as the morning of July 5 brightens, Canadian militia and Mohawk Indians begin popping away at the American camp from the shelter of the trees. The pugnacious Brown will not endure this annoyance long, and so he orders warhawk Porter's militia and Indians to go and abate this nuisance, assuring him that he faces none of the dreaded British regulars.

Porter, uncertain, nevertheless calls for volunteers and pushes off into the forest. He is walking into a buzzsaw. He does not know—nobody knows—that Riall is bringing his regulars south to attack the whole army. Riall, a fearless Irishman, is as combative—and as inexperienced—as Brown. These skirmishers in the woods are there to cover Riall's right flank, and Riall's regulars are moving across the open ground to Porter's right, outside the forest's edge. Riall has two regiments in line, the Royal Scots and the 100th, an Irish unit. A third, the King's, he keeps in reserve.

At first, Porter pushes back the Indians and Canadian militia. But then he runs into three light companies of British regulars, and his men quickly become unstuck. Porter's foray into the forest turns into a southbound footrace, devil take the hindmost, with the Mohawks whooping right on his heels. Leaving casualties and captives behind him, Porter escapes, humiliated but alive.

But now it is Scott's time, and he swings his brigade into line and begins to move across the open ground toward Riall's thin red ranks. Riall, deceived by the gray coats, at first writes off Scott's men as militia, the same rabble the British have routed again and again.

But then something about the swing and order and calm of these long steady lines begins to change Riall's mind. Those are no militia, not those; see them keep their alignment and their interval; see them close their ranks as British cannonballs smash men to bloody junk by twos and threes. Now Riall realizes what he is up against. "Those are regulars!" he says in admiration. "Those are regulars, by God!"

Scott's left-hand regiment swings through the woods, driving out the militia and Mohawks, flanking the red lines on the open ground closer to the Niagara. Scott's right overlaps the British front there, too, so that Scott's brigade begins to resemble a giant bow, with both tips curling around the flanks of the British force, three-quarters surrounding them.

The British artillery fire falls off as an American round detonates their powder supply. American cannon begin to rake the British ranks with torrents of grapeshot, so heavy that both leading regiments grind to a halt eighty yards or less from Scott's men. Torn by cannon fire, and by the steady, devastating musketry of Scott's regulars, the British ranks waver. Riall, riding fearless through the thickest of the fight, begins to realize he has bitten off too big a mouthful.

To make matters worse, Ripley's brigade is coming up on Scott's right, and the British loss in officers is ghastly. Riall reluctantly gives the order to retreat, with the King's Regiment fighting as rear guard. Back go the British, leaving a scattering of red dots in the fields behind them. It is a miraculous thing to see: the redcoat infantry repulsed in an open fight. Nobody present at Chippewa has ever seen British regulars beaten by Americans in any kind of equal engagement in the open.

But it has happened. Riall gets his survivors away, but they are badly battered. They are still disciplined, still under control, ably covered by the steady volleys of the King's, but they are leaving the field. He tears up the Chippewa bridge as he crosses, and the Americans cannot follow. But it has been a clear American victory, and the butcher's bill tells the tale plainly. American casualties total 328, almost all in Scott's brigade. The British have lost 415 men, with a high proportion of dead, probably the result of the murderous American grapeshot. Three quarters of the losses have fallen to the Irish and the Royal Scots. Partially encircling his enemy, Scott has used Wellingtonian tactics better than the British who invented them, bringing more muskets to bear than his opponents did. The result is a startling, satisfying victory.

Riall could not stay where he was. He was too weak to fight again, and the Americans were busily bridging the Chippewa somewhere upstream. It was time to go, and go he did, on July 8, falling back north toward Fort George at the Ontario mouth of the Niagara. His hopes were pinned on a junction with Lord Gordon Drummond, marching hard to meet him. If Riall could hold out at Fort George until Drummond reached him, their combined forces might fare better against these surprising Americans.

Brown had a plan of his own. He would march on to Lake Ontario, where he would join an American fleet under an officer named Chauncey. With Chauncey's fleet carrying the army's supplies, Brown could move quickly along the edge of the lake and take Burlington Bay, west along the shore of Lake Ontario. He might also seize Fort George, where the Niagara met Lake Ontario. Once supported by Chauncey, which Brown expected would happen by mid-July, he had every confidence that he could drive the British from upper Canada. He moved north to Queenston and went into camp, eagerly awaiting his naval ally.

Riall fell back before him, to Fort George and beyond, but along the way he acquired a very welcome reinforcement: the 103d Foot, later the Royal Dublin Fusiliers. The new troops were reasonably fresh; even better, they were close to full strength, some six hundred muskets. Riall reorganized his other battered regiments, watched Brown, and bided his time.

Brown would wait in vain for help from Commodore Chauncey, though Brown wrote with increasing urgency for the navy to hurry. Chauncey replied that he was ill. And anyway, he wrote Brown, he had not agreed to any meeting with the army at any time, let alone carrying its supplies. In any case, his pompous letter said,

> the Secretary of the Navy has honored me with a higher des-
> tiny—we are intended to seek and fight the enemy's fleet . . . I
> shall not be diverted in my efforts to effectuate it by any sinister
> attempt to render us subordinate to or an appendage of the
> Army.

In fact, from all appearances then and after, Chauncey plainly had a chronic case of what President Lincoln would later call "the slows." Worse, he seemed anything but eager to tangle with the British fleet. So much for naval cooperation.

Without it, Brown was stalled. He could see no reasonable course of action except to fall back to the Chippewa. There, he would resupply from his dump at Schlosser, on the American side of the river. He would then march overland to attack the British at Burlington Bay.

Meanwhile, Brown's militia and Indians were busily doing incalculable harm to the American cause, raiding loyalist farms (and, some said, without being particular about who was a loyalist). And on the nineteenth, an American detachment, commanded by a lieutenant colonel named Stone, burned the entire village of St. David's. Brown immediately dismissed Stone, but the damage was done.

On the twentieth, Brown broke camp and demonstrated busily before Fort George, placing troops with artillery on both shores of the Niagara. He hoped to induce Riall to fight in the open, where American numbers would overwhelm him, but Riall was too wise to tackle Brown again, at least not yet. For Drummond was on the way. And so Brown fell back across the Chippewa to draw his supplies, regroup, and then march north again.

Drummond arrived at Fort Niagara on the twenty-fifth, the day after Brown got back to the Chippewa. Riall had already detached a force of about eight hundred men to follow Brown, and this detachment occupied a promising position at the junction of Lundy's Lane and the portage road that wound around Niagara Falls. Lundy's Lane ran east and west and was flanked by the portage road and another track farther from the river. Both were oriented roughly north-south. Lundy's Lane ran generally along the crest of a swell of east-west high ground. This little ridge was little more than a pimple, only some twenty-five feet or so above the surrounding countryside. Even so, it was a fine defensive position; Riall occupied it.

Drummond had noted the vulnerability of Brown's base across the river at Schlosser, east of the river. British-held Fort Niagara provided Drummond with a solid base on the American bank of the Niagara, and from it he sent a six-hundred-man force south to Schlosser to destroy Brown's precious supplies. This thrust worried Brown, and it should have. If his provisions went up in smoke, or into British bellies, his campaign was over. He could only retire on Lake Erie and try to resupply his army.

Brown did not have to decide how to counter Drummond. When the British commander heard that Riall had reached Lundy's Lane, he marched to meet him, apparently fearing Riall might be overwhelmed by numbers and too far from support. Drummond recalled the detachment he had sent against Schlosser and marched south, calling in detachments as he went. A detached British brigade, delayed by conflicting orders, would not reach Lundy's Lane until dark, about nine P.M. that night.

As Drummond feared, Brown had indeed moved on Lundy's Lane. Anxious for his depot at Schlosser, the American commander had sent Scott's brigade forward to create a diversion, a demonstration to entice Drummond to recall his east-bank detachment and reinforce Riall. In the event, Brown's gesture worked exactly as he hoped it would, and saved his supplies; it also set the stage for one of the bloodiest small fights in American history.

General Brown, for all his scrappiness, has a blind spot: he is hard to convince, and harder still to unconvince after he has made up his stubborn mind. Colonel Henry Leavenworth, for whom a famous fort will one day be named, spots some British dragoons near the falls. He warns Brown that the main British army may be very near, especially as the dragoons have infantry with them. But Brown is not convinced; he sticks to his notion that Drummond's main force is east of the river. And so he sends Scott north with no more than twelve hundred men.

Scott approaches Widow Wilson's tavern—perhaps significantly, one of the few buildings the Americans have not burned. As the hostel comes into view, a party of British officers mounts its horses and rides away; one of them coolly waits until the Americans are within musket range, then formally salutes them as he departs. The widow, welcoming Scott, tells him that General Riall is close by, with "eight hundred regulars, three hundred militia and Indians, and two pieces of artillery."

Scott, eager to engage the enemy, takes the widow's word for Riall's strength. In fact, by this time the Irishman has reinforced to substantially more than eight hundred regulars; worse, he has seven guns and a fine defensive position. Scott, moving generally along the north-south river road, surveys the British position. This is what he sees:

On a little rise about one hundred yards to the left of the road sits a frame Presbyterian church, painted red. Just to the right of the church is a small cemetery. Just to the right of the graveyard, and nearer to Scott, is an orchard. The British have occupied the high ground and the ground on both sides, their guns in the center. Their line is concave, a crescent facing Scott's men. It is a solid position, even though Riall is even then considering withdrawal himself, believing he faces Brown's entire army. Drummond's arrival on the field changes all that: he will fight here.

Scott probably should have retreated. He did not. He might have had a touch of the delusion that sometimes strikes the best of generals, as it ailed Robert E. Lee at Gettysburg: after Chippewa, Scott might have thought his men could do anything. In any case, later in the afternoon he sends one battalion of the Twenty-fifth United States Infantry to swing through a dense wood on his right. They are to cut around the left flank of the British and block the road north behind them. Scott will lead a charge directly at the British lines.

The flanking battalion sets off, led by Major Thomas Jesup, and initially is successful. Jesup works through the woods, drives in a force of militia and dragoons, and approaches the road. He intends to swing in behind the British position and attack their artillery from the rear while Scott storms the rise from the south. Jesup's plans are spoiled, however, when, as night falls, he spots more British troops moving south down the road.

Jesup engages the newcomers in what is now pitch-blackness. Groups of soldiers on both sides blunder into one another in stygian gloom, lit only by the muzzle flashes of muskets and pistols. One small British party surrenders, surrounded by an American force under one Captain Ketcham. The British turn out to be Riall and his staff, the general already bleeding from a wound that will cost him his arm. When Captain Ketcham introduces himself to Riall, the general still has the grace to say through his pain: "Captain Ketcham! *Ketcham!* Well, you *have* caught us, sure enough."

Meanwhile, Scott's frontal assault has misfired badly. His three battalions have been badly bloodied by the British; two of them have broken and run. The slope and crest of this little rise are littered with bodies, British red mixed with American gray. The fighting has been head-to-head and hand-to-hand, close-range musketry and the chaotic, terrifying butchery of bayonet and musket butt. The British guns belch grapeshot into the faces of the Americans; the graycoats answer with musketloads of ball and buckshot.

Scott is left with one hurt battalion, plus whatever remnants of the other two he can rally. The British are being reinforced, too: Drummond himself has arrived, plus another detachment. Brown is going to have to hurry if anything is to be saved. Brown does. He is on the battlefield himself now, although he is still holding back some Pennsylvania militia in case Scott is not facing the whole British force. But Brown does send in Ripley's brigade, hurrying up through the murk to help out Scott's exhausted remnants.

One of Brown's fresh regiments—the green First Infantry—is quickly broken by the steady British fire. But in the confusion and darkness Colonel James Miller's Twenty-first crawls up the slope under cover of the undergrowth, until it is sheltering behind a rail fence only a few yards from the British guns. Then a point-blank volley kills or routs the British gunners, Miller's men surge forward in the night, and the guns are taken.

They have little time even to catch their breath when, out of the night, the British are back, coming in behind a fence of long bayonets, shimmering evilly in the flashes of the muskets. More and more men surge in from both sides, and for two hours the infantry hack and claw at one another, for most of the time no more than twenty yards apart. Brown is up with his men; so is Ripley, leading, driving, encouraging. In the darkness they can hear the British commanders doing the same, and Drummond himself, cool as ice: "Stick to them, my fine fellows!"

And stick the British do, charge after charge. They cannot recover their guns, but they will not retreat either, and so the slugging match goes on into the night. Units fire on other friendly units: Royal Scots volleys hammer their own sister regiment, the Glengarry Fencibles. It is a terrifying time for everybody, and it is too much for the Pennsylvania militia, who, having finally arrived, take a murderous British volley and take to their heels. Ripley is calling for help.

It is time again for Scott and what remains of his brigade. They are now the only American reserve. Only one battalion commander, Colonel Leavenworth, remains on his feet. Scott asks him whether the troops will stand another charge and then answers the question himself: "Yes, I know! They are prepared for anything! Forward and charge, my brave fellows!"

But this time is once too many, even for Scott's tough regulars. They are already bloody and exhausted, and now they run into the veteran British 89th Foot—later the Royal Irish Fusiliers—

who pour a terrible volley into Scott's ranks at no more than twenty paces and follow with the bayonet. In the confusion, other British units hold their fire, thinking Scott's men are their own. He escapes.

But Brown's men have shot their bolt. Everybody is exhausted, and many of the men still in action are wounded. Jesup is wounded and falling back, and Scott goes down as he tries to talk to Jesup. Scott has already fallen twice from his horse and been badly bruised by a spent cannonball. Now a British musketball tears through his shoulder, fracturing the joint. He is propped against a tree, gasping in pain and out of the fight. Leavenworth takes command of two hundred dogged regulars, all that is left of Scott's brigade.

Brown is hurt, too, pierced by a musketball and struck by a spent cannonball. With Scott down, too, he passes command to Ripley. One thing is clear to everybody, even the pugnacious Brown: it is time to go. The British are also exhausted, but still full of fight. Drummond has been wounded in the neck, but he is still very much in command; his men may come on again at any moment, and there is very little to stop them. And so the Americans prepare to drag off the captured guns and begin to round up horses to pull their prizes away.

It is too late. Before the party assigned to bring in the guns can hitch up their improvised teams, out of the night comes still another British rush: hoarse cheering in the gloom; grim, bloodied faces behind a line of leveled bayonets; a flash of muskets briefly lighting the darkness. It is too much. The exhausted men tugging at the captured guns are overrun and taken prisoner; their officer, mounted, escapes.

And so ended the fight called Lundy's Lane, with everybody back about where they started the day, those that were still alive. The American gunners got away with one British gun, which they may have mistaken for one of their own in the darkness; the British captured two American cannon. The redcoats were too worn out to pursue; many of them had marched twenty miles or more in July heat just to reach the battlefield; then they had fought half the night. They did what they could for their wounded and then flopped down on the battlefield to sleep among the dead.

The Americans were just as tired. They dragged themselves back to the Chippewa, to fresh running water and something like safety.

Like their British foes, they had suffered terribly, especially in officers, but General Jacob Brown was not through, in spite of his painful wound. Just after midnight, he sent for Ripley. Shake our men into some sort of order, he ordered, get them fed, and hit the British at dawn to retake the hill.

Ripley tried, good soldier, but he could find no more than fifteen or sixteen hundred soldiers fit to move, let alone fight. Moving north, he found a red battle line barring his way, its flanks anchored by the river on one side and dense woods on the other. Drummond had gotten his men up and organized, and he was waiting. There were more red coats over there than there were gray coats moving north, and Ripley made the right decision. He fell back.

Drummond did not pursue. Everybody was fought out, and neither side wanted to chance another battle. Ripley would fall back down the peninsula to Fort Erie, and still another invasion of British Canada would end in a whimper.

Lundy's Lane was a draw, a bloody, ferocious draw. Both sides lost almost nine hundred men apiece, dead, wounded, and taken prisoner. If the British had kept possession of the battlefield and frustrated another American invasion, they had not defeated the American field army. The combatants at Lundy's Lane had gained one lasting thing, at least: mutual respect. The surviving soldiers on both sides would long remember the sturdy infantry that fought them to a standstill. It may be that Lundy's Lane, like Chippewa, contributed at least a little to that most remarkable of achievements: the longest, oldest, unguarded border in history.

The United States Army owed Winfield Scott an enormous debt. More than any other man, even von Steuben, Scott laid the foundation for the long-service regulars. Once the war was over, Scott chaired a board of officers who produced a standard tactical drill, the "system of 1815." It remained standard all the way to 1834, when Scott himself modified it on Prussian tactical improvements. As changed, Scott's system prevailed until the very eve of the Civil War, when the murderous firepower of the rifled musket made sweeping changes mandatory.

Scott added to his laurels by leading the brilliant campaign that carried the Halls of Montezuma during the Mexican War. He ended his career, loaded with honors, as commander in chief of the army. Aged and corpulent, he retired early in the Civil War. But he left behind him the outlines of the strategic plan that would ultimately destroy the Confederacy, and a deathless tradition of excellence and professionalism.

If any man can be called the Father of the United States Army, Winfield Scott is that man.

CHAPTER TWENTY

THE VALUE OF AN EDUCATION

QUEEN VICTORIA'S LONG reign produced an astonishing collection of imperial commanders. A few were scoundrels, more than a few were sinners on the grand scale. Quite a number were unashamedly avaricious for both glory and wealth.

But they all had a couple of things in common. All of them were incredibly brave, walking into the jaws of death with a yawn and a bored expression. And they were gentlemen—Gentlemen with a capital G—to whom a classical education was a commonplace beginning, a phrase from Caesar or Horace an ordinary expression.

One of these Victorian lions was Sir Charles James Napier, scion of a remarkable family that made something of an industry of producing sons to fight Britain's wars. Napier had served with distinction through the Napoleonic Wars, even though he was so nearsighted he was never entirely certain where the enemy was. Nor did six major wounds diminish his appetite for imperial battle.

After serving Britain in our own rather silly War of 1812, Napier vegetated for some years until, in 1841, he went out to India. He was supposed to bring the blessings of Victorian civilization to Sind, a vast area of northwest India, most of which is today in Pakistan.

His principal opponents were the warlike Baluchis, who were not at all persuaded of the benefits of British rule.

The Baluchis' shortsightedness did not deter Napier. He knew what they did not: British governance would surely be more "humane" than what they were used to. "The great recipe for quieting a country," he wrote:

> the great recipe for quieting a country is a good thrashing first and great kindness afterwards . . .

And so Napier set out to thrash first and be kind after, taking with him about five hundred British troops and a little more than two thousand Indian soldiers. He was undeterred by odds of ten to one, and won a smashing victory at an obscure place called Miani in the early days of 1843. Miraculously—military miracles seemed to be the property of Victorian British officers—he routed the Baluchis. More victories followed, and in the final battle Napier killed five thousand Baluchis for the loss of only two hundred and seventy of his own soldiers.

And so Sind would henceforth be ruled—ruled kindly, of course—by benevolent Englishmen. The final thrashing was over, and history has Napier reporting his great success in the quintessential Victorian way.

Maybe the story is true, and maybe it isn't. True or not, it's too good not to tell. True or not, it speaks volumes about the cool, cultivated, self-assured Britons who built Victoria's empire.

"*Peccavi*," Napier's dispatch read, only a single Latin word. And in the wonderful Victorian way, that laconic pun was instantly understood.

"*Peccavi*" . . . "I have sinned."

CHAPTER TWENTY ONE

NUNC FORTUNATUS SUM

The Ordeal of Lucknow and Cawnpore

BENGAL WAS AFLAME. The unthinkable had happened, bloody, ugly mutiny the length and breadth of northern India, from Meerut all the way down the Grand Trunk Road to swarming Calcutta. A great many sepoys—native troops—of the Bengal Army had mutinied, and some had murdered their officers. More Indian troops would have joined the revolt had they not been speedily disarmed by British regiments and loyal native contingents. At least some of the sepoys remained loyal, in particular many Indian officers; and some old men, pensioners of the Bengal army, left their villages to help their former masters.

Nevertheless, the British East India Company was locked in a desperate struggle to keep any sort of control of its Indian domain. It was fighting against enormous odds, and just then—the spring of 1857—John Company looked like losing all of Bengal.

Across a thousand scorching miles British men, women, and children forted up, or fled for their lives, or were hunted down and murdered by rebellious sepoys, adherents of local princelings, and the scrapings of the bazaars. Delhi had fallen to the rebels, although there they had been deprived of much military supply by a tiny band of British who blew up the city magazine with themselves inside.

With Delhi the mutineers gained possession of the last of the moguls, a decayed old man called Bahadur Shah. Ancient he was, and doddering, but a useful figurehead nevertheless. Delhi had a sizable European civilian population, in addition to a small military contingent. Few survived.

And there was precious little to stop the killing and burning and looting. Along the Grand Trunk Road native soldiers outnumbered European troops—both company and queen's regiments—eleven or twelve to one. Communications were cut in many places, and many of the best British units were up in the Punjab, long marches away from the inferno.

The mutiny came as a shocking surprise. The governor-general found out the north was on fire only when he received a copy of a telegram sent by the British postmaster at Meerut. This unflappable functionary—expecting a visit from his aunt in Agra—wired that city to say Meerut was all fire and murder; he added, somewhat unnecessarily, "if aunt intend starting tomorrow evening please detain her."

Many officers in the path of the storm simply could not believe that *their* men would not be true to their salt. For some of these, that confidence would mean their death. This was not the first time, however, that native troops had mutinied. In 1824, a Bengal regiment had refused orders to travel to service in Burma. The troops' unwillingness had been summarily dealt with on that occasion by the local commander, who simply swamped the rebels with canister until the survivors saw reason.

Some of the company's best officers had been uneasy for many months, for there had been signs and portents. Most mysterious had been the passing from village to village of chapatis, cakes of unleavened bread. There was some enormous significance to this ritual act, though nobody—Indian or British, then or later—seemed to know just what it was.

There was also the ceaseless preaching and conversion attempts by Christian missionaries and laymen. Indeed, next to the military, more fathers of company officers were clergymen than followed any other calling. Many Indians—both Moslems and Hindus—dreaded the destruction of their religion and caste system. This fear fanned the spark that actually fired the mutiny, the matter of the cartridges.

For the company had newly introduced the Enfield rifle, an accurate, sturdy weapon that fired a Minie-type bullet very like the rifles that fought our own Civil War. It was a muzzle loader, which meant that its paper cartridge was greased to help the soldier ram it home. Before it was loaded, the soldier had to bite an end from the cartridge to pour the powder down the rifle bore. And therein lay the rub.

For the sepoys widely believed that the cartridges were greased with animal fat. The cow was sacred to the Hindu troops; to the Moslems the pig was unclean. To this day it is not entirely clear whether animal grease was actually used, and if so, what it was. And the company officers did what they could by way of damage control: a new loading drill was introduced in which the sepoys could tear the cartridges with their fingers, rather than biting them open.

But the damage was done, and the mutiny began at Meerut on the tenth of May. Here the company had its first piece of luck. The uprising had been timed to occur while the British troops of the Meerut garrison were on church parade, unarmed and away from their weapons. In the event, however, the start of services had been delayed an hour because of the heat, so most of the reliable British troops survived.

Moreover, there had been no serious trouble in either Madras or Bombay, although no man knew whether either or both might burst into flame at any moment. Even if they stayed quiet, the loyal troops in Bengal were desperately outnumbered by well-trained, enthusiastic mutineers and a horde of supporters.

Help was on the way. Troops were coming from England, troops in greater numbers than had been sent to the just-ended Crimean War, but it would take them a long time to arrive. And down from the Punjab, fighting most of the way, hurried small columns of British, Pathan, and Sikh troops led by such fabulous commanders as John Nicholson, Neville Chamberlain, and William Hodson.

A tiny British force "besieged" a much larger army of sepoys in vital Delhi, fighting constantly against heavy odds and plagued by bad water, bad food, blistering heat, and a variety of foul diseases, including cholera. In mid-September, for example, the British 75th Foot, almost four hundred strong, had only forty-three men "fit to turn out." Nevertheless, the handful of British, Gurkha, and Punjabi troops managed to hang on to the ridge, the high ground that overlooked the city. And when a train of siege guns arrived, plans were laid to deal with their much more numerous enemies.

And later on British storming parties came raging out of the night against the enormously strong walls of ancient Delhi. The vital city fell to the British in murderous street fighting, with heavy losses on both sides. The magnetic Nicholson was killed; Chamberlain and many other dynamic officers, leading from the front, were badly wounded.

But the city, focal point of the rebellion, fell, and indefatigable Hodson pursued and captured the aged shah. Next day, with only a tiny escort of Punjabi cavalry—his own Hodson's Horse—behind him, he shouldered aside thousands of hostile Indians, cut out the shah's three nephews, and personally shot each one. Strong medicine, that, and much criticized in peaceful England, but it destroyed three more possible rallying points for the rebels. Young Fred Roberts— later Lord Roberts and chief of the British Army—wrote that Hodson's act "seemed to the excited feelings of the army but an act of justice."

For now, however, until loyal troops first retook Delhi and then became available in sufficient strength to dominate the endless miles of Bengal, the besieged little bands of European survivors were on their own. There was no safety in flight, not in this vast land crawling with enemies. They would either hold out where they were or they would die.

For the Europeans of Cawnpore, trapped behind a system of flimsy earthworks outside the city, the end would be death. There were only about 350 men available to defend the place; of these only 60 were soldiers, and they were invalids. Nevertheless, they fought well, and held off ten times their number of sepoys for three bloody, scorching weeks.

The garrison suffered terribly from thirst, especially the women and children. There was only a single sixty-foot-deep well for all the besieged, and it was kept under fire day and night. Man after man was killed laboriously hauling precious water, bucket by bucket, from the depths of the well.

The British commander, General Hugh Wheeler, was an old man, but he was also a good soldier and, like most of his Victorian comrades, absolutely fearless. For a while, he beat back the sepoy attacks in spite of his enemies' superiority in numbers and artillery. The little garrison even sortied, bayonetting many sepoys and spiking their cannon.

Frustrated by Wheeler's spit-in-your-eye defense, the Indian commander, Nana Sahib, offered terms, safe conduct by boat down the Ganges River to Allahabad. Running out of ammunition and food—rations were already down to a handful of flour and split peas—and moved by the suffering of the women and children, Wheeler accepted Nana Sahib's smiling terms.

His trust was rewarded with treachery and massacre. For when the surrendered Europeans began to board boats for the trip downriver, they were murdered wholesale with musketry and grapeshot at point-blank range. As the boats burned and sank under the blast of grapeshot and rifle balls, most of the surviving British died in the shallows, chopped down by cold steel. In the end, only four men escaped to carry the hideous story downstream.

About 125 women and children survived . . . for a while, at least. It might have been better had they died in the butchery at the river. For in mid-July, with a British relief column on his very doorstep, Nana Sahib ordered their extinction. To their credit, his sepoys were reluctant to murder helpless women and children.

And so, after much ill treatment, all were murdered by a specially recruited band of city butchers. Their pitiful bodies were dumped down a well. Only a day later Cawnpore was retaken by a British column led by another of the extraordinary officers who turned the tide of the mutiny, Major General Henry Havelock.

Havelock beat successive rebel forces on his way to Cawnpore, employing his favorite turning action again and again. He was fearless, sitting his horse repeatedly in torrents of bullets and cannon rounds. His example inspired his men to one tremendous effort after another. From time to time, of course, even his best soldiers demonstrated an understandable care for their own skins, as when Havelock prepared to force a crossing of the Panda Nudi River under heavy fire.

Havelock was standing with the grenadier company of his Highlanders when a rebel round shot made mush of one man's head. The death inspired a little speech, a bit of vintage Havelock:

His was a happy death, grenadiers. He died in the service of his country.

One of his young Scots soldiers was quick to respond:

> For masel', sir, 'gin ye've nae objections, I wad suner bide alive
> 'i the service o' ma country.

At that moment the sepoys tried to blow the bridge over the river, and Havelock's men went roaring across the span to rout their enemy with the bayonet.

Havelock's men were sickened and enraged at what they found in Cawnpore, prison huts splattered with gouts of blood, a row of children's shoes with tiny feet still inside them, and the pitiful, stinking contents of the well. The whole area was littered with bloody women's and children's clothing, and

> One of the large trees had evidently had children's brains dashed
> out against its trunk . . . an eye glazed and withered could be
> plainly made out . . . smashed into the coarse bark.

Maybe worst of all was a blood-caked iron hook set into a wall: it was surrounded by bloody prints of little hands and feet, where a tiny impaled child had struggled for its life.

The British troops went berserk, and so did most of their officers. Captain Garnett Wolseley, who would later rise to the very top of the British Army, was typical:

> A more sickening, a more maddening sight no Englishman has
> ever looked upon. . . . The horror of the scene was
> appalling . . . it awoke in us . . . a fiendish craving for the
> blood of the cowardly murderers.

A group of perhaps a hundred Highlanders knelt together in one of the blood-splashed buildings, vowing to kill a hundred of the enemy for every woman and child who had died. Every man in Wolseley's company volunteered for hangman duties, a detail normally shunned by every soldier. Nobody seemed terribly concerned to sort out the guilty from the innocent; in the eyes of the British, all rebels were murderers; all were guilty.

And British vengeance was savage. Captured mutineers were blown from guns and hung in batches. Before they were executed, many were forced to lick a foot of dried blood from the floors of the dreadful Cawnpore huts. Newly arrived British troops were taken to see the huts, and from that time on a new, implacable note of anger and cruelty entered the war.

Havelock pushed on for besieged Lucknow as soon as possible, whipping a series of sepoy forces along the way. However, battle casualties and cholera, the perennial Indian killer, so diminished his little force that he was forced to fall back and wait for reinforcements. In mid-September he was back in Cawnpore, reinforced and ready to start, when he was superseded in command by Sir James Outram, another of the lions of the Raj.

Outram was an experienced soldier and a generous man. And so, feeling that Havelock had his plans made and ready, Outram put himself under Havelock's orders, at one stroke giving up both martial glory and the substantial financial rewards that relief of Lucknow was sure to bring.

Havelock's force was small but of high quality. With the reliable 78th Highlanders (later the Seaforths), he commanded the 84th Foot, the Madras Fusiliers, and a hard-drinking company regiment called the Blue Caps. There were also the 90th Light Infantry and a handful of Sikhs and cavalry. Havelock pushed off into the hostile emptiness for Lucknow, hoping he would be in time. Like Hodson and Chamberlain and Nicholson at Delhi, Havelock was the right man in the right place. He was sixty-two, a strict temperance man, and a highly professional veteran.

A poor man, he had been unable to purchase advancement (it had taken him thirty years to make lieutenant colonel), but he had learned his trade well along the way. If any officer could win through to the hard-pressed Europeans of Lucknow, it would be Henry Havelock.

Lucknow was by then fighting for its life. The British there had learned of the mutiny back on May 15. The Indians of the town and garrison were restless—a native regiment had been disarmed back on May 3 in front of frowning cannon crammed with grapeshot. Even so, the garrison had had time to prepare, in part because of the dynamic presence of the brilliant Sir Henry Lawrence, new commissioner of Oudh. Lawrence had smelled trouble coming, even though he had only recently come to Lucknow after a luminous career in the turbulent Punjab.

Lawrence could not hold all of Lucknow. It was a sprawling city of some 600,000, a maze of winding streets and walled palaces, mosques and gardens. And so, before the storm broke over Lucknow,

Lawrence moved all civilians to his residency, along with all the ammunition and supplies he could find.

The residency was a tough nut, a stone building overlooking the Gumti River, and Lawrence made it tougher, connecting it with some smaller buildings by lines of earthworks. When he was finished, he had enclosed an area of about thirty-seven acres, a perimeter a little more than a mile long.

Within it he brought his little garrison, including a number of loyal Punjabi soldiers and a few Bengal sepoys who remained faithful to the Raj. And the civilians, of course—men, women, and children from Lucknow and frightened fugitives from the countryside all around. Most of the civilian men were able-bodied, and they willingly pitched in to the hard work of fortification and the bloody labor of defense.

British and loyal native troops, civilians, hired coolies and chained convicts, all dug furiously, blocked up windows, built stockades, dug ditches that they filled with what we knew in a later war as punji stakes. Everything useful was put to use, even the library of a wealthy Englishman whose house was part of the perimeter; it soon developed that a volume of *Lardner's Encyclopaedia* would stop a musketball cold at page 120.

Repeatedly, deputations from the Lucknow citizenry tried to talk Lawrence out of fortifying the residency. One visitor came ostensibly to suggest that Lawrence should import monkeys into the residency, where they could be cared for by high-caste Hindus; this curious practice would, he said, placate the gods and make all right again. In reply, Lawrence led the visitor to one of his artillery batteries and laid his hand on a gun.

"See, here is one of my monkeys. There"—pointing to a stack of ammunition—"is his food. And that," said Lawrence, pointing to a sentry, "is the man who feeds him. Go and tell your friends of *my* monkeys."

Lawrence's improvised fort was hastily built and overlooked in places by taller mosques and temples. Lawrence decided not to tear down these holy places, even though he knew they would cost him casualties later on; he did not want to provoke the hurricane any earlier than necessary. At least the fortified residency gave the Europeans a fighting chance. And when the mutiny broke in Lucknow on May 30, Lawrence was as ready as he could be. His careful preparations had been some of his best work. They were also his last, for on the first of July a sepoy shell wounded him fatally. He lingered for two days, dying on a night of torrential rain, as screaming sepoys looted the city just outside the earthworks.

His successor was a tough, long-service officer of the 32d Foot named John Inglis. Inglis was a solid professional who knew how to lead and had no idea what the word *panic* meant. Inglis, then forty-three, kept his men under cover as much as possible and carefully conserved food, giving the fighting men a full measure of the reduced ration, women three quarters of that, and children half.

Almost worse than short rations, for the men at least, was the lack of tobacco. Supplies ran out early, and no reasonable substitute was ever found. "Coffee" could be made of roasted grain, and enjoyed if you had enough imagination, but there was no substitute for real tobacco. At auctions of dead men's effects, cigars and pipe tobacco were the most popular item.

When the besiegers attacked, Inglis' men hurled them back, women and wounded loading rifles for the troops on the firing line. Other defenders showered the sepoys with bricks and what with Victorian delicacy were called "other missiles of a very impure nature."

The British were given to cheering in the heat of battle, and in between they occasionally exchanged insults with the besiegers. One defender, so fluent in Hindustani that the enemy took him for a native, specialized in deep personal insult.

"Take that!" he yelled as he fired at the attackers. "Do you think I have eaten pigs' flesh like yourselves . . . take that, you son of a dog! Thou whose grandfather's grave I have dishonored!" A good line of insults helped pass the time. And who knew, perhaps an especially ingenious epithet might make an enemy angry enough to raise his head an instant too long.

Inglis needed every hand: by mid-August his little force was down to 350 European men—mostly soldiers of the 32d Foot—and 200 loyal Indians. There were almost 500 women and children to protect, and the sick list had reached 120. It was not long before both cholera and smallpox arrived to further diminish the little force.

Other ailments were also endemic: boils, colds, gastritis, scurvy. The latrines overflowed, millions of flies infested everything, and the camp was littered with the putrid corpses of dead horses and bullocks, all of which had to be buried in the darkness by already exhausted men. Inglis, who slept in his clothing for three solid months, was still on his feet, but his hair had turned entirely gray.

The garrison lived under daily bombardment, a steady shower of sepoy shells that killed and wounded indiscriminately. Among the wounded was the famous Dr. Brydon, sole survivor of the dreadful retreat from Kabul fifteen years before. Men of the garrison watched their wives and children go down dying or terribly wounded, and families mourned their men, sometimes killed before their eyes. As if roundshot and grape were not bad enough, the sepoys' missiles included copper coins, chunks of telegraph wire, carriage springs, and even monstrous chunks of wood fired from a sort of spigot mortar.

To add to the horrors of the steady artillery fire, the garrison soon found that the sepoys were digging, until many rebel attacks began with the roar of a mine going off under the battered line of earthworks. Fortunately, the 32d was a Cornish outfit (later the Duke of Cornwall's Light Infantry) and contained its share of experienced miners. Countermining found and destroyed many of the sepoy tunnels in troglodite struggles fought in subterranean gloom.

In spite of sepoy mines and storming parties and artillery, however, in spite of hunger and death and maiming, British morale remained high, and the garrison kept its offensive spirit. A particular thorn in the sepoys' side was one Private Cuney of the 32d Foot. Without orders Cuney and a sepoy named Kandial went night after night into the sepoy lines to spill blood and spread fear. On one occasion Cuney and Kandial slipped into a sepoy gun emplacement in the dark, bayonetting four gunners and spiking the piece.

Cuney was also part of a spectacular raid on July 7. The garrison had long suffered under sniping from a nearby house, including the deadly fire of a particularly good shot nicknamed ''Bob the Nailer.'' Under cover of their own snipers the raiders struck the house in the heat of the day, bayonetting fifteen or twenty sepoys and shutting down Bob the Nailer for good. The British lost only three wounded, plus a set of trousers blown off an otherwise undamaged officer.

As famous as Cuney was Captain Fulton, an expert in demolition. Fulton, followed everywhere by a huge Sikh carrying a barrel of powder on his back, made both work and hobby of surgically flattening enemy-held buildings without danger to the battered British defenses. In the end, like Cuney, Fulton, too, gave his life to keep Lucknow alive.

Not all these devoted defenders were human. Famous within the garrison was a dog called Bustle, who plainly understood the danger outside. When his tired soldier's attention wavered during the night watches, Bustle corrected the situation by jerking at the trooper's trousers with his teeth. On at least one occasion Bustle's vigilance woke his master in time to shoot down a prowling sepoy. Bustle survived the rebellion and the retreat from Lucknow, and was last heard of years afterward, living happily in England.

And so the tiny garrison more than held its own, and by September 24 the exhausted defenders could hear the thunder of Havelock's artillery. On the next day they were electrified by the wild skirl of bagpipes and the hammer of British musketry. That evening, amidst much cheering, tough Henry Havelock shook hands with Inglis. The beleaguered defenders cheered and cried, and Havelock's tough Scots hugged and kissed the scrawny children of Lucknow with tears in their eyes. "God bless, missus," said a Highlander. "We're glad we've come in time. . . ."

The garrison had held for eighty-seven agonizing days, but the ordeal was not over yet. Havelock's force had been all teeth and no tail. His ferocious infantry had the will and the firepower to break through to Lucknow but lacked the transport to get away the sick and wounded defenders, the exhausted women and children. Moreover, although Havelock had come loaded with ammunition, he had brought very little food.

The food problem was quickly solved. Miraculously, Colonel Robert Napier soon found a large pit full of good grain, apparently hidden by Lawrence before he was killed and unknown to anybody else. And now, with fresh veterans, defense became a relatively simple matter of killing sepoys in large numbers until more help came along. Outram took command, and he proceeded to carry the war to the rebels, designing raids and sorties to kill more of the detested enemy, spike his guns, and ruin his sleep. The amazing Private Cuney climbed from a sickbed to join these sorties, in one of which his astonishing luck finally ran out.

There would be fifty-three days more of this murderous, close-range fighting, more of the illness and the endless bombardment. And then, in early November, still another of the formidable British commanders took the road for battered Lucknow. By the tenth he was camped on the edge of the city in a vast pleasure park called the Alambagh, and he was ready to attack.

This extraordinary man was a grizzled Scot named Colin Campbell, veteran of more than half a century of service to the king. Campbell was another poor man who rose to the top on merit, a man so poor he had to borrow money to purchase promotion under the system of the day. He had performed brilliantly in the Crimea, and then, only about eight months back in Britain, he was contemplating a well-deserved retirement.

Campbell was born in the Hebrides, the wild western islands of Scotland. His birth name was McLiver, although his mother was surely a Campbell. When he was nine, he became the ward of his uncle, Colonel John Campbell, and when he was sixteen Colonel John introduced the youngster to the Duke of York, then commander in chief of the British army. "Another of the clan," said the duke, and the boy entered the army as Colin Campbell. The name would serve him well.

Campbell followed the sound of British guns across most of the world, serving in Barbados, Ireland, China, Gibraltar, the Crimea, the Punjab, and the Northwest Frontier. He had led brilliantly against the formidable Sikhs at bloody Chillianwallah. He was a bachelor, wedded to the army, an austere man whose quarters were always furnished in Spartan simplicity—and were never without a Bible. He was a hard-driving, hard-to-please trainer, a disciple of the great Sir John Moore, under whom he had soldiered in Spain. Any men he trained were experts at loading on the move and taking every advantage of cover and concealment.

He was utterly fearless under fire, leading always from the front, but never losing his cool, dispassionate soldier's judgment. At San Sebastian, during the Napoleonic Wars, Campbell led his soldiers and men of the Royal Scots in a desperate night assault on a breach in the city's walls. First into the opening in the walls, Campbell fell with a wound in the leg. Scrambling back into the breach, he was shot again in the groin.

And then, in the very heat and anger of attack, Campbell made the sober decision that would characterize the man for the rest of his career: he directed an orderly retreat. He would waste no more soldiers' lives on a hopeless enterprise.

Wherever he served, he acquired the reputation of a dour fighter, a fearless warrior chary of spending his men's lives. He excelled in peace as well. Commanding a regiment during the terrible Chartist unrest in northern England, he won a reputation for honesty and fair dealing with both sides.

He had been forty-six years a soldier, this "fiery old Scot," and he did not dream he would smell powder smoke again. Nevertheless, as the dreadful news from Bengal reached England, he found himself facing Lord Panmure, Queen Victoria's Secretary of State for War. Panmure came right to the point. It was the eleventh of July, 1857.

"Sir Colin," Lord Panmure said simply, "the government wishes you to take command. When can you leave for India?"

Campbell, surprised, was equally direct: "Tomorrow."

And so he did. On the twelfth he had an audience with Queen Victoria, and in the afternoon he met his staff at London Bridge Station. They took the boat-train for Paris, and Sir Colin was off to the wars again. He was needed.

Now, poised on the edge of Lucknow, Campbell had about thirty-five hundred veteran troops with him, and a mixed bag they were. His gunners were men of the Naval Brigade, sailors and Royal Marines manning six cannon and several rocket tubes.

The hard core of Campbell's force were the PBI—as the British would later call them—the Poor Bloody Infantry. The 53d was a Queen's Regiment—later the Shropshire Light Infantry, blazing in proper British crimson. With them were the 8th and 75th Foot, somewhat more drab in a nonregulation sort of gray drape material.

Campbell also commanded the 90th Foot, dressed in a bewildering collection of civilian and military hand-me-downs; the 90th had lost everything but their fighting spirit in a shipwreck on the way to Calcutta. Nevertheless, this regiment—later famous as the Cameronians—counted a large number of Crimean veterans in their ranks. They knew what they could do and how to do it. And last, but surely not least, were the 93d Highlanders.

This formidable outfit—later the Argyle and Sutherland Highlanders—was Campbell's favorite unit. They were the heroes of Balaclava in the Crimea, the "thin red streak tipped with steel." They were extraordinary fighting men, tough and devout—a sort of "military Highland parish," one of their sergeants called them. Just now they were furious and thirsting for action, for they, too, had seen the sights of Cawnpore.

The 93d was about a thousand strong, most of them veterans of the Crimea, where they had known Sir Colin very well indeed. And when they saw him again in Bengal they broke into wild cheering, and even quiet Sir Colin smiled. They were his own men, and he told them so, a tempered weapon with an edge that would not dull. They would be the point of his sword.

Young Roberts—one day to be commander in chief of the British army—had come down from Delhi in time to join this last push to Lucknow. He had moved with a column southeast from Delhi, steadily fighting its way to join Havelock before Lucknow. If the men of the column needed any further inspiration, they got it when they passed the skeleton of a European woman carefully propped up by a bridge. Anger mounted as the column moved on.

Now the column heard from Havelock, a message in Greek—one of the advantages of a classical education—secreted in the false bottom of a fakir's begging bowl. Havelock needed help, and quickly, and the column fought on. They were in Cawnpore in time to join Campbell's offensive.

Campbell keenly felt the need of some accurate knowledge of the sprawling maze of convoluted streets lying between him and the residency. As he approached the last perilous miles into Lucknow, he badly needed a reliable guide.

He got one, an ordinary man turned hero for the working day. His name was Kavanagh, and he was a minor civil servant with fourteen children. He must have known of the ghastly fate awaiting him if he were caught by the sepoys. Even so, he disguised himself in Indian dress, slipped out of the residency, and found his way to Campbell, bringing messages from Outram, maps of the city, and his own detailed knowledge of its winding streets. For his gallantry, he became one of the few civilians ever awarded the Victoria Cross.

Now Campbell had the intelligence he needed, and on the fourteenth of November, 1857 he went in to the attack. Against heavy odds, his veterans fought their way up to the Sikander Bagh, a monstrous walled enclosure. The Sikander Bagh was the key to Campbell's advance, and very strongly held. And so he called on the 93d, and spoke to them before the attack began:

We have to rescue helpless women and children a fate worse
than death. . . . Keep well together and use the
bayonet . . . Ninety-Third! You are my own lads. I rely on you
to do the work!

"Ay, Sir Colin!" shouted one of the Highlanders.

Ye ken us and we ken you. We'll bring the women and children
out o' Lucknow or die wi' you in the attempt!

Or something like that. Or maybe both Sir Colin and the soldier
said exactly those words, because men talked that way in those far-
off days. In any case, the regiment roared its approval and the assault
on the Sikander Bagh began.

On Campbell's orders, the Highlanders advanced in groups of
three: the point man cleared the way, and the other two men covered
his flanks. Nobody was to fire except as a last resort. Quarters were
too close for indiscriminate shooting—an Enfield ball might strike
down a friend as well as an enemy. Bayonets did not make the
same mistake.

The artillerymen started it, calmly serving their guns point-blank
in the open, hammering steadily at the thick walls while gunners fell
in dozens under the heavy fire from the defenders. Campbell stood
the torrent of fire with his cannoneers, suffering a bad bruise from
a round that tore through a gunner's body and struck Campbell in
the thigh.

While the 93d, the 53d Foot (Shropshire Light Infantry), and the
Punjab Rifles lay down awaiting the order to go in, the guns gradually
started a fracture in the walls. For forty-five terrible minutes gunners
died to hammer the thick masonry, at last opening a hole and finally
a small breach. The infantry were ready, straining at the bit:

"Sir Colin, Your Excellency," a sergeant shouted, "let the infantry storm; let the two Thirds at them!"

And Campbell gave his order.

The Scots, the 53d and the Sikhs went in yelling, the Highland
pipes skirling wildly through the roar of gunfire, all vying for the
honor of being first into the tiny breach. A Highlander named Don-
nelly was first into the Sikander Bagh and was killed immediately.
With him fell Subadar Gokul Singh of the Fourth Punjabis, and just

behind them died Sergeant Major Murray, a lieutenant named Cooper, and a fourteen-year-old drummer boy whose name has not survived.

A little way down the wall the stormers found a gate the enemy had not quite closed. As the sepoys desperately tried to haul it shut, a Punjabi soldier called Mukarrab Khan shoved his arm between gate and frame. When it was deeply slashed by a sword, he substituted his other arm, which was almost cut off at the wrist. But Mukarrab Khan jammed the gate long enough for his comrades to wrench it fully open, and a torrent of men poured into the enclosure behind it.

Meanwhile more and more men pushed through the breach, and some of them lived. At their head was the 93d's commander, Lieutenant Colonel John Ewart, swinging his broadsword beside his panting, shouting men. Now the crimson bayonets flashed deeper and deeper into the garden. In hand-to-hand fighting the Light Infantry, Highlanders and Sikhs cleared the garden and its pleasure bungalows, and they gave no quarter. It was time to pay back for the bloody little handprints on the wall at Cawnpore, and with bayonet and musket butt, broadsword, dirk, and tulwar, the attackers killed and killed and killed.

The sepoy dead, Roberts wrote later, were piled up

as high as my head, a heaving, surging mass of dead and dying inextricably entangled . . . the wretched wounded men could not get clear of their dead comrades . . .

And so fell the Sikander Bagh. Bloodied and tired, Campbell's men pressed on toward the next objective, a fortified mosque called the Shah Najaf. Campbell brought up the guns of the naval brigade to within twenty yards of the walls, but even the navy's heavy pieces could make no impression on the monstrous walls of the mosque. Finally, as casualties mounted, a rocket battery went into action, hurling its fizzing, flaming rockets into the mosque enclosure.

And that did it. As every British soldier knew, the rockets were a good deal more sound and fury than real danger. Royal Navy Captain Peel, commanding the naval brigade, put it exactly: "Well, you know rockets are rockets. If the enemy are only half as much afraid of them as we who fire them, they are doing good service."

Nevertheless, as the missiles whooshed noisily into the yard of the mosque the sepoys made haste to leave by the back gate, much as similar rockets had spooked raw American militia from the Bladensburg battlefield in the War of 1812. As the pipes of the 93d played "The Campbells Are Coming," the British occupied the whole of the Shah Najif.

A small British party now climbed to the top of the mosque with a signal flag, to show the residency the progress of the advance. Their flag drew both sepoy bullets and an acknowledgment from the garrison, and provoked an impromtu celebration by one of the flag party, a twelve-year-old drummer boy.

Excited by the triumph of his unit, the youngster stood on top of the dome in a shower of Indian bullets, waving his bonnet and singing "Yankee Doodle!" His NCO and officer were not pleased, since the boy had disobeyed an order to descend from his dangerous stage. Why, they asked, this unseemly demonstration high above the Shah Najaf?

It was simple, said the lad. Evidently a child of the regiment, he had been born while the 93d was stationed in Canada. His mother having been inconveniently visiting the United States when her time came, he had first seen the light of day south of the border, and was therefore an American. Hence, quite logically, "Yankee Doodle." One hopes the boy went on to be a general.

At last the enemy could stand no more, Campbell's men opened a path to the battered wreck that had been the residency, and Lucknow was relieved again. Amid scenes of wild celebration, Campbell met Outram and Havelock. It must have been an overwhelming moment for all three men, but they were Victorian soldiers to the core. Campbell lifted his cap in salute and the men shook hands. He greeted Outram and then Havelock: "How do you do, *Sir* Henry," he said, announcing to the delighted Havelock the knighthood he did not know he had won.

Wisely, Campbell did not try to hold the city. That could come later. For now, he would widen his corridor and evacuate the exhausted garrison, the women, the children, and the wounded.

And so it was. Sadly, Havelock, exhausted and riddled with dysentery, died before he could be brought out of the city. His profound faith sustained him to the last: "See how a Christian can die!" he said to his son. And then he smiled and was gone. For the rest, Campbell got them clear with little danger. Inglis, still on his feet and full of fight, managed the honor of being the last man out of the remains of the residency. Outram was with him, and senior to him, but Inglis had the last word: "You will allow me, sir, to have the honour of closing my own door."

And he did.

Only about half the gallant 32d Foot—backbone of the garrison— survived the siege, and many other graves remained behind in battered Lucknow. During the siege the Reverend James Harris, owner of the gallant Bustle, had conducted five hundred funerals. To keep a base in Lucknow, Outram remained behind in the strongly walled park called the Alambagh. Campbell got the rest out in a masterful fighting retreat across the Ganges to battered Cawnpore.

Once in Cawnpore, again threatened by a large army of mutineers, Campbell got his wounded and noncombatants safely off downriver to Allahabad. And then, with a substantial reinforcement, he fell on the major rebel army under Tantya Tope and Nana Sahib and smashed it. Leading from the front as always, Campbell led the final advance, walking his horse through a hail of roundshot in front of his faithful 93d Highlanders.

For Campbell there was still more fighting. The next March he was back in Lucknow, this time for keeps, leading a well-equipped army of some thirty thousand, a mixed lot of British, Indian, and Gurkha troops. And this assault was a reprise of Campbell's first attack. The Naval Brigade was back again, stolidly pushing its guns to point-blank range to open a breach for the infantry.

And then, in some of the most savage fighting of this conflict, famous for vicious hand-to-hand bloodletting, the infantry cleared the city. In fighting for the empress's palace, the 93d, in front again, fought from room to room, killing seven hundred to eight hundred rebels with the bayonet, for the loss of about sixty casualties of their own.

The palace was a scene out of hell, the ditch heaped with sepoy bodies. Inside, room after room was packed with dead, many bodies burning as their cotton clothing caught fire from point-blank rifle fire. The whole building stank of burning human flesh, and the floors were slippery with blood.

In ferocious fighting, Campbell's men smashed implacably deeper and deeper through Lucknow. Clearing one building after the last, the British hurled fused powder bags into rooms full of their enemies, flushing out the defenders, then closing with cold steel. A single Scots officer, a veteran up from the ranks, killed eleven sepoys in a row with only his sword. There was little quarter given. The memory of Cawnpore was still far too fresh; most of the rebels got a "Cawnpore dinner"—six inches of bayonet—whether they were willing to surrender or not.

The attacking forces fought their way from one strong place to the next, inexorably forcing the mutineers back against the river Gumti. "Here's another little palace," said Havelock's son, a major fighting with Campbell's forces. "We might as well have it." They did, and pressed on and on until the rebels broke and fled. By March 22 Lucknow was clear of the enemy. They left behind more than 3,000 dead. The victory had cost the British 127 dead and 595 wounded.

Lucknow had been a rich city, and much sepoy loot had been brought there as well. Most of it finished in the pockets of the victors, and one Englishman commented shrewdly:

> It was . . . suspected by the troops that certain small caskets in battered cases . . . contained the redemption of mortgaged estates in Scotland, England and Ireland . . . one deeply-encumbered estate was cleared of mortgage to the tune of 180,000 within two years of the plunder of Lucknow.

Much fighting remained before the last sparks of rebellion flickered out in Bengal. Young Fred Roberts rode through the thick of it, winning a Victoria Cross in a wild cavalry charge near Cawnpore, in which Roberts saved a Punjabi cavalryman's life, cut down three rebels, and captured a standard. During the fight, one mutineer pressed his rifle against Roberts and pulled the trigger. The weapon misfired, Roberts' saber didn't, and the young officer was saved to one day become Lord Roberts of Kandahar, Kipling's "Bobs Bahadur," idol and leader of the British army.

Lucknow was again British, and would remain so. And from March 1858 until the end of the British Raj, the ruined residency was the only place outside England where the Union Jack flew twenty-four hours a day. Havelock would have liked that.

Mindful perhaps of Napier's famous punning report on his conquest of Sind (*Peccavi:* ''I have sinned''), somebody invented a similar Latin pun for the doughty Campbell:

Nunc fortunatus sum, it read—''I am in luck now.''

CHAPTER TWENTY-TWO

THE SAVING OF THE RAJ

THE BRITISH VICTORY in Bengal seemed extraordinary even then, a divine judgment, a miracle, an astonishing triumph of a handful of Britons and loyal Sikhs, Gurkhas, and Indian soldiers over a horde of enemies. The rebel sepoys were well trained, after all, British-trained. There was no doubting their courage and fighting ability, either, and they had not only numbers but artillery.

Even without the horde of undisciplined local levies and civilians that swelled their numbers, they usually outnumbered the loyal troops. The British victory was indeed amazing, and there was in truth much to wonder at. But there were also very good reasons for the British success.

First there was the Enfield rifle. In part because of the greased cartridge controversy, many sepoys refused to use anything but the old Brown Bess, a smoothbore badly outclassed by the long-ranged Enfield. Many of the local potentates' troops were armed with primitive matchlocks, weapons even more inferior to British arms.

In the hands of steady troops, the 1852 Enfield was deadly far beyond the range of any smoothbore; there is reliable evidence that British riflemen did much killing at ranges out to five hundred yards. The Enfield was a rugged weapon made on American-built machinery, a percussion cap muzzle loader with three-groove rifling.

195

From a .577 bore, it fired a .55-caliber Minie-type bullet, a lead slug with a plug fitted into its hollow base. The explosion of the powder drove the plug up into its soft lead bullet, expanding the slug so that it engaged the rifling and flew true for hundreds of yards. The Enfield was durable, accurate, and tough, and it became a familiar weapon in the carnage of our own Civil War. Some eight hundred thousand of them were bought by North and South.

Second, there was leadership, probably the most decisive factor in the whole campaign. Prior to the mutiny, no Indian held high rank in the company army; none knew how to handle large bodies of men. The British had no such handicap. There was also a far more subtle British leadership advantage. These Britons *knew* they would win; they never doubted, or at least they never worried about death or defeat.

The Hodsons and Havelocks and Campbells and Robertses remind one a little of our own Farragut at Mobile Bay—"Damn the torpedos," he cried. "Full speed ahead!"—and they would have agreed with him entirely. They were certainly professionals, but they were also thoroughly imbued with a Victorian certainty that they would prevail, that right was with them.

That amazing self-confidence verged on arrogance and infuriated many who met them, but it carried them through astonishing trials with flying colors. It was also part of the wonderful talent for leadership that enabled them to lead and discipline fighting alien races, the quality that welded together units like the Guides and Hodson's Horse.

There is no better example of this Victorian spirit than the exploit of one Major Macdonald, commander of irregular cavalry at a place called Rohini. Macdonald, having tea with two other officers, was attacked by three mutinous cavalrymen armed with swords. The officers beat off these men with chairs, although all three officers were badly hurt.

Macdonald, with his scalp largely cut off, immediately convened a court-martial, at which he prosecuted, tried, and sentenced the men who had attacked him. In the presence of his unit, bordering on full mutiny, he discovered that the men told off to be hangmen would not follow their orders. Nothing daunted, Macdonald calmly hanged the attackers personally, and Rohini remained at peace.

Lastly, there was rage. The murders at Cawnpore had turned already formidable British soldiers into avenging angels. It is hard to understand the fury of those men until you read their letters, dripping with fury and soaked with the lust for revenge. It is a matter of record that the 93d Highlanders charged on at least two occasions with cries of primitive rage. These were not cheers—that was common to British troops—but the snarls of men who were determined on vengeance of the bloodiest kind. Other British troops felt the same way.

Matters of conscience were far clearer to Victorian eyes than they may be to us today; there were few shades of gray in 1857. Many of the British were profoundly devout, which may even have increased their horror of the killings at Cawnpore and elsewhere. Christian pity to the contrary notwithstanding, in the eyes of the British, Cawnpore called for Old Testament vengeance. Those bloody little handprints surely added a lot of extra muscle to the thrust behind the glittering bayonets forged in faraway Sheffield.

CHAPTER TWENTY-THREE

DO YOU SEE THOSE COLORS?

The First Minnesota at Gettysburg

DAN SICKLES HAD blundered, and a lot of men were going to die because of his mistake.

Sickles was a general in the Army of the Potomac, but he was hardly a professional soldier. Instead, he was a veteran of other kinds of wars, a Tammany Hall politician, a flamboyant man who had been a New York congressman, a successful lawyer, and a United States representative. And an assassin. In broad daylight on a Washington street, Sickles shot down a friend, one Philip Key, son of the author of "The Star-Spangled Banner," whose sin was a series of assignations with little Mrs. Sickles.

Sickles was acquitted in a sensational trial, ostensibly on grounds of temporary insanity. In fact, most people agreed that there were, after all, some things a man just could not put up with. Paradoxically, what got Sickles ostracized afterward, and very nearly destroyed his career, was his decision to forgive his wife and restore her to his hearth and bed. That, it appears, was just not done in the society of the day. Shut out of that society, Sickles seized eagerly on the chance for martial glory, and he raised a brigade of infantry on the outbreak of the war. By July 1863 he was a corps commander in the Army of the Potomac.

So Sickles was a political general, albeit a tough and courageous one, and maybe that accounts for his disobedience of orders. On this, the second day of Gettysburg, Sickles' III Corps had been told off to hold the left of the Union line, where the high ground of Cemetery Ridge petered out into rocky draws and little bunches of trees. Down there there wasn't much ridge at all, until you came to the little hills called Big and Little Round Top. On Sickles' right was Winfield Scott Hancock's II Corps, so that flank was safe enough. On Sickles' left was nothing whatever, nothing but thin air, and that was what worried Sickles. He understandably felt a little naked, especially because his two divisions were not strong enough to securely hold both the Round Tops and the rest of his sector as well.

So Dan Sickles worried. Out in front of his line was a little creek called Plum Run, and beyond it, to the west, the ground began to rise, up through a wheat field to a long, flat-topped hill with a peach orchard on it. Just behind the orchard ran the Emmitsburg Road, an almost-straight line from southwest to northeast, and farther west still rose Seminary Ridge.

The hill and orchard were a little higher than Sickles' own line, and he fretted that Rebel artillery up there might make his own position untenable. Perhaps more worrisome, a sort of ravine ran from the orchard off to the southeast toward the Round Tops. If a Confederate force moved down that way and got on the Round Tops, or south of them, it would be on or behind the Union left flank.

And so Sickles tried, unsuccessfully, to get army commander George Meade to ride down and see his problem. The crusty Meade would not come. Stay where I put you, he said bluntly, although he finally agreed to send artillery commander Henry Hunt down to give a second opinion. Hunt stayed a while, while Sickles sent a Maine regiment and Berdan's elite Sharpshooters out west toward the southern end of Seminary Ridge. There Berdan ran into a hornet's nest of Rebels—lots of them—and fell back to warn Sickles that there was big trouble out in front.

Sickles reacted immediately, pushing his whole corps out forward, a half mile or so in advance of the rest of the Federal line. He got men up on the hill with the peach orchard and bent his left back from the orchard, down through the wheat field, ending in the jumble of boulders and brush below Little Round Top, the place men called Devil's Den. The division commander on Sickles' left ran out of troops in a little valley just below the Round Tops, and there was no reserve. Officers of Hancock's II Corps watched Sickles' evolution in amazement and wondered whether they had missed some general order to advance.

Meade, hearing that Sickles had changed front, rode down at about four o'clock to see for himself, and he found Sickles' corps with both its flanks in the air. Meade instantly ordered his errant corps commander to get back where he was supposed to be. In this new position he was leading with his chin. He had no contact with Hancock on his right, and the peach orchard itself was a very vulnerable salient, sticking out to the west like a thumb in the enemy's eye.

It was too late. As the two officers were speaking, an explosive shell came howling in to burst in Sickles' lines, and the fat was in the fire. Forty-six Confederate guns flamed and thundered, drenching the orchard and the troops around it with roundshot. James Longstreet was over there to the west, and he was coming after Sickles. North, up the Union line, more Rebel guns hammered at the Federal artillery along Cemetery Ridge, filling the air with shell fragments, pieces of men's bodies, and jagged chunks of granite tombstone.

Meade knew big trouble when he saw it, and immediately countermanded himself. Stay put, he told Sickles; it's too late to go back. If Sickles tried to fall back now, Longstreet might catch him on the move and destroy him utterly. Better to fight here, and hope for the best. Then Meade galloped hard back up the line to his own headquarters, and there ordered tough regular George Sykes to get his corps down south, and get there quick.

Hunt helped Sickles all he could, sending batteries from the Union artillery reserve galloping down to Sickles' front, unlimbering into position in a little road just behind the peach orchard. The artillery of each side hammered and battered the other, with a good many dead and wounded on both sides, and then everybody along the Union lines looked westward, and there it was.

A long, breathtaking wave of gray infantry was rolling in from the southwest, tipped by a froth of gleaming bayonets, crimson battle flags waving gallantly out in front. It was coming on like Joshua, and the waiting Union soldiers could hear the high, keening howl of the rebel yell. This was John Bell Hood's famous division, and out in front rode Hood himself, that terrible fighter who looked like an Old Testament prophet.

Hood's men struck along the foot of Devil's Den, scouring the little valley at its foot, where a single Union regiment fought like demons before it dissolved under the weight of Hood's attack. In Devil's Den itself the fighting was fragmented; small groups of soldiers fired at each other in a cloud of powder smoke that covered everything. From that point, the Rebels began to roll up Sickles' line, overrunning the guns and scattering the infantry, and there were no reserves to stop them.

Sickles moved units from his right to his threatened left, but they came too late; they were smashed in their turn, and Sickles' whole line began to come unraveled. A Rebel brigade peeled off to the east, over toward Little Round Top, and it began to look like the whole Union left would dissolve and Cemetery Ridge would go, too.

And then George Sykes was there, coming down from the north in the broiling July heat, hurrying as Meade had told him to. One of his units—Strong Vincent's Brigade—went panting up the east side of Little Round Top at the double and went straight into action. Vincent would meet his death on Little Round Top, but he would save the hill and the army, largely through the heroics of Joshua Chamberlain and the astonishing 20th Maine.

But down below Little Round Top there was only chaos. Broken Federal units reeled back from Hood's ferocious assault, and two of Sykes' brigades were pounding into the maelstrom to help. The wheat field was lost to the Rebels, and then Hancock sent a division down into the smoke and took it back again; the division included what remained of the old, bold Irish Brigade, and there were dead men and screaming wounded everywhere.

Sykes' two brigades clung to the ground between the wheat field and the orchard—their division commander told them simply, "Boys, I want you to put in a few licks for Pennsylvania." And Sykes' men went in hard, and there was more killing, and the orchard changed hands six times. But all of it was for nothing, for there were too many Rebels. The Yankee left was now up against the better part of three big Rebel divisions, and the gray soldiers smelled victory and came in hard and fast.

The Confederates hit the peach orchard salient from three sides at once. Barksdale's Mississippi Brigade came in at the dead run, trampling a whole picket fence flat and routing the Union defenders on the other side. The peach orchard was gone.

By now the Union line was a series of fragments, all fighting madly whatever was in front of them, enveloped in a dense cloud of white powder smoke with no idea of what was happening anyplace else. And now, as Rebel bullets began to tear into them from their right and rear, the defenders began to realize that there was no longer any front. As one Union soldier put it to his commander: "Colonel, I'll be damned if I don't think we are faced the wrong way." And they were.

The Union line was collapsing, for all the dying and the desperate valor of Sykes' and Sickles' men. The Confederates were simply rolling it up, from the peach orchard down toward Devil's Den, and men in Union blue were streaming back toward Cemetery Ridge, leaving heaps of dead and wounded behind them. There was a monstrous hole in the Union line, all the way from the left of Hancock's line to the Round Tops. Sickles himself was gone, one leg torn off, smoking a cigar as he was carried from the field.

Farther north, along the line of the Emmitsburg Road, Union troops were pulling back in haste, attacked in front and from their left, where Sickles' people were supposed to be. Men fought on by instinct, often without orders, for officers and noncommissioned officers took hideous casualties, until often there was nobody left to command.

In the 11th New Jersey, for example, both the colonel and the major next in command were shot down in quick succession. The senior captain was killed as he heard that command had passed to him, and the next senior captain was shot immediately; as he was carried from the field, a second bullet killed him, and all four litter bearers were shot down with him. Still another captain was killed, and a corporal found himself commanding all that was left of a very good regiment.

For all practical purposes, there was nothing to close that terrible gap but bits and pieces of broken regiments, nothing between Longstreet and the rear of the Army of the Potomac. The only cohesive resistance came from a line of Union artillery up the slope behind Plum Run, commanded by a very tough Maine gunner, a combative lieutenant colonel named McGilvery. McGilvery built a flaming gun line out of reserve batteries and threw in whatever other fragments he could find to hold the lip of the fiery cauldron where Sickles' corps had been.

For a while, until McGilvery got his guns in line and going, the chief resistance came from a single battery, a green outfit from Massachusetts. Under a shower of artillery fire, with Rebel infantry crowding in all around them, the 9th Massachusetts held, firing triple canister loads in the faces of the enemy, cutting the fuses on shells so they would burst almost at the cannons' muzzles. The 9th lost most of its guns, half of its men, and all of its officers, but it bought McGilvery a little time to unlimber and get his pieces into action.

And so, when the Confederates were past the wreck of the Massachusetts battery, they ran head-on into the concentrated fire of a couple of dozen pieces, firing as fast as the crews could load, tearing gaping holes in the southern ranks. At one point a Rebel regiment got in among the guns, but the gunners drove them out again, swinging rammers and handspikes in the lowering smoke and the coming darkness of evening.

Hancock was everywhere as the evening came down, only one aide left with him, and that one wounded. The general was trying to rally fugitives and put together some kind of line—and not having much luck. The remnants of Sickles' men were simply fought out. They would not turn and face that gray infantry again this day, general or no general. Reinforcements were on the way, but Hancock's need was for troops now, troops to staunch the open wound left by Sickles' destruction.

And so the time of decision had come. If there wasn't much cohesive infantry resistance to the Rebel advance, the gunners were doing a lot of killing and holding their own for the time being. The Confederates were disorganized and tired and thirsty themselves, and there were a great many gray corpses behind them among the blue. Night was coming on, and if the shattered line could hang on only a few minutes longer, help would come, hurrying up from the Federal right and rear.

What the Army of the Potomac needed was a little time.

As the fate of the whole bloody day hung in the balance, General Hancock saw a Confederate infantry brigade heading toward him, emerging from a piece of low ground along Plum Run, a hundred and fifty yards or so away. The Rebs were headed for the fatal gap in the Union lines, and Hancock knew they had to be stopped. Trotting back to his rear, he saw one of his own regiments waiting quietly in line.

It was the 1st Minnesota Volunteer Infantry, a veteran outfit that
had seen most of the worst parts of this war, from the very start at
Bull Run through the terrible butchery of Antietam. The 1st Minnesota had started the day in line a ways to the north, but Hancock
had moved them south, about halfway between Cemetery Ridge and
Little Round Top, to help fill the gap left by Sickles' ill-fated move
out to the west. There they waited, in support of a regular army
artillery battery just north of them.

They lay down to shelter from the roundshot and shell screaming
by them, and watched Sickles' doom unfold, and wondered whether
they would be committed. They were about a half mile east of the
furious fighting in the peach orchard and had a grandstand seat for
the Union disaster unfolding in front of them.

They were understrength, only 262 strong, for three of their companies were detached to other duties. They watched the Confederate
brigades come closer and closer, watched Sickles' battle line come
unstuck. And finally, they watched in shame as hundreds of survivors
of III Corps ran past them in wild retreat.

At first some of the Minnesotans tried to rally a few of the fugitives, but they had no luck. At last they simply watched in horror
the disintegration of the line below them. "I felt that I would prefer
to die there," wrote one Sergeant Plummer,

> rather than live and suffer the disgrace and humiliation a defeat
> of our army would entail on us . . . We all felt bad, but resolved
> when our chance came to do our best to retrieve the fortunes of
> the day, hardly expecting to come out of the conflict unharmed.

Plummer's courageous sentiment was a colossal understatement in
every way, as Plummer was soon to learn.

Down below them the Confederate infantry came steadily on, still
holding their two-line formation, pushing through the smoke with
that wild banshee battle cry men called the rebel yell. They overran
a Federal battery and began to turn it against the remains of the
Federal line, and behind them Rebel guns were limbering up and
moving forward.

As the Minnesotans watched the pitiful wreckage of Sickles' corps
flowing around them, nobody had to tell these veterans that there
was nothing much left between Longstreet and the Union rear . . .

but the 1st Minnesota. Their time was coming, and coming fast. It came in the person of husky Winfield Scott Hancock, a big man on a big horse, his traditional spotless white shirtfront a bright spot in the gathering dusk.

He made straight for them, and one soldier heard the general's surprised exclamation: "My God, are these all the men we have?" But they were, and Hancock knew these veterans would have to do—if they could not hold the Rebels, for a few moments at least, then the day was lost—and so, probably, was the Army of the Potomac and maybe the war, too.

Out in front of the Minnesota column stood its commander, Colonel William Colvill III. Colvill was a lawyer and newspaper publisher back in Red Wing, and he had been the first man to enlist in the Goodhue County volunteer company all the way back in April of '61. Leaping over meeting hall chairs, he had outrun a friend for the honor of being the first name on the list. Elected captain of his company after the quaint custom of the day, he had fought with great gallantry over the next two long, bloody years.

In early May, Colvill had become the fifth colonel of the regiment. He was a big man, clean-shaven except for a luxuriant crop of muttonchop whiskers running down each side of his jaw. When he had taken command, his soldiers were not convinced he had any great military ability. But they liked him, and they would go wherever he led. Now, just two months later, Colvill was about to be tried in the hottest crucible any man could face; he and his veterans were about to find out what sort of steel William Colvill was made of.

Paradoxically, Colvill had been placed in arrest not long before. On the way to Gettysburg, some of his soldiers had disobeyed an order to ford a creek in ranks. Being sensible souls, they had found ways to cross dry-shod, as old soldiers will. You do not, as one of the author's sergeants used to say, have to practice to be miserable. Anyhow, Colvill had been blamed for this mild breach of orders, and this very day he had just been released from arrest and restored to command. He halted his men and looked up at Hancock. The general fixed Colvill with his famous flashing eyes.

"What regiment is this?" asked Hancock, and Colvill told him.

And now Hancock pointed to the Stars and Bars, waving out in front of the advancing southern brigade.

"Do you see those colors?" he asked. Colvill nodded.

"Well, capture them!" roared Hancock, and Colville turned to his men.

"Those colors" belonged to the veteran Alabama brigade of Cadmus Wilcox, out of A. P. Hill's corps, and they were as tough a bunch of scrappers as either army could boast. There were something like sixteen hundred of them, too, and the Rebel guns were firing over their heads at this tiny Union regiment that stood between them and Cemetery Ridge. Colvill, nothing daunted (or at least not showing it), turned to his men.

"Will you go along?" he asked, and the blue ranks roared "Yes!"

Colvill's boys were apparently in line already—"a beautiful line," one survivor remembered. Their long triangular bayonets were already fixed, and they carried their weapons at the "right-shoulder shift," a position like right-shoulder arms, except that the flat side of the stock was against the soldier's body, hammer facing away from him. They were ready, and there was nothing left but to get at the business of dying as well as possible. Colvill turned to his men: "Forward!" he roared. "Double-quick!"

And down the slope they went at a trot, bayonets fixed, jogging straight ahead into the gloom of the dying day, down a shallow incline toward the hollow of Plum Run and the smoke and flame of the Rebel fire. They were a forlorn hope, a lone regiment against a whole brigade, and they took terrible casualties as they ran in toward Wilcox's tough, ragged men, who were firing fast and accurately.

The Alabamians' musket fire knocked men down right and left, and sheets of canister ripped through the thin blue ranks from the Rebel artillery. "It seemed," wrote one Minnesotan, "as if every step was over some fallen comrade." And still they came on, running in an unnerving silence—no cheering, no shouting, no firing, nobody yelling orders. Up ahead there was only dense smoke and twilight gloom, and the flickering sparks of Rebel muzzle flashes. Behind the clouds of smoke glowed the baleful red eye of the dying sun.

At last Colvill bellowed "Charge!" The Minnesotans broke into a run, and those terrible bayonets swung down to the horizontal. Three times the 1st Minnesota's color bearers were hit, and three times other men picked up the precious flag and carried it on into the furnace at the bottom of the hill.

As they closed with the gray ranks at the bottom of the slope, running flat out, the Alabamians fired a terrible volley at no more than thirty yards' distance. More men fell, but what was left of the Minnesotans came in at the run with leveled bayonets, and the Confederates recoiled. Wilcox's men were tired, too, for they had seen much fighting and lost many friends this day. And, as one Minnesotan put it: "The men were never made who will stand against leveled bayonets coming with such momentum and evident desperation."

Not even the dogged veterans from Alabama. As the first Rebel line fell back onto the second, the Minnesotans reached the lip of the hollow and fired for the first time, a murderous volley almost in the faces of Wilcox's men. The Rebels staggered, but then they returned the fire, and for a little time the two lines traded volleys at point-blank range, standing up without cover, madly loading and firing. "But little ammunition is wasted," wrote a Minnesota man, "when the muzzles of opposing guns almost meet."

If the wild Union charge had stopped Wilcox's brigade in its tracks, the southern boys were not through. Sergeant Plummer, loading and firing as fast as he could, still had time to admire his dogged foes.

> . . . what surprised me most was to see some of the rebs, not
> fifty yards from us, standing out openly and loading and firing
> as deliberately as though they were in no danger whatsoever.
> Oh! There is no mistake but what some of those rebs are just
> as brave as it is possible for human beings to be.

As the two battle lines stood and hammered each other in the twilight, their muzzle flashes lighting the gathering darkness, the Rebels began to work around both flanks of the 1st Minnesota, and men began to fall pierced with musketballs from several directions at once. They found what cover they could in the dry bed of Plum Run, but the regiment was wasting away.

This kind of close-range murdering could not last long. There weren't many of the Minnesotans left by now, and they were fighting in little bunches and pairs and even single men hanging on alone. Colvill was out of the fight, hit hard about the time he reached the hollow. His executive officer, Lieutenant Colonel Adams, was also out of action, finally down with a ghastly wound in the lungs after he had staggered on with five less serious wounds.

Two other senior officers had been shot down, and a captain named Messick was commanding the regiment. In the darkness and the smoke and the flame, in the shambles of the creekbed, no man could do much commanding. And so Messick sensibly yelled to his men to find some cover and fire at will, and for a while they kept the Alabamians at bay.

The shallow creekbed was not much protection, for the Rebels had worked around the Union right flank and were pouring Minie-balls down the length of the little watercourse. Part of the 1st Minnesota had faced right to answer their fire. As the Confederate pressure on their right increased, the First's survivors knew it was only a matter of time before the gray infantry would be in their rear as well.

They were simply running out of men and firepower. More than a hundred blue bodies littered the ground on the slope uphill of the dry bed of Plum Run. In the creekbed itself, more men were being hit every minute. The Confederate fire was lethal, even though the twilight was turning to darkness and it was hard to see to shoot.

About then, however, the Minnesotans began to get some help. The redoubtable Lieutenant Colonel McGilvery had seen the Minnesota charge, and he began to sweep the lip of Plum Run with canister, ignoring the Confederate batteries that were pounding his own guns. McGilvery's fire began to rake the brush in which some of Wilcox's men had taken cover, and the Rebels started to take casualties from two directions themselves.

Fifteen minutes into the ferocious fight in the bed of Plum Run, there was almost nothing left of the 1st Minnesota. If they stayed where they were just a few minutes more, nobody would ever get back to Cemetery Ridge. Colvill, crippled by his wound, had still kept his consciousness and his head, and he told a captain to get the men out of that deadly place while there was anybody alive to go.

And so what was left of the regiment began to pull back, a trek that seemed to take forever up that bullet-swept slope to safety. "We dreaded to go back," one sergeant remembered, "for the danger of it, more than staying there." Now, so close to safety, falling back across that pitiless, coverless ground, the sergeant first felt afraid.

The order did not reach everybody at once, and so they straggled back by ones and twos and little groups, helping each other back out of that terrible gully. About fifty men of Company E fell back together, commanded by a sergeant, the sole survivor of all the officers and NCOs in the unit.

They had to leave their dead behind, of course, but men risked their lives to help back many of their wounded friends. Other hurt men hobbled out on their own. And the 1st Minnesota left not a single prisoner for the Rebels, a fact of which the regiment was intensely and justifiably proud—and about which it boasted as long as a single survivor lived.

Some of the last Minnesotans to leave the creekbed even brought a few Rebel prisoners with them and passed on the welcome news that this tough Confederate brigade had fallen back into the night. As one Union officer put it afterward, "What Hancock had given us to do was done thoroughly. The regiment had stopped the enemy . . . and saved the position."

And so it had. The Union line had held, held by the very narrowest of margins, and the 1st Minnesota had done it. But they had paid dearly. They had gone into action that afternoon with 262 men; they had come out of the cauldron with just forty-seven. But they still proudly carried their colors, the talisman of their military manhood, and they had not left a single unwounded soldier behind them in that terrible draw. Their 82 percent casualty rate was the highest butcher's bill for any unit for the entire war, a statistic of which the survivors were perversely but understandably proud.

And after what was left of the regiment rallied up on the ridge in the night, some of them, tired as they were, then went back down to the terrible creekbed and began to search for their wounded. Under the light of a full moon they prowled the heaps of dead and wounded by Plum Run, calling and calling in the warm, humid night.

They searched though many of the men they looked for and called for were past answering, past caring about anything at all. But many men still lived, and one by one the exhausted survivors began to collect them. Colvill was alive, lying there under the stars listening to his men calling for comrades and brothers and other relatives in the darkness. In due course his men found him and carried him carefully back up to Cemetery Ridge.

The searchers found Lieutenant Colonel Adams, too, miraculously alive with his six wounds, and a good many other men who were tough enough to survive their terrible hurts. Many of them would lose legs or arms, but they would live. And they would have memories of

this day that other men would listen to in envy across the years
to come.

Wilcox's Alabama brigade pulled back also. They had taken terrible casualties through the day, and they had no support, although
Wilcox had asked for it. They were tired and disorganized, and Wilcox made the sensible decision to break contact. There were too
many blue soldiers up ahead, plus McGilvery's belching guns. Like
the Minnesotans, the Alabama boys had done damage enough for
one day.

Up north of this witch's kettle, one Confederate brigade actually
got to the top of Cemetery Ridge, capturing some Union cannon
there. But Federal reinforcements came in at the charge, with Meade
himself out in front waving his hat toward the enemy, and Longstreet
had shot his bolt.

The terrible carnage of the second day was about finished at this
end of the line, save for some bickering of pickets in the darkness.
What remained was the terrible task of caring for thousands of
wounded, collecting bewildered stragglers and reorganizing shattered
units. From the northern end of the Union line came the rumble of
heavy firing, and the sky flashed and flickered with the flame of a
major fight around a pimple called Culp's Hill. Up there, men were
still killing each other, struggling in a stygian gloom lit only by the
flare of muzzle flashes. Down this way, it was over.

Here, in the south, there was only the moaning and screaming of
wounded men and horses, the rattle of guns changing front, and the
ceaseless calls of men looking for a comrade in the mess or trying
to find what remained of their regiments.

Weary as they were, the day was not finished for the 1st Minnesota. Once the wounded had been cared for, the pitiful remnant of
the regiment formed up and stumbled north through the darkness,
north along the ridge to the point where they had started the day. And
there they went into position and made themselves as comfortable as
they could, dozing through the night in a fine drizzle, camped among
the dead.

During the night the regiment was reinforced by the return of their
own F Company, which had been detached as skirmishers on another
part of the field. The men of F rejoined the regiment as it lay under
the stars along Cemetery Ridge, and they were horrified to count
only forty-seven comrades left out of all those they had left behind.

As they called to friends in what remained of other companies, they learned the full horror of the "awful calamity that [had] befallen the regiment."

Though they were exhausted and shot to pieces, the surviving veterans of the 1st Minnesota were too experienced to think that the battle was over for them. And it wasn't. As the daylight came on the morning of July 3d, the regiment sent men to the rear to organize coffee and carry it forward onto the ridge. The day got hot early, muggy and unpromising, and a mile or so across the way Robert E. Lee was still there.

As veterans will, the 1st Minnesota hoped for the best and prepared for the worst. They dug in as best they could, turning earth with their bayonets and piling it up with their tin plates onto makeshift barricades of fence rails, rocks, and brush. Their cartridge boxes refilled, their long rifled muskets cleaned, they lay back in the broiling sun and tried to rest. Many slept, as experienced soldiers will do at any opportunity, anywhere at all.

And then, as the broiling day wore on, there was movement over across the way, and finally a lazy puff of white smoke. The whole terrible pageant of Gettysburg's third day began with a single shell, a round from Lee's Washington Artillery. It came howling in and exploded about twenty yards away from a 1st Minnesota lieutenant as he read a Baltimore paper aloud to a group of his soldiers. "That," as one Minnesotan tersely remarked, "stopped the reading," and the regiment hugged Mother Earth like a second skin as the guns of both sides slugged away at each other.

The next two hours were a preview of Hell. It was the worst bombardment any of the regiment's men had ever heard, and it went on and on. For once, a kindly Providence spared the 1st Minnesota, although missiles howled and screamed past them by the dozen. Many of the Rebel gunners were shooting a little high, and the carnage behind the ridge was horrible. The infantry called these overs "quartermaster chasers," and they were killing men and horses in heaps on the reverse slope of the ridge.

If the canny veterans of the regiment hugged the ground, they mightily admired some who didn't. Tough John Gibbon, their division commander, was walking along his line, strolling calmly through the storm of artillery, and it gave his men a world of confidence. As one Minnesotan wrote:

Gen. Gibbons . . . walked along the line in front of us, seeming
to say, Boys, this is the way to face danger. We all noticed it
and many said, See there, see Gen. Gibbons.

And then the southern barrage began to slacken, and the veterans
knew what was coming next. Over across the way there was movement, and then a wonderful long wave of gray soldiers came out of
the distant tree line into the sun and began to roll across the mile-
long field west of Cemetery Ridge. The naked steel of bayonets and
drawn naked sabers winked in the afternoon sun, and behind dozens
of blue-and-crimson battle flags the Army of Northern Virginia was
coming on again.

It was a sight nobody on either side would ever forget, a grand
and terrible army with banners, and it was heading for a little clump
of trees and the corner of a stone wall not far away. If mortal men
could pull it off, the Rebs were going to break a gaping hole in the
Union line, and they aimed to do it just four hundred feet or so to
the right of the 1st Minnesota.

If any soldiers on earth could overrun John Gibbon's tough division, it was the men coming in long, beautiful ranks across that field.
They were Virginia and North Carolina men mostly, maybe the best
infantry there ever was. And pointed right at the little clump of trees
and the wall was Lo Armistead's Virginia brigade, with the general
walking in front, his hat held above his head, perched on the tip of
his drawn saber.

On the gray lines came, taking horrible casualties from the Union
artillery, closing their ranks as roundshot and canister swept men
away in twos and threes and bunches. Admiringly, the First Minnesota watched them come, three lines deep, breaking into the charge
as they closed with the Federal line. The First moved forward a few
paces, about 150 of them in a double line. The front rank knelt, and
waited, listening to their leaders calling "Hold low! Hold low! Shoot
at their feet!" (For the tendency of a soldier firing downhill is to
overshoot.)

And then Captain Messick roared "Fire!" and the 1st Minnesota
cut loose at an angle to their right, shooting at the legs of Rebel
soldiers whose heads and bodies were hidden in the dense white
smoke of their own musketry. Then everybody loaded and fired into
the gray ranks as fast as he could, biting off the end of his cartridge,

ramming it home, cocking the musket and slipping on a fresh percussion cap with hasty, fumbling fingers. Men went down in heaps at the spearhead of the Rebel charge, and the Confederates' return fire began to tear into the Minnesotans.

In the seething cauldron around the angle in the little stone wall, the fight had turned into a primordial brawl. It was a great milling free-for-all of grim, shouting, swearing men, faces stained powder-black like devils, mouths shouting soundlessly in the din, uniforms soaked black with sweat and splattered with other people's blood. And their own.

Nobody much was in command of anything, for the fight had gone far beyond commanding. Those officers who were still on their feet were down in the middle of the melee along with everybody else, shouting to their men and cursing and firing their pistols in the faces of the Rebels. And then an astonishing thing happened.

Apparently without orders anybody could hear, nearby Union outfits began to move down into the devil's foundry below, simply running down into the smoke and dust to help, without plan or purpose except to get into the fight and throw the Rebels out. Men shot each other point-blank, so close that the muzzle blasts set fire to the enemy's clothing. They stabbed each other's guts with bayonets and broke each other's skulls with musket butts. Those who couldn't see to shoot lobbed rocks over the heads of their comrades in front.

The Minnesotans ran down toward the angle with everybody else. Out in front, the last color bearer went down and the staff of their colors was shot in two. Corporal Henry O'Brien snatched up the precious flag and ran straight at the southerners, the rest of the regiment roaring behind him. And when O'Brien fell another corporal seized what was left of the colors and the Minnesotans went to join in the ghastly hand-to-hand brawl at the angle. And there they kept their own tattered flag and captured the colors of the 28th Virginia.

And when it was over, when what was left of the Rebels was falling back across that long, long field, the regiment had lost another fifty men. Half of these were dead or dying, and among those whose luck had run out forever was Captain Messick, come to the end of a long road that led all the way back to the Mexican War.

After Gettysburg the 1st Minnesota soldiered on, losing more men and gaining more honors at Bristow Station in the autumn of 1863.

By then some twelve hundred men had served with the 1st Minnesota; over time half of these had become casualties. The regiment passed into history at the end of April 1864, for its three years were up, and few remained of the original band of patriotic men who had marched south with such high hearts just three years before. Most of the regiment was replacements then, and only enough men reenlisted to fill up two companies. These became part of something called the First Battalion Minnesota Infantry Volunteers, and the old regiment was gone.

Except the memories.

CHAPTER TWENTY-FOUR

A NOTE FROM THE WHITE HOUSE

GENERAL GEORGE B. McClellan had just about every qualification for military success. "Little Mac" was a charismatic commander, and his troops developed a great affection for him. He was a fine trainer, too, and a favorite with the press. They called him "The Young Napoleon," and loved him especially on horseback (he had a penchant for big horses). Trouble was, the Young Napoleon had one fatal flaw: a marked disinclination to close with the enemy and slug it out.

President Lincoln was growing tired of much talk and little result. After the missed opportunities of the Antietam campaign, Lincoln lost all patience with McClellan's excuses for inaction. When McClellan explained away his failure to pursue Lee into Virginia by complaining that his cavalry horses were exhausted (which happened to be largely true), the usually patient Lincoln responded with uncharacteristic asperity.

> War Department
> Washington City
> October 25, 1862

Major General McClellan:

I have just read your dispatch about sore-tongued and fatigued horses. Will you pardon me for asking what the horses of your army have done since the battle of Antietam that fatigues anything?

> A. Lincoln

McClellan was relieved of command the following month.

CHAPTER TWENTY-FIVE

THEY WERE MEN INDEED

The Death of the Shangani Patrol

THERE WAS NO word for "soldier" in the Matabele language. This was so simply because every Matabele male *was* a soldier; young Matabele men had no other ambition in this year 1893, and there was plenty of soldiering to go around.

For the east African Matabele nation had the misfortune to find itself in the way of Cecil Rhodes, the visionary apostle of empire. Rhodes' Imperial British East Africa Company had been founded in 1888, in part to block German encroachment into the vastness of East Africa. In this it had succeeded, but it had also opened the area to farming and mining. The pioneer immigrants, British and Dutch, were right behind.

The Pioneer Column, sponsored by the company, moved into Mashonaland in 1890. The column comprised about four hundred white men, about half settlers and half company police, a well-armed paramilitary force alert for any trouble from the tribes. Along with the column moved its wagons, servants, and stock, and nothing in the world of the Matabele would ever be the same again.

As more and more whites trekked into what was to become Rhodesia, there was less and less land for the Matabele herds and less and less of the freedom of the good old days. Worst of all, there were more and more rules. Other tribes, notably the Mashona, had been the traditional prey of the Matabele. Year in, year out, as one settler wrote,

> The usual practice was to swoop down on the unaware Mashona . . . kill all the men and old women they found, and then carry off the cattle, young women and children. The excuse for the raid was that somebody in that part had offended His Majesty King Lobengula.

But the days of raiding and looting were fading, for the white man wanted peace and order. More threatening still, these British were willing to protect the Mashona, their women, and their herds. Such an infringement on the freedom of the Matabele was intolerable, especially to the young warriors, thirsty to wash their spears.

And so bloodshed was inevitable, or at least it seems so in hindsight. The warrior society of the Matabele was built around a life of movement and fighting, of raiding and killing their less powerful neighbors. The British settlers were miners and ranchers and farmers for the most part, and they needed peace and stability to prosper. In spite of their conflicting interests, however, neither the company nor the Matabele king, a big intelligent man called Lobengula, seem really to have set out to start a war.

The Matabele, like their Zulu cousins, were formidable opponents. They were big and strong and hardy and quick, but that was only half of it. They were also strictly disciplined, trained from birth to obedience and to the art of war. They maneuvered under orders, controlled by experienced officers, and they were consummate masters of cover and concealment.

A young Matabele was called up to military service when his year-group was ready, and in time was assigned to a regiment, a permanent fighting unit of his contemporaries modeled along the Zulu line but a bit smaller. He would stay with that regiment, live his monastic life with it, grow older with it, until at last his king consented to let the regiment marry. In theory no young man might marry until he had proved himself by "washing his spear" deep in the body of an enemy; in practice the king consented after a regiment had undergone years of seasoning.

Then there would be a great taking of wives, and the regiment would get a new kraal big enough for them and their women and the inevitable children. But it would remain a regiment, dedicated to war, renewed and reinforced in the fullness of time by its own children. So for the Matabele man soldiering was life and life was soldiering, and he gloried in it.

For his paramount virtue, his ideal, was *ubuqawe*—"courage." A man was judged by his warlike deeds, by his fighting ability, by the battle scars on his body. Death was infinitely preferable to any hint of cowardice. Like his Zulu relative, he would fight to the death without flinching. His leaders were men of experience and maturity, though there seems to have been no system of permanent small unit leaders, the NCOs who are the glue of every modern army.

The Matabele warrior fought always to close with his enemies, for his weapons were intended for hand-to-hand combat. He was not an archer or slinger, although toward the end of his heyday he obtained and used rifles with some effect. He carried lightweight throwing spears, usually two of them, and sometimes a knobkerrie, a sort of wooden club with a heavy head. This, too, was a short-range throwing weapon.

Even after the Matabele got used to firearms, however, his principal and favorite weapon, like the Zulu's, was the stabbing spear. It was called *usiba* or *isika,* and it had a long, slender blade of between nine and twelve inches mounted on a shaft from three to four feet long. The warrior wielded it overhand, destroying his enemy with a series of ferocious jabs, rather like throwing a javelin without letting go of it.

It was hard to tell *usiba* and *isika* apart. *Isika* was special, however, for it was the king's spear, which by tradition came from the ruler and had to be returned to him when the warrior died. Some warriors carried more than one stabbing spear, clutching the extra one in the left hand along with two or more throwing spears and the warrior's shield.

For while he was puncturing his enemy, the Matabele protected himself with an oxhide shield. He had no other defensive armor, and his shield was his pride, pointed on both ends like an elongated leaf and four or five feet long. A wooden staff ran vertically up the center of it, and the hair side was turned to the enemy. The warrior held it by a small handle, with two fingers.

Because the shield was a prized possession, the making of them was a respected craft in the Matabele villages, involving much soaking, pounding, and steeping in cattle dung. The color of the hide was important, white being the color of great honor, and the distribution of shield hides was at the discretion of the *induna*, the regimental commander, who passed out the finest hides to the best and bravest men.

Matabele tactics resembled those of the Zulu. Their favorite battle drill was the "chest and horns" attack made famous by the Zulu. The "chest" or center fixed the enemy in place while one or both "horns" or wings lapped around his flanks and encircled him. The *impi* ("unit") closed with a rush and destroyed the enemy in an orgy of ferocious hand-to-hand fighting with the stabbing spear.

The chest-and-horns was rehearsed over and over again, so that a regiment could execute it on as little as a hand signal from their *induna*. When possible, the horns deployed from the main body behind a hill or in a fold of ground, so that the enemy was shocked to find the *impi* closing on him from two or three directions at the same time. The evolution could be done by a single regiment or by several regiments together.

By 1893 the Matabele had a long, proud history of conquest behind them, but all of that was about to change. The Matabele had already learned about gunpowder to their cost, having lost many warriors to the rifles of the Boer trekkers. Still, they remained strong and independent, and they had acquired many guns themselves, including a good many modern Martini-Henry rifles. In spite of all their courage and all their confidence, however, they would soon encounter two forces much stronger and more lethal than anything they had faced before.

They were going to clash head-on with Cecil Rhodes' British South African Company . . . and they were about to meet the machine gun.

Lobengula had accepted a sort of boundary between his home country and the area settled by the British. This agreement, however, cut the Matabele off from their favorite raiding areas. The young warriors were angry and restless, for they had been deprived of the traditional rite of passage to manhood, the washing of their spears. Lobengula's rivals within the tribe conspired and whispered against him, and trouble was sure to come.

It first came late in 1892, when somebody began to cut the newly completed telegraph line between Salisbury and Cape Town. The Mashona seem to have been the culprits, hacking out chunks of wire from which to make bracelets and such. Or perhaps it was the Matabele—or maybe it was both. In any case, the company protested to Lobengula, who said he would deal with the problem.

That did not stop the wire cutting, however, and in time a further dispute arose over cattle given in payment for the wire (or seized by the company). This incident, too, was smoothed over, and peace continued. But in June a small Matabele *impi* raided native villages within ten miles of Fort Victoria, allegedly to punish the theft of the king's cattle. A small force of whites pursued and scattered the *impi,* and quiet returned . . . for a little while.

Real trouble arrived in July 1893, when an arrogant royal messenger, chafing against the king's restraint, exceeded Lobengula's orders and permitted the *impi* under his control to raid and ravage in and near the area settled by the whites. Some of these Matabele chased other blacks clear into the town of Victoria, stabbing them to death in the streets. Fires lit the night sky as Mashona kraals burned in all directions.

The white areas were flooded with panicked Mashona refugees fleeing from the Matabele, and these people and their stock were given shelter by the whites. This in turn infuriated Lobengula, who unwisely said that had he known his enemies would be protected he would have directed attacks on the whites themselves. Many Mashona were killed or kidnapped, and one British clergyman's comment spoke for most of the colonists. It was, he wrote:

> a sickening sight to see the number of human beings lying dead
> on all sides, mutilated by the Matabele . . . no Christian people
> can simply fold their hands and allow hundreds of their fellow
> creatures to be murdered wholesale.

Company police and volunteer units like the Victoria Rangers gathered, and the Cape Colony's Bechuanaland Border Police were alerted. Very short of horses, the British sent agents into the Transvaal to buy more. It was clear to everybody that the whole affair had gone far beyond talking. Words, stern or kind, were not going to change the old, aggressive ways of the warlike Matabele.

And so both sides were pulled into a bitter war, a war that neither side really wanted, except perhaps the young Matabele warriors. It was a war that could have only one outcome. For if the Matabele had the numbers on their side, the British had the firepower, and a courage to match the dogged bravery of the Matabele.

The British troops were local men by and large, members of the company's paramilitary police force plus local militia units and a number of volunteers. Most of these men were British, but some were Dutch and French Huguenot South Africans, mixed with a few men of other nationalities, for eastern Africa was still a frontier land, a land of opportunity that attracted the brave and the adventurous.

When they were not soldiering, some of these men were farmers, some ranchers, some miners. Some were hunters, like famed big-game man F. C. Selous. Some were simply adventurers, like American Frank Burnham, sometime scout in campaigns against the Indians in his own country.

Many of these men had been soldiers, and many had fighting experience against other tribes, in particular the pugnacious Zulus. Most were first-class riflemen and horsemen, some were expert trackers, and their leaders were, as a rule, able and daring officers. They took to discipline easily and could live roughly and move quickly.

They were the ideal instrument to combat the swift and disciplined Matabele. And, important for the company, they came cheap. They worked for nothing, in fact, but they were promised substantial land grants, the right to stake twenty gold claims, and a share of such cattle and other loot as might be taken.

The first big fight came at a place called Bonko early in the morning of October 25, when several regiments—about thirty-five hundred men—charged the night laager of a British column. Coming in fast, on the double, they ran head-on into accurate rifle fire and the murderous hail of seven machine guns and a light fieldpiece. By the time the sun was fully up the fight was over, and the Matabele had lost five or six hundred men. The British losses did not exceed sixty, mostly Mashona tribesmen.

The defeat was a terrible blow to Matabele spirit. Not only had they failed even to come to grips with their enemy, they had not even made him hesitate. Once the fighting was over and the battlefield cleared, the British column saddled up and marched off on its way—into Matabele territory. For all their courage, the confidence of the Matabele was shaken.

Bonko was followed quickly by the pivotal fight of the war, Ego-dade. King Lobengula had managed to gather an *impi* of some six thousand warriors. At least two thousand of his men carried firearms in addition to their traditional weapons, and about half of these were modern Martinis. Thus, in both overall numbers and in rifle power, Lobengula's men outnumbered the British column, which contained fewer than seven hundred men.

The British approached in two parallel columns two hundred yards apart, about twenty wagons in each. They were covered by some four hundred mounted troopers, and between the wagons flowed a river of oxen, three or four thousand of them driven by native herds-men. The waiting Matabele watched as the column went into camp in two separate laagers about a hundred yards apart on either side of a small native kraal. The white men began to cook their midday meal, sending their oxen and most of their horses to water and graze almost a mile away. It seemed a heaven-sent chance to the Matabele, a chance to strike hard while the Englishmen dozed.

But the Englishmen were not dozing.

The *impi* first learned their foe was alert when one regiment ap-peared on some high ground some twenty-five hundred yards from the British only to be greeted by seven-pound cannon shells lobbed into their midst. The warriors cleared quickly off to find cover in the rolling grassland. But they kept coming.

By this time the British had succeeded in driving their horse and ox herds back into their laagers, and their bugles sounded "pickets retire," calling their outposts back to the main body. They no longer wondered where Lobengula's main force was, if they had ever lost track of it. It was on its way toward them, rolling across the veldt in long, disciplined black waves.

Contrary to their long-cherished battle drill, on this occasion the Matabele seemed to have advanced slowly, firing steadily into the British wagon laager. Small groups of them would band together and rush the British, only to melt away before the white men's steady rifle fire, and the hammer of those terrible machine guns. The Mata-bele fell in heaps, leaving piles of dead in the wake of their advance and going nowhere. Their disciplined formation began to unravel, until they were fighting in bunches and gaggles, coming on "in the shape of a lot of locusts," as one English soldier observed.

By about two in the afternoon it was all over. Matabele casualties were somewhere between one and two thousand, and again British losses had been tiny. For many years afterward the bones and skulls of Lobengula's soldiers littered the grassy swales where the Matabele had fought so well and so hopelessly. Their swift retreat left them no time even to pick up the shields and treasured king's spears of the dead.

Worst of all, perhaps, they had again failed to come to grips with their enemy, and their own rifle fire, from which much had been expected, had been largely ineffective. Nothing, it seemed, could stop the remorseless advance of these deadly white men, covered by the terrible fire of the Maxim guns and the little cannon.

Nothing would. As long as they were careful, and they were, the settlers' columns could go wherever they wanted, burning kraals and crops. The Matabele could kill a few at immense cost to themselves, but in the end the result was foreordained. In time, hunger and misery would force surrender. Lobengula saw it clearly, and so he loaded his wives and his treasure into wagons and began to move his whole household north from his capital at Bulawayo, hoping against hope for some success against the whites, waiting for news.

But the news was all bad. It was news of the defeat and the terrible losses at Egodade. And as the king moved into the fever-ridden forests of the north, his bodyguard was joined by remnants and pieces of his defeated regiments, and a few relatively unblooded regiments as well. There was much grumbling, and soon bitter quarrels broke out between those who had seen much fighting and those who had not.

In the end many of Lobengula's men simply went home. Others, tired or sick or wounded, drifted away, some to die in the bush. Only a very few rejoined the king. And so, by the time the king's entourage had reached the banks of the Shangani River, his force was much reduced. Lobengula was tired and discouraged, too, and ill to boot: he suffered from an acute case of gout, which must have made traveling an agony. Lobengula was running out of options, for a small British column was not far behind him. It had fewer than 160 men, but it carried two Maxim guns.

On the north bank of the Shangani the king stopped, and his men threw up *scherms*—cattle enclosures—and wooden fences around Lobengula's wagons. And there the king took counsel with his advisers and captains. There was general agreement that further fighting was futile; too many warriors had been killed already. Lobengula decided to put an end to the war; he would surrender and negotiate the best peace he could.

Now the real tragedy began. Lobengula composed a letter to Dr. Jameson, the manager of the East African Company, and Cecil Rhodes' executive. In it he offered peace, and he included with it a bag of gold sovereigns, perhaps as many as a thousand pounds' worth, as an offering to Jameson himself. Letter and sovereigns were given to two dependable messengers, and these men set off to find an appropriate British officer or official.

What they found was two troopers, stragglers named Daniel and Wilson, whose eyes were dazzled by the shiny gold. The two men accepted both sovereigns and letter, but they kept the gold and disposed of the letter that might have ended the war. They told nobody of Lobengula's offer, not even their own officers, let alone Dr. Jameson.

Much later the story came out, and the British sent both men to prison. But now their avarice was about to cause the deaths of a good many brave men. And for nothing. So the stage was set for one more battle before peace came to Matabeleland, a storied fight that did great credit to both sides in this sad little war.

Forbes, the leader of the British column following Lobengula, was surrounded by great danger and knew it. All around him, on the south side of the river, were Matabele warriors, perhaps as many as three thousand. In the afternoon of December 3 he pulled his tiny force into a defensive perimeter on the banks of the Shangani and considered his next move.

Forbes knew that the heart and soul of the Matabele nation was its king. For all the dissension within the ruling classes of the tribe, the ordinary warrior revered his sovereign and would cheerfully die for him. The British commander knew these things, and knew that the king's capture or death might well put an end to the war. Accordingly, in spite of his own parlous situation, he decided to try to capture the fleeing king. Forbes correctly reasoned that Lobengula had crossed the Shangani toward the north; he incorrectly believed that the king had no more than a hundred fighting men around him.

And so Forbes sent a column splashing across the rising Shangani in the driving rain. It was a tiny force of fifteen troopers under Major Allan Wilson, an experienced, daring officer who spoke Zulu fluently and was an expert tracker. Wilson was a tall, handsome man with a thick mustache, popular with everybody who knew him, the sort of man who was the life of noisy drinking parties in that mostly male frontier world, even though he touched nothing more potent than ginger ale. He was a good leader, easygoing and calm, and men would follow him anywhere.

Riding with the raiders were two Americans, Pearl Ingram and Frank Burnham, the storied soldier of fortune. Burnham's story is one of the few surviving accounts of what happened to the Shangani patrol.

Once he had crossed the Shangani, Wilson's men began to encounter more and more Matabele. The day was dying, and as the darkness came on cooking fires began to spring up in the gloom, little red eyes in the night; there were a great many of them, and Wilson realized his tiny company was in the middle of a huge host of Matabele, outnumbering him many times. Still he pushed on, calling repeatedly to the startled warriors: "Put down your guns! The war is over! We want your king to meet our *induna*. Where is your king?"

All around them in the dark Wilson's men could hear the cocking of rifles, but nobody shot. One young warrior pointed the way to Lobengula's camp, and Wilson called to him: "Run on; we will follow you." Aside, he said softly to Burnham, "If he misleads us, shoot him."

But the warrior took Wilson straight to Lobengula's wagons, tucked away in an open glade, and enclosed by a little stockade of *mapami* wood. At every step they heard more gunlocks snicking around them in the night, but still nobody fired. Behind them masses of warriors gathered in the gloom, and Wilson's troopers could hear much stirring and shouting, much movement in the bush and trees. Above Wilson's men the pitch-black sky flashed and flickered with lightning, and thunder grumbled in the distance.

"The king is here," said their guide, but the wagons and the little stockade were silent. There were no fires. Still, Wilson tried, calling out in the night to Lobengula, using his honorific titles. "We are your escort to Bulawayo," he called, "where we shall make peace." But there was no answer, only more movement behind the column, more cocking of rifles, more shouting in the darkness.

Wilson now took his men deep into the trees. By then it was so dark that Burnham carried a white handkerchief as a marker to the men behind him. They kept moving until they reached a good-sized open glade, where they halted around a huge anthill to take counsel. As the rain came down harder and harder, the men moved under the fringe of the surrounding trees. They could sense the death all around them in the night.

Wilson called his officers around him, to talk in urgent low voices in the gloom. "We want to bring Lobengula in peacefully if possible," said Wilson. "If that doesn't work, our orders are to watch him until Forbes shows up with the rest of the column and the machine guns." And then Wilson sent a captain named Napier and two troopers off south to find Forbes. Napier was to urge Forbes to come quickly and bring the Maxims. Remove them from their carriages if need be, the message said, but bring them "at all costs."

One trooper pulled off his boot and felt across the sodden ground with his bare foot. When he found what he sought—the track of Lobengula's wagon—Napier and the other trooper, leading the horses, followed him south into the darkness, as he tracked by feel the way back toward the crossing of the Shangani. At the river, the trio remounted, plunged in, and fought their way across the swollen stream to find Forbes.

Historians have wondered why Wilson did not bring his whole patrol back across the Shangani. Wilson was a good soldier, and he had no illusions about the odds against him. Part of the answer is that he knew the power of the machine gun and must have thought that with them and the whole patrol it might be possible to defeat or overawe Lobengula's remaining warriors. Probably more to the point, three of Wilson's men were missing, and he would not abandon them.

And so Wilson took his little patrol back toward Lobengula's stockade. Out in front, Burnham led, feeling with his hands for the horseshoe prints in the damp ground. Wilson followed, leading both their horses, commenting coolly, "I want to see how you Yankees work."

Deep in the night, Wilson found his lost troopers, and the patrol settled down near the giant anthill to snatch what sleep they could in the rain. In a very little while Wilson waked Burnham, sure that he had heard something around them in the gloom. He had. Burnham, moving a little away from the bivouac, heard it clearly: it was the soft sound of a great many barefooted men moving in the night.

They were moving south, toward the river, where they would be between the patrol and Forbes.

Still, just before dawn, Burnham greeted a column of horsemen in the darkness and was answered in English. But it was not the column they had waited for. They were just twenty-two men under a captain named Borrow, and there were no machine guns with them. With daylight not far away, wrote Burnham later, "all of us who had ridden through the great camps and spent the night in the bush knew that the end had come."

Still, nobody panicked. Wilson called his officers together and asked what they thought the best move was. Burnham recorded their words:

"There is no best move," said Captain Kirton, sardonically.

Captain Fitzgerald agreed: "We are in a hell of a fix. There is only one thing to do—cut our way out."

Captain Borrow agreed: "We came in through a big regiment. Let's do as Fitzgerald says, though none of us will ever get through."

The experienced Wilson had no illusions. They would never reach the river, he reasoned. They might as well do as much damage to the enemy as they could before they died, and so he gave his orders. The column would try to find Lobengula, his royal bodyguard, and his *indunas,* his council; "and if we don't get him, at least we will try to kill his leaders and save our men in Bulawayo."

And so the patrol moved out. As they approached Lobengula's stockade in the first wan daylight, they found lines of warriors in front of it. The British column rode calmly through them in silence until they again faced the stockade. There Wilson again summoned Lobengula to surrender and was met only by silence, for the king was not there. Instead, an *induna* shouted "We are here to fight!" and fired on the patrol; and at that, all hell broke loose.

The patrol was being fired on by hundreds of rifles from all sides, and some warriors began to run toward the troopers, stabbing spears poised in their hands. One huge *induna* ran toward Burnham, shouting to other warriors *"Buya quasi!* [Come and stab!]" He fired and missed, and as he raised his stabbing spear Burnham fired his Martini one-handed, and the big .45-caliber bullet knocked the Matabele leader down, mortally wounded.

Wilson had no recourse but to fall back. Although his men miraculously suffered no casualties in the first firing, two horses were down, and one trooper ran in to cut loose the saddle pockets filled with rifle ammunition. They would need every round. Firing steadily, Wilson's men fell back to the great anthill, some twenty feet high. It was wide enough to give some shelter to the horses, and as good a place as any to make a stand.

All around them guns flamed and crashed from the forest. As one patrol member put it, "a thousand rifles and muzzle-loaders cut loose at us wildly from the timber," and he does not seem to have exaggerated. Even as men began to fall from this hail of bullets, Wilson and his men kept their marvelous British calm. When one slug knocked Burnham's rifle from his hand, a British officer handed it back to him with a smile: "Burnham, I think you lost something."

Wilson was still on his feet, even though he had climbed to the top of the anthill, where he stood directing his men. "Don't waste your shots," he called. "Pick your man." Dozens of Matabele went down before that terrible rifle fire, but Wilson quickly realized his men could not stay where they were and gave the order to fall back. Firing steadily, the patrol fell back toward the open glade where they had spent so much of the previous night.

At this point Wilson sent Burnham, Ingram, and a trooper named Gooding galloping back to the river in search of help. The mission looked suicidal, but death was everywhere, and the three men plunged back toward the Shangani, pushing their exhausted horses through thick scrub, pursued by hundreds of warriors. They had found a thin spot in the Matabele lines, however, and by doubling back over their tracks they managed to lose their pursuers.

Behind them they heard a roar of firing from the glade where Wilson had chosen to make his stand. Up ahead, across the Shangani, came the unmistakable hammer of Maxim guns: Forbes was also under attack. Burnham and his companions pushed their sagging horses into the river and fought their way across against the flood, finally making the south bank far downstream. They pushed on to join Forbes, kicking the "last little gallop" out of their mounts through a scattering of Matabele rifle fire.

Back across the Shangani, Wilson's men fought on, thirty-three against a thousand or more. As their horses were shot down the troopers took cover behind them. One of the white men, according to Matabele memory, never took cover, but remained on his feet throughout the fight: that could only have been Wilson, standing to see his enemies' movements better. A hail of bullets poured into the circle of British troopers from all directions, and one by one they died.

The fight could not last long. However hard the British tried to hoard their ammunition, each man had begun the day with no more than a hundred rounds for the Martinis and perhaps twenty revolver bullets. They had found some ammunition at Lobengula's stockade, but it could not have been much. For a while, though, Wilson's men held the Matabele at bay, and the roar of firing could be heard by Forbes' embattled men clear across the Shangani.

As the cartridges for the Martini-Henrys began to run out, the survivors fought on with their revolvers, until at last just seven men remained alive. And these few, according to Matabele legend, stood up together, took off their hats, and sang "God Save the Queen," or perhaps it was a hymn. The few remaining troopers then shook hands with one another and waited in silence.

One tale of Wilson's patrol says Wilson was the last to die, fighting from an anthill with a revolver in each hand. Maybe so, for another Matabele account says a single Englishman remained standing at the end. And then a final rush of Matabele closed over the patrol, and any man still living died under the spears. A few prayed at the end, one Matabele said, or covered their eyes with their hands.

It was over. Lobengula's men had killed without remorse, but they were deeply impressed by the courage of Wilson's men. This was the sort of *ubuqawe* they understood. And so, as a gesture of great respect, the warriors treated the bodies of the British as they treated their own dead: they were stripped, piled together and covered with a cairn of rocks. There they would lie until the next February.

And the Matabele had some three hundred of their own dead to attend to, for Wilson's men had sold their lives very dearly indeed. As one warrior admiringly put it:

We lost many more than the number of white men, for they were men indeed, and fought us for many hours.

Another story says that many of the gallant men with Wilson were very young. Standing over the bodies of their foes, the Matabele said:

These are but boys. If *umfaans* [children] can fight like this,
what will we do when the bearded men come to avenge them?

Then, certain that their good-faith peace offer had been rejected,
the Matabele moved west down the Shangani and turned north toward
the far Zambezi, trying to skirt the terrible forest infested with tsetse
fly, headed for what is today Malawi. Lobengula was safely ahead
of them, on the road to safety. Still harried by the Matabele rear
guard, the British did not follow.

Along the way Lobengula's people suffered terribly from both
smallpox and malaria, and in mid-January of 1894 Lobengula died.
Officially he died of smallpox, but a story persists among the Matabele that he committed suicide. He is buried today on the edge of the
Zambezi valley, and his grave is protected as a national monument.

Later in the year a British party traveled to the place of the fight
to bury what remained of Wilson and his men. Near their grave grew
a large mopani tree, and deep in the bark of the tree the British
carved a large cross and the simple legend "To Brave Men."

It applied to both sides.

CHAPTER TWENTY-SIX

THE BOOTY OF BERLIN

ANDREAS HADIK WAS Hungarian, a hussar general in the Austrian army, the very picture of the dashing cavalry officer. In 1757 his country was locked in combat with Frederick the Great's Prussia in the long conflict called the Seven Years' War. And in that year Hadik had a chance to live the cavalry officer's great dream, a daring raid deep into the enemy's country.

Frederick, outnumbered as always, was concentrated west of the Elbe River, moving against the French. Prussia was virtually denuded of troops. From Saxony, where Hadik lay with his units, an enterprising officer might thrust into the very heart of Frederick's domain: Berlin. Any strike would have to be lightning-quick, for Frederick would react speedily; if he caught up to the raiders, they would never see home again.

Hadik got his orders, and on October 10 he set out to the west. Behind him force-marched some three thousand Austrian troops, a mixture of horse, foot, and guns. About half of the raiding force was Hadik's own daredevil hussars. He moved fast, as he knew he must, marching 150 kilometers in less than five days, and Berlin could not resist him. Angry, afraid, embarrassed, the Berliners surrendered— and began to collect the loot Hadik demanded.

Hadik did not tarry. Frederick had found out about the raid quickly, and by the fourteenth help was on the way, help that included some of Frederick's crack cavalry. Hadik did not wait for it. He was encumbered with 425 Prussian prisoners, sacks full of more than 200,000 silver thalers, and the tribute he had levied on the people of Berlin. But by dint of hard marching and a good deal of luck, Hadik reached friendly lines ahead of Frederick's pursuit.

Hadik's raid had been a clever coup; the dashing hussar became a count in honor of his exploit. But the Berliners had the last laugh. Back inside the Austrian lines Hadik's men finally examined the thousands of pairs of gloves they had extorted from Prussia's capital as the price of ransom.

They were all left-handed.

CHAPTER TWENTY-SEVEN

NO MORE WATER

Hicks Pasha and the Kordofan Disaster

THE YEAR WAS 1883, and grim tidings filtered down the broad Nile from the heart of the backward wastes of the Sudan, tales of revolt and massacre and bloody murder in the holy name of God. For the Nile's life-giving waters were laced thickly with blood in these days. Ugly and terrifying things were happening far to the south of ancient Cairo, far, far across the cataracts of the river and the blistering deserts to east and west.

The Egyptian government, still in form an arm of the Sublime Porte, the Turkish government, was helpless. It proclaimed and declaimed, but did not act, knowing full well its officials were largely corrupt, its army venal and vicious and undependable. The Sudan, long tottering on the verge of anarchy, was a benighted, graceless place where life was cheap and the government's writ did not run beyond rifle range. And now things were even worse.

For the Moslems of the Sudan had found a savior, and the whole desolate region was aflame. He was one Mohammed Ahmed, once an apprentice boatbuilder from Dongola, later a religious leader, now the self-proclaimed Mahdi, the Expected One. He had declared his holy mission in August of 1881, and for those who wished to see them, all the signs were there.

234

His age and name were the same as that of the Prophet when he declared his mission, and his mother and father bore the names of the Prophet's parents as well. Between his front teeth appeared the *falja*, the V-shaped gap that meant good luck. His mission was to expel the hated Turk from the Sudan and then to carry the banners of Islam over the earth, killing all who opposed him. He proclaimed it and the Arabs believed.

And he was welcomed, not only by the ignorant, devout tribesmen, but by men moved by less elevated motives . . . the Arab slavers. For they had been deprived of their livelihood by this selfsame Egyptian government, whose instrument had been the charismatic, enigmatic British soldier Charles George Gordon, better known to history as Chinese Gordon.

Gordon had come to the Sudan in 1874—first as governor of a single province, later as governor of the entire vast region—with a reputation already made as a man who could deal with trouble in strange places. For Gordon had commanded the Ever-Victorious Army in China of the Manchus, and he had put down the most dangerous threat to the throne in centuries, the Tai-Ping Rebellion. He had come to the Sudan armed with little more than his reputation and a profound Christian religious faith. And he achieved prodigies.

For in only five years Gordon had destroyed the slave trade root and branch, terrorizing corrupt Egyptian officials, freeing miserable columns of chained black prisoners, shooting and hanging when he had to. In a single mass hanging he had executed the son of the Sudan's leading slaver and eleven of his lieutenants. Gordon was fearless, a father to the desperate poor enslaved by Arab masters and a scourge to their oppressors. His memory would long be green among the exploited black people of the Sudan.

But Gordon Pasha was gone from the Sudan, and the old corruption and oppression had immediately returned. The Egyptian officials were lazy and venal, the people again exploited and miserable. The whole region was a powder keg—and Mohammed Ahmed, the Mahdi, became the spark.

It started in a small way. Gordon's successor, an inept oaf named Raouf Pasha, made a halfhearted attempt to extinguish this new Mahdi early in his career, and the whole thing misfired. Raouf sent an officer and part-time slaver named Abu Saud to Abba, an island in the White Nile, to capture and bring back this religious upstart.

Abu sailed out to Abba on a cannon-armed steamer, taking with him two companies of Egyptian troops.

The soldiers were armed with the excellent Remington rolling-block rifle. The Remington was a splendid military weapon, hard to hurt and capable of destructive rapid fire in trained hands. The infantry and their Remingtons should have been more than enough, except that the soldiers had no heart inside them and were commanded in the usual shoddy Egyptian fashion of absentee leadership. Abu prudently remained in relative comfort on board his steamer, issuing no orders except to promise promotion to whichever company commander actually captured the Mahdi.

The two companies went ashore in the hot and humid night of August 12, 1881, and from that night one may date the explosion that would rip the Sudan to pieces. For Abu's troops wandered carelessly into an ambush, suddenly overrun in the dark by Mohammed's ragged followers, armed with spears and clubs and rocks.

The Egyptians left six officers and 120 other ranks dead on the island, a few survivors braving the current and the crocodiles to reach safety on the steamer. They also left behind their excellent Remingtons, the first of thousands the Egyptian army would donate to the Mahdi. It was an auspicious beginning for the movement Mohammed said would sweep the world.

Abu Saud cowered on the steamer, too afraid even to shell the Mahdi's little band with the steamer's cannon. On the island, the faithful celebrated around huge fires, and the few Egyptian captives kissed the Mahdi's feet and swore their allegiance to him as the Prophet's vicar on earth. The word of the Egyptian defeat would be carried across the Sudan almost overnight.

The fire spread. New recruits appeared in thousands, many of them experienced fighting men from the bands of discontented ex-slavers. Now the Mahdi's followers began to strike at isolated Egyptian units and province officials. These people, unreliable at the best of times, fled when they could and died when they were not quick enough. In December the revolt escalated, when the Mahdi destroyed a fourteen-hundred-man Egyptian force near Fashoda, hundreds of miles south of Khartoum, where the White Nile of high Africa joined the Blue Nile out of Ethiopia.

All these things were eons away from the government in Cairo, but even that slothful regime could tell that a bad situation was turning very rotten indeed. For the Mahdi's movement was spreading like the plague into Darfur, west of the river, and even to the town of Sennar, a couple of hundred miles up the Blue Nile toward medieval Ethiopia. A year after the revolt began, four thousand Egyptian troops were extinguished in south Kordofan, much nearer Khartoum. It was coming closer.

It was at about this time that an Egyptian officer named Ahmed Arabi Bey led a revolt against the somnolent, corrupt government of his native land. The khedive, the Turkish governor, was almost helpless, but the need for public order and the danger to the safety of some ninety thousand Europeans in Egypt had led to intervention by Britain and France.

Had Arabi compromised at this time and sworn allegiance to the khedive, he might have remained the power behind the government and led his country to a new day. But he overplayed his hand and remained intransigent. With that, the outbreak of a riot in which some fifty Europeans were murdered, and the general disintegration of public order, the European powers decided they had only one recourse. The result was invasion by British troops and the rout of the Egyptian army.

And so, neglected, the situation far to the south fell further into chaos. In September the Mahdi struck at El Obeid, the principal town of the western Sudan, the trade center of Kordofan. Repulsed by the Remingtons of the garrison, the Mahdi's people simply starved the town into submission, and in January 1883 it fell amid hideous scenes of torture and death.

The Mahdi's forces were now close to great Khartoum, and the little Egyptian garrisons, everywhere isolated, began to vanish without trace. With the fall of El Obeid all Kordofan was open to the Chosen One and his fanatic followers. And in the process the Mahdi acquired six thousand Remington rifles and five excellent Krupp artillery pieces to add to the ordnance he had looted from the other overrun Egyptian garrisons. He even formed a special unit of captured Sudanese soldiers—the *jihadiya*—an elite force experienced in the use of the captured rifles.

The Mahdi was by then all-powerful through most of the Sudan. He prescribed the most stringent rules of behavior for his followers, punishing such dreadful offenses as blasphemy by death, flogging fornicators, and separating adulterers from their heads. Drinking and

smoking called for public whipping. The Mahdi himself made do
with an enormous harem and drank his favorite tipple—date syrup
and ginger—from silver vessels, the booty of the sacked Catholic
mission at El Obeid.

The Egyptian government and its British advisers heard clearly the
calls for help from the south, but there was little they could do.
Britain intended to restore order in Egypt and then go home, and
anyway the Egyptian army had been disbanded after the defeat of
Arabi's rebels. But the government did send an English officer
upriver to report on the extent of the danger. The man chosen was
Lieutenant Colonel J. D. H. Stewart of the 11th Hussars, a first-class
professional whom Lord Kitchener called "the finest soldier I have
ever met."

Stewart minced no words. His matter-of-fact report was an appalling shock to the bureaucrats in Cairo. Professional that he was, he
saw clearly the extent of the developing disaster. Disgusted by the
indiscipline and unreliability of the Egyptian garrisons, he spoke
plainly of the military incompetence he had seen.

> Besides the gross ignorance of the Egyptian officers, nothing is
> more striking than their want of initiative . . . the officers are so
> ignorant, and so incapable of grasping the meaning of the simplest
> movement. Quite one-third of the troops are also ignorant of the
> use of the rifle, and they would be more formidable adversaries
> were they simply armed with sticks . . .

And Cairo finally acted. It was too little and too late, but at least
it was a beginning. Some ten thousand men of the old Egyptian army
were recalled to duty and sent south to defend the Sudan. They were
a wretched lot, some of whom had to be marched in chains to ensure
their arrival. Two of them threw lime in their own eyes, hoping to
avoid service in the Sudan by blinding themselves. One of their
British officers—Colonel J. Colborne—was advised by officers of his
regiment, the King's Royal Rifle Corps, to get himself a good, fast
horse. It was good counsel.

But at least some attempt was made to ensure that this demoralized
mob was professionally led. The Egyptian government hired Colonel
William Hicks, a retired officer of the Indian army, gave him a
handful of other British officers, and sent him into the Sudan as chief

of staff to the Egyptian commander of this rabble, one Suliman Pasha. It was emphasized, however, that Hicks and his officers were employed by the Egyptian goverment; Britain was sticking to her official policy of avoiding direct interference in Egyptian affairs.

Hicks, fifty-three, was not known as a brilliant soldier. He was experienced, however, having served thirty-four years in India, including the desperate days of the mutiny. If he was not a well-known military intellectual, he certainly was one of that solid class in which the Victorian military services were so rich: the stand-or-die, spit-in-your eye (genteelly) fighting officer. Hicks' kind of dogged courage and dedication had won many a field for Britain. Perhaps it could work another miracle in the Sudan.

As "reinforcements" arrived in the Sudan—their arms were thoughtfully shipped separately—a training program was begun. Hicks tried to weld this unpromising mass of reluctant humanity into an army. He could depend on his few British officers, at least, and he would have plenty of firepower if the troops could be induced to stand and fight. Besides the Remingtons, Hicks had some Krupp howitzers, some crank-fired Nordenfeldt machine guns, and even some rocket batteries. But the first drills were not promising.

> When the guns were attempted to be brought into action, dire confusion reigned. Men ran against each other; the ground was strewn with cartridges . . . No one appeared to have the slightest knowledge of how to feed, aim, or discharge the pieces.

The appalled British captain trying to organize this wretched mess worked so long and hard in the blasting sun that he was felled by sunstroke and sent downriver to Cairo to recuperate. He was one of the lucky ones.

It was also soon discovered that the Egyptians were unwilling to push out outposts to warn of the enemy's approach—because, as an Egyptian officer simply put it, "the men might get killed." With that sort of attitude endemic in the army, it took great effort to get soldiers to go on outpost duty, and once there to remain.

In addition to general Egyptian apathy and incompetence, Hicks was plagued by endless disorder among his irregular cavalry, the Bashi-Bazouks, a vicious lot of thieves and killers in the best Turkish Balkan tradition. There were also some curious Sudanese cavalry encased from top to toe in chain mail, war surplus left over from the Crusades. All in all, no matter how hard Hicks' officers pushed this menagerie, it remained, in the words of correspondent Frank Power of the *London Times,* "a cowardly, beggarly mob." Hicks' harassed officers agreed, and called them other things as well.

But strangely enough, the first major effort of this motley collection resulted in a victory, as Hicks had hoped. It happened at an obscure place called Al-Marabi, where several thousand of the Mahdi's people stormed the unwieldy square in which the Egyptians had to be marched. Hicks got his Nordenfeldts and Krupps and British officers out in front of the square, where the troops could plainly see them, and the hail of lead from the square killed several hundred attackers and drove off the rest.

It was a good beginning, and the Egyptian soldiers and Bashi-Bazouks made much of themselves. There were even the beginnings of a little pride, but the next campaign was to be a far more serious proposition. It was nothing less than a plan to clear the huge province of Kordofan of the Mahdi and his warriors. The odds were long and the distances enormous, and Hicks knew his command was unready.

But he tried his best. First Hicks had to gain some sort of clear chain of command. Suliman was an inert, superannuated product of Egyptian decay, determined to do nothing either energetic or dangerous. Hicks at last got Cairo to remove the dead weight of Suliman and send him away to rusticate in the hellish heat of the Red Sea. He also asked for reinforcements and money, for some of the garrisons had been long without pay, one for twenty-five months.

He got a little help, though not nearly enough. There was some money and a few reinforcements, the same sort of unwilling conscripts he had started with. But he could do nothing to change the inherent unreliability of his troops. Hicks cited just one doleful example in one of his dispatches to Cairo: "Fifty-one men of the Krupp battery deserted on the way here, although in chains."

Correspondent Power agreed:

> . . . even the most sanguine look forward to [this march] with the greatest gloom. We have here 9,000 infantry that fifty good men could rout in ten minutes, and 1,000 cavalry . . . that have never learned to ride . . . to beat the 69,000 men of the Mahdi. . . . I pity Hicks. He is an able, good, and energetic

man, but he has to do with wretched Egyptians, who take a
pleasure in being incompetent . . . delaying and lying.

Nevertheless, Hicks collected fifty-five hundred camels for transport, finished training his indolent, anxious army as best he could,
and finally turned west into the wastes of Kordofan in September
1883. He had a few Krupp guns, six or seven Nordenfeldts, and his
hard core of eight British officers. Along for the ride were Power;
one Baron von Seckendorf; Edmund O'Donovan of the *Daily News;*
Frank Vizetelly, an artist for the *Illustrated London News* and the
Graphic; a doctor; and a couple of Germans serving as orderlies,
one rejoicing in the name of Gustav Klootz. Powers' luck held; he
became sick early in the campaign and returned to Khartoum. The
rest—about ten thousand men and a couple of thousand camp followers—marched west into limbo. They would never be seen again.

For a month or so Hicks' dispatches reached Khartoum, and they
bore no good news. He could not bring the Mahdi to bay; that canny
desert warrior simply fell back before Hicks' plodding advance.
Water and reliable intelligence grew scarcer as the army felt its way
westward under a blazing sun. At last Hicks sent word that he was
leaving his supply lines, depending entirely on camel-borne
supplies . . . and then he was gone.

At first the march was uneventful, although water was a constant
worry. For a while it was found in rainwater pools and wells, although increasingly the enemy filled in wells and drove cattle through
the pools. All of the villages were hostile, and many of them had
been burned to deny his army any supply or shelter. Only a few old
people were left in such villages as remained. So Hicks decided to
abandon his plan to leave garrisons along his line of communication
and resupply. He would have to go it entirely alone, without connection to the Nile.

And then the column began to feel the enemy's presence. One
scout hunting water found a well and started back to report. He
realized he had forgotten his rifle—a comment on the military pov-
erty of Hicks' force—and turned back to the well. The column found
him the next day, sitting by the well with both hands cut off. When
water was scarce, some soldiers would break ranks to look for it or
to loot melons for their moisture. Some of them met the Mahdi's
scouts and were not seen again.

Halfway to El Obeid the army halted at a place called Akila, which had an excellent water supply. The army rested and drank its fill, but even there a group of men who wandered away from the *zariba*— the thorn fence around the camp—were slaughtered by the enemy. Just before the army pushed on, an officer's orderly was found . . . disemboweled.

There was worse to come. Next day, well on the march, the officers discovered that only about 30 percent of the water jars had been filled at Akila. Morale plummeted as four soldiers and over one hundred animals died of thirst.

On the eighteenth there was a skirmish with the Mahdi's followers. Little harm was done to anybody, but in the process Hicks found that the Krupp artillery had been so neglected by its Egyptian commander that it would not fire. There were also disputes over the reliability of the local guides, and further dissension between Egyptian and British officers.

Nevertheless, the army, more and more bedraggled, finally reached a place called Er Rehad, only forty miles from El Obeid, where there was water. A four-day halt was taken there, and a fruitless reconnaissance was attempted. Nothing concrete was learned, except that the Mahdi was near and was calling all the tribes to join him in the name of the Prophet. And they were coming. It was also said that the Mahdi had summoned forty thousand angels to aid the faithful in the final fight. And at Er Rehad Gustav Klootz deserted, preferring chains in the Mahdi's camp to what he foresaw for the army. He would survive years of captivity to tell his tale.

Morale was by now at rock bottom, destroyed by lack of water, the Mahdi's propaganda, and the terrible feeling of isolation, of enemies on every hand. Nevertheless, Hicks had only one course of action open to him: go on. There was certainly no retreat, and at last El Obeid was now close. On October 30 he pushed on toward the city. The water was running low again, and there was no more to be had.

Four days later he received a letter from the Mahdi. It offered life to anybody who would surrender and accept the authority of the Prophet and the Mahdi. Soldier to the end, Hicks pushed on, as Mohammed Ahmed must have known he would.

The conclusion was ordained. The Mahdi had a vast horde of fighting men with him, perhaps as many as one hundred thousand,

and on November 1 he marched from El Obeid. As he had done earlier in the campaign, he strewed the path of Hicks' force with leaflets urging surrender. Whatever other effect they might have had, they made excellent toilet paper, and the Mahdi was furious when he learned the use to which his inspired messages had been put.

Hicks' force was only fifteen miles from El Obeid when the terrible last act began. As the army reached a patch of dense scrub, a place called Shaykan, the *jihadiya,* the experienced riflemen, opened a murderous fire from ambush on the front of the Egyptian square. As the front of the square buckled and panic began to spread, the great mass of the Mahdi's men struck the flanks of the Egyptians, and a desperate fight continued through the afternoon. By nightfall, Hicks still maintained some sort of perimeter, although bullets thudded into his massed men and animals all through the night.

Next morning, Hicks kicked the remnants of his force into motion. They were terrified and desperate with thirst, but somehow he got them a mile closer to El Obeid before the full weight of the Mahdi's masses stopped the square cold and it began to come apart. Most of the surviving Egyptians took to their heels—and were cut down as they ran. Some tried to surrender, and a few survived by hiding under piles of their dead comrades—at least for a while, for most of the prisoners were killed in time.

One who survived was Hicks' cook, who managed to convince the Mahdi that he was a doctor and was accordingly spared. He appears to have practiced medicine—God help his patients—with the Mahdi's forces until he escaped five years later.

For Hicks and his officers there was no surrender. They made a stand together under a baobab tree and fought to the last, good men dying in a dubious cause. Hicks fought on foot with his saber, until he fell in a shower of spears. His head, with that of Baron von Seckendorf, was sent in triumph to the Mahdi. Hicks' courage so impressed the Mahdi that he was buried with honor.

Not so most of the rest of his forces. The dead, as many as ten thousand, were simply left, stripped of clothing and equipment, for the hyenas and vultures. The few prisoners, naked and roped together, were dragged in triumph into El Obeid, together with the captured guns and the rest of the booty, while the Mahdi's followers went crazy with adulation. "The Mahdi of God," they screamed, and so it must have seemed. Incredibly, his men had suffered only about three hundred and fifty casualties.

For a while nothing but awful rumors reached Khartoum. And then the ghastly news filtered back across the desert. Hicks had been betrayed by his guides, betrayed into an ambush, and his force had been wiped out. Nobody knew whether anyone at all had survived. All anybody knew was that not a single man of all those men had returned to tell the tale. The Egyptian government was in panic, and Europe was appalled. A modern, well-armed force of ten thousand had simply vanished without trace.

From that time onward, there were few anywhere in the Sudan who did not believe in the Mahdi's divinity and the infallibility of his cause. Recruits would flock to his standard, and his fanatic followers would carry on his vision long after his death. For Khartoum would fall to his faithful, and in it would die Chinese Gordon, sent back into the Sudan far too late to save it and without the resources to manage that almost impossible task. The Mahdi's explosive, visionary spirit would hold this whole bitter land in sway until the day in 1898 when the bubble burst forever before the magazine rifles and Maxim guns of another army, this time a professional, well-trained British one.

Colonel William Hicks, long dead, had in his way contributed to the final breaking of the Mahdi's cause. His death had been the catalyst that brought Gordon to Khartoum, and it was the shame of Gordon's death there, abandoned, that brought the army of 1898 to Omdurman, across the great Nile from Khartoum.

CHAPTER TWENTY-EIGHT

THE BRASH YOUNG CAPTAIN

BLACK JACK PERSHING was not known either for an even temper or for restraint in dealing with what he saw as inefficiency. And in France, in the autumn of 1917, he might have been particularly irascible: he had a big new army to train, after all, and little time to do it. Any less-than-perfect training was likely to cost soldiers' lives later on, and Pershing was determined to have nothing but excellence.

So it was that he castigated 1st Infantry Division's commander and chief of staff for what he perceived to be a subpar training demonstration in October 1917. Pershing was wrong, apparently, or at least far too hard on men working hard to train green soldiers and inexperienced officers.

Angry at the injustice of Black Jack's tirade, a young staff officer pushed forward and began to tell the general why he was so wrong. When Pershing began to turn away, the youngster put his hand on the general's arm and continued his passionate defense of his division.

Now in the Old Army, grabbing a general's arm was the grossest sort of breach of etiquette, and the young officer's comrades gloomily predicted he would surely be fired from the staff. The young officer was not dismayed. "All I can see is that I might get field duty

245

instead of staff duty," he said. "And certainly that would be a great success."

They were all wrong. Whatever other faults Pershing had, he admired spunk. He dealt with the brash captain by later making him his own aide, and saved the young man for greater things.

The captain's name was George C. Marshall.

CHAPTER TWENTY-NINE

A NASTY LITTLE WAR
Breaker Morant and the Bushveldt Carbineers

THE SOUTH AFRICAN War of 1899–1902 was probably inevitable, ordained by the vindictive gods of progress and modernity. Friction between the imperial, ambitious British and the standoffish, bucolic Boers was nothing new. For decades the two races had grumbled and growled at each other.

One old bone of contention was over Boer treatment of South African blacks—British abolition of slavery in 1834 had angered the Boers, who depended on slaves for cheap labor. Throughout the war, the Boers routinely shot black scouts employed by the British. Other irritants were Boer discrimination against British immigrants, competition over the great diamond and gold deposits, British imperial expansion, and the economic development of this whole, rich land. Two very different ways of life had met head-to-head, and one of them was bound to yield.

How the war would end was plain to anybody with eyes to see. The Boers—mostly of Dutch and French Huguenot descent—were fine horsemen and marksmen. They had to be: a man's horse and rifle meant life itself in this wild, dangerous country. The Boer units were mobile, without supply lines or depots, and they operated in a roadless land where most of the white population supported them.

Their weapons were rifles, mostly, Mausers and such Lee-Metfords as they could capture from the British. In the hands of an experienced marksman, they could reach out and pull down a man at a thousand yards.

And the British took the Boers too lightly, at least at first. The British army of the day was oriented toward little colonial wars, small, violent campaigns out on the fringes of the world, in which dash and initiative and cold courage counted for more than mobility and cover and fine long-range shooting. The British were in for a rude awakening.

For there was very little for them to attack. Their foe was elusive, a will-o'-the-wisp who struck and vanished and did terrible damage at long range. But the British learned, as they have for a thousand years. Somebody famous—I misremember who—once said that England always loses the first battle, and always wins the last one. By and large, that generalization turns out to be true over the years, and so it was in South Africa.

At the beginning, the Boers had much the best of the fighting. They besieged British garrisons in Mafeking and Ladysmith. The British would gallantly hold out in both places until they were relieved, but before that happened, British forces got a series of bloody noses. Advancing in the open simply did not work against fine marksmen shooting from cover. No amount of courage—and a couple of dozen Victoria Crosses would be won during the war—could protect a man against a Mauser bullet or shrapnel from a Krupp field gun.

But once the learning was done, the war wound down toward its inevitable conclusion. Lord Roberts, the scrappy little field marshal who rose from the ranks to tame Afghanistan, also crushed the bulk of the Boer resistance in South Africa. The major Boer forces surrendered, and some of the Boer leaders even served the British, commanding irregular units against their former comrades.

But there still remained the tag end of the war, the dregs of the poison cup, the final pacification. The ''bitterenders,'' as the last Boer resisters were called, fought on. Their hopeless—and pointless—guerrilla war spawned the worst days of the whole miserable conflict. For the Boers had no outside source of supply, and so they obtained their food and fodder from the isolated Boer farmsteads scattered across the endless expanse of the veldt. Whether the farm family favored the war or not, the Boer kommandos (literally, a "command," a generic name for any Boer unit) took what they needed.

The British reacted in the only way they could, in spite of a storm of protest in England and elsewhere in the world. The British commander in South Africa, Lord Kitchener, began to deny the last Boer kommandos the only support they had left. Over large areas, Boer families were removed from their farms, the buildings burned, the livestock confiscated or killed.

At first, under Lord Roberts, no farmstead was burned unless British troops had been fired on from its shelter. Then the burning was extended to the farms lying nearest the spot of any act of sabotage. In the end, Kitchener ordered the scorched-earth policy spread across hundreds of square miles, creating a desert in which, he hoped, the Boer kommandos could not long find either food or shelter. The policy created an outcry all over the world, especially in England herself: Winston Churchill called the devastation "hateful folly."

But it worked.

One Australian, writing home, reported the terrible extent of the destruction:

> In the eight days we collected eight prisoners of war, 62 men, 930 women and children, 354 horses, 28 mules, 5,688 cattle, 14,834 sheep, 133 waggons, and 108 Cape carts. . . . We cannot get the Boers to stand and fight, so we are going to starve them out . . . have burnt altogether about 60 farms during the past 4 days.

The Boer families, mostly women and children, were removed to protected areas from which they could no longer give aid and comfort to the remaining kommandos. They lived in what the British command called "concentration camps," a term that, in those more innocent days, connoted simply a bringing together, not a place of execution.

Still, many of the camps were grim enough, stark and cheerless even by the standards of the empty veldt, where the living was hard and dreary at the best of times. And people did die in the camps, many of them, for the living conditions were uneven, varying from reasonably comfortable to primitive in the extreme. They died of disease, mostly a result of poor management and abysmal sanitation; the most common killer was "enteric"—typhoid fever.

In fairness, it was also true that the Boer fighting men largely preferred to have the British look after their families. They could not take care of their women and children while they were on the run. Many of the camps were largely unguarded, and Boer kommandos would have had an easy time getting Boer dependents out had they wished to. They did not. As an American put it in a letter home: "The Boer women and children are in the Concentration Camps simply because their husbands and fathers want them there . . ."

Some of the farm removals were by way of help, assistance to those families who wanted no part of living on the open veldt for whatever reason; perhaps they had no stomach for war in the first place, or they thought they would be better off under British rule, or they had actually switched sides. During one Boer raid on a concentration camp, the Boer leader tried to recruit male Boers for his unit: of 689 men in the camp, only five joined the kommando.

Still, most of the inhabitants of the camps were Boer sympathizers. If they were left in their homes, they would provide a continuing source of supply to the diehard kommandos. Confined, they could provide no aid and comfort to the enemy. But the price to the British was high. As more farmsteads burned, as more people were removed to the camps, as the remaining Boer kommandos burned and looted farms themselves, the war grew increasingly bitter.

The vulnerable railroad lines were protected by small fortified posts, generically called blockhouses, scattered at intervals along the line. The spaces in between were gradually closed with wire fences into which British mounted units drove Boer kommandos like fish into a net. The fencing could be cut, of course, but the system did something to interrupt the mobility of the Boers.

The Boers, operating mostly in small groups, were highly mobile, and it took mobility to catch and destroy them. One British column rode 1,814 miles in 153 days of chasing Boers. Along the way it fought thirteen small engagements, losing 5 killed and 19 wounded. Boer casualties were 27 killed, 15 wounded, and 196 captured, and the British gathered in the usual swarm of farm animals and wagons. It was turning into a long, frustrating, weary war.

The British answer to Boer mobility and stealth was increasingly the use of cavalry, not only regular and colonial units but light horse outfits raised in South Africa especially for the purpose. Such a unit was the Bushveldt Carbineers. The carbineers were raised in early 1901 around Cape Town and Pretoria, and were not part of either the British or Australian regular establishment. Much of the original funding for the unit was subscribed by loyalist civilians in the northern Transvaal.

About 350 men enlisted in the unit, a hard-riding collection of British, Boers, and colonial soldiers. By way of example, one small group of Carbineers who messed together included two Australians, a London cockney, a Canadian, a Boer, a New Zealander, a Scot, and an American. Many of these men had served with the regular forces and had chosen the Carbineers for their second hitch in the war. They tended to be free spirits, adventurers, a breed of turn-of-the-century buccaneer. Among them was an extraordinary character, a veteran of South African service with an Australian outfit, a modern-day freebooter named Harry Morant.

When he worked in Australia, which was not always, Harry Morant was a horse breaker by profession, a good one, and thus he came by his civilian nickname, "Breaker." Morant was an engaging rounder, a poet of talent, always good company, forever ready for a fight or a frolic. Though he seldom paid his debts, most men forgave him easily and loaned him money again—the Breaker was the Breaker, after all, a sort of child of nature to whom money meant as little as danger. Even though Morant was a bit of a con man, and not above purloining somebody else's property if he fancied it, his own geniality and generosity made him a myriad of friends, most of whom he kept.

The ladies liked him, too, and Morant reciprocated, as one of his earthy poems suggests:

> *Let's toss a bumper down our throat*
> *Before we pass to Heaven*
> *And toast the trim-set petticoat*
> *We leave behind in Devon*

Morant was fearless, a first-class amateur boxer, and a superb horseman. He is said to have jumped a horse over a "stiff three-rail fence" in the dark of night, his only guide a couple of lighted matches stuck into the tops of fence posts. On another occasion—a hung-over Christmas morning, in fact—Morant jumped a blindfolded horse over two successive six-wire fences. He went steeplechasing as well, and played first-class polo, played with the upper crust of British society. In between games and frolics, he deeply loved music, and would spend his last shilling on concert tickets.

Still, Morant's rootless life took its toll on him. Too much drifting, too much whiskey, too many debts, too little decent food, all these things pulled Morant down body and soul, and he thought again of England, of going "home to the land of my forefathers and feed on fatted calf," as he put it himself. And then, in the fall of 1899, the South African War broke out, and the Breaker rushed to enlist in the South Australian Mounted Rifles.

For a man like Morant, the adventure of any war would have been a potent lure. This one was irresistible, for his country was involved, his native land. When Great Britain called, the Breaker would go. For even though Morant had lived in Australia since 1883, he was in fact an Englishman, and still considered England his home. He was proud of his heritage, and even embellished upon it, giving his occupation as "gentleman" and telling people he was the son of an English admiral (he was not; his parents managed a workhouse in the west of England).

Morant was a good soldier, too, a natural soldier. For all his independence, he could take orders—and he could give them, too. He sewed on the stripes of a corporal and kept them on, and in time would make sergeant. His superb horsemanship won him a job as a dispatch rider for a British general, and he and his unit were part of Lord Roberts' victorious campaign that turned the course of the war.

So far, so good. Morant's unit was mustered out in the summer of 1900 and returned to Australia, but the Breaker did not go with it. His pockets jingling with his final pay and a month's bonus, he mingled with the British elite in Cape Town. In the process, he ran up a substantial bill at Cape Town's finest hotel—a bill he never paid, in the best Morant style. His wit, his repartee, and his polo were his passport everywhere.

The Breaker went next to England (where he left yet another unpaid hotel bill), and there he became engaged to be married. He also made friends with a British officer, Captain Frederick Percy Hunt of the 19th Hussars. Hunt, another superb horseman with a freebooting streak, had also served against the Boers. And when the

British government called for reinforcements to finish the war, both Hunt and Morant answered the call.

Some men never get their fill of adventure; some cannot resist their country's call for help. No doubt both motives moved Morant and his new friend. In the Breaker's case, there may also have been the perennial problem of a flat wallet. Moreover, the course of his new engagement was certain to become rocky in time. Perhaps it had done so by the time he left, for Morant had a wife already, an embarrassing inconvenience not easily disposed of in Victorian England.

And so both Morant and Hunt returned to South Africa, where both enlisted in the Bushveldt Carbineers. The Breaker, thirty-eight and experienced in the ways of war, was quickly commissioned in April 1901, and then assumed the cares of command as Lieutenant Morant. Like his men, the Breaker wore British khaki but adopted the comfortable, utilitarian slouch hat as standard headgear. They carried the British Lee-Metford bolt-action rifle, a sturdy, accurate weapon that fed from a stripper clip pushed down into the magazine. Spare loaded clips were generally carried in a bandolier of leather snap-cover pockets worn diagonally across the soldier's chest.

The Carbineers, commanded by an Australian major, had a particularly nasty task assigned to them by the Intelligence Department of the British staff. They were to protect some 180 miles of vulnerable railway, a desolate stretch of track running north from Pretoria to the small town of Pietersburg. Boer kommandos struck again and again at the railway line, destroying track and wrecking entire trains.

The Carbineers' area of responsibility was huge and only sparsely settled. The Boer enemy was elusive and hard-core. He often wore British uniforms, and sometimes he was not above using those uniforms, or even a flag of truce, to lure British troops within striking distance. (Some of the Boers wore British khaki only because their own clothing was worn out and could not be replaced. Still, even for these men, scarcity was no excuse for not removing rank and unit badges from the uniforms, or for replacing them with other clothing at the first opportunity.)

The British reacted predictably to what they perceived to be misuse of both uniform and truce flag; the occasions on which either the uniform or the white flag had been misused by the Boers were multiplied by rumor. One Boer, left behind asleep when his kommando moved on, was caught by the British wearing the uniform of a British lancer regiment. They shot him.

An Australian unit, at the funeral of an officer shot by the Boers as he rode toward a Boer white flag, "joined hands together and swore most solemnly never to recognize the white flag." Equally short shrift was often given Boers caught carrying dumdum bullets, expanding ammunition that left ghastly wounds in human flesh.

Dynamiting of supply trains was commonplace. One soldier, wounded in the wrecking of such a train, later wrote that the attacking Boers robbed two female passengers, even taking the clothing from their babies. When the children's nurse hestitated to hand over her valuables, a Boer simply shot her down. The Carbineers retaliated by loading Boers on flatcars coupled ahead of British trains—if a contact mine was concealed under a rail, the kommando that laid it would be killing its own. And sometimes did.

And so the war got dirtier as tempers grew shorter and shorter on both sides. When a Boer schoolmaster shot two officers of an Australian outfit called the Tasmanian Bushmen, and then immediately tried to surrender, he got the ugly end of a bayonet for his pains, dying immediately and unmourned. On another occasion, a British patrol met two khaki-dressed Boers who called out "Don't fire, we are 17th Lancers!" The ruse worked just long enough for the Boers to kill the patrol leader and one of his soldiers.

No British unit with experiences like these ever forgot; they would not be twice deceived, and they were not quick to forgive. And the incident with the 17th Lancers had far-reaching consequences: Kitchener used it to justify his order permitting British units to shoot Boers captured wearing British uniforms. Remarkably, for all the anger and deceptions and reprisals, no formal allegation of deliberate torture was ever made on either side. There was, however, at least one informal charge, as we shall see; that incident turned carefree, smiling Breaker Morant into an avenging angel of death.

For the scattered British detachments, this guerrilla war was a thankless, dirty task: much hard riding, constant danger, few pleasures, and what to the soldiers often appeared to be irritating and unnecessary restrictions. As Morant put it in one of his rollicking poems:

> *If you encounter any Boers*
> *You really must not loot 'em.*

> *And if you wish to leave these shores,*
> *For pity's sake DON'T SHOOT 'EM!*

Still, for the most part, the war of the vast empty spaces remained reasonably civilized. As one bitter-end Boer soldier wrote later:

> Amid all the cruelty . . . there was one redeeming feature, in that the English soldiers, both officers and men, were unfailingly humane . . . there was never any hesitation in abandoning a wounded man to the mercy of the troops, in the sure knowledge that he would be taken away and carefully nursed . . .

And the Boers generally responded in kind. Still, there were exceptions. And as the war wound down, as the Boers lost more and more ground, as the tragic movement to the concentration camps continued, the war became gradually tougher. Brutality was still the rare exception, but when it happened it begat brutality in return. And that is what caused the tragedy of Breaker Morant and the Bushveldt Carbineers.

The great emptiness north and east of Pietersburg was a Boer-infested, fever-racked area generically called the Spelonken District. In June 1901 a Carbineer detachment hoisted the Union Jack and set up housekeeping in an old Boer fort some eighty miles north of Pietersburg. They called the place Fort Edward.

Morant led regular patrols from Fort Edward, and he hit the Boers hard again and again. On one expedition, at the head of twenty-two troopers, Morant brought in nineteen prisoners, evading a pursuing Boer kommando on the way. The Boers knew him by name, and they knew his ruthless pursuit. Many of them were little more than bandits, and therefore, as one officer observed:

> The Bushveldt Carbineers were specially recruited to deal with particularly desperate bands of men, and for this reason the regiment had attracted a rather tougher crowd than was normally to be found in these irregular units . . . .

This officer, who liked Morant, still characterized him as a "typical roystering hard case who took no heed for the morrow." But he added thoughtfully:

But for the existence of men of his somewhat ruthless calibre
during the eighteenth and nineteenth centuries, the British Empire would not now be the envy of all her neighbors. There
were many rough paths to be hewn out of the world between
1750 and 1900, and it was men of Morant's type who did the
work.

The same officer recalled Morant's softer side, his striking poetry,
and the slim volumes of Byron and Browning he carried in his
saddlebags.

Part of the force was an Irish-born captain named Taylor, an intelligence officer of deservedly ill repute. Men called him "Bulala"
Taylor. The word means "killer," and it fit Taylor well. Taylor had
lived in Africa for years and had served in the Matabele War. He
was also a well-known sadist and killer of natives, precisely the sort
of misfit to urge and sanction the killing of prisoners. "He was
notorious," a British officer wrote, "and distrusted by most white
men he came in contact with . . . his reputation stank to heaven."

And Bulala Taylor lived up to his name. In July 1901, he got
word that six Boers were coming in to Fort Edward to surrender. His
response, as temporary commander, was to order that no prisoners be
taken, no attention paid any white flag. Dubious and uneasy, the
sergeant major asked his commander whether he should follow Taylor's orders and was told he should, since Taylor was "commanding
officer at Spelonken."

And so, when the Boers arrived in two wagons, showing a white
flag, the Carbineers held their fire only long enough to make certain
there were no women or children in the wagons. There were none,
and so the six Boers were simply lined up and shot. When a Boer
Carbineer later pointed out to the dead Boers' wives the men who
had shot their husbands, he signed his own death warrant. Shortly
afterward, Australian Lieutenant P. J. Handcock shot the man while
on patrol. Oddly enough, neither Taylor nor the titular commander
of the detachment were ever punished for these killings.

Under Taylor's leadership, the Spelonken detachment lived like
freebooters, drinking moonshine from Boer farm stills and selling
confiscated stock back to the Boer farmers. When stories of poor
discipline and riotous living percolated south to headquarters, a new
commander was sent north to bring the detachment back to decent

military form. And headquarters sent an experienced, veteran officer, too: none other than Morant's English friend, Captain F.P. Hunt.

Hunt was a likable man, a superb horseman, a first-class polo player and dealer in ponies. At the same time, two new junior officers joined the detachment. One of them was another Englishman, Lieutenant Harry Picton. The other was a young Australian, George Witton.

Hunt was a fine leader and a no-nonsense officer, a very different character from shady, disreputable Bulala Taylor. Ably seconded by Morant, he destroyed the stills and abruptly ended the black-market dealings in cattle. Along the way, however, he made a number of enemies within the detachment, uniformed hoodlums who resented the reformation of their lawless little world. One, who had been arrested for selling uniforms, later said he would be "willing to walk barefooted . . . 100 miles, to be in a firing party to shoot Morant and Handcock."

For all the ruffled feathers among the sloppier soldiers in the detachment, Captain Hunt was good for the Carbineers. Tragically, for the unit, for Morant, and for himself, he did not last long. The last act for Hunt began when a German missionary named Reuter came to Fort Edward with the story that loyal farm families were being raided by a Boer officer named Viljoen, who was headquartered in his own farmhouse at a place called Duivels Kloof. With fourteen volunteers, Hunt rode out to deal with Viljoen, forty miles away; he did not come back.

Just what happened at Duivel's Kloof has never been entirely clear. Hunt and his patrol had dinner with the Reuter family and then moved against the Boer farm. Leaving their horses some distance away, they closed in on foot. Apparently, however, the Boers knew they were coming, and a ferocious firefight broke out in the blackness of the night.

The Boers had been reinforced, and Hunt's men were badly outnumbered. One soldier estimated the odds against Hunt at three to one; a lieutenant remembered that eighteen Carbineers fought at least eighty Boers in the gloom. The British patrol fell back, but in the darkness they could find neither Captain Hunt nor one of his sergeants.

Until the next morning. When the patrol again closed in on Viljoen's farmhouse they found the Boers had fled; left behind were the naked bodies of Hunt, his sergeant, and two Boers, including Viljoen. The sergeant was taken home (he was a loyalist farmer who lived nearby), and Hunt was buried in the garden of Reuter's mission station.

Morant arrived at Reuter's the next day, followed by Lieutenants Witton, Picton, and Handcock, and seventy troopers. George Witton, a brand-new officer, did not even know Captain Hunt. Picton came from a distinguished English military family and had served with the French Foreign Legion in the Congo; he had already won the Distinguished Conduct Medal in action against the Boers. Peter Handcock had been an NCO with an Australian unit, and had joined the Carbineers early in 1901.

What Morant learned at the mission station drove him nearly mad with rage. For he was told that Hunt had been repeatedly kicked while alive, perhaps kicked to death; a native witness said the Boers had broken his neck. Others remembered that the captain's legs had been slashed with a knife, his face stomped on with hobnailed boots. A Carbineer later said Hunt's head was

> pulp, his teeth were broken in, and his left eye had been kicked about. . . . we could see that they had simply knocked him to death. . . . They must have broken his neck by kicking at him . . . his kaffir boy, Joe, was sitting beside [the body] crying like a baby. Joe said that he had watched the Boers jumping on Captain Hunt's head. . . .

Next morning, Morant set grimly out on the track of the Boers who had killed his friend. Trailing the Boers to their first camp, the patrol found two fresh graves, but their quarry had moved on.

The next night, the patrol closed in on the Boers' camp and opened fire in the darkness. Leaving behind all their wagons and gear, the Boers again escaped . . . all but one. This man, named Visser, was wounded and unable to walk. Far worse—for him—he was wearing clothing that had belonged to Captain Hunt. It was his death sentence.

Visser was taken back to the Carbineers' base. There, after dinner, Morant convened a drumhead court-martial that quickly sentenced Visser to death. When Witton objected on behalf of some of the troopers, Morant said simply:

> You didn't know Captain Hunt, and he was my best friend; if
> the men make any fuss, I will shoot the prisoner myself.

And that was that. Since Visser could not walk, he was carried to
the riverbank to face a firing party of ten Carbineers commanded by
Lieutenant Picton.

Five rifles were loaded with ball ammunition and five with blanks,
so that no soldier could be sure he had killed. After the volley, Picton
gave Visser the coupe de grace with a shot through the head. The
Boer died on the spot.

Morant's vengeance was not complete. The next victims were eight
Boers captured by a Carbineer patrol. Morant took charge of the
prisoners, who were later shot by Morant, Witton, Handcock, and
three troopers—one of them, Botha, a Boer himself.

The next casualty was a missionary, German-born C. A. Daniel
Heese. Heese, who was very friendly with the Boers, was thought
to be a spy by some of the Carbineers, and he might have seen the
Carbineers shooting prisoners. In any case, he was followed by Handcock and later found dead on the veldt. The final murders were three
more Boers on their way in to surrender. The three officers and
Trooper Botha killed them all.

By this time British headquarters was becoming aware that all was
not well in the remote Spelonken. It was not long before Morant,
Picton, Handcock, and Witton were all arrested and taken to Pietersburg, where the allegations were tried by a series of courts-martial,
the first convened in January 1902. The charges were murder in the
separate cases of the three Boers, the eight Boers, Visser, and the
missionary. Bulala Taylor was charged with—and acquitted of—"in-
citing to murder" six Boers in a separate case.

The court-martial acquitted Morant and Handcock of the missionary's death. Both men were given alibis by Boer women, and the
prosecution's evidence was only circumstantial. The only possible
live witness, Morant's native "boy," was nowhere to be found. He
was last known to have left Fort Edward with Morant when Morant
took leave in Pretoria. Thereafter, he simply disappeared, and the
possibility exists that Morant himself removed the only sure witness
against him. Much later, Witton wrote that Handcock admitted to him
that he had shot the missionary, and that he did so on Morant's order.

As to the other charges, no amount of provocation could change what Morant and Handcock had done to anything but premeditated murder. Unless, and this was the officers' defense, they were justified by orders from their superior officers, orders they were bound to obey. They admitted the shootings; there was no question about what had happened. But was it criminal?

Morant defended himself on the ground that he fought the war in the only way in which it could realistically have been won. The only workable rule on the veldt, he argued, was war to the knife, and certainly there was no gainsaying the brutalities indulged in by the Boers themselves, not least on the wounded body of Hunt. "We were out fighting Boers," Morant told the court-martial, "not sitting comfortably behind wire fences. We got 'em and we shot 'em under Rule .303" (the caliber of the British service rifle).

"You can't blame the young 'uns," Morant testified. "They only did as I told 'em. They just carried out orders, and that they had to do." And then the Breaker stated the heart of his whole defense:

> They obeyed orders and thought they were obeying Lord Kitchener's. Captain Hunt told me not to bring in prisoners. He told me that they had said in Headquarters that they didn't want prisoners to flood the concentration camps. I did not carry out those orders until my best friend was brutally murdered. Then I resolved to carry out orders.

There it was: before his death Captain Hunt had ordered his men to "take no prisoners." He had apparently done so in retaliation for the death of a good friend of his—and Morant's—Lieutenant Best of the Gordon Highlanders, killed when the Boers wrecked a train. Maybe so. Assuming that were true, however, Morant was in command in Hunt's place when the murders were done. He had no duty to follow the orders of a dead man. The orders to do murder were his own.

Witton claimed that he had killed in self-defense, shooting down a "big powerful Dutchman" who had rushed him and tried to grab his rifle. Even his own account stated, however, that the Boer's attack came at about the time the Carbineers were shooting, or preparing to shoot, the Boer and his surrendered companions. And in a book he wrote much later, Witton admitted that he had "never had any qualms of conscience," for the Boer was "a most notorious scoundrel . . . head of a band of marauders."

And there could be no refuge in Kitchener's sanctioning of the shooting of prisoners caught in British uniform. That order might have excused the killing of Visser; he was wearing Captain Hunt's clothing when he was caught. It could not, however, excuse the killing of Boers trying to surrender.

And so the court-martial, in fact, had little choice. Murder had been done and proved, and there was no real defense. And so Morant was convicted, and with him Handcock, Picton, and Witton. For the first three, the sentence was death. Young Picton was cashiered from the service.

When the testimony and the judging were finally done, Morant stood convicted of three murders, Handcock of two murders and a manslaughter, Witton of one murder and one manslaughter, and Picton of a single manslaughter. All that remained was final action on the sentences; that was up to the commander in chief in South Africa, Lord Kitchener, the hero of the famous campaign against the Dervishes in the Sudan.

The officers who sat in judgment of the Carbineers seem to have had considerable sympathy for them. They were fighting officers; they understood something of the pressures of guerrilla war out in the vast empty spaces to the north. After Handcock and Morant were acquitted of the missionary's murder, two members of the court-martial sent them a half dozen bottles of champagne.

And after the death sentences were adjudged, the court-martial— including the president—recommended mercy, and did so very strongly in the case of Handcock and Witton, because they were acting under Morant's orders. To Morant's great credit, he tried hard to take all the responsibility for the killings on himself.

Witton was spared the firing squad when Kitchener commuted his sentence to life imprisonment (he was set free by royal order in the summer of 1904). Morant and Handcock would die.

Lord Kitchener has been accused of all sorts of unlawful command influence in the case, and of using the convicted officers as "scape-goats" to quiet the widespread criticism of his final brutal campaign against the Boers. Many officers also felt that there would have been little inquiry over the shooting of prisoners had it not been for the murder of the German missionary. Witton, deeply bitter, wrote later that "the German Emperor had to be appeased."

The allegations are probably unfounded, or at least exaggerated. No doubt Kitchener wanted to make an example of these men; he knew that the strictures of military law were being more and more disregarded as the war on the veldt got dirtier and dirtier. As a commander, he was surely out to stop it, as he had the duty to do. And the killing of the missionary probably had a considerable influence on Kitchener, since Imperial Germany was even then publicly attacking Britain's conduct of the war. If Kitchener was morally certain that the defendants had, in fact, killed the missionary, it appears he was probably right.

Kitchener certainly did err in throwing a veil of secrecy over the entire Morant affair, even failing to timely notify his superior, Lord Roberts. Kitchener was sensitive to the widespread criticism of his farm-burning, concentration camp campaign. He was also concerned not to arouse criticsm in Australia, whose leaders were always quick to intervene when Australians were imprisoned or tried.

If the court-martial felt compassion for the Carbineers, other officers also thought the sentences were an appalling miscarriage of justice, given the fury of the veldt war. Still others, however, felt no sympathy at all for the convicted men. Meeting Morant at Pietersburg, the officer who had gathered the evidence against Morant told him, "You are guilty as Hell, and I am glad to help send you there. Where is your boy . . . have you murdered him too?"

Plain as the defendants' crimes might be, one incident there was that might have moved Kitchener to mercy. During the trials, a Boer kommando attacked Pietersburg, where the garrison was weak. In the dawn of January 23, the Boers rushed the town, and the defenders needed every man. And so the accused Carbineers were released from confinement and given weapons, and Morant and Handcock fought together from the blockhouse that anchored the defense. The Boers were driven back, and their leader, Pretorious, fell to Handcock's cool shooting.

Kitchener was not moved to mercy, however, in spite of the Carbineers' courage in fighting for Pietersburg. Witton alleged that Kitchener deliberately made himself unavailable after the trial as senior staff officers searched for him with recommendations for mercy. Witton's bitterness is easy to understand, but his allegation is unlikely to be true. Surely no professional soldier—and Kitchener was very much a professional—would leave his headquarters without advising his staff of his whereabouts.

In the end, only Witton would be spared, but no further than commutation to life in prison. However, as Witton himself wrote later, Kitchener had in his possession a statement from Handcock that implicated Witton in the killing of the missionary.

For Morant and Handcock, there remained only a last sunrise— and a firing squad.

Breaker Morant went out the way he lived, unrepentant and flamboyant. He smoked a last cigarette and gave his cigarette case to the oficer commanding the firing party, saying, "I shan't be smoking any more of these." He refused the customary bandage to cover his eyes. And in the seconds before the Highland firing party squeezed their triggers, he stood up from the chair in which he had been seated and shouted to them, "There, boys, don't miss!" They did not.

Handcock also died well, still secure in the sincere conviction that he had only done his duty. "I will face my God with the firm belief I am innocent of murder," he wrote his sister just before he was shot. "I obeyed my orders and served my King as I thought best." And no doubt he believed he had.

Although a 1979 motion picture sympathetically portrayed Morant as the victim of high command influence, opinion at the time was sharply divided. Two colonial Carbineers, interviewed by an Australian paper, thought the killing ordered by Morant was nothing more than simple murder. Australian newspapers unanimously condemned Morant, and one referred to the Carbineers as a "mixed scallywag body" and called the killing "atrocious." Another congratulated its readers on the fact that Morant was not really an Australian but an Englishman.

So passed Breaker Morant, as one friend described him, "outcast, boon comrade, drunken beast, and brave man . . . what a sot he was in towns—what a mate in those long hours of night watch or day march." Another friend wrote what might have passed for the Breaker's epitaph:

> *A chivalrous, wild and reckless lad,*
> *A knight born out of his day.*

There was much to like in Morant. There was much to admire in his attempt to take the blame for his subordinates. There was much to sympathize with in his profound grief for his friend Hunt. The trouble was, Morant was a commander, with the soul-testing responsibilities that go with command. He was simply not ready for the awful burdens of leadership. Sadly, he remained more ''chivalrous, wild and reckless lad'' than officer, and it cost him and faithful Handcock their lives.

The tragedy of Breaker Morant was that he never entirely grew up.

CHAPTER THIRTY

AND SO GOOD NIGHT

Auf Wiedersehen, *Lili*

SOLDIERS AND GIRLS always went together. So did soldiers and beer. They still do. But even the happiest evenings have an end, and even young soldiers must sleep, for everything in every army starts early—at "oh-dark-thirty," as American G.I.s say.

And so, time out of mind, armies have called their troops to bed, first with drums, later with the bugle. "Tattoo," the British named their call, the last one of the night before the haunting "last post." Tradition says that *tattoo* was once "taptoo," and marked the hour when the publican or the commissary "tapped to" the bung in the barrel of beer, marking the end of the evening's festivities.

The United States Army also named its go-home call tattoo. Maybe the name simply followed British tradition; maybe it came from the same roots as the British call. American troops have never been shrinking violets when the time was ripe for celebration.

For German soldiers, the call was the Zapfenstreich. *Zapfen* means bung or spigot, the outlet for the precious beer. When the evening ended, the barman tapped the bung home and drew across it a chalk mark—a *streich*—marking its precise position in the barrel, lest some wastrel tap the keg further in the dead of night.

Like his American and British counterparts, the young German trooper left his beer and his girls and hurried to the kaserne, the courtyard that contained his quarters. He sang about those times, too, in the sentimental lines of "Lili Marlene," the haunting soldiers' song about the barracks harlot who stood each night underneath the lantern by the kaserne gate.

Lili Marlene struck a familiar chord in the heart of every soldier, a warm little note of comradeship and better times. During World War II it spread from the Wehrmacht to both the British and American armies. "The sentinel has already called," runs the song, "the bugle has blown tattoo":

Schon rief der Posten, die blasen Zapfenstreich
Es kann drei Tagen kosten, Kam'rad ich komme gleich

"Being late means three days' restriction," ran the song. "I'll be right there, comrade."

And the song ended with the wistful hope every young soldier treasured, the dream of reunion, safe at home. I'll be back, Lili (or Janet or Sally or Paulette). When all is made right I'll see you again: underneath the lantern by the barracks gate, "*wie einst,* Lili," the way it used to be.

And so good night.

CHAPTER THIRTY-ONE

RUSTY WARRIORS
The Q-ships

LODERER WAS DYING. The rusty tramp steamer was down by the stern, water pouring through a huge torpedo hole in her side, the cold gray sea reaching greedily for her. Her scruffy crew of terrified merchant seamen had already abandoned ship and now huddled miserably in the ship's boats. One crewman pathetically clutched the ship's mascot, a big green parrot in its cage. Down below, water rose steadily in the engine room; the grimy stokers abandoned their posts, climbing above the greedy water to temporary safety.

Loderer's sleek gray killer, U-83, was on the surface now, only three hundred yards away. On his conning tower her captain casually watched his sinking victim. But the German officer, savoring his kill, had only a moment more to live . . . for the scruffy men in the boats were a "panic party," acting out carefully rehearsed parts—the parrot was stuffed and the dirty tramp was a British man-o'-war. On the afterdeck, a twelve-pounder gun—the weight of the projectile— was neatly concealed inside a collapsible deckhouse.

Two more twelve-pounders lurked beneath the main deck, one on each side, with hinged shutters rigged to fall open outward when the order was given to fire. Two more guns were concealed in mock-up cabins on either side of the main deck, and two small cannon were

emplaced on the bridge and hidden by the bridge screens. Near the
funnel a machine gun was tucked away under a phony henhouse,
chickens being a familiar food-on-the-hoof on merchant ships in
those days.

On the bridge, Commander Gordon Campbell, Royal Navy,
watched under cover as the German boat cruised submerged past his
panic party, huddled in their lifeboats. Then the submarine moved
in close to crippled *Loderer* herself, so close that Campbell could
see the whole length of the U-boat gliding by under water. A huge
sleek shark, she passed no more than ten or fifteen yards away from
the tramp steamer's flank, carefully checking every detail of this
victim. And then, to Campbell's intense satisfaction, the enemy boat
surfaced, her conning tower opening. "Now," thought Campbell,
"now," and gave his order.

Just after ten A.M., February 17, 1917, the wheelhouse on *Loderer*'s stern collapsed outward onto her decks, taking down with it her
flagstaff and revealing her twelve-pounder deck gun with a Royal
Navy crew. At the same instant the concealed ports banged open
along her sides, unmasking the rest of her artillery, and the White
Ensign of the Royal Navy shot to the top of the bridge mast. The
Maxim-gun spat fire from the rickety chicken coop behind the bridge,
and hidden riflemen opened fire on U-83's conning tower.

The first cannon round killed the German commander, and U-83
never had a chance to dive. His Britannic Majesty's Ship Q-5, alias
Loderer, alias *Farnborough,* poured more than forty rounds of cannon fire into her, and the *Unterseeboot* vanished swiftly, taking with
her most of her crew. The British could pull only one officer and
one sailor from the cold, treacly sea.

On *Loderer*'s bridge stood her captain, quiet, pipe-smoking Royal
Navy commander Gordon Campbell. U-83 was his second kill, but
he had no time to enjoy it. He had a ship to save, for Q-5 was hard-
hit. Already the "panic party" in the boats was pulling hard back
to the ship and the gun crews were securing their weapons to fight
for *Loderer*'s life. It would be a close-run contest, and the gray
Atlantic very nearly won it. Q-5 had no steam, and her helm was
jammed immovably. Campbell at one point signaled his commander
at Queenstown, Ireland: "Q-5 slowly sinking respectfully wishes you
good-bye."

But the farewell was premature. For Q-5 was loaded with lumber, giving her great buoyancy, and Royal Navy help arrived quickly. Campbell called for twelve volunteers to work the ship, and the whole crew stepped forward. He made his choices and transferred the rest of his crew to destroyer *Narwhal*. The volunteers raised steam in a little auxiliary boiler, enough to get power to steer and get a tow cable aboard.

For a day and a half Campbell and his volunteers fought the sea, while Royal Navy warships towed them slowly toward port. At one point a depth charge in the flooded stern exploded, doing more damage, and Q-5 settled still deeper. But Campbell and his crew would not quit, and on the second night of their ordeal Q-5 made harbor. Her guts were full of water and her stern was eight feet beneath the surface of the sea, but she floated.

She was only one of many "mystery ships," as the British papers called them. The U-boat menace to Britain's supply lines was fought with every weapon at hand, for on it depended the outcome of the war. The Royal Navy's hard-pressed destroyers could not be everywhere, and the U-boats attacked everything from fishing trawlers to liners.

The device of the disguised warship was nothing new. In 1672 a Dutch privateer came up with a sloppily handled British merchant ship, only to find she was a man-o'-war. The same fatal error was made more than once by French privateers during the Napoleonic Wars. As soon as the U-boat danger was apparent, the Admiralty moved to equip all kinds of decoy ships. As early as January 1915, the first of them were at sea.

Success came slowly. The Navy had to learn to look scruffy, and it took time to perfect disguises. The fishing trawler Q-ships, for example, had to carry a cargo of fish to attract the cloud of gulls that invariably surrounded those little boats.

A single detail out of place was enough to warn off a well-commanded U-boat, for many German submariners had served in the merchant marine in time of peace. They had watched hundreds of British merchantmen, and could see easily through any imperfect disguise. Q-ship *Tulip* was torpedoed in the spring of 1918 by a submarine suspicious of the way her merchant flag was hoisted and of the fact that she had no defensive deck gun.

Sometimes a chance appearance changed a hunter's luck. When Q-ship *Penshurst* attacked a U-boat at the end of November 1916, her quarry escaped when *Penshurst* was forced to open fire at long range into the glare of the sun. And so that night *Penshurst*'s crew repainted their ship and altered the arrangement of her masts. With the dawn she was a different ship, and her crew's nocturnal labor paid off.

She was frustrated at first, as a British seaplane first fruitlessly bombed a U-boat she was stalking and then managed to crash in the channel. While *Penshurst* was retrieving the interfering aircraft and her crew, however, she was fired on by the submarine.

When the sub was within one thousand yards, *Penshurst*'s panic party abandoned ship. Their perfect performance was the key to success. U-19 now pulled up close to the ship's boats, apparently intending to pick up her papers. But all the German got was a storm of high explosives. The second round exploded in the engine compartment, and the fight was over. The *Unterseeboot* was gone in ten minutes, and half her crew went with her.

Three months later *Penshurst* got another one, stolidly taking casualties from German shelling until she was close enough to shoot with success. When she opened fire, her gunnery was superb, and U-37 sank with no survivors.

Penshurst remained on active service until her end came on Christmas Eve, 1917, without warning, from a German torpedo. The explosion knocked down the sides of her dummy lifeboat and false sternhouse, exposing two of her guns. Even then, the ship sinking beneath them, her gun crews waited grimly until the U-boat surfaced to finish the job with her deck gun.

Penshurst could shoot only six times, timing her fire to the roll of the sluggish ship, when the guns would bear. But she hit the U-boat twice, and although her quarry escaped that day, she was hurt, and apparently was sunk by a British patrol craft the next day. It was over for *Penshurst*. Her crew survived, but she died of her wounds late on Christmas Eve.

The odds were all with the U-boats. They could decide to kill a Q-ship by torpedo, without warning, and never surface at all. Even if the German surfaced, she was a tiny target, for she lay low to the water, while her crew had the whole exposed flank of the Q-ship to shoot at. Hitting the U-boat's conning tower or deck was useless, aside from inflicting casualties. The only certain mortal hit was one that punctured the pressure hull.

Beyond the risk of death and maiming, life at sea was very hard in the Q-ships. No more men could be visible on deck in daylight than were reasonable for a freighter's crew. The extra hands Q-ships carried had to remain out of sight all day, every day, for every commander had to assume he was always under observation. And there was often no rest at night. Because the Q-ships had to spend their time where submarines had been reported, or were often lurking, they had to change their appearance often. No German U-boat skipper would be taken in by the same steamer sailing back and forth in the same area without making port.

So the nights were frequently spent painting, moving cargo booms and auxiliary smokestacks, and setting up and taking down deckhouses, ventilators, signal halyards, and flagstaffs. Screens were erected to change the Q-ship from a "three-island" merchantman to a flush-decker, names were altered, and house markings painted and repainted on the funnels. Early in the war, before radio was common on merchantmen, the ship's antenna had to be concealed, too, often as a signal halyard or mast-brace.

Concealed pipes were fitted to pour out steam when the Q-ship stopped, simulating punctured boilers. Even deck cargo was simulated—and changed from disguise to disguise. One Q-ship carried four railway cars made of wood and canvas, easy to set up and take down depending on what ship her captain decided to be that particular day.

Concealed single-mount deck guns were standard equipment from the beginning, normally hidden in false deckhouses and behind hinged plates in the ship's sides. Machine guns were generally included, too. And as the war went on, some of the larger Q-ships added even heavier armament. In addition to their guns, they began to mount concealed torpedo tubes, and hidden away in the poops of the ships were depth charges, which could be pushed overboard through ports in the stern.

The Q-ship crews had to look their part in every detail. Gone were the crisp uniforms and holystoned decks of the navy. Now it was bowler hats and ratty suits, rust-streaked plates and chicken coops on the boat deck, and washing flapping on lines. Some unhappy young sailors even had to learn to dress as women, consistent with their panic party roles as the captain's wife. There was no saluting, no insignia, nothing to tell a suspicious U-boat commander that his quarry was anything but a down-at-heels tramp.

The panic parties rehearsed their parts precisely, down to the stoker who was "forgotten" and who ran to the rail and shouted until a boat returned to take him off. The play was the thing: every motion had to be perfect to fool an experienced and suspicious U-boat skipper watching carefully through his periscope.

The transformation to merchant mariner was especially hard for the regular navy men. Many of the crew came from the various elements of the Royal Navy Reserves, and some from the merchant marine. Others came straight from civilian life. But a large number, especially the officers and the gun crews, were regulars, and anything unwashed or unburnished was anathema to them. These men took some comfort from the fact that Q-ships, however disreputable they looked outside, were scrubbed spotless inside, Royal Navy style.

Nobody dared relax above decks, for at any second a periscope might be focused on their ship. Even radio transmissions had to be carefully watched, as the U-boats regularly monitored merchant marine wireless traffic. In time the radio itself became a weapon, and the Q-ships regularly sent hysterical distress messages as the panic party swarmed over the side and into the boats. None of the messages gave the ship's position, of course; no Q-ship skipper wanted a warship showing up and scaring away his quarry.

Q-ship *Stonecrop*'s use of radio was typical. Chased on the surface by a big U-boat in September 1917, she sent frantic SOS messages and finally radioed, in the clear, "Hurry up or I shall have to abandon ship." She then sent away her panic party, including two uniformed men representing the crew of the single defensive deck gun all merchantmen by now carried openly.

U-88 was completely fooled. She closed to within six hundred yards, and *Stonecrop* raised her white ensign and opened fire. It took her gun crews only three rounds to find the range, and then her gunners hit the submarine eight straight times. U-88 went under, surfaced briefly, then sank forever. With her went her entire crew, including her captain—Schwieger—who in 1915 had sunk the great liner *Lusitania,* killing over eleven hundred civilians.

The first decoy successes in the U-boat war came off Britain's east coast, where the fishing fleets harvested vital food. The little unarmed trawlers were cold meat for the submarines as long as no escorts were around, and the U-boats attacked on the surface with gunfire, as they often did to save torpedoes.

But on June 23, 1915, when U-40 opened fire with her gun on the trawler *Taranaki* east of Aberdeen, the tables were turned. For little *Taranaki* was not only armed but towing His Majesty's Submarine C-24, submerged but in contact with the trawler by telephone. Sighting U-40, the trawler slipped her tow and called her big sister.

The bugs were not entirely out of the system, so C-24 had to make her attack trailing a hundred fathoms of three-and-a-half-inch tow cable, and with the telephone line wrapped around her propeller. The mess hanging from her bow badly upset the British submarine's trim, but she shot straight, and her torpedo sent U-40 to the bottom with only a cloud of bubbles for a monument. Only three crewmen survived.

About a month later Q-ship trawler *Princess Marie Jose* was attacked by U-23. The little trawler took on the submarine with her popgun and held the U-boat's attention while C-27 dropped the trawler's tow, worked into position, and torpedoed the German boat. U-23 disappeared forever.

The first success by a surface Q-ship was scored by *Quickly,* an armed trawler with just two small guns. With a phony deck cargo, she operated off the east coast of Scotland, and on July 20, 1915, she caught a submarine on the surface and sank her.

The very next day the little collier *Prince Charles* met a U-boat in the icy waters off the northwestern coast of Scotland. The tiny coal hauler was manned by her peacetime crew, who had all volunteered to stay with her, and her diminutive sting was provided by four little popguns and a few rifles manned by Royal Navy crews. *Prince Charles* came upon U-36 on the surface, stopping a sailing vessel, and the submarine opened fire on her. At the first round the volunteer crew, playing "panic party," took to the boats. The U-boat bored in, still firing, and at six hundred yards turned broadside to the little steamer. The navy crew had their chance, and they made the most of it.

Lieutenant Mark Wardlaw barked his commands, the screens came down, and *Prince Charles* showed her teeth. Wardlaw steamed hard toward U-36 to close the range, and his gun crews hit the sub again and again. U-36 tried to dive, but her pressure hull was holed, and she was finished. She reached the surface again under a hail of British shells, and then went down again for keeps. Wardlaw was able to save fifteen men of the German crew of thirty-three.

In August 1915, SS *Baralong,* an undistinguished three-island tramp, was working the area between the southwest coast of Ireland and the mouth of the English Channel. Her crew was spoiling for a fight, for she had been at sea almost six months and had sailed some twelve thousand miles without firing a shot in anger.

This day would change all that, for in mid-afternoon she came upon U-27, busily shelling *Nicosian,* a helpless merchantman. *Baralong* did not react until the freighter was between her and U-27, blocking the German's view. Then down came *Baralong*'s gun camouflage and American colors, and when the Germans caught their next sight of her, she was flying the white ensign and ready to open fire.

For the German, it was far too late to react. *Baralong*'s twelve-pounders hit her repeatedly, and the Q-ship's ten Royal Marines took on her gun crew with their rifles. U-27 rolled over and went down in a matter of minutes, and *Baralong* turned her attention to U-27's intended victim.

Nicosian was still afloat, and her valuable cargo was intact; she was carrying mules out of New Orleans, critical transport for the British army. The situation was complicated by the fact that some of the German submarine crew had boarded *Nicosian,* which carried rifles and ammunition in her charthouse. This was a job for the marines, who carefully searched *Nicosian* until they found the U-boat men hidden in the engine room. That very morning the big passenger liner *Arabic* had been sunk not far away, and the marines were not in a forgiving mood. The Germans did not survive. *Nicosian* and her mules did. *Baralong* finished her day by towing U-27's victim safely to port.

Only five weeks later *Baralong* did it again. Sailing under a new captain, she encountered U-41 off the Scilly Isles. This time the U-boat was completely fooled, chasing this innocent tramp steamer, closing in, and demanding to see her papers. What U-41 got was a storm of steel—she had a few moments to see the white ensign snap to *Baralong*'s masthead and realize her error. And then U-41 was gone forever.

But it was not always so easy. A number of Q-ships simply disappeared, torpedoed and sunk, like other merchantmen, with all hands.

While as many decoys as possible were loaded with cork or lumber, even that cargo would not ensure staying afloat. Others fought indecisive battles with U-boats, losing their quarry when the submarine dived without being mortally hurt. But, even an indecisive fight often hurt the U-boat badly enough that she had to return to port for repairs, and that was a substantial victory, for the U-boat was out of the war for weeks or months.

In March 1916, U-68 just missed ragged old tramp *Farnborough* with a well-aimed torpedo. Frustrated, U-68 surfaced long enough to fire one round from her deck gun, and then partially submerged. The tired merchantman stopped and blew off steam, and her crew swarmed into their lifeboats and pulled desperately away. Satisfied, the German pulled closer and fired again, getting the range.

Lying on *Farnborough*'s bridge was the redoubtable Campbell, watching the U-boat through a slit in the bridge screen. Near enough, the officer decided, and gave his commands. The white ensign snapped to the masthead, and the submarine was instantly smothered in fire from *Farnborough*'s machine gun and the three cannon that would bear on the sub. U-68 was hit repeatedly and began to sink.

Leaving nothing to chance, Campbell steamed straight over her, and drove her to the surface again with a depth charge. As he passed, his aftergun hit the sub five times more, and she disappeared. For good measure, Campbell dropped two more depth charges, and the sea was quiet. A massive oil slick and some wooden debris were U-68's only memorial.

Campbell and *Farnborough,* alias Q-5 and *Loderer,* would go on to win fame as the champion Q-ship sub-hunters. Campbell would finish the war with three kills, best of all the mystery ships, and the Victoria Cross.

But there were other successful hunters, not least of which was *Prize,* an innocuous three-masted schooner typical of the many sailing ships still at sea when World War I erupted. A sailing ship was easy pickings for any U-boat, too weak to fight and too slow to run. But little *Prize* had sharp teeth.

She started life as a German ship, *Else.* Captured in the first days of the war, she was appropriately renamed *First Prize.* In time she was fitted with two small cannon and a couple of Lewis guns, and was drafted into the Royal Navy. At last, in April 1917, little *Prize* encountered her Goliath, U-93, a monstrous submarine carrying eighteen torpedoes and two 105-millimeter guns, both bigger than *Prize*'s armament.

U-93's commander was Freiherr von Speigel, an aristocratic and very successful skipper with eleven kills to his credit on this cruise alone. Eager to return to Germany, where he had horses running in Berlin in May, von Speigel nevertheless took time out to add this innocuous little sailing ship to his bag. He would be a long time getting back to Berlin.

Von Speigel was not a careless officer. Even after the panic party had left, he stayed dead astern of *Prize,* where none of her guns would bear, and shelled her to a shambles, holed repeatedly and with wounded below. But nobody moved on *Prize*. Her New Zealand captain, W. E. Sanders, lay motionless inside the steel cover of the companionway, watching the sub through small slits. Cool and competent, he would win the Victoria Cross for this day's work.

And at last patience paid. The German sub moved into the coverage of *Prize*'s guns, and the white ensign was raised. Sanders' two guns fired thirty-six quick rounds, nailing U-93 again and again, as the Lewis guns swept the German's decks. Let the German skipper tell it:

> . . . there was a loud whistle aboard the schooner. The white war ensign of Great Britain ran up the mast. A moveable gun platform slid into view. A roar and rattling and 7.5 cm guns opened up at us, and machine guns, too . . . one shell put our fore gun out of commission. [Then] we were up to our knees in water. A moment later we were swimming in the Atlantic. . . .

U-93 was gone, Sanders would receive the Victoria Cross, and urbane Freiherr von Speigel would spend the rest of his war in England. He was a professional, this cultivated German, and he did not stint his praise of the little schooner's crew: "The discipline of the German Navy is wonderful," he said, "but that your men could have quietly endured our shelling without reply is beyond all belief."

It was not known until much later that U-93 actually got back to Germany, absorbing incredible punishment and working her way home on the surface, unable to dive. Her remarkable survival was only a reprieve. She was rammed and sunk by a British ship one early morning half a year afterward.

At that, she lived longer than little *Prize*. *Prize* was saved that day, by her crew and four German captives working together, and she lived to sail again. Then in August *Prize* took on U-48, and in a short battle hit her twice. But the U-boat's wounds were not mortal, and her crash dive took her out of danger. Now she could stalk *Prize* submerged, and even with her auxiliary engine the little schooner could not sail fast enough to outrun the submarine. That midnight the squally blackness was torn by a roar and the brilliant flash of an explosion, and then another. *Prize* was gone, topedoed and sunk with all hands, including the gallant Sanders.

The fate that accounted for U-93 also overtook U-44, rammed and sent to the bottom in August 1917 by destroyer HMS *Oracle*. *Oracle* quite properly got the credit, but the U-boat's death was really due to the valor of another Q-ship, *Chagford*. Seven days earlier, *Chagford,* twice torpedoed, still fought U-44 to a standstill on the surface, and hurt her so badly that she could not dive for more than a few moments. *Chagford* went down, although her crew were saved, but she had killed the U-boat as surely as if U-44 had been sunk on the spot.

By late 1917 the Q-ships' day had passed. By then the U-boats were too wary, for the secret of the Q-ships was long since known. The submarines seldom surfaced to sink a ship by gunfire any longer, and when they did they were careful to stay at an angle to the merchantman that blocked fire from any concealed guns there might be. For the U-boat skipper, torpedoes were more expensive but a great deal safer; without the chance to engage on the surface, the Q-ships were almost helpless.

Even to the formidable Campbell, the ace of the Q-ship captains, there came at last a time of disappointment. For him it was the encounter with a U-boat some hundred miles west of Ushant. His ship, *Dunraven,* patiently enduring long-range gunfire from a submarine, took a hit in the stern that exploded a depth charge and set fire to the poop.

The flames licked ever closer to the ammunition stored there as Campbell waited; and at last, just before *Dunraven* had a clear shot at her tormentor, the stern exploded with a shattering roar, throwing the concealed gun clear into the air. Campbell's quarry dived, and *Dunraven* soon shuddered from the shock of a torpedo.

Campbell, still hopeful, sent the rest of his crew off, holding back two gun crews and staying on board himself. But the submarine was far too careful; now she knew she was dealing with a warship, and she surfaced only astern of *Dunraven,* where neither of the remaining guns would bear. Campbell's last hope, two Q-ship torpedoes, missed the submerged U-boat. The German was driven away by the approach of an American escort vessel, but *Dunraven* sank that night in spite of valiant efforts to tow her into Plymouth. Her crew was saved.

The last victory for the Q-ships was won by *Privet* just two days before the war ended. Attacking at night with gunfire and depth charges, she sent U-34 to the bottom and then herself sank, just short of sanctuary in Plymouth Harbor. She would be raised later and serve again.

The Q-ships have passed into history along with the gun-to-gun, single-ship tradition of combat at sea. But in their time they contributed immeasurably to British success in the battle of the sea lanes. They scored eleven certain victories and damaged at least sixty more U-boats. Those damaged limped back to harbor ahead of schedule, missing hundreds of days on station as a result, days when merchantmen sailed to England unmolested. Other U-boats used their precious torpedoes rather than surface to sink a merchantman with deck guns; every "fish" expended meant they would have to leave the shipping lanes that much sooner.

The Q-ships and their crews added a rich legacy to the tradition of valor and silent service that still imbues the Royal Navy. Though both ships and men are gone, their memory is evergreen.

CHAPTER THIRTY-TWO

DUST OFF

The Astonishing Major Brady

I HAVE NEVER met anybody who knew where the term "dust off" came from. It was just there, an expression everybody used and understood. And in Vietnam, I never heard anybody use the word in anything but a respectful voice. "Dust off" meant helicopter medical evacuation. It meant a quick, smooth trip to the best military medical care in the world. It meant an end to pain. It meant life.

A dust-off Huey came in and got me one dark night outside Pleiku. My affliction was not a combat wound, but I hurt like hell. The crew treated me as if I were made of glass, and I was delivered to the hospital pad in minutes. I have never forgotten the efficiency and the care. Neither have a lot of other men who are alive because dust-off helicopters flew into very bad places, under intense fire, in horrible weather, and got them out. And nothing illustrates the professional excellence and cold courage of the dust-off crews better than the story of a enormously courageous pilot named Brady.

Patrick Henry Brady first went to Vietnam in 1964, fresh out of flight school. In those days there were only a handful of Bell UH-1 Hueys in-country, and they were supposed to service all of Vietnam. Brady and the other youngsters with him learned their trade the hard way, pioneering night flying and repeatedly braving hostile fire to

extract hurt men from the battlefield. By the time Brady's tour was
over, he was one of the world's most experienced dust-off pilots—
his five-aircraft unit had moved over four thousand wounded men.

Brady returned to Vietnam in 1967 as Major Brady, executive
officer of the 54th Medical Detachment, a helicopter medevac unit,
forty men and six brand-new helicopters with brand-new pilots. The
birds wouldn't stay new very long; neither would the young pilots.
The unit settled near Chu Lai, on the coast of Vietnam's long skinny
waistline. The country to the west rose quickly toward the Annamese
Cordillera, a series of wicked limestone ridges covered with double-
and triple-canopy jungle. Below the huge teak and mahogany trees,
a tangle of brush and vines darkened the earth to a sort of permanent twilight.

It was bad country to fly in, especially in the fog and mist that
often covered the forest, especially in the downpours and drizzles of
the monsoon. Up there, Brady often flew night evacuations guided
only by flares popped on the ground; the eerie glare of the flares
gave him just enough light to see at least the outline of the terrain.
Other missions were flown in fog so thick that Brady kept his aircraft
level only by watching the tips of his rotor blades and the treetops
drifting past in the gloom of the fog.

The unit's average for battle damage exceeded 100 percent per
month, which translated into seven helicopters shot up each month—
and there were only six birds assigned. On the average, only three
Hueys were flyable at any given time.

The difficult was routine for Brady and his crew, but one amazing
day has got to stick out from all the rest. It began with a "fog
mission," under close-range enemy fire, to evacuate Vietnamese
wounded. Brady got it done flying low and sideways, following a
trail, his rotors blowing the fog aside ahead of him.

The day quickly got tougher. The next run was a rotor-blade-and-
treetop run to pull out badly wounded men from a fog-blocked valley.
Although two other helicopters had already crashed trying to reach
the wounded, Brady made four runs under North Vietnamese fire as
American soldiers cheered on a hilltop firebase nearby.

Brady's next run took him into another hot landing zone; he got
his wounded out, but the helicopter was finished for the day, its
controls partially shot away. Brady got a new bird and flew off on
still another mission. This one took him into the middle of a mine-

field, where another dust-off chopper had pulled out after a mine detonated. But there were still wounded there, and Brady gingerly set down his Huey where the other helicopter had been, on the thesis that there should be no more mines under the skids and the wash from the rotors would not set off nearby mines . . . probably.

Once on the ground, Brady's crew chief and medic began to carry wounded men toward the bird, heedless of their own safety. When a mine went off, the body the crew were carrying took most of the force of the explosion—Brady's men survived, but some of the blast struck the helicopter. Taking off with a full load of wounded, Brady watched the glow of warning lights on his instrument panel and wondered whether the Huey would last.

It did. Brady's wounded made the hospital and Brady's crew survived. Brady traded in his wreck for his third helicopter of the day and promptly flew back into the war. There were more wounded to save.

"It was a pretty full day," said Brady later with wonderful understatement. The army thought so, too. In the autumn of 1969, Brady added the Congressional Medal of Honor to his Distinguished Service Cross and four Distinguished Flying Crosses. It is pleasant to add that for all his daring Brady survived all the risks he so willingly took. At last count he wore two stars.

CHAPTER THIRTY-THREE

THE MEN WHO HAD NO NERVES

The Lost Battalion

THEY WERE AN odd lot, this 77th Division. An outfit like the 28th Division could accurately call itself all-Pennsylvania; the 82d Division (long before parachutes) was proud to be named all-American. But the 77th could best be called all-everything, for it was a melting pot in every sense of the word, and in that sense it probably represented the young United States better than any other outfit in France.

The 77th came from New York City, mostly, and although somebody figured out that it spoke forty-two languages, everybody rattled away in the abrasive, undefinable patois of the city's boroughs. There were immigrants from every place under the sun, including China: Germans, Jews, Italians, every race of the Near East, even some hillbillies who added their Appalachian twang to the babel of tongues. It was no accident that its shoulder patch was a white Statue of Liberty on a blue field.

The division was street-smart, cynical, intense, and very cocky indeed. It was tough, too, which was a good thing, for it was headed into a very bad place. In August 1918, the 77th went into line along the Vesle River, the stream that flows past lovely Reims. Up ahead were some very tough Germans, many of them well dug in, some of them deep in caves above the river itself.

The 77th was led by the right kind of commander, a general named Robert Alexander, a Scots mustang up from the ranks. He had done his familiarization tour with the veteran British 51st (Highland) Division, where he had learned a great deal about dealing with wire and trenches and hard-case Germans. Alexander had commanded one of Black Jack Pershing's regiments in the chase after Pancho Villa, and Pershing knew what this man was made of. It was inevitable that he would get a division command, and the 77th was it.

Alexander had not had, as he put it, "the advantages of West Point," but he was born to command men in battle. He was a soldier's general, the kind who terrorizes lazy cooks and arrogant billeting officers and uncaring doctors. After the war was over, a well-dressed New Yorker stopped Alexander in Manhattan one day. "Remember me, General?" he asked.

> I was the raggedy-assed corporal you saw on the Vesle. You asked me where the supply officer could be found and I led you to him. And then you said, "Why in hell don't you give this man a decent pair of britches to go to war in?" I got them that same day.

Which Alexander, being the kind of man he was, probably thought was the nicest compliment he had ever gotten.

Alexander recognized the quality of his new division, and its strength. He soon issued an order directing platoon leaders to capitalize on what he called the "gang spirit" of the men, and he promised his troops overwhelming artillery support on its next push (he delivered, too). He fired an influential general who did not deliver, and he looked out for his weary troops, first, last, and always. And Alexander had a certain panache that appealed to his rough New Yorkers. He made his rounds with a shepherd dog sitting beside his limousine driver—a German shepherd, of course, who would ultimately abandon Europe to live out his days in Brooklyn with the general's driver.

This was just the man to command this Tower of Babel in its hour of trial. And a trial it was to be. For the next month the 77th fought through the toughest of the Aisne-Marne offensive, and it did very well indeed. It fought with a sort of underplayed gallantry, learning its trade the hard way, pushing forward with a species of grumbling good humor characteristic of New Yorkers.

Aisne-Marne had been tough, but the Argonne would be tougher. By the first of October, the 77th was facing a bristling defensive area called the Palette Pavillion, the 28th Pennsylvania Division on its right, a French division to the left. The pavillion's high ground commanded the dense woods of the south Argonne, but also the open green valley through which the French troops next to the 77th would have to advance.

The 77th itself was ordered to push through dense woods and rocky ravines, a riot of vegetation so thick that it was always twilight under the dense branches. There the thickets were tangled with barbed wire and hidden chicken wire screens, and everything was swept with interlocking machine gun fire. The Germans had had lots of time to fortify this ground, and they had wasted none of it. If one outpost line was overrun, you could count on another defensive line waiting farther uphill, and then another. To the men of the 77th, veterans by then, that hill country looked like a very bad place indeed.

It was.

The division jumped off at six-thirty on the morning of the first of October—and met trouble immediately. Among the units in the first wave was the First Battalion of the 308th Infantry Regiment, commanded by a skinny, reserved major named Charles W. Whittlesey. Whittlesey's battalion was at about half strength, perhaps between 350 and 400 men on line, spread thinly across a brushy, wooded front big enough to accommodate an entire regiment.

Bespectacled, quiet Whittlesey had seen a lot of war by that time, albeit from a headquarters perspective. He was not a professional soldier, but he had learned. A Wisconsin native, he had been a New York lawyer before he joined up in 1916 . . . as a private. He had been a dedicated peacetime soldier, too, a graduate of the officers' training camp at Plattsburg, New York, an operation set up in the naive days before the war spread to America.

Plattsburg and other camps like it were designed to give some rudimentary training in tactics, marksmanship, and other basics to men who might have to command raw new soldiers in a vastly expanded army. As they labored through the last palmy days of peace, these dedicated men could not dream how quickly their time would come.

Those who ridiculed the idea of ever fighting another war, those who liked to laugh at soldiers, the isolationists of the Wilson administration, all made fun of the earnest Plattsburg students, sweating through the long hot days of training, often on their own money. In the event, however, Plattsburg and other camps like it produced a cadre of men with at least the rudiments of military training.

Whittlesey was a quick study, rising to captain by the time his outfit sailed for France in the spring of 1918. This bespectacled Harvard man served as the regiment's operations officer until he was chosen to command the First Battalion. He would prove to be an inspired choice.

Whittlesey's men were supported by detachments from the 306th Machine Gun Battalion and by Captain George G. McMurtry's Second Battalion of the 308th. McMurtry was another Harvard lawyer, another Plattsburg graduate, and an ex–Rough Rider to boot. His battalion was also understrength, about the same size as Whittlesey's. McMurtry was a solid soldier, too, tough and fearless, but he labored under the same difficulties that plagued Whittlesey.

In the first place, his battalion and Whittlesey's were the whole regiment. The Third Battalion had been pulled out into brigade reserve; its own regimental commander no longer had any control over it. Worse, the terrain was awful, even for the Argonne. The regimental sector was split by a deep, brushy ravine that ran diagonally across the sector. Whittlesey had his A, B, and C companies in line to the east of it; D Company was isolated on the west.

Behind Whittlesey's men, McMurtry's battalion was similarly split: F Company supported Whittlesey's D; his other three companies followed Whittlesey's A, B, and C. Companies A and C of the 306th Machine Gun Battalion went along, the crews lugging the Hotchkiss guns and their heavy tripods.

It was a recipe for disaster.

Whittlesey's 1st Battalion jumped off at six-thirty A.M. behind an artillery barrage that—like all barrages—was supposed to pulverize enemy resistance and, of course, did nothing of the sort. The battalion ran into heavy resistance, methodical and deadly machine gun and artillery that halted the attack quickly and everywhere. On the American flanks, the French were stopped cold and the Pennsylvanians bogged down in front of the caves called Le Chene Tondu. By ten

A.M. the wheels had come off the American attack and casualties were very heavy.

But the day was not over. Don't worry about your flanks, Pershing had ordered; don't look back; push on. And so General Alexander sent the 77th in again an hour and a half past noon. Now Whittlesey found a crevice in the German line and hammered at it, and suddenly he was through, breaking through belts of barbed wire with comparative ease and overrunning German trenches. They took only about thirty prisoners, however, and no more than three of those deadly machine guns, and they took ninety casualties getting through.

It quickly became obvious that the Germans were falling back, in order and without panic, holing up in prepared positions along a line of high ground farther south. Whatever meager success the Americans had had, it was all to do over again. As for Whittlesey, however, at least he was close to his objective, the Charlevaux Mill, and he had found a place in which to dig in. It was called the Ravine de Charlevaux, and Whittlesey could not know then that he would be there an almighty long time.

There was a road, winding along a sort of bench cut into the slope of the hill, with a cliff above it some twenty feet high. The road therefore lay in dead ground that many of the German guns above them could not reach. There was a little stream, too, flowing from east to west, and a spring, so Whittlesey's men would not lack for water. He was in touch with McMurtry's men, behind him and in a tolerable defensive position.

His men were well supplied with ammunition, but food was a problem; before their attack they had packed only a single day's rations of hard tack and corned beef. To make matters worse, two companies had jumped off to attack without time to collect and issue rations. Those who had food shared their meager supply with these men. It was cold, too, and the men were without blankets or coats, left behind at the jump-off line for the attack.

And so Whittlesey posted his machine guns out on the flanks, and his men dug their "funk holes" as best they could in the hard and rocky earth. Whittlesey tied into his regiment's reserve battalion through relays of runners and waited for the inevitable German counterattacks. What he needed most, however, was what he could not have: the regiment's Third Battalion.

For there was a gaping rupture to his left, a void of about a mile that he had supposed would be filled by a French division. The plan had looked good on paper, except that now the French were not there. They were not even close. Not only had they not come up on line with Whittlesey's men, they had stopped some fifteen hundred yards to the rear. They might as well have dug in on the moon.

As soon as he learned that the French had failed to link up with Whittlesey and cover his flank, Alexander did what he could: he ordered up the missing battalion of the 308th and called for the reserve battalion from his other brigade. They were to fill the hole to Whittlesey's left, plugging the gap where the French were not.

Except that they never got there. War is confusing at the best of times, and these were the days of uncertain communications; radios were unreliable and too heavy to carry, so men made do with carrier pigeons and human runners. There was no certitude. And so, for this reason and the general fog of battle, neither battalion got where it was supposed to go.

Wandering about in the night, they lost their way entirely, one battalion bumping its nose straight into the flank of the French in the gloom. Only one company of the 307th Infantry found its way to Whittlesey, led by a tough and enterprising captain named Nelson Holderman. And that was all.

Meanwhile, if neither the French nor the reserve battalions could find the hole in the American front, the Germans could and did. Whittlesey discovered that they had when he sent one of McMurtry's lieutenants back to find and bring in his lonely D Company and McMurtry's F from across the ravine. What the lieutenant found was not the missing companies but tangles of brand-new barbed wire and a profusion of Germans, including heavy weapons.

This was the Germans' home ground, after all. They had held it a long time, and they knew it well. Not only did they infest the ground on Whittlesey's flank, they had broken his chain of runner relays, his only contact with his own rear. The lieutenant shot his way out of trouble and brought the ominous news back to Whittlesey. By the time he got back, the Germans had extended their tentacles across Whittlesey's rear. The Americans were surrounded. Carrying parties sent back for more rations disappeared.

Their opponents were elements of two German divisions. One was the 76th Reserve Division; the second was the 2d Landwehr, a unit of middle-aged reservists who weren't supposed to be first-line soldiers. They held the high ground, however; and although they were fighting on the defensive, they did it very well indeed.

Whittlesey had no more than six hundred men in his little pocket, an egg-shaped cauldron about 350 yards long and 70 deep running along the hillside bench and its country road. He also had eight carrier pigeons, two of which he promptly flew off to Alexander asking for what he needed, which was about everything from food to help. The only thing this skinny New Englander neither asked for nor needed was determination. Whittlesey had never learned how to say "surrender," as the German army was about to learn.

Early the next morning, the division tried to punch through to Whittlesey. It went in with both brigades abreast in a thick fog—and got nowhere at all. It was like attacking, as one company commander put it,

> in a blind world of whiteness and noise, something like the surface of the moon. One literally could not see two yards and everywhere the ground rose into bare pinnacles and ridges or descended into bottomless caverns, half-filled with rusty tangles of wire . . . the thickest jungle I have ever seen and it seemed to go on forever . . . .

The Germans had their machine guns registered on every yard, their fields of fire interlocking and complementary. If one gun were overrun, there were always more to sweep the same deadly ground. Visibility in the mist and thick brush was nearly zero, and casualties steadily mounted. Another American attack went in at four o'clock that afternoon and achieved nothing but two hundred or so more hurt men and corpses.

Even where runners could successfully wiggle, squirm, and sprint from one unit to another—assuming they did not lose their way, their life, or their liberty—messages still arrived garbled, losing coherence as they were passed from man to man in the noise, confusion, and fear of combat. This was a special problem for the 77th, with its astonishing babel of dialects and broken English. General Alexander later recalled one message that began life as "Watch out for shell holes" and finished as "The captain says to go wash yer clothes."

Whittlesey was now in serious trouble, and the United States Army was bending on every effort to bail him out. Corps commander General Hunter Liggett summoned his division commanders and issued his directives. The obese Liggett was a tactical genius—"There is no fat above my collar," he once told Pershing, and he was right. He had his work cut out for him.

It was now October 5, and Whittlesey was out of both medical supplies and food. He still had enough rifle ammunition, but his grenades were almost gone. Worst of all, some 50 percent of his men had been hit. McMurtry was dragging himself around on a knee filled with German shell fragments. The formidable Captain Holderman had been wounded three times; even so, he remained in command with a chunk of stick grenade handle imbedded in his back.

As Whittlesey's men huddled on their bench along the road, the Germans showered grenades down from the high ground above them. The Americans could hear the sergeants counting, *"Ein, zwei, drei,"* so that everybody threw together, and then would come a deluge of stick grenades and a storm of fragments. German artillery and mortars added to the hell of explosions along the narrow hillside bench.

The Germans followed up with infantry probes, which the battalion threw back with losses. There were barrages by massed machine guns, phony orders called to Americans in English, and a Teutonic voice crying "Gaz masks!" "Gas masks, hell!" yelled one American, who fired in the direction of the voice and silenced the caller permanently.

Some of the American and French artillery support struck the Germans pressing the battlion closely on every side; some of it fell on Whittlesey's men themselves. It got so bad that Whittlesey flew off another of his precious pigeons:

> We are along the road parallel 276.4. Our own artillery is
> dropping a barage directly on us. For heaven's sake, stop it.

The story goes that the valiant pigeon, a bird named Cher Ami, carried its vital message back in spite of losing an eye and a leg in the storm of metal above the battlefield.

Many of the American wounded lay all day without help, for no one could reach them in the face of the heavy German fire. After sundown soldiers would crawl to those who still lived, take their canteens and refill them at the spring, then crawl back again with the life-giving water. Going for water was terribly dangerous even at night, for a German machine gun was registered on the spring.

The Germans could hear American wounded crying out and moaning below them in the gloom; they were equally powerless to help. As one German regimental commander wrote:

> The losses of the surrounded enemy in the "Amerikanest" are very heavy . . . Divisional headquarters desires to see them capitulate, for a good number of these Americans are sons and grandsons of native Germans.

Many of the American dead were unburied, and the stench was dreadful. Nobody liked to leave a comrade unburied, but the ground was very hard and the men grew steadily weaker from lack of food and rest. During daylight, when the work might have been marginally easier, nobody dared stand up to dig. Standing erect in the ravine meant death.

The living suffered agonies, for only two medics remained unhurt after the first two days. These men crawled from one wounded man to another, laying their lives on the line over and over again. They stripped blood-soaked dressings from dead men and reused them. It was that or strips of filthy uniform . . . or nothing at all. The German cordon was drawn so tight that no resupply could get through on the ground. Whittlesey's and McMurtry's men were as isolated as if they had been in Tierra del Fuego.

Except for the air. Nobody ever found out who the pilot was who flew low over the German positions, signaling to the American artillery, "Fire on me!" Other American pilots of the 50th Squadron flew mission after mission through intense ground fire, trying to find and resupply Whittlesey's desperate men.

Whittlesey put out such cloth panels as he had, but the American pilots were never able to spot them in the confusion of brush, trees, smoke, and dust. They dropped their parcels of food and ammunition blind into the maelstrom below, but in spite of their selfless heroism, not a loaf of bread or a clip of ammunition reached the lost battalion.

Two American aircraft were hit, crashing between the lines. A third, flown by two enormously courageous lieutenants named Goettler and Blackley, made pass after pass at only two hundred feet until their luck ran out on their second trip, and German fire crippled their aircraft. Even so, the gallant Goettler managed to land the plane near a French front-line unit. When the poilus ran to the downed bird, they found only two corpses sitting bolt upright in the cockpit. Both men were awarded the Congressional Medal . . . but still no supplies had gotten through.

By this time the press had learned that an American outfit was cut off and fighting for its life up on the pavillion. Whittlesey's desperate fight and the repeated efforts to break through to him made wonderful copy. And along the way somebody came up with a nifty phrase to catch the fancy of the readers back home. So the two battalions of the 308th became "The Lost Battalion" in the papers, notwithstanding the obvious fact that they were anything but lost.

On the fifth of October there was a moment of optimistic excitement when a French unit drove onto the Palette Pavillion to Whittlesey's left. The brief hope died quickly, however, when the American counterattack intended to break through to Whittlesey failed under heavy German fire, and German flank attacks drove the French off their new-won ground on the Palette.

Alexander blamed the American failure on the colonel who had commanded the left-hand regiment of the attacking brigade. He relieved the commander and appointed a fire-eating captain named Lucien Breckenridge to lead the regiment. But the advance was still stalled, and up on Whittlesey's bench it had rained during the night, so that his men were lying in mud and water. His effective strength was fewer than four hundred by then, and many of these had been wounded one or more times.

The American offensive remained stalled on the next day, October 6, although Liggett was attacking all along his line. For the first time, however, messengers got through from Whittlesey—a lieutenant and two privates who had alternatively snuck and shot their way through the German encirclement. Now, for the first time, the American command had precise information about Whittlesey's precise position, and more intelligence about the surrounding German units.

Lieutenant Colonel Eugene Houghton, commander of the 307th Infantry Regiment, listened closely; then he told Alexander he thought he could punch through to Whittlesey the next morning—he would strike at what appeared to be a hole in the German wire barrier. Houghton knew what he was talking about, too; he had been at this war for three years, serving in the Canadian army since 1915.

Before the attack could be launched, however, Whittlesey was presented with what must have been his greatest temptation. Through his lines came a captured American carrying an invitation from the German commander to surrender and save his wounded further suffering. The message carrier was a kid named Lowell Hollingshead, one of McMurtry's men, and he must have been longing to get back to his own people. Even so, Hollingshead at first refused to carry the message at all. Finally, he said he would go, but only if the German officer wrote the right kind of note. And so the major scribbled:

> The bearer . . . has been taken prisoner. . . . He refused to give the German Intelligence Officer any answer . . . and is quite an honorable fellow . . . believing that he is doing wrong to his country to carry . . . this . . . letter. . . . He is quite a soldier. We envy you.

One tale, apparently told by Damon Runyon, said that Whittlesey himself answered, calling out to the German commander to go to hell. But that was not in Whittlesey's character, nor is there a record of any reply by Whittlesey at all. He handed the German's note around to Holderman and McMurtry, and the three men smiled at this appeal "to your humane sentiments." Otherwise, Whittlesey's only reaction was to roll up his tiny white aircraft recognition panels—he wanted nobody to think the battalion was showing a white flag.

In fact, Whittlesey's men seem to have answered for themselves once they learned of the surrender offer, shouting all manner of suggestions in both English and German, all of them rude and most of them obscene. One soldier seems to have spoken for everybody: "Come over and get us, you Dutch bastards!" Which, if not strictly accurate, was answer enough.

And so, about a half hour later, the Germans put in an attack in force on the American right flank. At the point of it were five flame-throwers, the dreaded *flammenwerfer*, which could fry a man alive. Of the American machine gunners' nine Hotchkiss guns, only one was still operable. The last gun, however, caught all five flame crews and cut them down, the thrashing muzzles of their weapons belching flame across the attacking Germans and setting the thick brush afire.

The hard rocks of the defense were still at it, still leading, still calling out to their men: Whittlesey, McMurtry, and Holderman (who hobbled about using a pair of rifles for crutches in spite of a German slug in his shoulder). The astonishing Holderman at one point stood erect in the open on his crutches, shooting Germans with his Colt .45 as they rushed an American machine gun. And when another German push came in from north and northeast, it too fell apart before the concentrated fire of the American Springfields.

Every time a German infantry probe went in behind the potato mashers and the mortars, it was met with deliberate, well-aimed rifle fire. None of the German attacks made any appreciable progress in the face of those deadly Springfields, and the Germans were deeply impressed with the solid professionalism of the trapped Americans.

One German lieutenant put it pretty well. The Americans absolutely lacked nerves, he said: "Our men were jumpy and worn out; the Americans did not seem discouraged at all." The German would have admired the American private, shot in the stomach, who managed a smile for McMurtry. "It pains like hell, Captain," said the soldier, "but I'll keep as quiet as I can."

And then, behind them, Whittlesey's men began to hear the unmistakable clatter of Chauchat automatic rifles, the French weapons with which so many American units were equipped. When it worked, which it did sometimes, you could always recognize a Chauchat. Now they sounded like the bells of heaven. These were friendlies, and they sounded close.

They were. A whole brigade was battering its way through the German circle, its fifty-seven-year-old commander out in front of the first wave. The first Americans most of Whittlesey's troops saw were the leading elements of 3d Battalion, 307th Infantry. Among them was a nonchalant doughboy carrying a sack full of canned corned beef hooked to his bayonet. It must have looked like the nectar of the gods.

Houghton had made it, and his men were soon tossing their own combat rations to Whittlesey's famished survivors and tending to the wounded, almost two hundred of them. The survivors were close to exhaustion, as the adrenaline drained away, and many of them had stomach cramps from eating tree bark. One of their chief concerns—American to the core—was the fate of little Cher Ami, the tiny pigeon that had carried their last message.

The pigeon was all right, they were told; he was getting the best of care, a wooden leg and all the grain he could handle. Cher Ami was being retired, they said, and Whittlesey's men no doubt answered that that was more than they were getting, and laughed. But at least they were alive, and they had full bellies for a change, and the abiding comfort of cigarettes. And no doubt they were proud, too, as they had every right to be, for they volunteered to remain in the line for the rest of the Argonne offensive.

Of the 554 who had started in the pocket, just 194 fell in at the foot of the hill after the shooting stopped—and many of these were wounded. General Alexander walked among them and saw their spirit, and he visited Whittlesey, who was busy making sure his men were all fed.

Then Alexander went back to his headquarters and telephoned General Liggett, and then he called back forward to tell Whittlesey that he was a lieutenant colonel and McMurtry was a major. They were both getting the Congressional Medal of Honor, he said, and so was the indestructible Holderman.

Suddenly they were famous, too. Damon Runyon's "Go to hell" line had made Whittlesey an instant and permanent celebrity, even though the major never said it. The fable was probably born, in fact, when Runyon asked General Alexander how Whittlesey answered the German summons to surrender. "Why, he told him to go to hell, of course," said the plainspoken general, never dreaming Runyon would take him literally.

But he did, and so did America, and if the story was a fable it was a damned good one, the sort of thing Americans have always warmed to. And Whittlesey's force would always be "the lost battalion," even though it wasn't a battalion, and even though Alexander said pithily that Whittlesey's men were neither lost nor rescued. Alexander's comment on the battalion's fight was all army—and very close to the actual truth:

Major Whittlesey and his command held the position to which they had proceeded under my order and were found by me, when I visited them on the very early morning of October 8th, an organized command, in good order, and in excellent spirits.

For Whittlesey the war was over. He was shipped back to Fort Dix, New Jersey, to train troops for the rest of the war and was horrified to find himself a national icon. He was idolized wherever he went and was deluged with invitations to speak at all manner of events. Whittlesey paid dearly for every speech he made, however, for each one of them dredged up the terrible memories of the death on the slope of the pavillion. The attention and adulation never stopped, even after the war was over. Even a return to civilian life and to his law practice could not wipe out the memories of the dreadful days and night in the Argonne.

In 1921, after a speech on "the lost battalion" for the Red Cross, Whittlesey bared his soul to a friend. "Raking over the ashes like this," he said,

> revives all the horrible memories. I'll hear the wounded scream-
> ing again. I have nightmares about them. I can't remember when
> I last had a good night's sleep.

On Armistice Day in 1921 Whittlesey was again recognized, serving as one of the ceremonial pallbearers for the Unknown Soldier at Arlington Cemetery. It was a great honor, but it seems to have been the straw that broke the camel's back, for just over a week later Whittlesey sat down to write a will and several letters to relatives and friends, including McMurtry. And then, on the morning of November 26, he left New York on the steamer *Toloa,* bound for Cuba. That evening, unusually, he talked animatedly about the war to other passengers.

And then somewhere in the night far out at sea, Whittlesey climbed over a deck railing and stepped out into the foggy autumn night. No trace of him was ever found.

At last he could sleep.

CHAPTER THIRTY-FOUR

THE MAN WHO USED HIS HEAD

ROWAN WADDY WAS an Australian, part of a select commando force engaged in giving the Japanese fits all across the Pacific. Waddy was tough and smart, and a survivor, but he had an unusual problem: how was he to display his most impressive decoration for achievement in combat? Ribbons and medals are easy enough to display . . . but how do you conveniently show off a smoked head?

The head had once been part of a Japanese soldier—a member, in fact, of the dreaded secret police, the Kempei Tai. Now, properly shrunken and smoked, it belonged to Waddy, for its owner had engaged Waddy in a brief firefight and come in second.

In this summer of 1945, Waddy was in Sarawak, organizing the ferocious Iban headhunters to strike at the Japanese. The pro-British Ibans were delighted to assist. Not only did they detest the Japanese, but they were invited to collect heads once more, an old and treasured tradition forbidden by British law before the war. Happy days were back again.

The Ibans were an engaging people, cheerful, hospitable, and murderous, and they were impressed by Waddy's killing of the secret policeman; he was their kind of fighting man. As a token of professional respect, they painstakingly prepared the head and presented it to Waddy with speechmaking and feasting and dancing. He was a warrior of warriors, and the Ibans were willing to follow him against the Japanese enemy. With their loyalty Waddy would perform his mission with great success.

Which is what comes of using your head—or somebody else's.

CHAPTER THIRTY-FIVE

THE RAID THAT NEVER WAS
The Calcutta Light Horse at Marmagoa

CAPTAIN ROEFER PULLED down hard on the alarm cord, and the shriek of *Ehrenfels'* siren split the muggy night. The alarm howled out over the steaming darkness of the harbor, screaming that the *verdamnt* British were in the harbor, alerting his crew, calling for help from ashore. The German captain spun around as the door to his cabin burst open. Framed in the door were two middle-aged, slightly paunchy men in khaki dungarees.

These were not the young, tough Royal Marine or Royal Navy boarders Captain Roefer expected. These men looked like typical British businessmen, too old to serve in war. Captain Roefer would never know that was exactly what they were, for they were the last thing the captain saw on earth. As the captain and his mate reached for weapons, a Sten gun clattered from the door, and the ship's officers died quickly in the crowded cabin, crumpling under the gaze of a portrait of Adolf Hitler glaring down from the bulkhead.

On this night of March 9, 1943, one of the most astonishing raids of all time was under way. It was under way, moreover, on neutral territory, in Marmagoa, harbor of Portuguese Goa, on the west coast of India. Any violation of this tiny Portuguese enclave ran the horrible risk of offending neutral Portugal, with the consequent loss of extremely valuable privileges, such as the right of transatlantic flights to refuel in the Portuguese Azores.

But risky or not, something had to be done about Marmagoa—or, rather, about the German freighter *Ehrenfels,* interned in Goa since the early days of the war. She lay at anchor with her sister ships, *Drachenfels* and *Braunfels,* and the Italian merchantman *Anfora.* Any of the four ships, loose at sea, would be useful to the Axis, especially if they could make Singapore, where the Japanese might fit them out as commerce raiders.

But *Ehrenfels* posed a far greater danger, for concealed aboard her she carried a powerful radio transmitter. And she used it regularly, for she was no less than the control for German U-boats ravaging Allied shipping all across the vastness of the Arabian Sea and the Indian Ocean. To *Ehrenfels* were delivered the reports of the Axis spy system in India, reports of sailings and arrivals, many of them provided by Indian traitors.

Protests to the Portuguese fell on deaf ears. Officially, *Ehrenfels'* radio equipment had been removed when she was interned, and that was that. The Portuguese colonial officials did not want a confrontation with Germany or anybody else; they wanted no fuss and bother at all. Some things it was better not to know, such as the presence on *Ehrenfels* of another powerful transmitter, able to reach far out to sea, to the waiting ears of lurking U-boats.

Raiding in neutral harbors being desperate business, the British first tried simple kidnapping. Two officers of SOE—Special Operations Executive—drove across the Goan border in civilian clothing and casually snatched one of the major German secret agents in all of Asia. His code name was Trompeta, and it was to him that reports came in of British ship movements. Trompeta then relayed the information to an officer on *Ehrenfels,* in Goa, and more vital Allied shipping died at sea.

The two Englishmen approached the problem directly: they jammed a pistol into Trompeta's belly, conducted him and his screaming wife to their car, and drove off under the nose of a shouting policeman. Once out of town, the two cut the telephone lines to the border, injected both their captives with a powerful sedative, and drove on to the crossing point. While one Englishman visited the border officials' shack, the other sat in the car. He was prepared to throw a bag of rupees into the road if there was trouble; the idea was to smash straight through the wooden border barricade while the Goanese were distracted by the money.

But there was no alarm, and the two amateur kidnappers returned safely to India with their prizes. It was neatly done, and it knocked an important cog out of the German intelligence machinery, but it did not fix the problem. In spite of this daring coup, and British arrests of a number of little fish, other agents continued to pass shipping information to *Ehrenfels*.

No, jailing spies was not enough; something had to be done about *Ehrenfels* herself, and done quickly. The German freighter had to be attacked directly. There were several options: in the best Nelson tradition, she could be cut out and sailed out of the harbor, the ideal solution; or her radio system could be entirely destroyed; or she could simply be sunk in the harbor. One way or another, she had to be silenced. Allied merchant shipping—stretched thin all over the world—could not stand U-boat losses at this rate.

The prickly question of Portuguese neutrality made conventional raiding an unacceptable risk. A strike by Commandos or a Navy boarding party was the obvious answer to the *Ehrenfels* menace, but if it went sour, there would be hell to pay and no pitch hot. So regular forces were out of the question; the job had to be done by somebody without official connection to Britain, somebody who could be disavowed if the raid failed, somebody expendable.

It was also desirable that whoever struck the Portuguese port have a suitable—and real—civilian cover, and that they come from far away, to lessen the chances of discovery. With these requirements in mind, the British intelligence community cast about for another tool, and in the end its hand fell upon a military unit both available and eager. It was, however, a somewhat unlikely instrument for a delicate, supersecret foray against an enemy on neutral ground.

It was called the Calcutta Light Horse, a reserve cavalry unit of ancient lineage that had (and has) its own monument in St. Paul's Cathedral. Its battle honors reached all the way back to 1759, and it had known great days. The rebels of the Indian Mutiny had called it *Shaitan Pultan*—"regiment of devils"—and on formal occasions of state it performed with dash as the viceroy's escort. More than fifty of its men had been killed in action in the two world wars, and six of its members had won the coveted Victoria Cross.

Between wars it had provided a warm and pleasant social center for British civilians in Calcutta, a place where a young man might ride and race, and meet and become part of the British community. It had elected its own officers since 1857, but new men started always as ordinary troopers regardless of their civilian office or profession. Promotion was entirely on merit—and on the vote of the regiment.

Just now, however, it was a slightly rusty sword, reduced to being largely a social club, for nearly all of its younger members were already on active duty with British forces all over the world. Its average age in 1941 was almost forty, and growing older. The men who were left were either too old for active service or too vital to spare from their jobs as company directors and civil servants. Most of them had already volunteered for active duty and been rejected, and all of them chafed at being left out of the war. They still trained regularly and enthusiastically, but gradually their hope of getting into the war was fading away.

The colonel of the Light Horse, Bill Grice, was just the sort of man to entrust with a wild, forlorn hope like the Goa raid. As a young man he had served in HMS *Vindictive* in the daring British strike on Zeebrugge, on the last St. George's Day of World War I. He had lost none of his taste for action in the years between, and began to quietly gather Light Horsemen for what promised to be, as the British put it, a very rum go indeed. Grice could not take more than about twenty men, and the four Axis ships' companies would outnumber his skimpy force many times over.

It would be a shoestring operation in other ways, as well. Small arms and plastic explosive were plentiful enough, but a ship was another matter. British shipping was stretched to the breaking point already, and a warship could not be used in any case. In the end, after much searching, Grice's men fell upon *Phoebe;* she was unglamorous, a thirty-year-old, Glasgow-built gondola barge designed for the pedestrian job of dredging channels through the shifting sands of India's Hoogly River.

Phoebe was not bred for blue-water service, but she was willing, and with her came a couple of resourceful Royal Navy hands to keep her going and the redoubtable Bernard Davies, ex–Royal Navy destroyer officer. Could he get her to Goa, asked Grice. Certainly, said Davies. He'd have to stay close to land to keep the Indian crew from panicking, and he'd have to pay his lascar seamen double wages, but it could be done. How much time did he have? Almost none, answered Grice. Good, said Davies, because the monsoon was coming, and once it hit, *Phoebe* could not survive in the open sea.

On that cheerful note, Grice chose his boarding party from a crowd of eager volunteers, including in his force four men from another reserve outfit, the Calcutta Scottish, with whom there had long been much good-natured rivalry. Grice put his chosen men, paunches and all, through a crash course of refresher training under the hard eyes of two somewhat dubious regular army sergeants. "Here they are, then," said one unimpressed NCO. "If these are the Light Horse, what must the heavy mob be like?"

Whatever their reservations, the sergeants pushed the Light Horse hard, driving them through long sessions of hand-to-hand combat and physical conditioning. Hard training had become even more important because Grice had received word that the Axis ships were expecting an attack, and their decks were now littered with a hideous assortment of incendiary and explosive traps. Even if the enemy did not have firearms, even if Grice achieved surprise, his men could be engulfed in an inferno as they came aboard.

In addition to bearing the pain from creaking joints and muscles long unused, the Light Horsemen also had the anguish of inventing more-or-less plausible reasons to be away from Calcutta. At least one wife wondered whether her husband of many years was visiting a lady elsewhere, and a newly engaged reservist had to go to the trouble to write a series of love letters to be mailed at intervals by a friend at a place very far from Goa.

At last, however, March arrived, the torrents of the monsoon held off, and *Phoebe* sailed south. Grice and his strike force followed by train, rolling across the length of India to the southern port of Cochin. There they somewhat dubiously boarded *Phoebe,* already a veritable Ark of lascar crewmen, crates of gear, cackling chickens, and odoriferous goats.

For most of the raiding party, their first glimpse of *Phoebe* was not entirely reassuring. They went aboard as casually as possible, in small groups, and carefully tore up anything to connect them with the Light Horse and home, even their bills from the Cochin hotel where they had stayed.

And in the afternoon little *Phoebe* slipped quietly out of Cochin Harbor until she struck the swells of deep water and turned south. Only after dark did the little dredge turn again, this time to the north, running through the dark without lights for Goa. There was no moon, and the night was thick and heavy with heat.

Meanwhile, in Goa itself, the critical first part of Grice's operation was unfolding, the operation designed to cut down the terrible odds against *Phoebe*'s boarders. Even if the raiding party could achieve the advantage of surprise, there were far too many German and Italian crewmen in Goa for Grice's tiny group to take on alone. The crews had to be thinned out, and the Light Horse had thought up an ingenious way to do it.

And so down to Goa came a remarkable man named Jock Cartwright, in civilian life an executive with a jute company. Physically disqualified for the raiding party itself, and bitterly disappointed that he could not go along, Cartwright had pleaded for a part in the operation. His only son was missing in action, and he ached for a chance to get into the war. Very well, said Grice, you shall, and what you will do will be essential to success.

In Goa, Cartwright did two things. First, he called on an influential Portuguese official to encourage that avaricious and pliable man to see to it that both a city fiesta and a gala government reception were given on a certain night in early March. To these festivities he might well invite local dignitaries of all sorts, and, of course, he should include the officers of all ships lying in the harbor. Cartwright, ever helpful, had even seen to it that proper invitations were printed, and he produced a sheaf of them, carried safely into Goa in a box welded to the frame of his car.

For this small favor, he told the official, he would be most grateful. He might be of some help, too. He knew, for example, that the official's two children went to school in India and that the expense of keeping them there was considerable. He felt quite certain that their tuition might be paid in full in return for the official's kindness. Also, of course, the expense of the fiesta and reception would be defrayed; neither the government nor the official would be out a peseta.

Did they understand one another? They did, especially when Cartwright handed the official an envelope, stuffed with banknotes, for his "immediate and personal expenses." The Goan had one question, however: why was the reception specifically set for ten P.M. on the ninth of March?

"That I cannot tell you," said Cartwright politely. "And I think

it would be unprofitable and unwise to ponder too deeply upon it.''
If Cartwright's reply was less than satisfying, the Portuguese clearly
understood the undesirability of further inquiry.

Cartwright's next move was a curious one for a God-fearing, middle-aged, middle-class Englishman: he strolled into the town to visit
one of Goa's multitude of brothels. His conversation with the keeper
of the house went something like this:

Did the *senhor* wish particular pleasures? Everything was available, and of course at a reasonable price.

No, the *senhor* did not wish pleasures of that sort, but there was
a matter of business to discuss. He was, ah, an ex-sailor and wished
to do something brotherly for those who still went down to the sea
in ships. He would be willing, for example, to fund a free night in
Marmagoa's leaping-houses—this one and all the others—for sailors
of all nations. Could that be arranged?

It could, of course. The *senhor* was most generous. Was there a
particular night on which the sailors should be welcomed?

There was, in fact, a particular week in March. And the prices of
all the girls would be paid every night for that week.

The brothel keeper beamed. It would be an honor to assist the
senhor. Could he offer a brandy to seal the bargain? Certainly, said
Cartwright, and the deal was done.

And so it was that many of the German ships' crew members
were ashore on the night of the ninth of March, enjoying the oldest
of pleasures. At the same time many of their officers mingled with
the elite of Marmagoa in a great house high above the steamy town.
It had been a pleasant evening, a formal-dress night of music and
wine and good conversation . . . until the howl of *Ehrenfels'* siren
tore the night apart.

Up above the harbor, the guitars ceased abruptly; gone was the
pleasant clink of champagne glasses and the hum of polite conversation. The dancing and the flirtation also ceased, stopped dead by the
howl of *Ehrenfels'* siren shrieking out of the blackness of the harbor.

"It's the British!" a German officer swore. Surely not, said the
Portuguese police chief; this is a neutral port and everybody here is
under Portuguese protection. Perhaps it is some harmless prank? It
is not, said the German. It is the enemy, and he and the other Axis
officers started to run frantically downhill toward the harbor. Above
their own panting they began to hear firing out in the darkness, single

shots and the hammer of automatic weapons. And then the gleam of fire began to light the gloom of the harbor.

It was indeed the British. Little *Phoebe* chugged in out of the sticky night blacked-out and undetected, her only marking a hand-made Jolly Roger flying at her stern. The boarders' Sten guns were cocked and ready, their pockets crammed full of assorted saps, pistols, knives, and plastic explosive. One boarder thoughtfully wrapped up his glass eye in a piece of cloth and tucked it away in a pocket for safekeeping.

Phoebe was nestled against *Ehrenfels'* huge steel flank before a crew-member challenged: Who were they? They were a harbor barge, a Light Horseman answered in German. "Why are you sailing without lights?" shouted the German, but he got no answer, only a wave of strange men with blackened faces pouring up and over *Ehrenfels'* steep cold sides, swarming up rickety bamboo ladders handmade while *Phoebe* was at sea.

Other Light Horsemen tossed grappling hooks over *Ehrenfels'* rail, locking the two ships tightly together. For just a moment, *Ehrenfels'* searchlight bathed *Phoebe* in a noonday glare, until a burst of automatic fire put out its brilliant eye. Their faces blackened with camouflage paint, *Phoebe*'s boarding party spread out across the big German ship, moving almost soundlessly in boots with half an inch of felt glued to the soles.

Two of the raiders shot out the lock of *Ehrenfels'* old radio room, just seconds too late to prevent a German officer from throwing an incendiary grenade into the ship's codebooks. One Light Horse boarder tackled the German; the other clubbed him with the butt of a Sten. The blow put the German down, but the codes were past saving; the Light Horsemen ran on, pausing only to put a revolver round through Hitler's picture on the wall.

On deck a German crewman fired a flare pistol into one of the incendiary traps, and *Ehrenfels'* whole afterdeck burst into a maelstrom of flame. A Sten blew the German over the side, but the boarders could not reach the stern anchor cable to blow it loose from the ship. Worse, a party of raiders in the engine room discovered that the engines had been disabled. There was no way to cut *Ehrenfels* out and sail her away. She would have to be scuttled.

First, however, the same raiding party that had been disappointed at the condition of the engines finally had some luck. They also found a locked steel door marked "Danger—High Voltage," and quickly ripped it open with plastic explosive to reveal *Ehrenfels'* secret transmitter. The Light Horsemen tore a list of wavelengths from the front of the set, then smashed and shot the radio into useless scrap metal.

On shore, a mob of German and Italian officers were milling about in confusion at the harbor's edge. Across the black water they could hear the clatter of automatic weapons and the boom of explosions. From *Ehrenfels'* deck a fire flared brilliantly in the gloom, leaping up almost to masthead height. Men were dying out there in the darkness—and ships too—and there was absolutely nothing they could do about it.

They had run all the way to the water, but such small boats as there were along shore now lay on their sides in the mud of low tide. Nor were the Portuguese authorities at all eager to sail out to investigate, either. The police would make inquiries, they said, yes, assuredly, but there was no reason for haste.

In fact, they were right; all need for haste was past. For *Ehrenfels* was dying, her Kingston valves opened to the sea by her own crew as part of the German plan to deny her to a British cutting-out expedition. And Bill Grice was getting his people out. The mission was accomplished; the radio was junk; *Ehrenfels* was going down. It was time to leave before help arrived from shore or from the other Axis ships.

There remained a brief scuffle on *Ehrenfels'* deck as German crewmen tried to close with scattered members of the *Phoebe*'s crew. Three Germans were driven off by a blast in the face from a fire extinguisher, and two others were knocked down and handcuffed. A few were dragged onto *Phoebe* as prisoners. *Phoebe*'s little siren shrieked in the night as a last recall to the boarders; the job was done.

And then, as *Phoebe*'s hammering engine pushed her slowly away from burning *Ehrenfels* and out toward the welcoming dark of the open sea, more explosions tore the night of Marmagoa Harbor. By now, the crews of the other Axis vessels knew *Ehrenfels* had been attacked. Assuming they were next, their crews fired explosive charges to blow out their bottoms, and set massive fires on deck.

Gradually the other Axis ships settled into the shallow water of the harbor, listing, lighting the night with crimson and yellow fire. On Italian *Anfora* an entire on-deck garden slid gracefully over the side into the sea. The water was full of debris and swimming Germans and Italians, and from *Anfora* a flotilla of hogs had abandoned ship and was heading for shore.

Davies kept *Phoebe* close inshore for cover, and everybody pitched in in relays to shovel coal to the laboring engine. After what seemed an eternity, *Phoebe* began to pitch and yaw to the waves of the open sea, and the glare of the fires of Goa faded away. They maintained radio silence, except for a single message: "Longshanks," they signaled; "Longshanks." And back in India the SOE men rejoiced: *Ehrenfels* was finished.

Phoebe was well clear of the Portuguese coast by then, and the Light Horsemen broke out the last of their whiskey ration and began to sing. They had earned it. Behind them, standing in the sticky darkness of Marmagoa town, Jock Cartwright lit a cigar and watched the flames dancing out on the black water. Cartwright was deeply satisfied; the raid had gone perfectly. And he had another reason to enjoy the night and the fireworks. Just hours before, Cartwright had gotten a call through to his wife in India: his son, she told him joyfully, had survived; he was a prisoner of war, but he was alive.

Far out in the gloom to the west, U-181 surfaced at the appointed time, a sleek dark shark gliding through the black water and listening, listening in the gloom for news of new quarry to hunt, new ships and men to kill. But this night there was only silence and a little static; there was no message from Goa, and there would never be again.

The U-boats were blind. In the first eleven days of March they had sunk twelve Allied ships, British, American, and Norwegian. For all the rest of the month they would sink only one more. And in April thirteen submarines destroyed only three merchantmen. The Calcutta Light Horse had earned their whiskey.

It was all the reward they would get. Even after the war their feat went unrecognized, even by award of the general World War II campaign medal, worn by a lot of other people who had never been close to danger. The only decoration the Light Horse got was a curious one they designed themselves, a little sea horse wearing a sun helmet. The little creature appeared in *Gallop,* the regimental magazine, and was even made into jewelry given to wives and girl-friends. For long years only the Light Horse knew what the little mascot meant.

After the raid, British intelligence immediately circulated prepared press releases that stated plausibly that low morale aboard the Axis ships had prompted the crews to fire and scuttle their own vessels. Indeed, said later releases, the conflagration's root cause was a quarrel between Nazis and anti-Nazis among the crew members. Papers across the world picked up the story. The Germans knew better; surely the Portuguese suspected. But neither country had much interest in printing anything like the truth.

The Calcutta Light Horse passed away with the ending of the Raj in 1947. Quite fittingly, it was disbanded with great respect and ceremony by its honorary colonel, the last viceroy, Earl Mountbatten of Burma. The regiment left behind a rich history of service—more than six hundred of her men had fought in two world wars, not even counting the fights of the old colonial days. Many Light Horsemen gave everything they had; they are buried all over the world.

Earl Mountbatten, writing in later years, gave the regiment its finest accolade. After praising its service in its many wars, he added, somewhat cryptically: "But it was not in this country that the Calcutta Light Horse was to fulfil its destiny. . . ."

The average reader would have taken the earl's line to mean service across the world in two world wars, but the Light Horse guessed, probably correctly, that Mountbatten meant a dark harbor in a little foreign place called Goa.

CHAPTER THIRTY-SIX

AMERICAN EAGLE
The Saga of Old Abe

THE 8TH WISCONSIN Volunteer Infantry was a tough, cocky outfit. They were good and they knew it, and for them no ordinary mascot would do.

And that is how Old Abe the bald eagle came to join the regiment.

The story goes that Abe appeared in Eau Claire as an orphan chick at just about the time the regiment was getting ready to leave for the Civil War in the west. "Let him enlist!" roared the soldiers, and Abe became a member of the 8th Wisconsin. The regiment named him for the greatest of presidents, and the little eagle began his service.

After that Abe traveled with the regiment through more than thirty fights, sitting atop his own perch as bullets ripped the air around him. He was carried into action by the regimental eagle bearer, right between the regimental flag and the national colors. A red-white-and-blue shield adorned the perch.

Abe loved action. In the midst of battle he would fly up from his perch to the end of his sixteen-foot tether, his screams of patriotic defiance answered by thunderous cheers from his regiment. He ignored Rebel shouts of "Buzzard!" and other snide Southern comments, and paid no attention to two minor wounds and some tail feathers lost to the enemy's bullets.

309

Abe's wages were paid in chicken, mostly provided by the scroungers of the regiment. As one veteran put it, "He was fonder of chicken than the chaplain and not half so particular about the cookery"; and he grew big and handsome. His soldiers normally provided his chicken for him, for he was secured to his perch by a sixteen-foot tether. Occasionally, however, Abe got loose and successfully hunted on his own, always returning to his perch and his regiment, full of chicken and ready for more military duties.

Among these duties was recruiting. From time to time Abe returned to Wisconsin with some of his soldiers, and there he dutifully attended various functions for the benefit of the troops. Always he returned to the wars and his own "Eagle Regiment."

He served with the 8th Wisconsin until 1864, when he was retired, to settle in Madison as a permanent guest of the state. Abe lived in a two-room suite at the state capitol; he had several perches, his own bath, and a regular supply of succulent rabbit.

Abe never lacked for visitors, either. He was famous, and all manner of people came to see and admire this elegant bird who somehow symbolized their own country and their own pride. Abe got to travel to various postwar patriotic gatherings, too—even to the 1876 Philadelphia Centennial.

Abe passed on to Valhalla in 1881, but he is immortal on this earth too. At Vicksburg, one of Abe's battles, there is a fine memorial to the Wisconsin troops who fought there. And on top of the memorial, proud and fierce as ever, sits Abe, six feet tall and solid bronze.

And if you look at the shoulder patch of America's 101st Airborne Division, you'll find Abe again, still gallant, still defiant. He is the original Screaming Eagle, pride of a very tough, very good division with a long and gallant history.

You have to think this is the honor Old Abe would like best.

CHAPTER THIRTY-SEVEN

A FEAT OF ARMS

Après Moi le Déluge

As EARLY AS the late 1930s it occurred to some ingenious Royal Air Force operations officer that destroying the power sources feeding Germany's critical Ruhr factories might prove even more effective than pulverizing the factories themselves. Much of this Ruhr industry was driven by coal, but some of it was hydroelectric. And that meant dams. If they could be breached, power might be cut or diminished over much of the Ruhr, to say nothing of the extensive damage that the resulting floods might cause to towns, bridges, and farmland.

Thus was born Operation Chastise, nothing less than an attack on the major dams that controlled the influx of water into the river Ruhr itself, and thereby the water supply for power stations and other industrial operations that required water, such as coking ovens. Major targets were the dams on the Moehne and the Sorpe, both of which penned up enormous reservoirs to feed the vital factories in the valley below. The Moehne Dam alone held something like 130 million *tons* of water.

Several other dams were also targeted, including the Eder, which controlled the flow of water into Kassel. Kassel lay outside the Ruhr but was still a booming industrial town, specializing in the production of vital railroad rolling stock.

The concept was attractive, although RAF bombardment chief Arthur "Bomber" Harris was not convinced it would work. RAF commander Air Chief Marshal Portal endorsed the idea, however, even though the practical problems of taking out the dams were prodigious. In addition to the customary flak, there was the almost insuperable problem of precisely hitting the dams from above. Even with a solid hit, conventional bombs had virtually no chance of cracking an enormous pile of steel-reinforced concrete.

The crucial Moehne was a monster, 25 feet thick at the top, tapering out to a gargantuan 112 feet at its base. It was more than 800 yards long, and the lake behind it stretched for 12 miles. Built mostly of limestone, the Moehne Dam held back some 134 million cubic meters of water. It had been formally opened by Kaiser Wilhelm with great fanfare back in 1913, and it seemed to be as solid as the day it was built. So did the Eder, a similar concrete pile even larger than the Moehne.

The Sorpe Dam was smaller and of somewhat different construction, stone-faced earth packed around a thirty-foot concrete core. But even it seemed invulnerable to conventional weaponry. Somebody suggested torpedoing the dams, but the Germans had already thought of that: steel nets were already in place to protect the dam faces.

And so the RAF turned to one of the legitimate geniuses of World War II, Barnes Wallis of the giant Vickers firm, designer of, among other things, the highly successful Wellington bomber. He had worked on all sorts of theories about attacking mines and dams, and was designing an enormous "earthquake bomb" for use against Germany. As early as 1941, Wallis had experimented with explosives on models of the Moehne Dam.

Barnes Wallis thought it could be done. What about a sort of depth charge, he said; a large mine detonated under water, flush against the face of the dam? The right kind of blast might crack that massive concrete, and the tremendous weight of water behind the dam would do the rest. Maybe a pilot could skip the depth charge over the nets if he went in very low over the lake behind the dam, so that the bomb's angle of descent remained very shallow.

Wallis knew that both RAF and American aircraft had used skip-bombing with success against shipping, and at some point he learned that old-time Royal Navy gunners had deliberately skipped roundshot off the sea's surface to increase its range. Trying it out for himself, he experimented at his own home in Surrey, using a catapult to fire his small daughter's marbles across the surface of a water-filled tub. The idea worked.

Barnes Wallis went to work at his infernal machine, now code-named "Upkeep." It soon developed that building a bomb that would skip to its target would not be a great problem. It could be a sphere, thought Wallis, although in time he would come to realize that a cylinder would be a more workable shape.

The major difficulty was in knowing precisely when to drop it, for the bombardier would have to trigger his load at a precise height—too low to depend on an altimeter—and at a precise distance from the dam's face. The pilot would have to fly straight and level and at an exact speed on his bombing run, no matter how many tracers were flying past his cockpit.

Even touchier was the problem of keeping the bomb flush against the face of the dam as it sank to the correct depth. Nobody knows just what started Wallis thinking about putting backspin on the bomb, although the idea may well have had its genesis in a conversation between Wallis and another Vickers employee about spin-bowling at cricket.

Wallis solved this difficulty by designing a device driven by an auxiliary motor on board the bomber. This rig would start the bomb spinning at about five hundred revolutions per minute as it hung crossways under the aircraft. The bomb would continue to spin after it was dropped, so that when it skipped up to the face of the dam its backspin would keep it against the concrete until it reached thirty feet of depth. At that level, a hydrostatic device like a depth charge pistol would fire the bomb. Barnes Wallis got some practice bombs made and tried them out at Chesil Beach in December 1942. They worked.

Wallis did not have an easy time selling his theory. "Bomber" Harris, never a man to mince words, roared at Wallis before he could say anything in their first interview:

> What the hell do you damned inventors want? My boys' lives
> are too precious to be thrown away by you!

It was not an auspicious beginning, but Harris mellowed a little once he realized Wallis had not come to talk about attacking German battleships with his huge bomb. Harris was not convinced, nor would he ever be. Still, when Air Chief Marshal Portal endorsed the plan, Wallis and the RAF could get on with the Moehne raid.

Now "Chastise" went into high gear, for the optimum time to attack the dams was late spring or early summer, while the water level was at its maximum height. The RAF chose its commander first, and it chose well. He was an extraordinary twenty-four-year-old, already a Wing Commander, a tough, pleasant pilot named Guy Gibson. Gibson had already flown more missions than most pilots of any nation would fly in the whole war: 170 of them, including two tours of duty in bombers and one in night fighters.

Gibson was a driving, single-minded professional who already wore two Distinguished Flying Crosses and two Distinguished Service Orders. 617 Squadron was officially born on March 17, 1943, and Gibson became its commander the next day. On the twenty-first his new crews began to report to the RAF station at Scampton. Their experience level varied greatly: although the RAF had laid down that all 617 crews were to have finished all or nearly all of two bombing tours, some of those who reported had not completed even one.

They all had, however, one essential quality: they were volunteers. Some were already well-known as superior aircrews: one was headed by Squadron Leader H. M. Young, an Oxford rowing star married to an American, a veteran and respected pilot with two tours behind him. He would command one of Gibson's two flights and serve as squadron second in command. The other flight leader would be another veteran, Squadron Leader H. E. Maudslay, DFC.

There was Flight Lieutenant J. C. McCarthy, an American who had joined the Canadian Air Force early in the war, like Young and Maudslay a holder of the Distinguished Flying Cross. Flight Lieutenant H. B. Martin, DFC, was an Australian, well-known for his expertise in low-level operations. The others came from England and Scotland and Wales, and from every other corner of the empire and commonwealth.

Gibson would settle for nothing short of perfection, and he began training as his crews joined his brand-new squadron. Two of his aircraft were fitted with amber coverings for the cockpit windows; the crews would wear blue-tinted goggles. Night flying training would go on through the day as well.

But it was the night that counted most. Gibson's crews hammered through the English skies at all hours, startling people, pigs, and especially cattle, which protested the racket by declining to give milk. The squadron had started with the idea of warning municipal governments of practice operations, but that idea was soon overwhelmed by the necessities of training; Gibson had only ten aircraft on which to train all his crews. As soon as an airplane became available, a fresh crew took it up, and damn the advance notice.

The chosen aircraft was a much-modified variant of the Lancaster, with its four dependable Rolls-Royce Merlins and big bomb load capacity. The upper turret had been removed to save weight. The bomb bay was covered with a fairing and a couple of arms installed outside, looking rather like a couple of huge cymbals, to hold Upkeep.

These changes left the aircraft looking, as one pilot put it, "rather like a gutted fish." The addition of this great lump of a bomb did little for the lines of the Lancaster. It looked, Gibson thought, "like a pregnant duck." Inside, mechanics would install the mechanism that would start the bomb spinning. Outside would hang the bomb, an object "about the size and shape of the front wheel of a steam roller."

Which was a pretty fair description. Barnes Wallis had discarded the sphere he had started with in favor of a cylinder. Tests at Reculver Beach in April confirmed that the cylinder was a better choice. It was an ugly thing, rather like a huge gasoline drum, a monstrous, cumbersome affair with none of the smooth, tapered grace of a normal bomb. It was about five feet long and almost that thick, and it weighed a staggering five tons. It was tested with success on the Kent coast, but the tests raised another complexity: to make the thing skip as it had to do, and to keep it from breaking up when it hit the water, it had to be dropped no more than sixty feet off the surface.

As Barnes Wallis and RAF officials wrestled with the mechanics of the bomb and its delivery, Gibson and his men flew hundreds of hours of hair-raising practice runs, hammering across lakes and lochs all over England, Wales, and Scotland, right on the deck in the dark. You had to be good to fly even the practice flights, for the big Lancaster was not designed to fly fighter sweeps at treetop level.

From the beginning, the Lancasters returned from practice flights with chunks of branch crammed into their air intakes, and there were many close calls. Placid lakes that were blue in daylight turned

deadly black at night, distorting the pilots' depth perception. Gibson
was forced to give his eager deputies a cautionary instruction:

> You've got to stop this or else someone will kill himself, and
> I might also tell you that the Provost Marshals have already
> been up to see me about reported dangerous low flying . . . for
> God's sake tell your boys to try and avoid going over towns
> and aerodromes and not to beat up policemen or lovers in a
> field, because they'll get a rocket if they do.

There were other problems, notably communications. The somewhat crude bomber radios of the day were not good enough for
instant, reliable contact between aircraft: Gibson wanted state-of-the-
art VHF fighter equipment, and he got it. Gibson and Young, his
second in command, carried two sets apiece.

Extensive damage was still being suffered in rehearsal. Lancasters
returned to Scampton with their bottoms swathed in foliage. And if
an aircraft dropped its monstrous bomb a trifle too low, a huge
column of water smashed against the underside of the airplane, twisting metal, fracturing control surfaces, cracking turrets. It was, Gibson
wrote, "a miracle some of them got home." The ground crews labored mightily, repairing extensive damage, getting the big airplanes
ready to fly again. They were working against time.

But the training never stopped. As spring came, and the rehearsals
wound down, Gibson and his men had flown some two thousand
hours of low-level practice and dropped twenty-five hundred dummy
bombs. Over in Germany, the water level at the target dams was
almost at the top of the concrete, optimum conditions for the raid,
and 617 Squadron was ready.

Meanwhile, another delivery problem had also been solved, the
question of maintaining a precise sixty feet above the surface of the
lake. The chief of research at the Ministry of Aircraft Production
recommended bolting two spotlights to the underside of the Lancaster's fuselage. The spotlights, tied to a switch operated by the pilot,
were set at an angle, so that their beams touched in a figure-eight
pattern when the aircraft was precisely sixty feet off the water. As
long as the pilot could keep the two pools touching below his Lancaster, the altitude was right.

One of Gibson's men was unimpressed. "I could have told you

that,'' he said. ''Last night Terry and I went to see the Ensa show, and when the girl there was doing her strip-tease there were these two spotlights shining on her. The idea crossed my mind then and I was going to tell you.'' Sadly, there was nothing to the wonderful fable that the happily married Wallis got his idea from the same source.

Which left the most perplexing problem of all. The bomb had to be dropped a precise distance from the face of the dam. Going like a bat out of hell on the deck in the dark, with flak flying everywhere, how was anybody to know where the drop point was? Simple, said an RAF aeronautics expert named Dann, and went off to find a piece of scrap plywood and some nails.

The result was a simple plywood triangle with a wooden handle on the bottom. A nail was driven upright in each of two corners and a simple peephole was placed at the apex. The peephole is your sight, Dann explained. The Germans had conveniently built a tower on each end of the Moehne Dam, towers on which now sat light flak guns. When the outside nails cover those towers, you drop. A piece of cake.

In practice, some bomb aimers were not enamored of the Dann sight. In a Lancaster leaping madly about at zero feet, the sight was hard to hold in one hand and use accurately—the bomb aimer needed his other hand for the release toggle. And so some of the crews made their own sights, based on grease pencil markings on the inside of their windows and a piece of cord attached to the window and held taut against the bomb aimer's nose. These contraptions were not pretty, but they were functional.

And so, with scrap wood, grease pencil, string, and a bit of elementary geometry, the worst and final problem was solved. With the requisite number of big Lancasters converted to carry Barnes Wallis' creation, with Gibson's aircrews trained to a gnat's eyelash, all that remained was permission to go. That came to Bomber Command at High Wycombe on the morning of May 15 and was passed on down to 617 Squadron. The operation was on.

The crews were briefed by Barnes Wallis, among others, and at last 617 Squadron got a clear picture of the immense task for which they had volunteered. Wallis, ''detailed and clear,'' told them what the bomb would do and why it was important. Gibson finished up with operational details, and then the crews had a little while to reflect on the mighty undertaking in front of them.

Tired as they were from their nightly low-level practice runs, and in spite of their professional instinct that this mission would be enormously dangerous, the crews were eager. One crewman chalked his thoughts on one of the bombs: "Never has so much been expected of so few." It seldom had, and the man with the chalk might have had a premonition: he would not come back from the raid.

Dinner in the mess was a subdued affair. They were eating eggs, standard fare before an operation, and often served as well to those who managed to get back. There was the usual quiet joking, too. Young asked Gibson if he could have his egg if Gibson didn't come back, and got the usual ribald response. Joking softly with his boss, Young could not foresee what lay ahead of him that moonlit night over Germany. It was as well that he could not.

Gibson, practical and undramatic, showed his sentimental side for just a moment shortly before takeoff. His treasured, beer-drinking black Labrador had been killed by a car just the previous night, and Gibson missed him deeply. "Chiefy," he called to his warrant officer, and then asked that his dog be buried at about midnight. Gibson knew where he would be at that hour, and knew better than anybody else the odds against surviving at sixty feet over a black lake in the Ruhr.

Otherwise, the departure was not without its light moments. Gibson described one of them, involving the big American, McCarthy: "Our favorite Yank, F/L McCarthy, caused quite a disturbance":

> He arrived at his aircraft and after finding she had hydraulic trouble, came dashing back to our only reserve aircraft . . . he had no compass card and came rushing back . . . frantically screaming for one. He had also pulled his parachute by mistake and the white silk was streaming all over the ground, trailing behind him. With perspiration dropping off his face, good old Mac ran back to his aircraft with everyone behind him trying to fix him up with what he wanted. He got off just in time.

And so, on the evening of May 16, Gibson led his first wave into the gathering dusk over Scampton Air Station, nine heavily loaded Lancasters in three vees of three aircraft each. Pulled into tight formation, they droned east across the North Sea in the darkness, flying within one hundred feet of the calm dark water.

The 617 Squadron would use a system of code words, short, simple transmissions that would advise England of the progress of the raid on the Moehne. Most of the less desirable reports were "Goners." "Goner 1" was a bomb that did not go off; "Goner 2" meant the bomb had overshot; "Goner 3" was a bomb that blew over one hundred yards from the dam, and so on. Only "Goner 10" would create much joy in England: that meant a large breach. These reports would be transmitted on the group frequency; Gibson would save his squadron frequency for his own orders and the reports and warnings of his aircraft commanders.

Gibson's men knew precisely what they were up against and what they would do when they attacked. They knew there would be at least three minutes between each single-handed run, enough time to allow settling of the turbulence caused by the bomb of the aircraft ahead. Each Lancaster would fly a counterclockwise circuit over a prearranged area, keeping very low to blend with the earth, waiting for Gibson's order to attack the dam. Each crew would fire a red Very flare as its aircraft cleared the dam.

Just then, however, Gibson's airplanes were hammering east through the night, and each man was alone with his thoughts. Everybody tried out the crucial spotlights, and several navigators dropped flame floats into the placid sea, little beacons from which their rear gunners could estimate drift. There was virtually none. To the north the aurora borealis flickered across the great dome of the sky.

They crossed the Dutch coast in moonlight, threading their way around the heavy German flak defenses emplaced on the Dutch islands. They had made their landfall without attracting the attention of the antiaircraft batteries and night fighters, and they flew on into the night over occupied Holland. They were so close to the deck that from time to time Gibson's crew had to warn him to pull up to clear trees and power lines. Along the way, one of Gibson's vees fell behind.

Gibson's men now crossed the German border, still in bright moonlight, and droned on into the valley of the Ruhr, on through the night to the mighty Rhine—"Happy Valley," to the crews of Bomber Command. They swung around the industrial hive of Duisburg and its forest of antiaircraft guns and flew up the river itself.

Armed barges on the Rhine cut loose at the bombers as they loomed
suddenly out of the gloom above the river, and the Lancaster gunners
drenched the German gunners with tracers in return.

Behind Gibson's flight, the three aircraft led by Squadron Leader
H. E. Maudslay were suddenly flooded in light as bright as noon,
searchlights assigned to the protection of a German airfield so new
it had not been marked on their maps. The British gunners hammered
away at the searchlights and the darkness returned, but it was too
late for one Lancaster.

One account says its pilot, blinded by the lights, lost control and
augured into the ground. As the aircraft struck, its bomb exploded,
and the Lancaster and its crew vanished in a brilliant flash of light.
Other versions say the aircraft was caught in two converging streams
of tracers and was last seen on fire. Moments later an explosion
rent the gloom, and Pilot Officer Bill Astell and his whole crew
were gone.

About the time Astell's Lancaster died in the darkness behind
them, Gibson's vee finished its twisting route on up the river, passing
Dortmund and Hamm, until at last one of Gibson's crew caught sight
of the Ruhr hills.

"We're there," he said simply.

"Thank God," said Gibson, more simply still.

And there was the dam, massive and monstrous in the moonlight.
"God," said one crewman, "can we break that?" Nobody knew
whether they could or not . . . but they were about to try.

The Germans were ready, and the antiaircraft began to come up
as Gibson started down toward the lake in front of the dam. Lazy
strings of tracers arched through the night, deceptively pretty neck-
laces of yellow, red, and green. Gibson thought he was being shot
at from five different positions, maybe a dozen guns in all, either
20- or 30-millimeter, perhaps both. They were, as he put it, "nasty
little things."

Gibson called to his flight:

> Hello, all Cooler aircraft, I am going to attack. Stand by to
> come in to attack in your order when I tell you.

At this the rest of Gibson's Lancasters dispersed, each one orbiting
in its preplanned area out of the direct sight of the dam's defenders

and obscured from the view of any night fighters that might happen by. Gibson himself turned in to attack, boring in low over the eastern end of the lake, the moon behind him. The view was clear and perfect, and the bombardier ("bomb aimer" in the RAF) was delighted. "Good show," he said happily as the deadly tracers arched past him out of the dark; "This is wizard."

For a while Gibson's Lancaster was fairly well sheltered from the German defenses. A spit of land pointed straight at the dam, a tongue dividing the Mohne and Heve rivers as they ran into the lake upstream of the dam. The high ground of the spit gave good cover . . . until the attacking aircraft cleared the spit of land. Then each Lancaster would be naked, in plain view from all sides, its spotlights telling the blindest German gunner where his target was.

Gibson's big plane cleared the landspit, and the German flak reached out for him across the lake. The single-barreled 20-millimeter Flak 38 could spit out 480 rounds a minute at a target over a mile away. Gibson had at least that far to fly, straight, low, and level, before he could skip his bomb over the torpedo nets, which lay from one hundred to three hundred feet in front of the dam. The attack run seemed to last forever.

While the flight engineer carefully monitored the big plane's crucial airspeed, the copilot handled throttle and flaps to ensure that the Lancaster never deviated from the proper speed. The navigator watched the dark water below the aircraft to make sure the two spotlight beams kept their fragile figure eight on the lake's surface. Gibson, feeling the cold sweat under the rubber of his oxygen mask, kept the aircraft centered on the dam, alone in the night with his thoughts: "In another minute we shall all be dead—so what?" And then: "This is terrible—this feeling of fear—if it is fear." And then, as the dam grew monstrous through the perspex canopy of the Lancaster, Gibson spoke again to his copilot, very calmly: "Better leave the throttles open now, and stand by to pull me out of the seat if I get hit."

And so the big plane closed with the dam, which looked huge and unbreakable, flickering muzzle flashes dancing on the flak towers on both ends. Up front, the Lancaster's forward power turret flamed and hammered; the airplane filled with the biting stench of cordite powder as Gibson's gunner poured a stream of tracers into the tower on the left-hand end of the dam.

In a cloud of antiaircraft fire, Gibson finished his run across the flat waters of the reservoir. And then, from his bomb aimer: "Mine gone!" And there it went, Barnes Wallis' pet monster, skipping and spinning its way toward the dam. The bomb skipped true across the flat, smooth surface of Moehne Lake, dived down the face of the dam, and exploded somewhere below the black water. A gigantic waterspout leaped into the air along the face of the dam.

But nothing happened; the huge concrete structure did not seem to have been disturbed in the slightest. Gibson pulled up sharply, turning left over the dam and the big power station behind it, clawing for height and still chased by the merry faerie lights of the flak tracers. The water roiled and surged around the face of the dam, but no crack appeared.

"Goner," Gibson transmitted. "Goner 68": bomb exploded five yards from the dam, no apparent damage.

As he called for the next Lancaster in the bombing order, Gibson banked sharply back into the maelstrom of flak, deliberately drawing the Germans' fire to his own airplane, his gunners firing burst after burst into the flak positions along the dam and the edges of the lake. The night flashed and flared with streams of brilliant fire, for the Lancaster had two guns forward and four aft, each tube capable of about ten rounds a second.

Gibson's gunners had loaded their belts with all tracers for its psychological effect, and their volleys looked like solid bars of fire reaching out for the flak gunners at the dam. In the next few minutes, Gibson's rear gunner alone would fire almost twelve thousand rounds into the flak positions around the dam.

The next aircraft was flown by quiet, softspoken English Flight Lieutenant J. V. Hopgood—"Hoppy" to his many friends—and Hopgood was quickly and repeatedly hit by the flak. At least two engines were struck, and a gout of flame quickly engulfed the airplane. Hopgood never wavered, but closed in and dropped his bomb anyway. But something was wrong, perhaps a wounded bomb aimer, for the big bomb skipped completely over the dam, exploding down toward the power station behind it.

His run finished, the veteran Hopgood struggled to gain what height he could, fighting in his last seconds of life for a few more feet of altitude to permit his crew to jump. "For Christ's sake, get out of here!" they heard him call, and then at five hundred feet the flaming Lancaster exploded, a brilliant smear of crimson and yellow in the night.

Miraculously, Hopgood's courage did save two of his crew, both of whom opened their parachutes and *then* jumped. Hopgood went down with his aircraft in a blazing pyre beyond the dam. Near the flaming wreckage of his aircraft the huge oil-filled transformers of the wrecked power station were burning, too.

Gibson's monstrous gray enemy continued to stand unmoved after Australian Flight Lieutenant Mick Martin dropped his bomb. Again an enormous waterspout rose high above the dam, but Martin's bomb had veered off course to the left. "Goner," signaled Martin, and then he too swung back over the lake to add his firepower to Gibson's attack on the flak batteries.

As depression mounted back in England, Gibson continued to fly back and forth across the dam, drawing the fire of the flak in the towers and on the shoreline, his gunners hammering away at the German gun crews while Gibson calmly talked his next crew in on their single-handed run. This time it was the Lancaster flown by Squadron Leader H. M. Young, another double DFC winner.

Young bored straight in across the lake, with Martin flying beside him to distract the flak, and Young put his bomb in exactly the right spot. Again, as the huge waterspout leaped into the air and began to settle back, the great gray dam still stood, defiant.

Now Gibson called for his fifth airplane, with Flight Lieutenant F. J. H. Maltby at the controls. Maltby got his line and height, and then, as he tore in across the water, he saw it: the dam was cracking, crumbling, and rupturing, and a monstrous gout of water jetted out down the valley toward the Ruhr, far below in the night. Young's bomb had done the job. Maltby finished his run anyway, and his bomb bounced four times, struck the dam's face, and blew, sending a monstrous column of water and mud hurtling up against the brilliant moon.

As the waterspout from Maltby's run subsided, somebody shouted over the radio, maybe Martin: "Hell, it's gone! It's gone! Look at it, for Christ's sake!" And now Gibson saw the dam begin to go, water pouring through the chasm in its face "looking like stirred porridge in the moonlight." Gibson and his men, and the other aircrews, cheered and yelled over the intercom and the radio, like a rugby team that had scored its winning try in the last seconds of their match. "We began to shout and scream," wrote Gibson later, "and act like madmen on the R/T," for this was a "tremendous sight, a sight which probably no man will ever see again."

Downhill of the ruptured dam, a monstrous wall of water roared toward the village of Himmelpforten—Heaven's Gates. The hamlet disappeared beneath a raging flood, and the village priest died ringing his churchbell in futile warning. Other villages died as well, people by the hundred who never got out of their houses and farms, livestock by the thousand.

Back over the ruins of the Moehne, Gibson's flight had ceased their celebrating and turned back to grim business. With the night long spent, the Eder Dam still remained. And so, with Squadron Leader Young and those of his aircraft that still carried bombs, Gibson now turned for the Eder, some fifty miles away in the blackness. As he did, he told Scampton in the clear that the dam was gone.

And Scampton went wild with joy, for now they knew the whole thing had been worth it: the Moehne was gone. It was time for congratulations, and Bomber Harris turned to Barnes Wallis: "I didn't believe a word of what you said when you came to see me," he said, "but now you could sell me a pink elephant."

Meanwhile, deep in the darkness above the Ruhr, Gibson's Lancasters swept in over the Eder Reservoir. Gibson sent them in one at a time again, just as they had attacked at the Moehne. There was no flak, but the Eder approach was very difficult, for each bomber had to dive steeply in over Waldeck Castle, turn hard left over a point of land, then quickly find its sixty-foot height and drop. After the bomb was away, there remained a steep climb to clear a bad piece of high ground just behind the dam.

Gibson's first Lancaster, under the command of Flight Lieutenant D. J. Shannon, made repeated runs at the dam but could not find the right attack line. Maudslay took over and made two runs but had the same problem. Shannon, very young and very tough, then tried three times more, and on the third pass he dropped his load precisely. As the monstrous waterspout receded, however, the dam still stood.

Squadron Leader Maudslay then made another run. As he bored in, Gibson could see something hanging beneath his aircraft, probably the result of flak damage on the trip in. Maudslay's bomb aimer dropped too late, directly on the upper rim of the dam, and in the blinding flash and waterspout the Lancaster disappeared. The other aircraft were sure they heard Maudslay transmit once after that, very faintly, and then there was only silence.

The third and last chance, carried by Australian Pilot Officer L. G. Knight, bounced lazily across the flat black surface, ducked under the dark water, and blew up in the blackness thirty feet below. Whether Shannon's bomb had started a crack or not, this bomb finished the job.

A huge hole appeared in the face of the dam, and another huge jet of water roared off downhill, headed for the valley of the Ruhr. One of the aircrew thought it looked like water gushing ''as from a large hose.'' Gibson's crews could see car headlights disappearing beneath a colossal black wave of water in the valley below the dam. The Eder was breached. Gibson sent the code word for success— ''Dinghy''—and then, with the night far gone, it was time to turn for home.

There was still no word from Maudslay, and there never would be again. At the time, most people thought his Lancaster had gone down in the explosion of his bomb on the top of the dam. It is probable, however, that his battered aircraft survived, badly damaged, and he tried to nurse it home. He was probably shot down by light flak near Emmerich, along the Rhine, not far from the Dutch border, with all his crew.

And somewhere in the night the gallant Young and his crew, the men whose bomb had actually broken the Moehne Dam, simply disappeared without a sound. They would not return to Scampton that night, or anywhere else in England, ever. They almost made the sea, but were knocked out of the air by flak on the Dutch coast. They crashed in the ocean, and only a few bodies were ever found.

Gibson flew safely home by way of the Moehne, landing at about 0415. Shannon, Maltby, and Martin were already on the ground. Knight was not far behind. The sky was growing light in the east. It would be a clear, beautiful day.

As Gibson was hammering the Moehne Dam, the Sorpe group of five Lancasters ran into a storm of heavy flak. Two were shot down. One Lancaster's bomb exploded as it struck the ground; a brilliant flash of light lit up the gloom, and then there was nothing. The second plane simply disappeared in the night.

The flight leader also turned for home, his aircraft badly damaged by flak and its radio shot away. A fourth turned back after it lost its bomb, scraped off the aircraft as it tore across Holland's Zuider Zee at wavetop height. These disasters left only a single airplane, which had taken off late and flown alone, to hit the Sorpe.

The pilot of this lone Lancaster was the big American, Flight Lieutenant J. C. McCarthy, DFC, and McCarthy did his level best. Because of the earth construction of this dam, it was to be attacked lengthwise, and McCarthy put his bomb dead on in the center of the dam. But the structure held, and there were no other aircraft to follow up. McCarthy turned for home and made it.

There remained only Gibson's reserve of five Lancasters, whose mission was to strike any dam left standing after the bombs of the first wave. They flew out of Scampton about two hours and thirty minutes after Gibson and his men were airborne and quickly came to grief. Two aircraft were shot down in the night; one was damaged and turned back with its bomb still on board. A fourth attacked a small subsidiary dam without result.

The remaining Lancaster was flown by Canadian Flight Sergeant Ken Brown. Responding to radioed orders, Brown attacked the Sorpe. Flying through mist and darkness, the persistent Brown made five passes over the dam. On the sixth, finally satisfied, Brown dropped his load squarely on the top of the dam—without result. It was a disappointing end to a brilliant exploit.

Next day, 617 Squadron, what was left of it, got some leave. Only Gibson stayed on at Scampton, taking two more days to finish the grimmest duty of any commander: writing the families of the men who would never come back to England. And he insisted on hand-writing every letter, fifty-six of them altogether.

One hundred and thirty-three British aircrew flew the raid. Of these, about a third of them Canadian or Australian, fifty-three died; three survived as prisoners of the Germans. Nineteen Lancasters of 617 Squadron had flown off into the night for France; eleven had gotten through to make their bombing runs; eight had not made it back to England. Back at Scampton, his exaltation drained away, Barnes Wallis unashamedly wept for the men who had carried his bomb to glory and now would never come home again.

Gibson spent what remained of his leave at home with his wife, whom he had told he was at some sort of flight training school. Martin was badgered for a newspaper story by a pretty girl named

Wendy, but would say nothing until she had lunch with him; in time, she would become Mrs. Martin.

For the survivors of the raid, there was much honor. They had not only flown with enormous courage and professionalism, they had totally wrecked two of their three major targets. And they had done so on a night so brightly lit that few other Allied missions could be flown; the entire complex of German defenses could concentrate on 617 Squadron. And still they had pulled it off, in spite of everything the Germans could throw at them, regardless of their terrible losses.

Gibson was awarded the Victoria Cross, Britain's highest award for gallantry. In addition, there were five Distinguished Service Orders, fourteen Distinguished Flying Crosses, and eleven Distinguished Flying Medals. Included in the men so honored were six Canadians, an American, a New Zealander, and eight Australians. Some of the awards, sadly, were posthumous.

The moral impact of the strike was enormous on both sides of the English Channel. The material effect of the raid is much harder to judge. There was considerable damage to agricultural land, utilities, towns, bridges, and the like; eleven factories were wrecked and more than a hundred others damaged. However, thanks to their traditional careful planning and efficiency, the Germans were able to turn to alternate sources of power and water, thus minimizing long-term industrial shutdown.

Even so, thousands of additional workers—including troops—were needed to repair the widespread damage; these workers were desperately needed elsewhere. Twenty thousand men were pulled in from Normandy alone, where they had been building fortifications intended to defeat the cross-channel invasion the Germans knew was coming.

The bomber offensive had other far-reaching consequences. Albert Speer, the genius of German war production, saw the danger clearly:

> That [second] front was the skies over Germany. . . . Defense against air attacks required the production of thousands of anti-aircraft guns, the stockpiling of tremendous quantities of ammunition . . . and hundreds of thousands of soldiers.

Speer estimated that the ceaseless assault from the air ate up nearly twenty thousand antiaircraft guns, which "could almost have doubled the anti-tank defences on the Eastern Front." Even at the Ruhr dams, antiaircraft units needed elsewhere were diverted to beef up the dam defenses, and an intricate web of steel cable was built to obstruct any future attacks. Too late.

The raid had other positive results as well. It marked the debut of the "master bomber" system, a single experienced leader controlling the approach and attack of other aircraft. Gibson would share his ideas and experience with a galaxy of RAF bombing stars, who would use his system to carry death and misery deep into Germany. The master bombers would vastly improve accuracy and hitting power in the huge night raids to come. They succeeded, as one writer put it, "in converting . . . Bomber Command from a bludgeon into a rapier."

Barnes Wallis' exotic bomb was succeeded by even bigger and more deadly conventional bombs. Tallboy, at six tons, gave way in time to Grand Slam, a monstrous 22,000-pounder. Tallboy sank the superbattleship *Tirpitz* and battered a variety of other targets, including German missile sites and 617's old enemy, the Sorpe Dam. Grand Slam destroyed the great railroad viaduct at Bielefeld and was destined to ravage Japan when the war abruptly ended in a mushroom cloud.

The 617 Squadron had been born and bred for a single mission, and now that mission was over. But the squadron was not finished. In spite of its casualties, almost 50 percent, the dam raid had proved its usefulness, and Bomber Command wisely kept it in being for future use, a decision richly rewarded by time.

Before it finally stood down for the last time, 617 Squadron would successfully attack a variety of critical and special targets, including concrete E-boat pens, the lethal V-weapon sites in north Germany, and the mighty *Tirpitz* in a Norwegian fjord. One hundred and thirty-three boats were destroyed at Le Havre and Boulogne; the V-sites were left a wilderness of craters; *Tirpitz* remained at her anchorage, no more than a lifeless, capsized chunk of battered steel, a metal tomb for half her crew.

The 617 Squadron's raid was an extraordinary stroke, another nail in the coffin of the Ruhr, an astonishing shock to the German leadership, a wonderful tonic for British morale. The British papers made much of the raid, helped by superb aerial photos of the broken dams and the swamped lowlands below them. And 617 Squadron got a visit from the King and Queen, during which George VI congratulated Shannon on his twenty-first birthday. The King also decided the winner of the squadron motto competition; he chose a most appropriate paraphrase of Marie Antoinette's famous dictum—*"Après moi, le déluge*—[After me, the flood]."* The patch that went with it depicted a broken dam.

Barnes Wallis, the father of the whole idea, was appropriately praised and honored, and after the war he was awarded ten thousand pounds in gratitude—he promptly gave the money away for the benefit of the families of men who had died serving the RAF. When friends urged him to accept something for his contributions to the war, Wallis answered them with a quote from the Book of Samuel: "Is not this the blood of the men that went in jeopardy of their lives?"

Wallis' favorite accolade, however, would certainly have come from his eldest daughter, who had participated in the marble experiment back in Surrey: "Hooray, wonderful Daddy," she telegraphed from school, and that said it all.

Guy Gibson richly deserved a little rest; for months he had been living on borrowed time, considering the life expectancy of an RAF bomber pilot. To the physical strain of low-level flying he had added the crushing cares of command. He should have been assigned to a quiet desk job out of harm's way, and the Royal Air Force gave him one. Winston Churchill even took Gibson on a trip to the United States and sent him on a tour of American bases to talk to USAAF pilots.

But Gibson would have none of peace and quiet. In spite of his spectacular long history of combat operations, he wanted more. He made a regular and persistent pest of himself until the RAF threw up its hands and agreed to send him back on operations again.

Gibson was the ultimate professional, the dedicated warrior, the civilized man wholly committed to the destruction of his country's enemies. He represented the cream of the public school system, the sort of man who would always be the captain of the team. He was willing to give everything he had for England, and in the end, one dark night over Holland, he did.

He was flying a pathfinder Mosquito, the Plywood Wonder, roaring in at low level to drop phosphorus and high explosives, marking targets for the heavy bomber stream behind him. Gibson marked this mission, and marked accurately, and the other bombers heard him call: "Okay, chaps. That's fine. Now beat it home." But then, somewhere in the night, his luck ran out. Wing Commander Guy Gibson, VC, crashed into a hill in Holland, his aircraft probably crippled by flak.

The Dutch buried him there.

If Barnes Wallis wept for the men who would never come back to England, he was proud of them, too, and so was Britain—and so was the Royal Air Force, from top to bottom. Even the restrained, stiff-upper-lip RAF official history could not resist an exultant comment on the Ruhr dam raid. It was, the historian said "the most precise bombing attack ever delivered and a feat of arms which has never been excelled."

And so it was.

CHAPTER THIRTY-EIGHT

OF RICE AND LEADERSHIP

Orde Wingate Trains His Chindits

BRIGADIER MIKE CALVERT was a Chindit, fabulous commander of one of the British long-range penetration brigades inserted deep behind Japanese lines in Burma and supplied entirely by air. He was also a disciple of Orde Wingate, the charismatic leader whose brainchild the Chindits were.

Wingate insisted on using ordinary British and Indian battalions in his Chindit units; he wanted no elite forces because he believed these rank-and-file soldiers, properly trained and led, could beat the Japanese in their own jungle. Wingate was right, as his Chindits proved, but implementing his ideas sometimes took some doing. Here is one such case, just as Mike Calvert told it to me one pleasant day in London:

The Indian companies were based around the cooking pot. They carried a huge cooking pot, which would take two and a half hours to cook the rice. So sometime midday everything had to stop while they cooked this rice. I'd seen this on the retreat from Burma. And I told Wingate this, and so he had us—we had the 3/2 Gurkhas with us, and they were pretty junior. In my column I only had one Gurkha officer who was over the

331

age of twenty-two. I remember meeting them, and they were all twenty-one, nineteen, eighteen, so on.

And so Wingate called the battalion around, young Gurkhas sitting around the bottom, then the older Gurkhas, then the British officers were around the sides. They were shaking their heads; they didn't think Wingate could teach them anything. And Wingate took some dried sticks from out of his pack. And he showed us—this was Boy Scout stuff—after you made a fire you picked up a sufficient number of sticks for the next fire. He was ready.

And he put these sticks on the ground and he lit them with a match. He measured out some water in a normal can, waited till the water boiled, and then he took a sock out of his pocket, measured out some rice and put it in. Then he set his alarm clock for twenty minutes and he just sat there on his haunches and everybody else watched in absolute silence and then after twenty minutes he took it off and showed it to them, and then sifted it and put some salt on it.

And he took a spoon and—I was looking at the Gurkhas' faces—and he got a spoonful of rice and munched it, and a terrific smile spread across his face, and they all smiled and then he handed the can around. According to their religious customs they're not supposed to do that kind of thing, but they all took a bite. And it was all right.

So in less than an hour he had converted the whole battalion to how to move and then of course you cook your own rice and that makes all the difference in your movement and maneuverability. You couldn't send out small parties before. It converted the whole battalion so they could be self-reliant.

And that is what good officers call leadership.

CHAPTER THIRTY-NINE

LEAD FROM THE FRONT

General of Armored Troops Hermann Balck

THE GERMAN INFANTRY were exhausted. Nobody had eaten all day; many men had nothing to drink. Casualties had been heavy, especially among the officers, and ammunition was running low. Bouvellemont, the battered village ahead, was another hornet's nest, spurting fire, looking as far away as the moon. The soldiers in dirty field gray were worn out.

It was May 15, 1940, and First Infantry Regiment had been the point of the German spear from the beginning of the thrust into France. Part of the fabulous First Panzer Division, the regiment had already accomplished prodigies, forcing a crossing of the Meuse under fire to drive the French from the crucial high ground south of the river. Without engineers, this truck-borne regiment had handled the assault boats itself, the regimental commander out in front with one of the leading companies.

After that, the regiment had driven on by night and day, fighting off a French counterattack, carrying village after village, and it ached for just a little rest. One frontal attack on Bouvellemont had already failed. Now one of the regiment's battalions was hammering at the rear of the little town, but here, too, the exhausted Germans could make no headway. Without orders, the troops began to dig in.

The regimental commander, as usual, was with the battalion at the point of attack, and he hastily called the surviving officers together. This tough young lieutenant colonel was named Hermann Balck, and he could see what his tired subordinates could not. He was sure that beyond Bouvellemont there was only empty air, an open road into the Champagne, into the very heart of France. The way there had to be opened now, this day, before the French could reinforce, before they could dig in further and bar the way.

He faced his surviving officers, speaking quietly and calmly: "Gentlemen, either we attack now or we give up our final victory . . ." Then he heard his exhausted leaders say what he already knew: the men were hungry, they were short of ammunition, they were terribly tired. Balck nodded. "Fine. Whoever wants to stay here can stay here. I'm leading the attack on the next village."

And then, armed only with a stick, he marched out into the open toward Bouvellemont . . . alone. His astonished soldiers watched, horrified.

"D'you see the old man? Are you going to let him go on alone?" And they began to get to their feet, grabbing weapons and grenades. Let the regimental adjutant tell the rest:

> . . . dead-tired, half-sleeping men sprang electrified from their slit trenches, and all of a sudden they had caught up with the regimental commander. They charged past him and burst into the enemy's very last position with cheers.

By personal example, Balck had gotten the last bit of effort from his men, just as he had done over and over during the fighting advance into France. It took an hour and a half of bitter fighting through Bouvellemont's houses and gardens, but the regiment's tired men at last cleared the hamlet of French defenders for good.

Balck was not through. His men got a little rest that night, but next day Balck had them on the road again, driving on to the west. When the sun went down on the sixteenth, First Infantry Regiment had covered an incredible 130 kilometers more, all the way to St. Quentin, on the river Oise.

That day Balck's men were visited by their corps commander, Heinz Guderian, a man who knew a thing or two himself about leading from the front. Guderian visited every company in the regiment, and by the seventeenth the whole unit knew that Balck had received the Knight's Cross of the Iron Cross for his dynamic leadership under fire. He had made another contribution, too. His recommendations were part of the reason that, after Sedan, German armor and infantry generally operated in combined arms teams.

Urbane, straightforward Hermann Balck would be the last man to see anything unusual in what he had done. He came of a famous family, a family of soldiers and statesmen, born to lead. The Balcks were Finnish originally; a Balck had been Bishop of Abo in 1308. Balck's part of the family had moved to Germany before the Thirty Years' War and settled in Hannover. Another Balck had moved to Britain and served with distinction under Wellington in the peninsula against the French.

Balck's own father had also been a general, a winner of the coveted Pour le Merite, the "Blue Max," Germany's highest decoration for valor. He authored a well-received book on tactics, which was used in the United States in translation. It was the senior Balck who in World War I had saved a young Lieutenant Guderian from serious trouble by having him quickly transferred after he accused a senior officer of cowardice.

Hermann Balck, forty-seven years old in 1940, had entered the German army in 1913 as a Fahnenjunker, an officer candidate, in a Jaeger regiment, the Goslar Rifles. He fought throughout World War I on the Western Front and in Russia, Italy, and Rumania. Collecting seven wounds and the Iron Cross, First Class, Balck showed the steel will that would later drive his exhausted battalion through the French in May 1940.

At one point during the Kaiser's War, he commanded his company for days with both arms in slings. And, facing French machine guns on Mount Kemmel in April 1918, then Captain Balck called for supporting fires from a German mortar platoon. "No," said the platoon leader, "I will fire only when the attack actually begins. Moreover," said he—and perhaps this was the heart of the problem—"if I fire I'll draw artillery on myself."

Balck reasoned quietly with the mortar commander; in his words:

I drew my pistol abruptly. "I'll count to three—then there'll be a shot, either from your mortars or my pistol. One, two . . . !" With a crack one of our mortar bombs landed slap among the

French machine guns. All further preparations for the attack
went ahead undisturbed . . .

Balck returned from the war to a cold and hungry Germany, a
land full of workers' and soldiers' councils, seething with discontent
and revolution. The Goslar Rifles was one of the few units that
retained its cohesion, helping to put down communist unrest in the
Ruhr in 1920. Commanding a company in the same battalion was
another bright veteran captain, another man who would rise to high
places—Heinz Guderian.

Guderian and Balck would cross paths again and again. The out-
spoken, brilliant Guderian, whose admiring men would call him
"hurrying Heinz," was a stormy petrel in constant trouble with peers
and superiors alike. Saved from disgrace by Balck's father, Guderian
continued his honest and acid ways. On one occasion he was con-
fronted by a citizen's complaining letter:

> When I went in to my maid's bedroom last night, I found two
> riflemen of your company in her bed, sir! . . . I ask you, is my
> house a brothel?

Guderian answered:

> Even in the days of the Kaiser, it happened that riflemen were
> found in servant girls' beds. . . . As regards . . . whether your
> house is a brothel. . . . You are in the best position to judge
> this for yourself.

The response was not calculated to sooth the good burgher, and
Guderian was in hot water again. "I gave an objective answer to an
objective question," he told his superiors, and survived. He was
Balck's kind of soldier.

Balck paid tribute to Guderian's contributions to the theory of
modern armored warfare. But to Balck, Guderian contributed just as
much in upgrading vital field communications. It was Guderian who
added another man—a radio operator—to German tank crews and
gave the panzer division a signal capability that allowed its commander to command from anywhere. Later, as he rose to higher and

higher command, Balck made the most of Guderian's enormous contribution:

> I always located my Chief of Staff in a headquarters to the rear. I commanded from the front by radio and could thus always be at the most critical point of action. I could transmit my commands to the Chief of Staff, and then it was up to him to make sure that they were passed on.

Balck moved from assignment to assignment during the interwar years, including service with the excellent Finnish army. He turned down a chance to serve with the Hungarians, a job he considered "poodle-training." Promoted to lieutenant colonel in 1938, Balck was moved to the new Inspectorate of Mobile Troops, where he worked with both cavalry and the trucked infantry and recon elements then attached to the horse troops.

Balck worked hard to mechanize Germany's new divisions. He also did what he could to add mobility to "leg" infantry divisions, mounting their recon units on horses and bicycles—not as comfortable as motorcycles, maybe, but much, much quieter. To the cavalry, he added mules to carry crew-served weapons and other loads:

> I chose mules in preference to asses, because most of the asses available . . . had too few legs—most of them had two legs rather than four.

Chafing unhappily in Berlin, Balck missed the Polish campaign of 1939. In October of that year, however, he was given command of First Infantry Regiment, then at Weimar. He knew the unit well, having helped equip it in his job with the Inspectorate of Mobile Troops. He would do wonders with it during the thrust into France.

After his breakthrough at Bouvellemont, Balck was moved to command of First Panzer Regiment. He showed the same driving leadership there that had pushed his First Infantry Regiment so far, so fast. Handing over to another unit a bridgehead on the Somme, Balck showed the same impatience and same sense of urgency that had carried Bouvellemont. He curtly refused to waste time in a formal relief, and told the commander of the replacement unit:

I'm advancing on Amiens. If you lose the bridgehead, you must just retake it. I've done it. And what's more my field kitchens will stay with you for a while.

And he left in a cloud of dust. By the middle of the same morning, Balck's leading elements were almost sixty kilometers down the vital road to the west, on the edge of Amiens.

After the collapse of France, Balck commanded still another panzer regiment, this time in the conquest of Greece. Bouncing over terrible roads, Balck's advance guard bumped into a tough New Zealand rear guard blocking the main road entirely at the Vale of Tempe, below Mount Olympus. Balck, always the daring, driving leader, swung a motorcycle battalion and a rifle battalion around the flank of the dug-in New Zealanders.

The Germans moved at night over rocky terrain slashed with ravines, cutting in on the flank of the defenders and clearing the pass. Throughout the Greek campaign, Balck's men pushed on remorselessly, regardless of fatigue, losses, or the forbidding terrain over which they had to operate. As a New Zealand report admiringly concluded:

> The German Panzer Regiment 3 knows no going difficulties and negotiates terrain which was regarded as absolutely safe against armor . . . Seldom in war were tanks forced through such difficult country, or had foot soldiers, already with over 500 kilometers marching behind them, pushed forward so rapidly under such punishing conditions.

During the Greek campaign, Balck came to a conclusion he held firmly for the rest of the war: wheeled vehicles did not belong in an armored division, not even to resupply. Everything should move on tracks. In an army still short of even wheeled transport, dominated by horse-drawn supply and artillery, it was a daring conclusion. Sadly, it would never come to full fruition.

After Greece, Balck was appointed a general of mobile troops. In late 1941, Von Brauchitsch, Wehrmacht commander in chief, sent the new general to Russia to assess the situation there. Balck lost no time in consulting his old comrade, Guderian, and in personally inspecting the Russian T-34, at that time by far the best tank of the war.

At about this time Hitler dismissed Brauchitsch and made himself commander of the army. It was to der Fuëhrer, therefore, that Balck reported on December 30, 1941. For two hours Balck related his impressions of the crisis in the east. For all the controversy that has since surrounded Hitler's "no retreat" order to the troops facing Moscow, it was an order with which the experienced Balck entirely agreed.

That was, in fact, the advice Balck gave Hitler. Because of the terrible cold and deep snow, Balck felt that organized retreat was not possible; he also doubted that it would be feasible to prepare new defensive positions. In the course of their conversation, Balck struck sparks when he interrupted Hitler, contradicting *der Führer's* figures on tank production. Like other courageous Wehrmacht officers—"Papi" Wenck is one notable example—Balck was not afraid to cross the Supreme Warlord on military matters.

In May 1942, Balck took command of 11th Panzer Division. Bringing this famous division up to strength, Balck commanded it during the great Kursk offensive that summer. In two months of almost constant attack, 11th Panzer destroyed more than five hundred Russian tanks.

When the Stalingrad front cracked wide open in December 1942, Balck and 11th Panzer—now part of 48th Panzer Corps—played fire brigade, repeatedly cutting into the flanks and rear of Russian columns breaking through the patchwork German defense behind the Chir River. On the nineteenth of December, Balck watched calmly as a Russian tank force rolled south past his headquarters. Behind them moved another armored element, twenty-five tanks altogether.

Until the second wave of tanks opened fire, it never occurred to the Russian leading elements that the armor supporting them so closely might be German. It was, in fact, Balck's 2d Panzer Regiment, and the maneuver was vintage Balck.

Leaving forty-two Russian tanks silent and burning in that frozen desolation, Balck's panzers turned into a depression and waited for the second wave of Russian armor. 2d Panzer Regiment caught this second wave on the skyline—within a few minutes the Russian attack was dying, a bloody shambles, sixty-five more tanks burning or broken. Balck's men had not lost a single panzer.

Up in front, as he had always been, Balck was fond of commanding from his *Kübelwagen*, the fragile, vulnerable German jeep. He
and his worried officers knew he would be safer in a tank, but Balck
would have none of it. "Oh no!" he said, "from a tank you can't
see anything!" On one very dangerous occasion, he was persuaded
to ride in a subordinate's tank only when that officer—an urbane
nobleman—smilingly suggested it would be discourteous for Balck
to refuse his invitation. Laughing, Balck agreed.

As the German front stabilized, Balck was promoted to lieutenant
general and was awarded the swords to his Knight's Cross. Both
promotion and decoration were richly deserved. The rapier thrusts of
11th Panzer Division had done much to blunt and bloody the massive
Russian assaults. On one occasion Balck had put snowplows out in
front of his tanks, then roared clear around the Russian advance to
raise havoc on the airfield that was the hub of his enemy's supply
line.

In January 1943, Balck was moved to the Commanding Officers'
Reserve—or so he thought. Before he could even get back to Ger-
many, he was pulled from a train to command the famous Gross
Deutschland Division. He led these elite troops until May, took a
brief leave, then substituted briefly for the commander of 14 Panzer
Corps, falling back ahead of the British in Italy.

When the Allies came ashore at Salerno, Balck's five-division
corps moved to contain the landing. Hurrying to visit his men up
forward, Balck had nearly every rib broken when his Fieseler Storch
crashed and flipped over. The injury was a reprieve to the Allies,
trying to consolidate their shaky landings, for the Germans had
massed every man they could spare for a decisive stroke at the
beachhead.

Years later, Balck still believed the battle might have ended differently had he been able to command at, as he put it, "the point of
action." His radio-intercept services had even heard General Mark
Clark talking about evacuating the beachhead. Balck recognized two
important German errors in dealing with the Allied landing. First,
powerful and persistent American airpower had caught German aircraft on the ground and crippled the Luftwaffe. Second, as Balck
put it,

> some silly ass on the staff of one of my divisions, without my
> knowledge, ordered loudspeakers installed at all the strong

points of the defense . . . intended to order the Americans to surrender. The American troops might have laughed themselves to death when they heard the loudspeakers but I can imagine no other possible effect.

A mere plane crash could not deter Balck, even though it kept him out of the Salerno fight at a critical moment. By mid-November he was on his way back to Army Group South in Russia, where crisis followed crisis. Manstein, commanding, knew how to use his calm, brilliant tank leader: Balck took over 48th Panzer Corps, outside Kiev.

Attacking with 1st Panzer Division and the SS Leibstandarte—two of the German army's finest units—Balck slashed into the flank of the Russian advance, stopped it cold, and carried the vital town of Zhitomir. Then, reinforced with three more panzer divisions and an infantry division, Balck pressed the Russians, making progress until the famous Russian thaw struck and the battlefield turned to bottomless mud in which everything bogged. Among other critical material, his men had captured some six hundred antitank guns. Balck urged that such weapons be rebored to German calibers and organized en masse—into what he called "antibreakthrough divisions"—to be assigned to army group level and committed only to cut off large enemy penetrations. The idea never got a real tryout; it might have made a difference.

Balck was a popular commander, a favorite with troops, who were confident of his care for them and his tactical expertise. Balck had no patience with rigid defense lines and resistance to the last man. To him, the ideal defense against the Russian hordes was a system of scattered outposts screening the main defense line—a line held well back out of effective Russian artillery range. He organized his artillery so that he could easily mass its fires, and maintained mobile reserves of assault and antitank guns.

Even the SS recognized his brilliance and followed him happily. Once, when Leibstandarte was returned to Balck's command after a six-week absence and received its first messages from him, that famous division let Balck know its happiness at being back under his command: "Hurrah!" Leibstandarte signaled. "Hurrah, we hear our Master's Voice!"

Balck knew the value of speed and mobility, the factors that repeat-

edly won German victories against enormous odds. Fighting outside Chir on the Stalingrad front, at seven o'clock one evening,
Balck was engaged in counterattacking Russian formations. In the
midst of battle, higher headquarters called with urgent orders to
drop everything and stop a breakthrough in another part of the
front.

Balck immediately disengaged his men, then marched twenty kilometers through the night. "I marched with the units," said Balck
simply: "After all the men were dead tired and nearly finished. I
rode up and down the column and asked the troops whether they
preferred to march or bleed." They marched. Balck struck the Russians at five o'clock the next morning. Attacking with complete surprise, his panzers destroyed seventy-five Russian tanks without losing
one of their own.

By early 1944, Balck was at Tarnopol, trying to repair a monstrous
hole with 7th Panzer Division and the Leibstandarte—and nobody
on either side of them. Improvising, using whatever troops came to
hand, Balck threw the Russians back from Tarnopol until reinforcements arrived to seal the hole.

So Balck had held again—but increasingly the fragile German
front sprang leak after leak under the intense Russian pressure. By
the end of July, the Russians were over the Vistula, and Balck and
his battered units had retreated into the Carpathians. In the west, the
Allies were preparing to break out of the Normandy beachhead, and
heavy bombers pounded the Reich day and night.

Balck took over Fourth Panzer Army at this desperate time, and
by early September he was attacking north, into the flank of the
Russian thrust surging out of its Vistula bridgehead at Baranov,
pointed like a knife at the heart of Silesia. In vicious fighting, Balck's
men again smashed the Russian spearheads, attacking always into
the flanks and rear of the Russian penetrations. As the Russian attack
lurched to a halt, Heinz Guderian knew who had worked this latest
miracle: "Thanks to Balck's indestructible energy and skill, in the
end we were once again able to ward off extreme catastrophe."

Balck went on to wipe out two Russian bridgeheads using small
combined-arms assault forces, but massing nearly every piece of
artillery for miles to hammer Russian resistance to pieces. An inter-
cepted Russian radio conversation told the story:

Hold your position!

I am finished.

Reinforcements are moving up.

To hell with your reinforcements. I am cut off. Your reinforcements won't find me here anymore.

. . . I would prefer you to shoot your own people than allow the enemy to shoot them.

Tovarich . . . perhaps you will grasp the situation when I tell you that I have nobody left I can *shoot, apart from my wireless operator.*

One job well done begat more responsibility. This time it was Army Group G, on the western front, trying to hold Alsace with very meager resources. Hitler briefed Balck on his way west and told him he would not be reinforced. Such new troops as there were would be saved for the Ardennes offensive. Ever the realist, Balck wrote that he had never commanded "such a mixture of badly equipped troops" as his ragtag army group. Ever the professional, however, Balck would do all he could with this blunt tool.

And so he did what he could to straighten his line, launching a successful series of local, limited attacks. Once that had been done, he sent men to "comb out the most attractive villages and towns" in his rear areas. In this way he moved his tank workshops out of comfortable rear-area billets up close to the units they supported. And he generated replacements—every army has lots of what Bill Mauldin called "garritroopers: too far forward to wear ties; too far back to get shot at." He personally oversaw formation of small mobile division reserves, and with these he launched local counterattacks as his units slowly withdrew, fighting.

Balck also made imaginative use of minefields to slow up the massive American advance. Most of the mines were dummies, each containing enough metal to register on a metal detector. American armor had to slow up to deal with them. "After all," said Balck,

when a tank moves out and sees signs of [mines] he can't know
whether they're fake or real. So he's got to stop and get the
mine field cleared, even if it has lots of dummy mines . . .

But in December, Balck was relieved of his command, the victim—or so Guderian thought—of Himmler's plotting. Balck was
abruptly sent to Budapest, there to command Sixth Army and two
Hungarian armies. By this time, the handwriting of defeat was on
the wall—both east and west, the German defenses were already
coming unstuck.

And now Balck, who had worried all his life about his men's mail,
and food, and health, worried about them again. He was determined
to surrender his forces to the West, not the hated and barbarian
Russians. As the battered German forces fell back into Austria, he
made his decision.

Balck called for a parley and spoke—in English—with his counter-
part, commander of American XX Corps: "We do not want to be
taken by the Russians," he said. "But if necessary we will attack
the Americans." The American commander, General McBride, understood. He did not consult his superiors but simply accepted
Balck's surrender, saving countless German soldiers from death or
endless captivity.

It was fitting. No whisper of brutality or barbarism had ever
touched Balck. He represented the best of the old-line German regular
officer, who admired courage and civility and returned, as he said,
"fairness against fairness." Balck's longtime chief of staff, von Mellenthin, a perceptive writer on war in his own right, probably knew
Balck better than anyone else. His verdict is worth repeating:

> He was one of our most brilliant leaders of armor; indeed, if
> Manstein was Germany's greatest strategist during World War
> II, I think Balck has strong claims to be regarded as our finest
> field commander.

Hermann Balck was indeed the finest type of armor commander.
In the wild confusion of tank warfare, he seldom had to wait long
for fresh, accurate information. Because he spent much of his time
far forward, he either saw for himself or was close enough to the
action to get news almost in real time. He coupled that leadership

from the front with great tactical skill and energy, seeking always the vulnerable flank or rear of his enemy.

Finally, when Balck struck, he struck to kill, with everything he had: Balck subscribed fully to Guderian's famous maxim: "Don't slap 'em, smash 'em!"

And smash them he did.

Like many high-ranking German officers, Balck remained in detention into 1947. Released, he took what work he could to feed his family—from working in a warehouse, he rose to be a manufacturer's representative. In the end, Balck went to work for his old comrade, chief of staff, and biographer, F. W. von Mellenthin, prospering as a representative of a South African airline. He settled in Stuttgart.

CHAPTER FORTY

LEADING

LEADERSHIP FROM THE front has always been a hallmark of the best and most successful officers. It is a tenet of the modern United States army, and paid substantial dividends during the Gulf War. The British army fights the same way; Britain's astonishing success in the Falklands was attended by disproportionately heavy officer and NCO casualties—including a battalion commander killed in action—but that is part of the price of successful leadership.

German leadership from the front was a major reason for the Wehrmacht's smashing success in 1940. Although it tends to be overlooked in all the talk of tanks and Stukas and blitzkrieg, the fact remains that forward, daring leadership is one of the characteristics of "lightning war." The casualties suffered by XIXth Panzer Corps—the unit under which Balck and his regiment served—illustrate this principle quite clearly.

Between the beginning of the campaign and Dunkirk, the corps' losses were 6.99 percent, including 1.16 percent killed, light enough, surely, for all that its units achieved. Among officers, however, the rates were significantly higher: 16.07 percent wounded and 3.53 percent killed.

Daring and courage are expensive.

CHAPTER FORTY-ONE

AMBUSH
The Death of Groupe Mobile 100

IT WAS HOT, oppressively hot, and terribly silent. There was no sound; there were no people; there were no animals, not even birds. There was only the brazen sun and the empty road—and a sense that there was danger everywhere.

The sweat-soaked troopers of the Battalion de Marche of the 43d Colonial Infantry had halted near kilometer 15. First Company, in the lead, smelled trouble. Captain Leouzon, the CO, looked out over a bend in the road, a left turn through an open area covered with thick, yellow-green elephant grass, six feet tall.

Leouzon conferred with Major Muller, his battalion commander. He was uneasy about the curve with its dense cover, and he wanted to sweep the area some distance from the road for a possible ambush. Muller was uneasy, too, but there was no time for a reconnaissance in force. Behind them, far down the road, east toward An Khe, stretched the vehicles, guns, and plodding infantry of the rest of Groupe Mobile 100: three more battalions, a convoy of trucks loaded with supplies and ammunition, a handful of armored cars and half-tracks, two or three hundred terrified civilian refugees.

Muller, understandably, did not want to wait. Eleven kilometers ahead lay Mang Yang Pass; French troops there were ready and waiting to receive this long, unwieldy snake of a convoy. And he knew the column was being chased. The Viet-Minh were out there somewhere, invisible and eager for the blood of the men sweating along the road.

The column had left An Khe before dawn that morning, behind them tall columns of greasy black smoke from burning ammunition dumps. Dien Bien Phu had fallen, and the French were pulling out of their An Khe post forever. Most of the equipment and civilians had already been flown out, and the Groupe commander, Colonel Barrou, dared not wait to finish the destruction and evacuation.

For he had hard intelligence that the Viet-Minh Regiment 803 was heading for this road, Route Coloniale 19. The Viets would know that he was heading west from An Khe, and they would move swiftly to cut him off from the highland capital of Pleiku, on up the road to the west. And so he had decided to move on this twenty-fourth of June, 1954, a day ahead of schedule.

The column would move the entire twenty-two kilometers in a single bound. Covering so much ground in one day, he could not make the painstaking recon he would ordinarily insist on, but he reasoned that if he moved quickly he might beat the 803d to Mang Yang Pass. Once there, he would have enough strength to bloody almost anything the Viets might throw at him.

Barrou was an experienced officer, and he did what he could to avoid surprise. A light recon aircraft—the French nickname was *mouchard* (''snooper'')—was always near the column, flying low to spot movement approaching the road and the convoy. Out in the bush, north of the road, prowled Captain Vitasse with his detachment of Bahnar tribesmen. If he could not avoid the 803d, Barrou reasoned, at least the *mouchard* or Vitasse's Montagnards might give him enough warning to prepare for the Viet attack.

Barrou had divided his artillery battalion so that each infantry battalion had a battery of its own. He would travel in the middle of the column, where he could exercise maximum control, and he kept close to him his tiny platoon of armored cars and half-tracks.

He was confident in the quality of his foot soldiers. The 43d was a veteran colonial outfit of both French and Cambodian soldiers. The rest of the infantry were the 1st and 2d Korea battalions, the famous soldiers who had fought so well beside the United States 2d Infantry Division in Korea.

The men of the Corée Battalions were all professionals, many of whom had taken a reduction in grade in order to fight in Korea. They still proudly wore the American unit's patch. For a while there they had been commanded by an amazing fifty-nine-year-old legionnaire called Monclar—a nom de guerre. Monclar pretty well typified the soldiers of the battalion, for he himself had given up three-star rank to lead the Korea battalion as a lieutenant colonel.

These men had made a name for themselves in Korea for derring-do and professionalism. They had won an American Presidential Unit Citation there for an action in which they had held vital ground against enormous odds, retaking one critical ridge "with bayonets fixed and screaming like madmen."

Vietnam had been a different sort of war, however, a six-month traveling slugging match. The Korea battalions of GM 100 had traveled some two thousand miles and fought again and again, but this time in a country of dense bush and jungle, a place of silence and endless empty spaces and sudden violent ambush.

But so far, here on R.C. 19, the Groupe's *baraka*—its luck—had held. The rear guard had taken a few casualties from automatic weapons fire at kilometer 6. Two kilometers farther on, another man had gone down to a poisoned dart, fired silently from a blowgun. But otherwise, the retreat had been a walk in the sun. The experienced Colonel Barrou was satisfied, but he was not comfortable.

Besides the threat posed by the Viet-Minh 803d, Barrou was particularly concerned about one unit in the column, a Vietnamese agglomeration called the 520th Tieu-Doan Kinh-Quan (TDKQ). It was a so-called commando battalion, but it was anything but. Far from being commandos, the TDKQ were an ineffective, frightened rabble, a liability rather than an asset. Barrou knew he could depend on them to hide or run, but never to fight.

Barrou also had serious shortages in personnel. The Groupe had already suffered heavy losses, the latest in a mass ambush on April 4 at this same kilometer 15. Even before that clash, Barrou had been short seventeen platoon leaders, some twenty radio operators, and a variety of other specialists. In that fight, two companies of 1st Korea had lost over half their strength, including many NCOs and officers.

And then the radio crackled in Barrou's headquarters element and the colonel was listening to Captain Vitasse, a tiny voice somewhere in the emptiness north of the road. Vitasse's report was urgent. The

803d *was* on the way, and Vitasse had seen them only three kilometers north of the road. At almost the same time a *mouchard* saw another Viet-Minh unit north of kilometer 11. Then, just a little later, the *mouchard* reported a barricade made of light rocks across the road at kilometer 15, although the pilot saw no people near it. The ring was closing.

And here an odd omission occurred, an oversight that would cost Groupe Mobile 100 much blood and torment. The reports from Vitasse and the *mouchard* were duly passed on to each element in the long column—everybody, that is, *except* the 43d Colonial Infantry, and it was leading the long column.

And so Leouzon's men pushed off across that ominous bend in the road, alert as always, but without the critical intelligence that might have saved their lives. They were moving toward a little pimple of a hill, a place from which they might at least see farther than a foot or two in the tall grass. And then Cambodian Sergeant Li-Som stopped and called urgently for absolute silence. As the men behind him froze, Li-Som's practiced ear heard clearly a soft clicking from the long tough leaves of grass.

Li-Som knew that clicking. It was the sound the grass makes as it vibrates back into place after something large has pushed through it. And Li-Som knew: the Viet-Minh were already there. Whatever Vitasse and the *mouchard* had seen, the ambush was already in place. Li-Som, veteran NCO, reacted instantly, pushing forward into the grass, calling for his platoon to follow him, pulling the pin on a grenade as he moved.

As he did, two Viet machine guns opened at almost point-blank range, and Li-Som threw his grenade at the sound. One Viet crew died in the flash of Li-Som's grenade, but the second gun tore the little sergeant's chest wide open. First Company went automatically into its battle drill, patching up a perimeter defense under a hail of mortar, automatic weapon, and recoilless rifle fire. It was precisely 1420.

Leouzon was convinced they would all die in that stifling patch of grass by the bend in the road, but he and his men were determined to do it like soldiers. His men deployed smoothly and began to return the torrent of Viet fire. They did it calmly and with panache, as befitted a veteran outfit. Leouzon's 57-millimeter recoilless rifle gunner dropped prone next to his commander.

I hope you won't mind, *mon capitaine*, but I'll have to kick up quite a bit of dust.

Back with the headquarters element, Colonel Barrou heard Li-Som's grenade and the hammering of machine gun fire. Before he could react, smoke and dust and fire enveloped the headquarters vehicles and the armored platoon just ahead. Viet mortar and recoilless rifle fire rained down on the road, and within seconds vehicles lurched to a halt and began to burn.

Within five minutes the radio truck was a flaming pyre, cutting Barrou off from his battalions. In those flames died the radio crew, the only men who might have said why the 43d was never told of the danger into which they marched. The armored platoon was gone, too. Three half-tracks and an M-8 armored car were in flames almost immediately, their ammunition exploding amid the din of nonstop firing from both the Viets and the convoy.

For a little while the lone surviving M-8 fought on alone, raking a Viet hillcrest machine gun position with canister from its 37-millimeter gun. Under its fire, Barrou and Captain Fievet, the Headquarters Company commander, rallied a few men for a counterattack on the machine guns. For a moment, against all hope, it looked like the counterstroke had a chance. But then Barrou was down with a bullet in the thigh; Fievet was dying, his chest torn open; and the last M-8 ceased fire, its gunner killed.

As the attack broke down, Barrou tried to drag himself onto the M-8 to get its gun back in action. Hit again, this time in the other leg, he fell from the silent M-8 and rolled into the roadside ditch. Barrou had done all he could. Headquarters Company was finished. He had conferred the Legion of Honor on the dying Fievet—and on Lieutenant Colonel Lajouanie, commander of the Korea Regiment, mortally wounded as he, too, tried to get to the machine guns that were killing the column.

Now Barrou tore off his rank insignia and destroyed his identification. Masses of Viet infantry were running down toward the road. He could hear their cries—*"Tien-len, tien-len* [Forward, forward]''— amidst the roar of firing.

Many of the surviving truck drivers had run for their lives, leaving the road solidly blocked with their vehicles, many of which were burning and exploding. Some of them had been carrying loads of ammunition, and the thunderous blasts of their dying rocked the valley. The wretched TDKQ had run also, leaving the few remaining headquarters men to fight alone. Up ahead, the 43d still held together, fighting with very little hope but doing it professionally still. They were still a unit, but their casualties were high. It was 1530.

And then, with the headquarters element in its death throes, the survivors heard heavy firing from the rear of the column, and men of the lst and 2d Korea began to fight their way through the mael-strom of smoke, dust, flame, and explosion. One battery of the artillery battalion had gone into action on the road in spite of murderous casualties from the Viet mortar fire. Though many gunners lay dead and dying in the road, the men still on their feet were pouring point-blank fire into the onrushing Viets.

Two companies of 2d Korea fought their way through to the 43d, and Major Kleinmann, commander of 1st Korea, took command in the pocket. At about 1620 he and Major Guinard, commanding 2d Korea, decided they could hold enough ground for an airdrop. Ominously, ammunition was running out, and casualties were every-where. But for the time being they threw the Viets back—and received some unexpected help.

For down the deadly twisting valley flew B-26s of the French air force, their noses loaded with guns. Everybody on both sides hugged the ground, for the two sides were so closely interlocked that the fire from above threatened French and Viet alike. A radio in Headquarters Company crackled as some hard-pressed soldier made the classic infantryman's comment on the rain of ordnance from the air. What he said was typically French: "This goes to show you again—this whole aerial warfare business isn't quite perfected . . ."

And so the column fought on, and at last the endless day began to draw toward sundown. Guinard and Kleinmann conferred again. They had driven the Viet infantry back with heavy losses, but mortar fire still rained down on the burning vehicles and the desperate wounded. Their own howitzers were silent, their ammunition gone, their crews dead. There was no more water. Kleinmann had authority from higher headquarters to break out toward kilometer 22 with what-ever he could bring, and it seemed to him that to stay longer in this evil place would produce nothing but more casualties. His brother officer nodded: it was time to go.

What tore at both officers' hearts was the question of the wounded.

Unless they could walk, they could not go. The only way out was through the bush, hostile, vast, and largely trackless. Each stretcher case needed eight men just to carry him. No, these two veterans knew, the seriously wounded would have to stay.

But not alone. Any medical personnel who would volunteer to do so would remain with them. It was time to tell the doctor. Down behind some overturned trucks, little Major Varme-Janville, the column surgeon, had been fighting for men's lives all through the baking afternoon. Exhausted and covered with blood, he heard his commander's decision.

Varme-Janville understood; he was a soldier. He simply nodded and said

> Gentlemen, I don't think I can be much further help in this. They've got good doctors up in Pleiku, but my men need me here. I'll stay. . . .

And he went back to his wounded.

Up the road, the remains of the 43d had already smashed a hole in the circle around them and begun to move. Now 1st and 2d Korea began their own preparations. As darkness came on, at about 1900, they crammed thermite grenades into howizter tubes and set fire to what undamaged equipment remained. And then, as the wounded who could still shoot fought on to hold off the Viets, Kleinmann's men struck off into the trackless jungle.

They broke out cleanly. The veteran Kleinmann had wisely chosen to go straight south, avoiding the short, obvious western route closest to kilometer 22 and safety. Once out of the trap and into deep jungle, the men broke into platoon-size groups, each commanded by an officer or NCO. Heavy columns do not move well in the jungle.

They plodded on through the night of the twenty-fourth, hacking at vines and brush, unable to move silently in this wilderness, wondering each minute when the night would explode in a torrent of bullets from ambush. And some of them simply sank to the ground, exhausted. Their comrades could not carry them; their friends could not wait. And so they died there in the silence alone, slowly of hunger and thirst, or quickly under the knife of a tribesman eager for loot.

The rest went on, step by agonizing step, through the creepers and vines and thorns, dragged down by thirst and exhaustion, driven by the certainty that the Viets would try to cut them off. For the victorious Viet-Minh had to know where they were headed—sanctuary lay in only one direction, up the twisting road toward Pleiku.

But when dawn broke on the twenty-fifth, the little groups still held together, still carried their weapons. Some men carried an extra weapon, so that the walking wounded could sell their lives dearly if they were caught by the Viets. They were haggard, hungry, and dead tired, but they were still soldiers.

And then they began to encounter resistance, groups of Viet-Minh probing for them, met almost point-blank in the jungle. 1st Korea led, and four times between 0630 and 0830 men of the battalion bloodied Viet-Minh probes and drove them back. The men of 4th Company opened the final Viet block with a wild charge: ''Corée!'' they roared; ''Corée!'' And the Viets ahead of them broke, leaving a dozen corpses behind. The way was open to safety.

And then at last, at about noon, the survivors began to see blue sky above them and feel a breeze. The point of the advance froze, ready to fire, as a voice challenged them. But the voice was French:

Qui va là? [Who goes there?]

Ne tirez pas. Francais!—[Don't shoot. We're French!]

And the exhausted men of lst Korea fell into the arms of paratroopers of lst Airborne Group. The ordeal was over . . . at least for a while.

The Airborne Group did not intend to stay at kilometer 22. They were there only to collect whoever might have broken out of the trap back at kilometer 15. Among them were the survivors of 1st Company of the 43d, still led by the formidable Leouzon, although the indestructible captain had lost his pants to thorns somewhere back in the jungle. The last of the GM 100 men straggled in at about nightfall that evening; there would be no more.

The wounded were trucked up the road to Pleiku. The survivors who could still fight trudged on up the road to Mang Yang Pass, where lay Groupe Mobile 42, composed mostly of Montagnard tribesmen. There was reason to hurry, for the 803d Viet-Minh regiment was close behind. Reinforced with a full additional battalion, the

Viets would follow, intent on destroying every French unit along the road.

And so the remnants of GM 100 fell back, along with the elements of GM 42 and the airborne group. With them was a welcome reinforcement, some tanks of 5th Armored Cavalry, a famous unit whose nickname, Royal Poland, dated from the great days of Napoleon's Grande Armee. They moved slowly and carefully, the infantry combing the sides of the road as they pushed toward Pleiku.

By the night of the twenty-sixth they had safely reached a place called Phu-Yen, some ten kilometers west of Mang Yang Pass. After a night's rest the column pushed on toward a stream, the Dak-Ya-Ayun, smashing through a Viet ambush on the east side of the crossing. 1st Korea, leading on the approach to the Dak-Ya-Ayun, took fifty-nine dead, but with the tanks opened the road to the bridge.

The next day, June twenty-eighth, the country around the road began to broaden, and at last the troops began to see peasants and cultivated fields. Pleiku was not far now, and there lay safety.

But as the head of the column closed in on the junction of R.C. 19 and R.C. 19-b, the sense of great danger returned. There were the same ominous signs the men knew of old: rocks piled on the road, no birds, total eerie silence. The leading units, including two companies of the 43d and what was left of 1st Korea, looked to their weapons.

And just before noon it came, the same barrage of mortar and recoilless rifle fire, the same automatic weapons fire from the bush near the road. This time, however, the leading troops pulled into a perimeter, howitzers in the center, and poured fire on the charging Viet infantry. This time their enemy was Regiment 108, reinforced by another first-class battalion.

Down the road the convoy's trucks were blasted by bazookas and mortars, and instantly some began to burn and explode. But this time the native drivers did not jump and run. This time they accelerated, roaring on through the fire, pushing burning vehicles ahead of them off the road. This time they made it to at least temporary safety in the perimeter, though they left ten trucks blazing on the road behind them.

And then, at about 1215, a human wave attack struck the long-suffering survivors of First Company, 1st Korea. There were only sixty of them left, and they had no heavy weapons, but they stood

their ground and fought it out with ten times their number. Until
finally the wave of screaming little men simply drowned them, and
First Company ceased to exist.

But they had held up the Viets for a quarter of an hour or so, and
that was enough. Now three platoons of Second Company struck the
Viets in flank in the same kind of hell-bent-for-leather charge that
had so astonished the Chinese. "Corée!" they roared; "Corée!" And
they went in hard, the tanks with them, the howitzer gunners firing
point-blank into the faces of the Viets.

They stopped the Viets cold, piling them up short of the guns,
and as they did, the air was full of the roar of aircraft engines. The
B-26s came in low, all the way from Nha Trang on the South China
Sea, and they caught the Viets away from cover. Splashed with great
sheets of flaming napalm and slashed by the nose guns of the bombers, the Viets broke and fell back into the bush. Even in the heart
of this carnage, the French kept their famous savoir faire. Sniffing
the stench of burning Viet, one 1st Korea man remarked: "It would
even smell like fried pork, but it's that awful gasoline stench which
spoils everything."

It was over. The Viet-Minh had had enough and were gone into
the bush, leaving heaps of dead behind. And for a while, at least,
the road to safety lay open. What was left of GM 100 reached Pleiku
on the twenty-ninth without further fighting, ragged, exhausted, suffering from dysentery and jungle sores. But they were still soldiers.

The losses had been staggering. The three infantry battalions, 1st
and 2d Korea and the 43d Colonial, had had a paper strength of
834 men each. When they counted noses at Pleiku, they numbered,
respectively, 452, 497, and 345. There were 215 gunners left out of
474, and their commander lay dead at kilometer 15.

Dead also were the badly wounded men left at Kilometer 15. The
gallant Dr. Varme-Janville could not help them. They were collected
by the fighting units of the Viet-Minh and returned to An Khe. But
there the doctor looked directly into the soulless face of communism.
His captors were the commissars, the politicals, not the fighting men
of the 803d.

And so Varme-Janville had to sit and watch his wounded die, all
of them, and die in the middle of a fully equipped hospital the French
had deliberately left undamaged. The commissars simply forbade him
to treat the suffering men:

You are no longer a doctor, but simply a dirty imperialist officer. Our wounded have no doctor. Your wounded have no doctor.

And so they died, one by one, while in Geneva diplomats in clean, starched shirts droned on and on about ending the war. The little doctor passed into Viet captivity, survived the death march to northern POW compounds, and was repatriated at war's end. His health was destroyed by his ordeal. So, it is said, was his spirit.

Colonel Barrou lay in his ditch for two days, crawling finally to a wrecked vehicle to find a little water. He was found at last by other Frenchmen, survivors of the deadly ambush, and these faithful men built a litter and began to carry their colonel up that bloody road toward Pleiku. They did not get far, for the Viets had kept watchers on the road. Barrou and his saviors would also become prisoners.

Premier Mendes-France had publicly promised an armistice by July 20, and there was some reason to think he would keep his promise. It was not too much for the remains of the Groupe to think their war might at last be over. Even though there had been some replacements, by rights the exhausted survivors of GM 100 should have been left alone to watch the war sputter out in some sort of safety.

But down at Nha Trang, Zone Headquarters insisted on another offensive effort. The Battalion de Marche of the 43d was gone, and 2d Korea had the job of defending Pleiku, the province's capital. And so it fell to the battered 1st Korea to saddle up and move south down the R.C. 14 to help clear that vital road to Ban Me Thuot, another important provincial capital.

The battalion was still tired, worn out with war. Two of its companies were commanded by junior lieutenants, and most of the platoon leaders were sergeants. The men of 1st Korea had no illusions about this operation, ominously named "Forget-me-not." One corporal spoke for them all: "My God, they want to kill us to the last man. Haven't we done enough?"

They had, of course. More than enough. But being good men and good soldiers, they went off down Highway 14 with GM 42, the Montagnard Groupe, a few guns, and some armored vehicles of Royal Poland. And about halfway there, in the bowels of a narrow gut called Chu-Dreh Pass, a little after noon on Bastille Day, the curtain finally fell on 1st Korea.

It was another ambush, sprung after all of GM 42 had passed through the pass to the south. 1st Korea, closing the long column, took the full weight of it. Fourth Company died in the middle of the pass where there was no cover, cut down by carefully laid machine guns firing down the road.

Professionals to the last, First and Headquarters companies pulled into a rough perimeter west of the road and began to inch back toward the northern end of the pass. From there they fell back by bounds, covering one another and dragging with them their wounded, including Major Guinard, the battalion commander. They left behind a trail of dead.

At last, a suicidal rush by tanks and half-tracks of Royal Poland roared back north through the pass, relieving some of the pressure at the cost of burning half-tracks, reeking with the awful, unforgettable smell of burning flesh. And at about 1400 the guns finally fell silent as the Viets pulled back once more. The Geneva cease-fire was only three days away.

When it was all over, and the stragglers had worked their way back to Pleiku, the gallant 1st Korea counted 107 men. Half of even these were hospitalized. The battalion was dead. It is pleasant to relate that it later found resurrection as a conventional infantry battalion of the French army. In its new incarnation it left Vietnam a year after the Chu-Dreh ambush . . . for Algeria and another war.

Groupe Mobile 100 was officially abolished by the French Command on the first of September. The Groupe's last commander, Colonel Masse, pronounced its epitaph in his last order of the day. He put it pretty well:

> Beyond the diversity of your origins, nationalities and unit traditions to which you remain deeply attached, you have succeeded in acquiring a collective soul which has given its unity to G.M. 100. . . .

Indeed it had. And that soul had acquired a measure of immortality. For when men talk who admire courage and loyalty and professionalism, GM 100 will be remembered. That memory is probably its only monument. As late as 1964, there was a simple memorial near kilometer 15: *"Mort pour la Patrie,"* it read. "Fallen for the Fatherland."

But who knows whether it is still there.

AMBUSH II

The Legacy of Groupe Mobile 100

MANY YEARS AFTER the ambush of GM 100, there came a distant echo of the roar of gunfire and the cries of pain, an ugly memory of the blood and flame at kilometer 15. It rang out as the days were beginning to run out for the Republic of Vietnam, with masses of North Vietnamese regulars poised for the last offensive south.

Many of First Korea's survivors had died trying to open the road to Ban Me Thuot. Now, in mid-March 1975, that important town had fallen to NVA tanks and infantry. And communist shells were also falling on Pleiku and its airfield. It was plain that the nation was in crisis, and at last even Nguyen Van Thieu realized that something had to be done. Without action, the country was lost.

And so he flew to Cam Ranh Bay, and there he conferred with three other Vietnamese in the white house with a sea view that had been built for Lyndon Johnson's 1967 visit. With him were General Ngo Van Truong, commander of the northernmost provinces; general staff chief General Caoa Van Vien; and General Pham Van Phu, who commanded in the highlands. The meeting was grim.

Thieu had already decided to pull back to Saigon the Airborne Division, his best soldiers, and to give ground in the north to save something farther south. Now he had to decide what to do about Ban Me Thuot and the highlands.

General Phu was not encouraging. The NVA was four divisions strong in his area, with tanks, and all major routes into the highlands were blocked. And then Thieu asked the ultimate question: Could Phu recapture Ban Me Thuot?

Yes, said the general. Yes, but only with heavy reinforcements of all kinds.

Thieu turned to the chief of staff.

"Yes, General. And what do we have in reserve for General Phu?" Vien was direct. "Nothing."

And so the die was cast. It would be evacuation, and quickly, the idea being to pull all regular troops back from Pleiku and Kontum to the coast, to regroup for the recapture of Ban Me Thuot, lynchpin of the highlands. The local irregular troops, nearly all Montagnards, would not be told of the retreat. They would, in short, be thrown away to cover the departure of the regulars.

All this was bad enough, but even worse was the choice of an abandoned logging road as the route of retreat. Phu chose to use this route, called Interprovincial Route 7-b, even though the road was in terrible condition and had been mined at various times by Saigon troops, the communists, and the South Koreans.

Phu had fought in French uniform at Dien Bien Phu and had suffered terribly afterward in Viet-Minh captivity. Critics later said that he feared communist capture again. And so, when Vien reminded him of the killing at kilometer 15—as Vien certainly did—perhaps those memories of captivity and bloody ambush moved him to choose 7-b instead of 19, the main route. Vien said later that he mentioned Groupe Mobile 100 only to remind Phu of the hazards of a retreat down a similar road in similar terrain.

Whatever the truth may be, for whatever reasons, Phu chose 7-b. The result would be a butchery vastly eclipsing kilometer 15. For the retreat soon turned to rout, a desperate flight down a gauntlet of murderous NVA fire. Vietnamese dead and dying littered the road in many thousands, and of these perhaps the majority were civilian refugees, including thousands of women and children.

When it was all over, Phu's survivors could not come close to retaking Ban Me Thuot. Much worse, they could not hold the coastal enclaves either, and the wheels came off the entire Saigon defense structure almost literally overnight.

Perhaps the choice of a withdrawal route would have made no

difference in the end. In all probability the sands had run out for South Vietnam no matter what Phu chose to do. But it is tragically ironic that the ghosts of kilometer 15 apparently rose from their graves a generation later to lead an undecided officer into another bloody ambush on a twisting mountain road.

CHAPTER FORTY-THREE

THE ANGEL OF DIEN BIEN PHU
Genevieve Galard

HER FULL NAME was Genevieve de Galard-Terraube. The press, fond of coining dramatic names, called her "the angel of Dien Bien Phu." That was all very well for the front page of *Paris-Soir,* but nobody referred to her that way in that ghastly valley. The soldiers who adored her called her simply "Genevieve."

They would have walked through fire for her, too, all those soldiers of the old Colonial Army. Some of them were mainland Frenchmen, with all the gallantry and wit of that breed. Many, however, had never even seen La Belle France, and barely spoke her language. They were Algerian tirailleurs and infantry soldiers of the Moroccan Tabors, and shy Thai partisans from the wild hill country of the north. They were big, cheerful Senegalese gunners and Germans of the Legion, who sang "Westerwald" and "Annemarie" and the sentimental songs of the German army in the watches of the night.

But all of these men, speaking their babel of languages, revered the elegant, quiet, blue-eyed aristocrat named Genevieve. She was more than a healer; to the tough fighting men of the Colonial Army, she also represented goodness and mercy and peace. She was just a touch of all the good things men dreamed about down in the muddy, bloody valley called Dien Bien Phu.

Genevieve was a flying nurse, one of the women who regularly flew with the lumbering C-47 medevac aircraft. She had not been part of the World War II resistance, but she was eager to serve France in Indochina. Daughter of a viscountess, she felt called to serve France—after all, her noble ancestors had been doing just that ever since the Crusades. They had followed Joan of Arc, these de Galards, and the fighting blood of Genevieve's ancestors ran true in her veins. Their passion was hers:

> I guess it was a hereditary thing. I thought, 'I am young and free, and I should be helping the effort' . . . it was no longer a colonial war, but a fight for freedom—against Communism.

In Indochina, she belonged to a seven-woman team of nurses who flew missions of mercy all over the vastness of Tonkin. Wherever a C-47 could land, they went, through the blinding torrents of the monsoon, around the jagged peaks that lurked malevolently in the mists for these old radarless aircraft.

They were shot at again and again, these nurses, but they kept on flying, day in, day out. They flew to Cao Bang and Na San and Lang Son and a host of other places nobody remembers anymore, and they faithfully brought out the wounded. And they flew mission after mission into the worst place of all, the bloody valley of Dien Bien Phu.

"It seemed as though you were landing in hell," she said: "There in the darkness lay the men waiting to be evacuated, staring at you with sunken eyes from pale, exhausted, unshaven faces."

Genevieve flew into Dien Bien Phu again and again, returning to Hanoi with loads of terribly hurt men, fighting for the lives of her charges along the way. She made thirty-nine trips into hell, into the valley French soldiers called "the chamber pot," and got safely away with her charges.

On the fortieth run, her luck ran out.

She had landed in the valley on March 26, but Viet fire was so heavy that her Dakota could not stop to load the waiting wounded. In a storm of mortar shells, the pilot poured on the power and took off again for Hanoi. And so, when it came time to fly the next run into the valley, Genevieve insisted on going. The last flight had not been complete, she said; they had not gotten the wounded they went for, so she was still first in the rotation. In the face of those steady blue eyes and that determined chin, her superior gave in.

And so it was that on March 28, 1954, Genevieve de Galard, instead of the woman next on the list, climbed aboard the two-hour night run for Dien Bien Phu. Not long past midnight, hospital C-47 number 434—nicknamed Delta Coca—of Transport Squadron Bearn, lifted into the night from Hanoi's Gia-Lam airport, bound for the valley. By this time, Viet-Minh antiaircraft fire had made the Dien Bien Phu strip untenable during daylight hours—any aircraft was fair game to the Communists, and the red cross was no protection. When the night blinded the Viet gunners, however, a daring pilot still might land long enough to load some of the worst of the wounded.

This night Delta Coca landed just before 0600, settling in safely through a storm of Viet flak. Taxiing through the pitch-blackness, the aircraft tangled with a mass of barbed wire and lurched to a stop, apparently undamaged. Twenty-five wounded were hastily loaded, and Delta Coca turned to take off. Before she could clear the runway, however, the pilot discovered that the landing collision had puntured an oil line. The wounded were quickly off-loaded and laid in slit trenches to await repairs to the plane. Genevieve suffered for the wounded:

> Because of bad weather, these poor men had been waiting to leave for three nights . . . They thought it was the end of that hell for them and it wasn't.

Dien Bien Phu's mechanics, unable to work in the blacked-out gloom of the valley, pushed Delta Coca into the place of a wrecked C-47, a derelict with which the communist gunners were long familiar. They left the wreck where Delta Coca had come to rest and hoped for the best.

It almost worked. Delta Coca was repaired successfully, and it was not until the wounded were ready to load and the plane's props turned over that Giap's gunners discovered they had been fooled. The torrent of fire that followed left Delta Coca just one more burned-out wreck on the battered airstrip. No more aircraft would land in the valley—not this day, not the next, not ever. The crew of Delta Coca were stuck in Dien Bien Phu to stay.

Major Paul Grauwin looked up from his bloody surgeon's work

to see Delta Coca's crew enter his subterranean hospital. They carried with them a wounded legion soldier who had been helping in the evacuation. "And in the background," wrote Grauwin later, "there was a young girl in blue, with a wing in gold on her breast, the flight nurse. . . . I recognized this one—her name was Genevieve de Galard."

Genevieve went to work at the main hospital of Dien Bien Phu, working shoulder-to-shoulder with Grauwin, the fabulous chief doctor of the tortured valley. From that day on Genevieve worked day and night in the purgatory of the underground hospital, jammed with hideously wounded men, crawling with millions of huge white maggots. She and Grauwin lived like troglodytes, emerging from their burrow only long enough for a quick cigarette and a gulp of rain-laden air, reeking with the sick-sweet stench of hundreds of putrefying corpses. Just outside one entrance yawned a pit full of amputated arms and legs, slowly rotting away in the mud.

Below ground, the scene was straight out of hell. Grauwin and Genevieve were surrounded by hideously wounded men: men with amputations, often double, even triple; men with gaping abdominal wounds; men with their brains showing through rents in their skulls; blinded men; men crying out for their mothers; men with holes where their private parts had been. Through all this horror Genevieve moved quietly, smiling, healing, and soothing. Grauwin marveled: "The flight nurse, the girl who had joined our ranks a few days before, moved through this fantastic world, gentle and efficient, silent."

In a hideous world in which high courage was an everyday virtue, Genevieve's quiet gallantry shone like a flare in the night. As the shells crashed down on top of the hospital dugouts, she calmly put on her helmet and walked into the terror outside. It did not occur to her to stay under cover when there were hurt men in the open. She simply shook her head at Grauwin's pleas: "But . . . I must go outside. I'm sure I'm needed."

Under the terrible pressure of the flood of wounded men, time quickly began to lose its meaning for the staff of the hospital. At one point in the siege Grauwin lost complete track of day and night, dragging himself exhausted to the mouth of the hospital tunnel, woozily working out that he had lost three complete days. As he sucked in the air and feasted his eyes on real sky and clouds, he heard a quiet voice behind him in the murk of the tunnels: "Oh, I would so like to go to sleep and never, never wake up again."

It was Genevieve, and she was crying quietly to herself, leaning against the filthy wall of the underground hospital. Even the bravest know times of desperation, and this was hers. Still, her horror at the suffering around her could not kill her devotion to the wounded huddled in the grime and blood of the underground hospital: "I felt I could not have left anyway. Not after those three days. I wouldn't have wanted to go."

And the depression did not last. She got a telegram out to her mother in France: "The boys have invited me to stay for the battle." And she laughed at her mother's answer: "I am relieved. At least there you will not run the risk of being killed in a plane crash." It seems reasonably certain that the aged French lady, a descendant of fifty generations of fighting ancestors, guessed pretty accurately at her daughter's danger; the message was her blessing.

Genevieve cared especially for some of the worst cases in the hospital, dealing with protruding intestines and hideous burns with a quiet smile and those marvelous eyes that sometimes calmed where morphine could not. She spent what extra time she had with some of the worst cases in Grauwin's hospital, like the soldier who had lost both arms and a leg. Propped up by this slim, tough woman, the soldier hopped on his remaining leg to a tunnel opening for a breath of fresh air, promising to take Genevieve dancing one day when the shooting was over.

When she could, Genevieve visited the wounded in other scattered bunkers. Her boss, Major Grauwin, fretted over her reckless gallantry:

> Genevieve, don't go so far, there are shells going off every-where. I don't need another patient.

But neither the murderous shellfire nor anything Grauwin could say would stop her. She did not even consider being hit. "Oh, no!" she said.

> If only you could have seen how happy they were and how pleased I was! Everywhere they were saying, 'Mademoiselle,

who are you? A nurse—that's marvelous . . . You must come and see us often.'

Before long she was no longer "Mademoiselle de Galard" to Grauwin and the men of the hospital. She was simply Genevieve, and the men around her scrambled to make this astonishing little woman as comfortable as possible. Boots and a paratroop uniform appeared, and other items of clothing. Pierre Langlais, the tough Airborne Group commander, found her a sleeping niche and furnished it with a bed covered with parachute silk. Others brought her precious cigarettes, which she passed out on her incessant rounds among the wounded.

There was virtually no privacy for a cultured woman in this crowded, hectic world of mud and death and bursting shells. The men around her did everything they could to honor her private moments, and she kept her sense of humor even about her most embarrassing times:

> . . . going to the bathroom. I had to climb out of the trench into the open, behind the sandbags and barbed wire. I was very frightened that I would be wounded, and I really didn't want to be wounded in that position!

When Genevieve contracted a monstrous boil on her shoulder, the pain finally forced her to seek help from Grauwin. By the time the doctor saw it, the boil had become a huge carbuncle, and Grauwin knew he had to operate immediately. Quite aware of the pain she would face, Genevieve staunchly refused pentothal—as usual, thinking only of her suffering patients: "I'm not going to be off duty for a whole day just because I've got a little boil!"

By that time, the "little boil" was as big as a man's hand. Even so, Genevieve said not a word as Grauwin lanced it, only clenching her small hands tightly against the edges of the operating table. And then she went quietly back to work, to the stinking colostomies, the oozing stumps of legs and arms, the maggots, and the mud.

Whatever the press said later, Genevieve was not the only woman in the mud and misery of Dien Bien Phu. There were even a few families there, wives of the Meo partisans who had taken refuge in the valley as the red tide submerged all northwestern Tonkin. And there were the women of two BMCs—Bordel Mobile de Campagne—the official military brothels that followed the French army nearly everywhere. These Vietnamese and North African prostitutes also nursed and comforted; they brought a little spark of decency into the squalid, stinking pesthole of Dien Bien Phu.

But it was little Genevieve in her cut-down paratroop uniform who became the heart of the defense. After all, how could any man lose heart when this quiet, brown-haired woman carried on with a smile in the terrifying filth and suffering of the hospital tunnels?

On the twenty-ninth of April, as the shadows descended on the defenders of Dien Bien Phu, Genevieve was summoned to the command post of Colonel Langlais, commander of GAP 2, the airborne element in the valley. As she pushed through the blackout curtain, she was astonished to find not only Langlais but also Brigadier General de Castries, the valley commander, and other officers, including Major Marcel Bigeard, the lion of the Airborne, fabulous commander of the 6th Colonial Paratroops.

De Castries called to her: "Genevieve, I've got something for you." And he pinned to her uniform shirt both the Croix de Guerre with Palms and the coveted, vivid red ribbon of the Knight's Cross of the Legion of Honor. The hard-bitten men of the valley were commending one of their own, and they had gone to considerable trouble to do it. Langlais had fished his own battered Croix de Guerre out of the bottom of a canteen, and the Legion of Honor ribbon was the gift of a paratroop lieutenant who had recently won it as his own.

The next day brought more commendation for the little nurse. It was Camerone Day, the holy feast day of the Foreign Legion. On this day, all across the world, the Legion celebrates the astonishing stand of a Legion company in Mexico in the spring of 1863, and the courage and panache of its commander, Captain Danjou of the Wooden Hand. And on this day—usually a sort of orderly orgy given to much red wine, blood sausage, and roistering—it was the Legion's custom to create a few carefully selected honorary Legionnaires.

This Camerone Day, little Genevieve was one of the few honored. She stood proudly beside de Castries, Bigeard, and Langlais to become a Legion PFC, entitled to wear her Legion rank ever after and to carry the serial number of her Legion sponsor. Genevieve's sponsor was the orderly to Langlais' chief of staff. Genevieve was intensely proud of the honor the Legion had paid her, and said so to her sponsor: "If we ever get out of this alive, I'll pay you a bottle of champagne no matter where we meet."

There was little with which to celebrate Camerone Day, no blood sausage, just a few drops of real wine, only cups of the vicious Vinogel, the foul-tasting, constipating wine concentrate that had to substitute for the "pinard" so beloved of the Legion. And even the Vinogel had been hard to come by. The last airdropped supply had been lost, drifting off into the bullet-torn wilderness east of strongpoint Eliane. To leave it there on Camerone Day, undrunk, was, to the Legion, unthinkable.

And so a force of Legion volunteers had retrieved the precious Vinogel, striking the Viet lines in a night raid that left a number of Communist casualties without a single Legion loss. It looked fine in the daily briefing, and it was not until much later that the French command in Hanoi learned the whole operation had been mounted solely to retrieve the Vinogel.

Back at the hospital, Genevieve showed off her new insignia to Grauwin, delighted to have been recognized by the men she cared so much about. And then she made the rounds wearing her Legion rank, to the applause and congratulations of the wounded. In a gesture typically French, Grauwin unearthed ten bottles of hoarded champagne in honor of the diminutive new Legionnaire. And Genevieve made sure every wounded man got at least a sip.

But no amount of heroism or élan would save the valley. The skeletal companies of the Legion and the paras hurled themselves again and again against hordes of Viet infantry, attacked and counterattacked in the rain until only shadows remained of the elite units of the defense.

By the end of April the monsoon squatted malevolently over the valley, pouring torrents of water into the valley, collapsing bunkers, turning trenches into little rivers. Down in the hospital bunkers the mud rose gradually to knee depth. In the gloom of the operating room, the doctors had to jerk their feet clear of the gluelike muck in which they stood hour after hour.

Everything rotted; everything was covered with mold and mildew. And with the damp and heat came a plague of flies, crawling in their millions over the helpless wounded. Their maggots writhed inside the bandages covering open wounds, slithered at night over the bodies and faces of sleeping men. Grauwin soothed his wounded as best he

could, reassuring them that the repulsive worms could only do them
good: "It's a very good thing. These grubs eat everything dirty, even
dead bone. So they leave you with a nice clean wound; they do a
better job than a pad of ether."

By Easter Day it was plain that the end could not be far away.
Nevertheless, mass was celebrated in the valley and in the charnel
house that was the hospital. Genevieve was there, with Grauwin and
other medical personnel, and staunch Father Heinrich administered
Holy Communion to the terribly wounded men crammed into the dark,
oozing tunnels. A parachute drop of desperately needed supplies and
food raised everybody's spirits, although the wounded continued to
pour into the crowded hospital.

As the Viet lines closed down around the few remaining strong-
points in the valley, badly wounded men began to leave the hospital
for their units. Dying with one's friends was better than dying in a
dark hole, they said—and anyway, a man with only one arm or one
eye could still shoot and be useful. Genevieve sent them off with her
quiet smile, although it must have torn at her heart to see them go.

By this time, Genevieve had given up her own little shelter, turning
it over to more badly wounded men. She was sleeping in her clothes
on a muddy stretcher, exhausted and thin, dark rings etched around
her brown eyes. The hospital was overflowing; even the muddy pas-
sages were stacked with men in agony. New wounded poured in
from everywhere, and with them came men driven from local aid
stations by the advancing Viets, naked men, men without arms or
legs, who dragged themselves through the muck, still hoping for
salvation.

On May 4 Hanoi transmitted the last private message to Dien
Bien Phu. It was addressed to Captain Desire of the Thai partisans,
announcing the arrival of his new daughter. The little girl, so far
away, had been named Anne-Marie, the name of the strongpoint
Desire and his Thai irregulars had held through all the bitter weeks.
One wonders: After Dien Bien Phu, how many soldiers' daughters
were named Genevieve?

On the night of the sixth of May Genevieve slept a little, curled
up under a table on a pile of muddy parachutes. On the morning of
the seventh she was up, worn but smiling, slogging again through the
maggots and filth, talking softly to the wounded, giving something to
drink, changing dressings, administering medication . . . and sorting

out the wounded from those already dead. Some of the corpses were unwounded—Grauwin thought they had simply fought on past the point of endurance. They had died of sheer exhaustion.

And so, late in the afternoon of May 7, the firing died away to a spiteful spattering of individual shots. In his dugout, Langlais burned his papers and pictures, even his treasured red paratroop beret, kissed Genevieve, and waited. The indomitable Bigeard wrapped a silk map around his ankle and tore off his badges of rank. He was already thinking of escape.

Grauwin collected his personnel, made certain everyone wore medical insignia and a red cross armband. And then he waited, too, Genevieve standing beside him. At last, watched by Viet-Minh soldiers in battle dress, they emerged blinking to bright sun and a brilliant blue sky. Grauwin's hair had turned completely white.

On Viet orders, Grauwin and his staff went back to their hellish hospital. Although the Viets took much of their remaining dressings and medicine, at least they could make conditions a little better for the worst of the wounded. The shells no longer fell, the electrical plant still operated, and parachuted medical supplies lay scattered everywhere for the salvaging.

Grauwin, Genevieve, and the rest of the French medical staff had no notion of the progress of the Geneva talks. For all they knew, the Indochina war would go on forever, drag on and on while wounded men died for lack of care. Even so, Genevieve held out for ten days against two female Viet commissars who pressed her to sign a special appeal asking clemency for the French wounded.

Genevieve could see clearly that the "appeal" was purely a propaganda ploy, and she dug in her heels. At last, out of fear for his terribly wounded charges, Grauwin courageously took the responsibility and ordered her to sign. Fearing for her wounded, she reluctantly obeyed; she was also compelled to sign letters to Ho Chi Minh thanking that murderous little tyrant for his "clemency" to the French wounded. With characteristic courage, Grauwin signed a similar appeal, chancing his reputation for the sake of his wounded. It is impossible to blame either of them.

Late in the evening of May 24, Genevieve stepped off an aircraft in Hanoi, still wearing her paratroop uniform, the mud of that filthy valley still on her boots. Exhausted, she insisted on spending two days in the Hanoi hospitals, visiting the men for whom she had cared in the valley of Dien Bien Phu. In the process, she met a captain named de Heaulme; they would meet again.

For quiet little Genevieve de Galard-Terraube, it was the end of four years in Indochina. She had flown 149 medevacs in those four years. Forty of them had been to the dreadful valley of Dien Bien Phu. Ahead lay an official trip to the United States, where she received a hero's welcome. President Eisenhower, who knew something about war himself, presented her with the Medal of Liberty.

In time, Genevieve would find some happiness and peace. She returned to France after the agony of Dien Bien Phu had ended and married a French officer—de Heaulme—who had not served in that terrible valley. They lived in Madagascar for a time, returning to France with their three children in the 1960s. They settled in a beautiful Paris apartment that had long been in Genevieve's family.

On Armistice Day in 1980, Genevieve de Galard became a Commander of the Legion of Honor, receiving her decoration under the Arc de Triomphe from the hands of the French president himself. It was the ultimate honor, but it is certain that Genevieve appreciated many times more the smiles of hurt men to whom she had brought a little sunlight in the gloom of the tunnels of Dien Bien Phu. It may be that she also thought of another sort of recognition, a chance meeting some seventeen years before.

For in 1963, on a Paris street, little Genevieve saw a familiar face in the passing crowd and called out. She had seen the Legion soldier who had stood her sponsor on Camerone Day a decade before and a world away, in the dreadful valley of Dien Bien Phu. She remembered the valley and the men, and she remembered the promise she had made on Camerone Day.

The Legionnaire got his champagne.

CHAPTER FORTY-FOUR

THE LUCK OF THE DRAW

JOSHUA CHAMBERLAIN WAS surely one of the most memorable officers to wear Union blue—or anybody's uniform, for that matter. His fame would have been assured by Little Round Top alone, the broiling July day when he and his 20th Maine were the far left of the whole Yankee army; the day he led his wild downhill bayonet charge that scattered Hood's hard-bitten Rebels; the day he saved the Union flank, and the battle, and the whole Gettysburg fight.

Chamberlain went on to command a brigade, and finally a division. It was fitting that he and his men took the surrender of the Army of Northern Virginia at Appomatox. And it was characteristic of the gallant Chamberlain that he called his men to present-arms as the sad remnants of their old adversary went trooping by on that dismal April day.

Maybe the Lord had his hand on this biblical warrior. Perhaps he was being saved for the years to come, the years in which he became president of Bowdoin College and governor of Maine. For Chamberlain had come close to death at Little Round Top. He was wounded there, and knocked down by a bullet that slammed into his saber scabbard. He would be wounded again, too, but he never came closer to death than he did at the end of March 1865, in a field near Petersburg, at a place called Lewis' Farm.

Leading his brigade from the front, as always, Chamberlain reeled in his saddle as a southern Minie-ball tore through his horse's neck and slammed into Chamberlain's chest. The round had hit Chamberlain right over the heart, and it seemed obviously mortal. He fell forward over his horse's neck, and his commander, tough Regular Charles Griffin, rode up beside him and put his arm around Chamberlain's shoulders. Griffin was obviously moved. "My dear general," he said, "you are gone."

Chamberlain looked up at him. "Yes, General," he replied, "I am gone." So saying, Chamberlain kicked his horse into motion and rode forward to rally his men and drive the Confederates from their position. For the bullet, slowed by its passage through the tissue of the horse's neck, had torn into an orderbook and a mirror tucked into Chamberlain's breast pocket. The impact had knocked him senseless for a moment, but it had done no lasting damage.

General Joshua Chamberlain would live for almost half a century more.

CHAPTER FORTY-FIVE

A LOUSY PLACE TO FIGHT A WAR
The Ridges of Dak To

I LAY IN my shallow hole watching North Vietnamese mortar rounds burst on both sides of the airstrip below me. Along the far side of the strip two American transport aircraft burned furiously, pouring great gouts of black oily smoke into a peaceful pale-blue sky. The mortars—and maybe a 75-millimeter pack howitzer—had got them, too, after they had unloaded their troops and before they could take off again. A third aircraft had just gotten clear of the strip, moving too fast for the enemy gunners to track it.

"Cherokee's pissed off," said a small voice in a neighboring hole. No doubt about that: the Fourth Infantry Division commander in the valley was after those communist tubes with everything he had. Artillery around me was shaking the earth, pouring rounds out into the hill country around us, searching for the weapons that had caused so much grief down here in the valley. Over to my right I could hear the *bam-bam* of 40-millimeter Dusters, beating at the tangled green slopes above the valley.

Overhead four F-4 Phantoms were starting runs along the ridge where the mortars were. They were carrying napalm, long, graceful silver canisters tucked away under the stubby wings. As I watched, the first Phantom dropped its load and great sheets of yellow-crimson flame leaped up against the green ocean of jungle, waves of jellied gasoline that would fry anything in their path. The other three F-4s followed the same path, and the tortured earth along the ridge became a boiling inferno. The hostile fire stopped.

I was safe enough in my hole, close to the valley floor. My lair wasn't very deep, but deep enough that a mortar round would have had to land practically on top of me to do any real harm. Most of the shells were landing farther down toward the strip anyway. The real hell was up above, up on the hills above the valley. Up there, a lot of Americans were locked in a bloody, ferocious, close-range fight for their lives.

This was the valley of Dak To, a benighted place in the highlands of Vietnam. It was November 1967, and out along the jungle-covered limestone ridges, the fourth, last, and biggest of Vo Nguyen Giap's "border battles" was reaching its thunderous height.

The first of the communist offensives had been badly bloodied by the marines around Con Thien, up around the DMZ. The next attack had been repelled by the South Vietnamese at an unappealing place called Song Be, over against the Cambodian border. The third round had been fought at Loc Ninh, also near the Cambodian frontier, where Giap's insect army left almost nine hundred dead strewn in front of the American positions.

In all of these offensives, and here at Dak To, there had been an element generally lacking in other VC and NVA operations. Communist elements showed a willingness to stand and fight in spite of appalling losses, instead of fading away as they generally had in the past. A communist order captured at Dak To laid out their objectives, which included destruction of a "major U.S. element," and exercise in massed attack. Although none of the offensives achieved the first objective, the NVA got plenty of practice in the second.

The Dak To country was, as an infantry friend wryly commented, "a lousy place to fight a war." And if there is no such thing as a good battleground, this terrain is as foul as it gets. It is a merciless land of steep limestone ridges, some of them exceeding four thousand feet. The sharp ridges are covered with double-canopy, sometimes triple-canopy, jungle.

This nightmare vegetation reaches up to blot out the sun with teak and mahogany that tower a hundred feet and more above the rotting jungle floor. The draws between the ridges are dreary tangled places of perpetual twilight, where a thousand growing things struggle to the death for light and air. The jungle is laced with vines and thorns, and in it live divers snakes, a zillion leeches, and about half the mosquitoes in the world.

The village of Dak To—and the nearby Special Forces camp—lay in Kontum Province, in the Central Highlands, some thirty miles from the Laotian border. There was a French post there in the 1950s, and for years French officers and NCOs and Montagnard partisans waged a vicious, silent ambush war against the communist Viet-Minh. In February 1954, Viet-Minh attacks in battalion strength submerged the little French garrisons north and west of the provincial capital of Kontum. One of those tiny posts was at Dak To.

And so this grim, unforgiving country all around Dak To is littered with dead men's bones: French soldiers, Viet-Minh, native partisans of both sides, Vietcong, American Special Forces troopers, and their Montagnard soldiers. There are ghosts everywhere in this dark, brooding country.

The battle around the valley of Dak To had been building up since early summer, when the enemy moved against the Special Forces camp. Two battalions of the American 173d Airborne Brigade had been flown in to help out. The sequel was a series of ferocious fights in the drizzle and mists of the monsoon. In one of them a paratroop company was overrun by a North Vietnamese Army battalion, losing seventy-six dead, many of them murdered by the NVA as they lay helplessly wounded.

In the months that followed, elements of the 173d, Vietnamese paratroops, and a brigade of the American First Cavalry Division worked over the wild country north and west of Kontum. In clash after clash, they piled up an impressive tally of communist dead, but the enemy continued to reinforce and push east. There were a great many of them out to the west, and they were coming out to fight. The communists needed a victory, and they intended to get it by overrunning Dak To.

This enemy was not Vietcong, by and large, but North Vietnamese, real and actual regiments with much modern equipment, trained and organized along Russian lines. They carried AK-47s and the excellent RPG rocket launcher. Some wore steel helmets, and they were plentifully supplied with grenades, mortars, and a world of ammunition.

They were tough and they were motivated, and they could stand a lot of hardship.

The enemy carried their rice ration in a plastic roll slung over the shoulder, and they slept in hammocks slung between trees in the jungle. They knew a great deal about camouflage, too; many of them carried a contraption of concentric bamboo rings, which fit over the shoulders on elastic straps. The rings could hold branches of whatever vegetation flourished around them erect above their torsos and heads.

Most important, perhaps, they were masters of the shovel; they preferred to fight searching American troops from deep, long-prepared bunkers, often situated deep under cover about halfway up a steep slope. Sometimes they had dug their bunkers so long in advance of a fight that the rioting jungle had grown completely over all trace of their antlike burrowing. Often they had dug so deeply that bombs and rockets could not touch them; their bunker complexes were interconnected and mutually supporting. They were, altogether, a formidable enemy, especially in defense.

The American command knew they were coming. LRRPs (long-range reconnaissance patrols), Vietnamese agents, airborne "people sniffers," and other sensors confirmed that the regiments of the so-called B-3 Front were moving from their hideouts near Cambodia, moving fifty to one hundred kilometers northeast into central Kontum Province. Fourth Infantry Division's 3d Battalion, 8th Infantry patrolled deep into the limestone ridges around Dak To, uncovering new enemy base camps and ammunition dumps. The NVA was on the way.

At the end of October, Fourth Infantry Division's 1st Brigade moved to Dak To. The 173d had moved on, east to the sea, except for the 4th Battalion of the 503d Infantry, which was attached to Fourth Infantry. Supplies poured into the valley of Dak To, the engineers improved the tired road and repaired destroyed bridges into the valley, and cargo aircraft shuttled in and out of the airstrip.

American and Vietnamese patrols continued to find evidence that the enemy was present—and in great strength. Trails had been improved and heavily traveled, and trees had been cut. That activity suggested both that the enemy intended to fight near Dak To and that he was building elaborate field fortifications. Both conclusions turned out to be correct. The NVA were on the ground in strength, and as 4th Infantry commanding general William Peers later wrote:

> Nearly every key terrain feature was heavily fortified with elaborate bunker and trench complexes. He had moved quantities of supplies and ammunition into the area. He was prepared to stay.

He was. Early in November, the NVA's intention to fight at Dak To was confirmed by a deserter, a sergeant from an NVA artillery team selecting sites to emplace heavy mortars and rocket launchers. At least four infantry regiments were committed to the valley, he said, plus an entire artillery regiment armed with mortars and 122-millimeter rocket launchers. Together, they made up the NVA 1st Division. Among them were a great many veteran soldiers, including survivors of the vicious 1965 Ia Drang Valley fight against the Seventh Cavalry. Their targets were Dak To and the new Special Forces camp at Ben Het, some eighteen kilometers to the west.

Things quickly heated up. As NVA regiments were identified to the west and southwest, on the move, friendly units and masses of supplies continued to build up at Dak To. Up along the ridges, the paratroops and units of Fourth Infantry encountered larger and larger NVA elements in bitter fighting. Two more battalions of the 503d were flown in.

The jungle-covered limestone ridges took a physical toll even without the lung-busting effort of combat. A load for an American soldier on the move might weigh as much as fifty pounds all told. Typically, he lugged at least five hundred rounds for his M-16, loaded eighteen or nineteen to a magazine. He was issued belt pouches to carry his magazines, but he often packed some of them in canteen covers or in a cloth claymore mine bag for easier access.

He carried three or four quart canteens of water, four or more fragmentation grenades and a couple of smoke grenades, a knife or bayonet or machete, and usually a belt for one of the M-60 machine guns or a LAW antitank rocket for busting NVA bunkers. He often carried one or two claymores as well. He sometimes packed as much as three days' C rations—in tin cans—although on short patrols he might carry only a single meal in a bootsock tied to his harness. Add in the weight of his steel helmet, tack on more pounds for his

M-16 or M-79 grenade launcher or M-60 machine gun, and the soldier had plenty to sweat about before anybody fired a round.

The early battles were for control of the critical hills overlooking Dak To itself, and the critical supply routes snaking into the valley. In ferocious close-range fighting, the Fourth Infantry's 3d Battalion, 8th Infantry and 3d Battalion, 12th Infantry took vital Hill 724, looming above Dak To and its critical airstrip, leaving 232 NVA bodies and several dozen weapons scattered across the slopes of the hill.

The tempo and pattern of the fighting above Dak To is well described by the story of what happened to Task Force Black, a company and a half from 1st Battalion, 503d Airborne Infantry. Task Force Black was inserted into a landing zone (LZ) on a densely wooded hilltop called 823, west of Dak To and south of Ben Het.

Hill 823 was a bad place. Three companies of 4th Battalion, 503d Airborne had fought a ferocious battle earlier in the month in the same area. At a cost of fifteen dead and forty-eight wounded, the paratroops had mauled a part of the NVA's 66th Regiment, which left behind them over a hundred dead and more than fifty weapons. Now the Americans were back on 823, and this time it was going to be even worse.

During TF Black's second night on the slopes of 823, the paratroopers could hear movement all around them in the gloom, and watch the tiny red and green fireflies of NVA lights moving like wills-o'-the-wisp in the valley below.

TF Black—about two hundred men strong—was commanded by a tough West Virginian captain named Tom McElwain. McElwain was a mustang, up from the ranks, and immensely popular with his men. He'd been a soldier from the time he was seventeen, and he was a stranger to panic. It was just as well he was.

McElwain's mission was to find the enemy, and he lost no time getting at it. On the morning of November 11, Veterans' Day, he pushed off from the LZ down a well-traveled trail with most of his force. Lieutenant Gerald Cecil, his lead platoon leader, not only ensured vigilance on the point but carefully patrolled the heavy brush and bamboo on both sides of the trail.

Only two hundred meters from the LZ, the point man killed an enemy soldier, an NVA dressed in a clean, fresh uniform and carrying a brand-new AK-47. Pushing on into a twilight depression beneath the towering trees, Cecil could feel the enemy all around him. He pushed on a little way farther, then pulled his flank squads into a hasty perimeter with the rest of his platoon. It was dead quiet, and the platoon leader "sensed that we were standing right on top of them." They were.

Cecil's instincts were perfectly accurate, and he acted on them, ordering his men to open fire into the scrub, starting near their own feet and working outward. All hell immediately broke loose as NVA regulars hidden in holes and vegetation returned Cecil's fire from all directions; other communist soldiers began to drop grenades from the trees above the American column. Cecil's troopers hosed the trees and vegetation around them with everything they had, and NVA soldiers began to die.

As the NVA recoiled from the massed American fire, some of Cecil's men quickly set up claymore mines and blew them as the NVA came in again. The deadly little plastic mines sent a scythe of steel balls tearing into the charging NVA, and a communist soldier disappeared as he tried to grab a claymore in the moment of detonation. Cecil then began to pull his platoon slowly back up the trail, dragging his wounded, reaching back for contact with the rest of McElwain's men.

The whole American column pulled together into a long, skinny perimeter perhaps a hundred yards in length. They were getting mortar fire, very heavy and very accurate, and automatic weapons swept their lines from both flanks. McElwain was up against a whole battalion at least, and he called in the platoon he had left behind at the LZ. The lieutenant in command there buried the company's mortars and shot his way forward to help his boss. He and his men had to crawl part of the way, but they made McElwain's perimeter and began to fill in the gaps left by the dead.

McElwain called in friendly artillery within twenty-five meters of his own position, but its effect was minimized by the high canopy of the jungle and the NVA tactic of "hugging" the American perimeter as closely as possible. Air support was virtually helpless, for the thick green tangle that covered the ridge all looked the same from the air. The fighter-bomber pilots could see nothing to attack, and attempts by TF Black to mark their perimeter with smoke on the ground were frustrated by NVA releases of the same color smoke.

McElwain's troopers fought on. One soldier cut an NVA literally in two with two rounds from a twelve-gauge shotgun. Some of the wounded, many of them hit again and again, were saved further agony when an enemy mortar round bounced in among them . . . and proved to be a dud. A gallant kid named John Barnes saved more lives and earned a posthumous Congressional Medal when he dove into a group of American wounded to stifle an NVA grenade with his own body.

McElwain, running out of ammunition, his perimeter clogged with wounded men, was in desperate straits. A gallant helicopter pilot's attempt to resupply TF Black misfired when his chopper took thirty-five hits and its slingload of ammunition fell into enemy territory.

All the gallantry and all the suffering, all McElwain's leadership, could not have saved TF Black alone, but help was on the way. One hundred and twenty men of another paratroop company were airlifted in some eight hundred meters away from McElwain's fight. Loaded with extra ammunition, they pushed down into TF Black's old camp, preceded by a violent artillery barrage that walked ahead of them. Then they shot their way up the trail to McElwain's perimeter, calling out loudly so McElwain's tired men would know they were friendly.

By four in the afternoon it was over. American losses amounted to 20 killed and 154 wounded. Two men were missing. NVA dead were four or five times the American KIA, and the enemy, with all the advantage of surprise and numbers, had failed to destroy TF Black. Said Lieutenant Cecil, who won the Distinguished Service Cross for his gallant day's work, "The North Vietnamese in eight hours were unable to accomplish what should have taken them thirty-five minutes." Cecil was right, and what he said spoke volumes about the grit and courage of TF Black's paratroopers.

Much of the fighting around Dak To was at ranges as short as ten or fifteen yards in the thick, tangled vegetation. Through the whole battle, medevac dust-off helicopters flew mission after mission to get out the worst wounded men. The dust offs were hit again and again; some didn't make it, but the others kept trying. Air force pilots flew hundreds of missions with cannon, bombs, and napalm; up on Hill 1338, Charlie Company, 3d of the 12th, was calling in air strikes fifty feet from its own perimeter. But it took the hill.

Down below the rugged hilltops, a massive logistics effort kept the guns fed. Transport aircraft, helicopters, deuce-and-a-half cargo trucks, lowboys—even engineer dump trucks—kept supplies and men pouring into Dak To. Even a blown bridge along the vital road did not interrupt the flow of the army's lifeblood. Down on the Dak To strip, regularly hit by NVA mortar fire, supply loads were quickly broken down and flown forward by Huey slicks—cargo helicopters. Anybody around, regardless of rank, lent a hand to the loading and unloading.

On the thirteenth of November two companies of the Second Battalion, 503d Airborne locked horns with a whole NVA battalion in ferocious fighting at point-blank range. On and on through the night it went, as American helicopters flew daring low-level runs to drop ammunition on spots marked by flashlight beams. When the smoke blew away the next morning, opposite sides of one single log sheltered the bodies of six NVA and six Americans; all were dead.

On the fifteenth, as the two transports burned out on the strip, NVA mortars hit the ammunition supply point, producing a monstrous explosion that literally shook the earth. So good were American logistics, however, that the guns never stopped in the valley. American troops continued to seek out the enemy in increasingly savage fighting, and devoted dust-off helicopters flew desperately wounded men out of hilltop firebases under heavy fire.

The weather at least had improved: the torrential rains were gone; even the postmonsoon mists, the *crachin,* had largely disappeared. Helicopter gunships—"hogs," in GI parlance—and fighter-bombers could help out the infantry at almost any time. That is, if they could see the grunts' marking smoke drifting up through triple-canopy jungle and sort it out from smoke grenades popped by the NVA to confuse the issue.

The culmination for the fight at Dak To boiled up on the eighteenth, centering on a pimple called Hill 875. That day a Special Forces Mike Force ran into big trouble—an NVA regiment deeply dug in on the east slope of 875—about twelve miles west of Dak To itself. The enemy occupied deep, interconnected bunkers built months before, so long before that the natural vegetation had grown back over the whole complex, shrouding it and its defenders in the best of natural camouflage. The Green Berets and their Montagnard troopers wisely pulled back and called for help.

The job of dealing with the hornet's nest on Hill 875 fell first to the Airborne soldiers of 2d battalion, 503d Infantry; their mission, stated with deceptive simplicity, was: "Move onto and clear Hill 875," a job far beyond the ability of any single rifle battalion in the world. They were very good soldiers, these paratroopers, but they soon were fighting for their lives, outnumbered, against an enemy that seemed to come from everywhere, under a rain of mortar shells and rifle grenades.

By the afternoon the Americans had pulled back and closed in to a rough defensive perimeter, dragging their wounded with them and finding whatever cover they could. Casualties were very heavy, particularly among officers and NCOs. The entire command group of one company were killed together. One sergeant, hit seven times and down in the open, shouted to his lieutenant, "For God's sake, don't come out here; there's a machine gun behind this tree!" Three times the officer tried to reach his NCO; three times he was hit himself.

Father Charles J. Watters, the battalion's chaplain, showed an incandescent courage that stood out even among the dozens of acts of shining valor that illuminated Hill 875. Major Watters, unarmed, had gone back again and again into the teeth of the NVA firestorm to help hurt men, men lying helpless on that ghastly mountainside. Watters administered Last Rites, carried wounded men to safety, and brought water and comfort to wounded men, paying no attention to pleas from other paratroopers not to take such desperate chances.

To add to the battalion's agony, American artillery rounds began to fall around the perimeter, and at last an errant air force bomb struck the center of the defensive ring where the wounded had been collected; at least twenty men died in the blast, perhaps as many as forty, and some thirty more suffered terrible wounds. Father Watters died with the men he was comforting, but he would live on in a great many memories . . . and on the roll of the Congressional Medal of Honor.

But what remained of 2d of the 503d fought on, on through a hideous night of close-range grenade exchanges. American artillery was adjusted to hammer the area outside the battalion's perimeter, and down below, the 4th Battalion of the 503d loaded itself down with extra ammunition and got ready to help. Helicopter after helicopter tried to land to take out the worst wounded, braving almost point-blank NVA groundfire. Bird after bird was hit; six were shot down; but the Hueys kept trying.

By the next night, 4th Battalion had fought their way through to 2d battalion, and on the morning of the twenty-first enough of a landing zone had been cleared to fly out the rest of the badly wounded. That same day began the smashing of Hill 875, the intense preparation that should have been done before 2d Battalion ever tried to take the hill in the first place.

For seven hours U.S. firepower rained destruction on the hilltop: artillery, bombs, more than seven tons of napalm. It did not seem that anything could live in that inferno, but when the airborne went in again that afternoon it immediately ran into heavy fire from the tunnels and bunkers that honeycombed the NVA position. Covered with logs and earth up to fourteen feet deep, protected inside by blast walls and escape tunnels, the communist bunkers were almost impossible to destroy . . . except by the bare hands of men.

One by one, these miniature fortresses had to be extinguished, and most of the extinguishing had to be done by the infantry. Antitank rockets often failed to do the job, even when they hit a firing aperture, for the defenders fell back into tunnels behind the fighting compartment of the bunker, running back to fire or throw grenades at American attackers after the rockets had exploded.

The NVA counterattacked again and again. During one of these assaults, on the twentieth, a four-man outpost was struck by an entire NVA company, part of a Viet attack on a lone American company. Young PFC Carlos Lozada stopped the NVA company in its tracks with murderous close-range machine gun fire, leaving at least twenty bodies piled in front of his gun. He then fought on alone to cover the company's withdrawal. Lozada was mortally wounded on that hill, but he took dozens of the enemy with him, and a lot of paratroopers lived because of his single-handed stand.

In the end, the reduction of the NVA defensive complex was done by men, soldiers who pushed satchel charges through the firing ports or who took out bunkers with napalm concentrate poured inside and then fired with grenades. Supporting trench lines were taken with rifle and grenade, and NVA attacks on the American flanks and rear were beaten off with the same weapons.

Within 250 feet of the crest of 875, the paratroops pulled back on the evening of the 21st, and on the next morning the air force drenched the hilltop with more napalm and high explosive. Two fresh American companies from 4th Infantry Division's 1st of the 12th Infantry reinforced the 503d, and on the morning of the twenty-third the infantry went in again. This time, there was little resistance, for what was left of the NVA regiment was gone. They had fought to cover the retreat of the rest of the North Vietnamese, and their mission was finished.

It was Thanksgiving Day.

On Hill 875, amidst the devastation and the stench, the surviving troopers ate their dinner, flown in, turkey and all the fixin's. The battle for the hill was over. So was the vicious fighting around Dak To, at least most of it—at least for a while. American forces had hammered the enemy with more than 150,000 rounds of artillery, more than 2,000 close air support sorties, even B-52 strikes.

In the end, however, for all the might of modern war machinery, for all the magic of logistics and communications, the essential job was done by the men with rifles in their hands, by the sweating gunners, and by the iron-nerved helicopter crews. Five Congressional Medals were won at Dak To. One of them went to PFC Carlos Lozada.

The North Vietnamese offensive had cost them dearly. At least four enemy regiments had been badly mauled, conservatively losing over sixteen hundred dead. These units would be rested and reinforced and resupplied in Cambodia, but they would never be the same again. Off to the west, toward Cambodia, the battered remnants of NVA regiments trudged back to the sanctuary permitted them by an astonishingly inept American political leadership.

The trail of the NVA was marked by bloody dressings, dying soldiers, and the roiling smoke of repeated American artillery and air strikes. NVA medical support was sparse and primitive, and their seriously wounded died by scores and by hundreds during the retreat. The real count of enemy dead may have been as high as three or four thousand; nobody will ever know.

Months later the trails west of Dak To still stank of death from dozens of graves full of North Vietnamese corpses, graves hastily dug as their comrades fell back into Cambodia. Nobody knows how many are buried out there; as one American company commander put it to me: "I didn't lose anything down those holes; my folks have better things to do than diggin' 'em up."

America had her own dead to mourn; there were almost 300 of them, plus more than 70 Vietnamese killed in action. Hill 875 alone had cost the Airborne 158 dead, maybe more than there would have been had even greater use been made of artillery and tactical air instead of human bodies. American troops had won a major victory

over a tough and aggressive foe, but the sense of winning could not
erase other, uglier memories. One officer remembered:

> We were there three days, couldn't get the helicopters in. The
> bodies were rotting in the sun. They got this cargo net. There
> must have been thirty bodies. As the cargo net swung back and
> forth, fluid and blood sprayed down from the sky. Arms and
> legs were falling out. . . .

The 173d Airborne remembered their comrades with their traditional memorial service. It was celebrated in front of long somber
lines of boots in carefully dressed ranks, one pair for every dead
trooper.

The lines of boots were terribly long.

Index